Alfonso Gálvez

Seven Letters to Seven Bishops

First Volume

New Jersey
U.S.A. - 2024

Seven Letters to Seven Bishops, First Volume by Alfonso Gálvez. Copyright © 2024 by Shoreless Lake Press. American edition published with permission. All rights reserved. No part of this book may be reproduced, stored in retrieval system, or transmitted, in any form or by any means, electronic, mechanical, photocopying, recording or otherwise, without written permission of the Society of Jesus Christ the Priest, P.O. Box 157, Stewarstville, New Jersey 08886.

CATALOGING DATA

Author: Gálvez, Alfonso, 1932–2022
Title: Seven Letters to Seven Bishops, First Volume
Library of Congress Control Number: 2024910899

ISBN: 978-1-953170-41-5 (hardcover)
978-1-953170-42-2 (e-book)

Published by
Shoreless Lake Press
P.O. Box 157
Stewarstville, New Jersey 08886

INTRODUCTION

The *Apocalypse*[1] is a prophetic book; the only prophetic book of the New Testament.[2] The Bible closes with a *farewell* that is more an *until–we–meet–again,* since every prophecy is a look into the future; in this case, into an *after* that will give meaning and fulfillment to all that comes before.

But the simple fact of calling it a prophetic book poses from the beginning diverse and serious problems. Said problems have to do with topics such as the following: prophecy always refers to the future; it uses a veiled and dark language; it requires, therefore, interpretation.

It is proper to all prophecy to be dark and to not reach clarity until after its fulfillment. That darkness is yet deeper when the prophetic announcement is presented through symbolic images which hide the object more than they reveal it, as is the case of the Apocalypse.[3]

For any of the items indicated above, problems accumulate almost *ad infinitum* if we add the multiple opinions provided by schol-

---

[1]In Greek, *Revelation.*

[2]This does not mean that the remaining books of the New Testament do not contain other prophecies. We omit here any reference to the unending list of Councils, both National and Ecumenical, that have defined the authenticity and canonicity of the Book of *Apocalypse,* including all corresponding anathemas for those who deny them. Only in Spain, the IV Council of Toledo (633) excommunicated those who denied its authenticity and refused to recognize it as sacred, including those who would not preach about it at Masses during the liturgical times from Easter to Pentecost (Can. XVI).

[3]DTC, I, *Apocalypse,* V.

ars throughout the centuries. And having gone through twenty centuries of diverse interpretations, the possible solutions have grown considerably in number. And it can be supposed, as well, that any opinion on any of the topics affects the others.

We could begin, for example, with the consideration of what is peculiar to a prophetic book: its reference to the future. Everything would indicate that the fact that the *Apocalypse* would refer to the future should not pose any problem in this sense; after all, it is a prophetic book. This said, we must keep in mind that we are dealing with an intricate and difficult Prophecy: one that contains, among other things, a multitude of symbolism applicable to innumerable and various events in History. It is not surprising, then, that scholars have frequently opted for the easy path. Hence rationalism has attempted to deny the *Apocalypse* its status of prophecy since the second half of the eighteenth century. For the Philosophies of Illustration, the author of *Revelation* is, in effect, merely making History and only speaks of his own time; more concretely, he speaks of the struggle of the Church against the pagan Roman Empire, symbolized in this case by Babylon and the Beast. The seven heads of the beast would then be the seven emperors, while Nero would be for the author of the Book the Antichrist.

Before continuing, it is advisable to warn that this Commentary on the Letters to the Seven Churches of Asia does not pretend to be, either in part or in whole, an exegetical study of the *Apocalypse*. This is why problems of textual criticism will not be addressed nor will we elaborate on the diverse commentaries on the *Apocalypse* that have taken place over time. Here we simply pretend to outline some forays into the matter, more as an essay than with a desire for erudition, in regard to certain questions that the Sacred Book poses with the simple purpose of procuring the spiritual benefit of those who long for it. Or, if you prefer, with the plain hope that this foray will serve as amusement for some reader who disposes of the necessary time as well as sufficient animus to read it.

Here it goes without saying that we consider as fact the prophetic character of the *Apocalypse*. Twenty centuries of venerable tradition without the least doubt in that regard make something more than a tough difficulty for those who would attempt to sustain the contrary. Moreover, the Book of the *Apocalypse* itself solemnly proclaims this both at the beginning (Rev 1: 1–3) and at the end (Rev 22:19); almost as if to take on the subject completely and eliminate any uncertainty about it.

In this regard, for example, while the theories that maintain that the Letters to the Seven Churches of Asia (Ephesus, Smyrna, Pergamon, Thyatira, Sardis, Philadelphia, and Laodicea) make reference to the tribulations that those Communities had to face at the end of the first century in order to serve as a consolation to them could well be accepted as true; however, *it is not probable that they take into account the entire truth*. The *Apocalypse* is far too important to reduce such a fundamental fragment of it to a series of events that took place at the same time the Book was written with no further projection and no other significance for the future. Numerous centuries have gone by throughout which the faith of the Christian People has seen something truly transcendent in those *Letters*; they refer, of course, to the seven Communities of Asia *but have a reach that goes far beyond what would be merely contemporaneous*. And it would be difficult now to admit that this faith has been nothing more than a mistaken belief. It would suffice to read closely the recommendations that the Spirit directs to the *Angels of the seven Churches* to convince oneself of the contrary: a mere narrative chronicle to make those particular Christians know they were not alone...? It is evident that the attempt to *diminish* has always been an obsessive fixation of all sects and heresies even from times prior to Christianity.

It turns out, though, that *reductionism* in History, whether in reference to events occurring in time, space, or whatever form, always winds up manifesting its falsehood.

This is what happened, just to mention a case, to the most ancient of interpreters and commentators of the Apocalypse (including some of those who came later), who believed to find in Nero the figure of the Antichrist. It is only natural that such a fateful character should represent for them the worst and most perverse that the human mind could imagine. However, for those who live in the twenty-first century, after twenty centuries of Christianity and after having known other comparable historical figures, Nero seems more like a Jesuit novice. Without the need to go too far back in History, it would suffice to cite some of the great criminals and genocidal figures of our time, such as Hitler, Lenin, Stalin, Mao Tse-Tung, Ho Chi Minh, Fidel Castro, or Arafat, to quickly get an idea. For some of them their crimes can be counted in millions of human beings;[4] and yet, they cannot be considered the worst. Because we should add to this list those who, using the most sophisticated means of modern technology, manipulate and destroy minds and souls: *Do not be afraid of those who kill the body but cannot kill the soul; fear him rather who can destroy both body and soul in hell.*[5] Besides, Nero sent souls to Heaven, while the latter, authentic murderers and annihilators of Humanity, throw them into Hell. With regard to Spain

---

[4]Curiously, only the crimes of Hitler seem to be remembered; nevertheless, he is amply outdone by some of the cited butchers, while the crimes of the others are systematically silenced. Curiosities, achievements, and mysteries of the strange world of Leftist ideology.

[5]Mt 10:28.

Introduction 5

specifically, Polanco's media empire dedicates twenty-four hours a day, seven days a week, to pouring TV trash and rot of the worst kind into a multitude of homes. If to this is added that practically all the television channels in the country belong to him, in addition to almost all the radio stations and the most important newspapers, it will be easily understood that comparing Nero with this individual is a matter of laughter. Of course, no one who thinks seriously is going to believe that Polanco alone is the responsible person; it is well known that there are camouflaged Powers, behind him and above him, acting in the shadows. Freemasonry is not something so occult as to go completely unnoticed, no matter how hard it tries. Only God is capable of knowing the damage and destruction caused to an entire generation (or several) by this means. Those who are quite aware of such manipulations know, however, that, although human Justice cannot or does not want to do anything about it, such Powers and individuals will not be able to escape divine Justice.

On the other hand, therefore, it is not possible to identify these genocides and criminals with the Antichrist, for the same reason used to *vindicate the memory of Nero*, pardon the irony. Here we should remember the old saying that *someone else will come that will make me look good*. It is true that it would be quite difficult to overcome such criminals; nevertheless, nobody knows what History still has in store for the future which only God can see. In any case, it does not seem a bad idea to allow historians and exegetes historical seriousness, advising them to abandon the tarot definitively to the hands of individuals to whom it belongs, such as fortune-tellers, haruspices, necromancers, palmists, and all the rest in the gamut of charlatans.

And something similar should be said about the mania for identifying the Babylon of the *Apocalypse* with Rome. While it's true that today's Rome is considered one of the most corrupted parts of the world, such a thing does not seem reason enough to make it the place to which the terrible visions of the Sacred Book refer. The Protestant Reformation, as is known, has been always inclined to identify both cities. A curious theory to which many Catholics, some excessively traditionalists and others deeply concerned, have adhered in modern times. Despite this, it should be repeated, there are no reasons to confuse them. When it comes to the interpretation of prophecies, the concrete determination of places and times is usually slippery ground. Throughout the centuries there have been too many dates set, with alleged accuracy, for the Appearance of the Antichrist based on the data of the Apocalypse; and all of them have been outrageously false. Everything seems to indicate that the incarnation of Evil, as it appears in the various characters who have emerged throughout history, tends to manifest itself more intensely as time goes by; and hence the degree of perversity of ancient criminals is much lower than that of modern ones. From which two things could be inferred; first, the worst has not yet come; second, when the Antichrist appears, whoever or whatever he may be, there is no doubt that he will be something more serious than what Christians have been imagining until now.(A)

* * *

(A) Attempts at *reductionism* with respect to the revelations of the *Apocalypse*, as we have said above, have become more frequent in modern times. Perhaps the most important of all revolves around the mysterious announcement of *new heavens and a new earth*. In reality, what lies at the bottom of such a reductionism is the desire to build an earthly Paradise and forget forever the Celestial Paradise, in which by the way no one believes anymore. In other words, it is about stopping thinking about the *utopia* of Heaven and starting to build the *reality* of an Earth tailored to man. Logically, modern progressive theology does not use such a rude and stark language; it would be a clumsiness that would easily reveal the traces of Marx and Engels, and of the numbers of epigones, continuators, disciples, and followers who have appeared later. A moment will come, is what is usually said, in which man will be able to *enjoy* a *new Earth*; the same in which, at last, *justice* will be definitively established. Once this proclamation is made, without further additions, it will be enough to let it spread on its own. Indeed, *it sounds good*; it has a pleasant flavor of renovation, modernity, and even revolution. Hence no one is likely to dare oppose it; for such a thing would mean adopting an attitude that would easily be branded as scandalous, recalcitrant, conservative, and, despite everything, also belligerently rebellious.

The rather big problem arises with respect to what progressive theology usually understands by *justice*. It happens that a long list can be made of concepts drawn from the core of Christianity (all authentic values, natural or supernatural, are based on Christ) that have been reduced to purely human categories, once stripped of their supernatural projection and scope. Truly speaking, they have been emptied of their content, rather than falsified or mimicked. This is what has happened with ideas as lofty as justice, human nature, human rights, peace, charity (now solidarity), generosity to others (now social commitment), freedom (now exemption from all human law and above all divine law), etc. It is understood that nobody is going to accuse modern Pastoral activity of disbelief. Nevertheless, the fact that it is the offshoot, more or less consciously, of a theology impregnated with Modernism, it frequently adopts ambiguous positions that could be dangerous. Consequently, as the outpost and motor of Christianity that it is supposed to be, it can only claim for the faithful what is in accordance with a better world, namely: greater human maturity, as they usually say. Thus, it is just one step away from being exclusively concerned with those issues which may be more in tune with Christianity: such as justice, peace, or perhaps solidarity... although almost always understood in such an ambiguous or *progressive* way as to run the risk of misunderstandings. With the consequent possibility that some Christians remain, with respect to such concepts, *at ground level.*

Unfortunately for Modernist theology, the Bible has never shown any interest in agreeing with it. An issue as important as *justice*, for example, has very different connotations in one and the other. The reduction of justice to social justice, understood in the Marxist way, has nothing to do with the Bible;[6] in spite of which, it paved the way to the ideal of finally implanting justice in this world, *and only for this world.* The consequences follow by themselves: the new heavens and the new earth that Christians expect do not mean a new universe, but a merely *transformed* world. It is no longer about waiting for a change, but for the simple transformation that an improvement causes. In other words, we do not expect a substantial change, but only a transformation from less to more, or from good to better, although always remaining within exclusively human parameters. At last, a *transformed* Earth in which the values of social justice, human rights, and, in general, everything that leads to the well-being of man will have become a definitive reality: but without any consideration for supernatural fantasies that exist only in the imagination of dreamers. In a

---

[6]Modern Catholic Pastoral activity is quite permeable to the socialist concept of justice. Hence, the supernatural meaning of this virtue has been blurred in this Pastoral, giving way instead to a reductionism with respect to its biblical significance. Probably this occurrence was influenced by the phenomenon that has affected the Church since the end of the nineteenth century and throughout the twentieth century: the abundance and extraordinary proliferation, at all levels, of ecclesiastical Documents on *Social Doctrine*. There was even a time when any Bishop felt compelled to make his contribution to the issue, with the intention, perhaps, of completing the social Encyclicals of the Popes, already lengthy in themselves. All this is a consequence of the monomania of socialism that invaded the Western world during this time, probably caused by an inferiority complex whose antecedents would have to be sought in a crisis of faith.

few words: the Marxist utopia, which has ceased to be such, to become a reality.⁷

However, the data contained in Revelation runs along different paths. There is no need to insist that the biblical concept of *justice* has nothing to do with the corresponding Marxist concept.⁸ What Scripture states about *the new heavens and the new earth* is foreign to the presuppositions of Modernism. Saint Peter is clear about it, and he does not seem to refer to a mere *transformation* or simple change, horizontal in nature, in the living conditions of men: *But the heavens and the earth which are now, by the same word are kept in store, reserved unto fire against the day of judgment and perdition of the ungodly men. But the day of the Lord shall come as a thief, in which the heavens shall pass away with great violence, and the elements shall be melted with heat, and the earth and the works which are in it, shall be burnt up. Seeing then that all these things are to be dissolved, what manner of people ought you to be in holy conversation and godliness? Looking for and hasting unto the coming of the day of the Lord, by which the heavens being on fire shall be dissolved, and the elements shall melt with the burning heat? But we look for new heavens and a new earth according to his promises, in which justice dwelleth.* ⁹

The first statement referring to the present heavens and earth — *reserved unto fire against the day of judgment*— is not easy to harmonize with a merely better world according to human standard. If this affirmation lacks something, it is precisely confused and easy optimism which

---

⁷Modern Modernist Pastoral, of course, cannot show itself in such a crude and radical way, as has been insinuated before. But if its background is carefully examined, the reality of its content is soon discovered.

⁸It is well known that one of the tricks most frequently used by idealist philosophies (and more specifically Marxist ones) consists in making use of Christian words, attributing to them a content and meaning different from the original. Because people tend to dispense with analysis and distinctions, they simply accept what they are told, albeit in the way they have always interpreted it; very soon, however, more or less consciously, they end up assimilating the meaning intended by the false ideology. A weakness that the System has always known how to take advantage of.

⁹2 Pet 3: 7.10–13.

thinks that it can do without God. Before the events that are to take place, Saint Peter does not insist on the task of working to establish definitively the Terrestrial City (without waiting for any other); instead, he advises *leading a holy and pious life, awaiting, and hastening the coming of the Lord.* As for the new heavens and the new earth that are to come, he is careful to point out that *justice will finally dwell in them.* Although it is very doubtful that Petrine justice has anything to do with social justice understood in a *progressive* way if one also considers the clarity with which the biblical texts exclude the authentic virtue of the present eon.[10] And the Apocalypse is much more forceful about this issue: *And I saw a new heaven and a new earth. For the first heaven and the first earth was gone, and the sea is now no more.*[11] If indeed the whole creation groans in labor pains until it might be freed from its slavery to corruption (Rom 8: 21–22), then we must acknowledge that it is very difficult to imagine such liberation in a Modernist (Marxist) fashion.

* * *

As was said at the beginning, since darkness is something proper and normal to all prophecies, the prophetic message cannot be fully understood until the moment of its fulfillment.

As far as the *Apocalypse* is concerned, this is not to say that the book is an impossible set of riddles, hieroglyphics, or charades. For it would not be logical or admissible for God to speak to men with the intention of not being understood. It is normal, in effect, that the prophecy appears wrapped in a certain darkness, more or

---

[10] It is interesting to note the way the Beatitudes pose the problem. Poverty, suffering, purity of heart, meekness, etc., are for the present eon: *Blessed are the poor... those who cry..., the pure of heart...* The same does not happen with justice. In its case nothing can be done now except waiting for it with longing and hope: *Blessed are those who hunger and thirst for justice.*

[11] Rev 21:1.

less intense. Which does not prevent it from always *containing a meaning that, in its deepest content, transmits a message to men which by no means should unintelligible.* As the Apostle teaches, *all scripture, inspired of God, is profitable to teach, to reprove, to correct, to instruct in justice.*[12] Saint Peter, for his part, counsels that, in addition to the need to pay attention to the word of the prophets, we should not forget also that no prophecy of Scripture depends on any private interpretation (2 Pet 1: 19–20). The Bible, of course, has been written to reveal to men what is necessary or convenient for their salvation; consequently, it is not a book of enigmas or logogriphs. Jesus Christ Himself, having finished the list of His darkest prophecies, which are those referring to the destruction of Jerusalem and the end of History together with His Second Coming, after enumerating the signs that will precede such events, He ends by assuring that these signs will not be so enigmatic as to be unrecognizable: *And from the fig tree learn a parable: When the branch thereof is now tender, and the leaves come forth, you know that summer is nigh. So you also, when you shall see all these things, know ye that it is nigh, even at the doors.*[13] Which, paradoxically, will not be an obstacle so that, despite the forcefulness of the signs, men do not know how to understand them or guess its meaning: *And as in the days of Noe, so shall also the coming of the Son of man be. For as in the days before the flood, they were eating and drinking, marrying and giving in marriage, even till that day in which Noe entered into the ark, and they knew not till the flood came, and took them all away; so also shall the coming of the Son of man be... Watch ye therefore, because ye know not what hour your Lord will come... Wherefore be you also ready, because at what*

---

[12] 2 Tim 3:16.
[13] Mt 24: 32–33.

hour you know not the Son of man will come.[14] A catastrophic and disastrous end which cannot be blamed on the prophecy but *on the men who have freely decided to turn their back on the truth and choose error.*

Perhaps this is the key to understanding the meaning and significance of prophecies. Although the prophetic message is normally obscure, once admitted that it has been pronounced for teaching and the edification of men, it is then impossible to qualify it as unintelligible. Whence it is necessary to admit in it two elements to consider: the reason for its obscurity and its relative but undeniable intelligibility.

The reasons that justify the darkness of the prophecy are impossible to explain in an entirely satisfactory way. It is evident that the obscurity must have reasonable foundations since God never acts arbitrarily or capriciously; but it can already be assumed that the investigation will not lead beyond the field of hypotheses. At any rate, we are going to attempt here some interpretation, rather as a venture, and without intending to delve too deeply into the depth of the mystery.

Perhaps we can use, as a key, certain words of Jesus Christ addressed to His disciples as an answer to a question posed by them: Why do you speak to people in parables?

And the answer given by Jesus Christ is so long and profound as to require, in turn, another series of explanations. Which does seem ironic, and most probably it is: like a kind of endearing joke that God would have taken pleasure to play on men. Anyway, G*od always has a reason for the things He does, for He continually pursues the good of His creatures, which should not be forgotten.* In short, the response addressed to the disciples reads as follows:

---

[14]Mt 24: 37–44.

—Because to you it is given to know the mysteries of the kingdom of heaven: but to them it is not given. For he that hath, to him shall be given, and he shall abound; but he that hath not, from him shall be taken away that also which he hath. Therefore, I do speak to them in parables: because seeing they see not, and hearing they hear not, neither do they understand. And the prophecy of Isaias is fulfilled in them, who saith:

> *By hearing you shall hear, and shall not understand;*
> *and seeing you shall see, and shall not perceive.*
> *For the heart of this people is grown gross,*
> *and with their ears they have been dull of hearing,*
> *and their eyes they have shut:*
> *lest at any time they should see with their eyes,*
> *and hear with their ears, and understand with their heart,*
> *and be converted, and I should heal them.*[15]

The introductory sentences to the quote from Isaiah do not seem to be connected: (a) *to some it is given to know the mysteries of the kingdom of heaven: but not to others*; (b) *he that hath, to him shall be given, and he shall abound; but he that hath not, from him shall be taken away that also which he hath.*

The meaning of the first affirmation offers no difficulty: to some it has been granted to know the secrets of the Kingdom of God, but not to others. Of course the word *to know* must be understood here in the sense of *going deep*, since the statement refers to secrets which, because they are intimately connected with the Kingdom of God, always preserve their secret status. On the other hand, it is evident that, as far as the prophecies are concerned, some people reach a

---

[15]Mt 13: 11–15.

deeper understanding than others; as happens with the degree of knowledge of the Gospel and the teachings of Jesus Christ, which is very different for diverse people (Rom 12:3). It all depends of the various graces, always different in quality and degree, granted to each one by the Holy Spirit. He leads to the complete truth (Jn 16:13) and brings to memory everything Jesus said (Jn 14:26). In this sense, it is necessary to recognize that there are those who manage to reach a certain *intuition* regarding the content of the prophecy (which could also be called *premonition*).[16]

However, one might ask: Why is it granted to some to have more and understand better, while others receive little and understand less? And which is which?

The second of the sentences of Jesus Christ considered here, although not too clear either, perhaps can provide some explanation to those questions: *For he that hath, to him shall be given, and he shall abound; but he that hath not, from him shall be taken away that also which he hath.* These statements seem to point out that he who has a heart will be even more fulfilled; while the one who skimps or gives little will be left with nothing. After all, love is a bilateral relationship of mutual giving: *one lover* gives it all away; and since *the other* does the same, each receives in turn all that belongs to the other: *All things whatsoever the Father hath, are mine.*[17] *All my things are thine, and thine are mine.*[18] As for love,

---

[16] Certain terms must be used in order to try to qualify a knowledge that is known to be *imperfect*, or perhaps rather *incomplete*; well understood that words such as *imperfection* or *insufficiency*, applied to this case, are also unable to express what really happens here, because such intuitive or *premonitory* knowledge of the Word of Revelation, obtained under the lights granted by the Holy Spirit, can actually reach such a magnitude as to be qualified as ineffable.

[17] Jn 16:15.

[18] Jn 17:10.

giving little or with measure is equivalent to not giving anything; in which case, and since love is reciprocity, nothing is received and then love vanishes: *to him who has little, even that little will be taken from him.*[19] From which it could be deduced that he understands more who loves more; likewise, he also receives more pardon who has more love (Lk 7:47).

Now, what comes next seems more logical and better connected with what has been said above. Jesus Christ Himself provides an explanation about His speaking in parables: *Therefore, I do speak to them in parables: because seeing they see not, and hearing they hear not, neither do they understand.* Which in a more intelligible sense, though entirely faithful to the original thought, should be translated like this: *Because seeing they do not want to see, and hearing they do not want to hear or understand.*[20]

They neither see nor understand because they have closed their eyes and ears to the truth and have chosen error. Which is precisely what has been explained above: the darkness of prophecy becomes more intense the darker the heart of man: *And if our gospel be also hid, it is hid to them that are lost, in whom the god of this world hath blinded the minds of unbelievers, that the light of the gospel of the glory of Christ, who is the image of God, should not shine unto them.*[21]

---

[19] In the Sermon on the Mount according to Saint Luke, Jesus Crist utters these words: *Give, and it shall be given to you: good measure and pressed down and shaken together and running over shall they give into your bosom. For with the same measure that you shall mete withal, it shall be measured to you again* (Lk 6:38).

[20] The prophecy of Isaiah quoted immediately after confirms this meaning: *For the heart of this people is grown gross..., they have been dull of hearing..., and their eyes they have shut.*

[21] 2 Cor 4: 3–4.

Collective and voluntary anesthesia, with respect to the Word of God, in order to not listen to It and to follow one's own inclinations, is much more common than it seems. Most commonly, it is caused and fostered by the System itself, in order to manipulate the masses and keep them in an attitude of docile deception. But this does not imply an exemption from guilt; for the deceived, since any abandonment of the truth is always guilty, one way or the other. As regards the truths that refer to salvation, only those who consent to error can be deceived; hence the Apostle says that God sends a seductive power to those who did not want to accept the love of truth (2 Thess 2: 10–11).

Saint Paul also referred to this collective and freely accepted anesthesia when, alluding to the end of time, he said: *For when they shall say, peace and security; then shall sudden destruction come upon them, as the pains upon her that is with child, and they shall not escape.*[22]

At present, everything seems to indicate that the Church is immersed in a situation of collective unconsciousness, which is much graver than any other before in her history. She finds herself steeped in Neo-modernism, when it seemed that the Modernist heresy had been definitively banished; afflicted with a serious crisis in all her scopes (the Magisterium has been discredited and put into question; mass desertions from consecrated life and almost a total absence of vocations; disrepute and dishonor of the priesthood; general confusion in the laity with respect to their role in the Church; widespread crisis of faith in the dogmas and abandonment of the practice of the sacraments; *de facto* legitimation of divorce and con-

---

[22] 1 Thess 5:3.

Introduction 17

traception;²³ bewilderment and confusion about fundamental concepts of the Natural Law, with admission of aberrations such as homosexuality; radical ecumenism, animated by a total surrender which has led Catholics to believe that all religions are equally valid; anarchy and desecration of the liturgy; etc.), while contemplating, however, a general environment in which the faithful breathe with satisfaction the well-known triumphalism of the so-called *Springtime of the Church*.(B)

* * *

(B) These claims may seem exaggerated and, consequently, uncomfortable for those who would qualify them as *alarmist*. Times of triumphalism and smiling *Springtime* do not usually welcome those who denounce evils and dangers, whether they are present or future. The final destiny of the doomsayers, from the prophets of the Old Testament to the present, is none other than being rejected, often with violence.

However, according to the very words of Jesus Christ (and it would be very difficult to term Him as pessimistic or melancholic), there must come a time when, by the extraordinary abundance of wickedness, the charity of man will grow cold (Mt 24:12). And Saint Paul also speaks clearly saying that, toward the end times, the *great apostasy* will take place (2 Thess 2:3).

Of course, to point out certain times for these events would be quite reckless, and even the Apostle himself warns us not to make calculations in this regard. Although there is a fact, despite everything, which provides us with a key that we cannot doubt: according to Jesus Christ Himself,

---

[23]The legitimation of divorce has been carried out through a mere change of name: nullity of the bond in its origin. And contraceptives have been admitted *in fact* in almost all confessionals; and even *de iure* by many Shepherds (including Bishops and Cardinals) who usually allege the defense against AIDS as the main pretext.

when the time comes for His Second Coming, He will *hardly find faith on earth* (Lk 18:8).

Regarding the post-conciliar crisis, and the widespread post-conciliar aphorism *post hoc, non propter hoc*, used to drive away ghosts, it should be remembered that it was already discussed elsewhere to show its inconsistency. According to Menéndez Pelayo,[24] the aphorism *post hoc, ergo propter hoc* is nothing more than a sophism. And so it is indeed, since it tries to prove something by means of an argument that actually does not prove anything: the *post hoc* thing is clear, obviously. But the *ergo propter hoc* would have to be previously demonstrated, since, otherwise, by itself it lacks content. Something curious happens here, however, which is that, on little examination, it is soon discovered that the same reasoning can be applied to the helpful *post hoc, non propter hoc*.

* * *

The conclusion to which the above considerations would lead, as a practical summary, could perhaps be that the darkness of prophecy is necessary. The believer must test his convictions in the crucible of Faith and examine the authenticity of his love, so that, in this way, he can also share with Jesus Christ the madness of the cross. *Crede ut intelligas.* The strength of Faith is the only thing capable of making manifest the totality of Love, of putting man in a one-to-one relationship with God. It is not for nothing that faith is *sperandorum substantia, rerum argumentum non apparentium.*[25]

But, as stated above, it is also necessary to consider in prophecy, in addition to its obscurity, its undeniable (if relative) intelligibility, since it is impossible to think that God speaks to men with the intention of not being understood at all.

---

[24]Marcelino Menéndez Pelayo, *Historia de los Heterodoxos Españoles*, I, IV, Preamble.

[25]Heb 11:1.

In this regard it is important to distinguish between *obscure* language, peculiar of prophecy, and *ambiguous* language, widely used in modern Pastoral activity and in the language of many theologians who support it. In reality, both Pastoral activity and *progressive* Theology use ambiguity, although according to different variants.

One of them is typically used in the written language of Theological Manuals. It consists in making more or less orthodox statements, not clearly condemnable, to usher in, right afterwards, others of contradictory appearance and which, at best, leave the reader submerged in doubt. The procedure, very peculiar to Rahner, manages (under the most favorable circumstances) to cast some doubt upon the subject, with the feeling that it is under review.

A simple and intelligent resource that has a double quality: it is not likely to be condemned, on the one hand; and it enjoys prestige in advanced intellectual circles, on the other.

Although the most significant and accomplished use of *ambiguous* language can be found in some texts of important Documents of the Second Vatican Council. Not to mention the enormous amount of legislation issued later for the application of such Conciliar Documents.

Actually, they amount to several hundred Documents and *Instructions*, which usually take full advantage of the ambiguities contained in the conciliar texts. The procedure followed is generally converting the exception (admitted for *pastoral needs*) into a general norm, and the general norm into exceptions. The logical end is to leave even the exception far behind to make way for the inventiveness, the ridiculous, and even the sacrilegious. This is not the place to deal with a problem to which serious studies have already paid attention.[26] Suffice it to say here that the procedure, driven perhaps in large part by a strange sense of *Ecumenism*, offered an opportunity for the later application of such texts to cause abundant confusion amongst Catholics, mass defections and the general decline of faith.[27]

Another form of ambiguous language is generally used in both preaching and the written paraenesis of some Shepherds addressed to their faithful. It basically consists of speaking without saying anything, or saying very little, avoiding everything that can be compromising for the speaker or unpleasant to the listeners. Hence the peculiar way of expressing himself using ingenious balances and successively agreeing with one trend and the opposite. Juggling operations that usually go accompanied by the curious peculiarity of emphasizing the rights of the *bad ones*, while leaving rather in the shade what could favor the *good people*; with the naive intention, it seems, to make it clear that the Church is understanding and in no way authoritative. Jaime Campmany called this way of addressing the faithful *episcopal language*, thus putting into circulation a clever epithet that became very successful since it expressed, in a graphic manner, the way Bishops usually exercise (at least in Spain) their sacred magisterial mission.

---

[26] See, for example, the important and exhaustive work of Michael Davies, in three volumes, *Liturgical Revolution*, Angelus Press, Kansas City, Missouri: already in its sixth edition in 1992.

[27] We do not intend to say that the Conciliar Documents contain *errors in faith*; although it is demonstrated, however, that the authors introduced in them *ex profeso* ambiguous expressions (it is not appropriate here to judge intentions). The procedure is well known: a correct expression, *of first intention*, is likely to accommodate other possible meanings which, according to their virtualities, are capable of later handling in order to draw *other possible conclusions*.

The problem, unfortunately quite widespread, is likely caused by a variety of reasons whose examination does not belong here. Nevertheless, there is no doubt that this way of proceeding has little in common with the character that Scripture assigns to the Word of God: *take unto you the helmet of salvation, and the sword of the Spirit, which is the word of God,* said the Apostle.[28] *For the word of God is living and effectual, and more piercing than any two edged sword; and reaching unto the division of the soul and the spirit, of the joints also and the marrow, and is a discerner of the thoughts and intents of the heart.*[29]

Indeed, that which is *more piercing than any two-edged sword and reaching unto the division of the soul and the spirit, of the joints also and the marrow* certainly is the opposite to a dull blunted instrument. Jesus Christ exhorted His disciples to speak loud and clear: *That which I tell you in the dark, speak ye in the light: and that which you hear in the ear, preach ye upon the housetops.*[30]

It is true that the Word of God must be preached with love and not in a *guerrilla* way, but by taking into account, as Saint John the Apostle said, that *perfect love casts out fear.*[31] Obviously one thing is not incompatible with the other and the faithful need that the food of the Word of God that is offered to them is not adulterated or decaffeinated. Love cannot be missing in the proclamation of the

---

[28] Eph 6:17.

[29] Heb 4:12. The inferiority complex is a corrosive disease of the spirit which has been tormenting the Church since the early days of Marxism. It has also had a lot to do with the fear experienced by many ecclesiastics (apparently not of robust faith) before the technological achievements, reaching extremes so regrettable as to seem ridiculous. At present (early years of the twenty-first century) the complex does not seem to be in the process of healing.

[30] Mt 10:27.

[31] 1 Jn 4:18.

Word if the preaching is to make sense; just as clarity cannot be missing either, and for the same reason: *I thank God that I speak with all your tongues; all the same, when I am in the assembly I would rather say five words with my mind, to instruct others as well, than ten thousand words in a tongue,*[32] said Saint Paul. It is certainly not good to try to conceal the sins of the faithful and hide them under the rug; since in the end, as always happens with garbage, the bad smell ends up disclosing its presence.

The seven *Letters* included in the *Apocalypse*, destined to the seven Churches of Asia, contain a heading addressed to each one the seven *Angels* who preside over them. It would be unwise to not accept the common sentence shared by almost all the Fathers and theologians throughout the centuries who see in them the Bishops who govern such Churches. Of course, it is certain that they are men, since their actions are worthy of praise at times or recriminations at other times.

We have here another of the eminent notes of the Church founded by Jesus Christ. She is clearly made up of men, praiseworthy at times and occasionally blameworthy. After all she is an itinerant and militant Church, still on the way and in a period of struggle. Hence, her members still suffer the consequences of original sin, despite having already been redeemed. And yet, contrary to what one might think, such a thing does not constitute a reason for scandal, but is rather a reason for joy for men; thanks to Jesus Christ, of course. He has granted His followers the opportunity to contribute to His salvation through their own struggle and effort, as well as that of suffering and dying, sharing the existence of their Master.

Therefore, here we have Shepherds placed by the Spirit to govern the Churches. Men after all, with virtues and defects; it could not

---

[32] 1 Cor 14: 18–19.

Introduction 23

be otherwise. On the other hand, it is clear that it is possible to address the issue without scandal or surprise to anyone. This is simply what happened in the times of the Apocalypse; and perhaps now also, although there may be doubts...(C)

* * *

(C) In modern times the System has used, with no small success, the strategy of promoting the personality cult of the Shepherds of the Church. To that purpose, the System has manipulated and adulterated the concept of magisterial infallibility, giving rise to the idea of absolute perfection and inerrancy of the Shepherds. Making them appear infallible, both in deed and in word, whatever their actions or proclamations may be.

Simultaneously the System has fine-tuned an intelligent undermining work to weaken their authority. The instrument used with the greatest success in this regard has been the Episcopal Conferences, which have basically deprived the bishops of their decision-making power. This undermining seems to have taken place through Pressure Groups, whose operating ability is greater through the Assemblies than with individual bishops who are scattered over wide territories and independent in their respective dioceses. Nevertheless, the System had a truer and deeper purpose. We are referring to its determination to cripple the hierarchical and *monarchical* constitution of the Church as was established by Divine Law. The *democratization* of the Church is a powerful dissolving element, as the already long post-conciliar practice has shown.

Here the problem would no longer focus merely on a question of Political Law about which would be the best system of government and the one better adapted to the present moment. Such a question would lead to a trivial discussion; what is really important here is the *attack carried out against Divine Right*, with consequences easily predictable and then confirmed by the facts.

To put it plainly, it is the attempt to do away with the Hierarchy and what lies at the bottom of this paradox of the cult of the person of the

Shepherds (without sparing indiscriminate adulation whenever necessary), on the one hand, and the manipulation to undermine their authority, on the other.

The System has worked hard to create confusion around such an important issue as that of Pontifical infallibility. Through misunderstandings, half-truths, ambiguous explanations, manipulated doctrines, and even palpable lies, it has managed to spread a smokescreen over the mentality of most Catholics. Any statement or activity of the Pope, no matter how far from meeting the conditions required for the infallibility of the Magisterium, have been or are considered as *dogmas of faith;* endowed, therefore, and without possible appeal, with the halo of infallibility.

This creates, among other things, insoluble situations and problems for the Catholic who is aware of the History of the Church; one filled with facts and events that would be impossible to explain and which could destroy the infallibility of the Magisterium of the Pope.

It is impossible to build a healthy doctrine on the basis of lies or mistakes. Pontifical infallibility is a doctrine of the Universal Church, defined in Vatican Council I. It is true that there are necessary conditions which acts of the Pope must meet in order to be considered infallible which have been specified clearly enough in the declaration of the Council and are easy to know.

If the Pope, for instance, travels to a country or makes an appointment, it is evident that these activities and others like them are not infallible; in fact, they have nothing to do with the Magisterium. Something similar can be said if he speaks or writes as a private theologian or makes statements here or there without intending to act solemnly as Supreme Pastor of the Church (statements to journalists, speeches before certain gatherings of people, occasional homilies, etc.), not to mention interventions or provisions that constitute the framework of what could be called *Vatican politics.*

The tendency to *universalize* Pontifical infallibility is an unfortunate policy that can be traced to the time of the Reformation and did not exist before then. The faithful had clear enough ideas, thanks to which their loyalty to the Holy See did not suffer exceptions. The new doctrines are the consequence of an explainable reaction against the Reformation, which have been cleverly manipulated in modern times by the System.[33]

The apparent zeal for catholicity, with which some have pretended to intensify the authority of the Pope, is really nothing more than a wish to destroy it. Once the falsity of the affirmation that the Pope is infallible in all his words and actions is discovered (not a difficult thing to do), all his Magisterium (the Ordinary and the Extraordinary) is dismantled. The Christian People, always simple and now less educated than in antiquity, does not know much about distinctions. But meanwhile the attempt has served as an effective gag used against those who claim to honestly defend the principles of sound doctrine and have tried to warn about possible actions or statements not magisterial at all, and therefore susceptible to being clarified or discussed. This kind of behavior, since it never caused scandal or aroused scruples, was always practiced by ancient Christians.

The only effective way of fighting abuses is to clearly expound sound Christian doctrine. As History proves, one cannot expect good fruits from erroneous teaching introduced though deception and manipulation.

The infallibility granted to the Supreme Pastor of the Church is a gift to the *office*, never to the person. To enjoy which the Pope has to speak expressly and intentionally as Supreme Pastor of the Church on matters of faith or morals. But, as has already been said above, pretending that everything the Holy Father says or does is a dogma of faith unequivocally leads to the *destruction of the Magisterium*.

When ideas are clear, difficulties are not insoluble. It is hard to imagine that God would have arranged the task of paying due assent to the Pontifical Magisterium, according to its various degrees, as if it were about solving a puzzle. The good Catholic knows how to distinguish in the Pontifical Magisterium the so-called Ordinary, the Extraordinary, and of course the Solemn. Which does not mean that the mere Ordinary Magisterium is not for him a teaching worthy of respect, veneration, and due obedience. An

---

[33]Let us stress the fact that this operation has been accompanied by other apparently opposite attempts used to undermine Pontifical authority, introducing doctrines such as conciliarism (more or less disguised), the need to democratize the Church, etc.

Encyclical, for example, although it is not an infallible Document in itself, may very well contain *infallible doctrines*; to the extent that its teachings are consistent with those always imparted by the Church and made her own at all times. It is precisely the case of the Encyclical *Humanæ Vitæ*, of Pope Paul VI, so reviled and disobeyed by so many Shepherds and progressive theologians. And the same can be said of the *Creed of the People of God*, also of Paul VI.

The Ordinary Magisterium of the Pope does not enjoy the privilege of infallibility, consequently it is not irreformable, except when it is in accordance with the teachings which *semper et ubique* (always and everywhere) the Church has taught, in which case it would be practically *unshakable*, even if it cannot be termed *infallible*. The same could not be said of an Ordinary Magisterium that contradicted the teachings of a previous one (also Ordinary) which, on the other hand, is already part of a Body of Catholic Doctrine practically traditional. In the hypothetical case of such an event, there is no doubt that it would raise serious problems with regard to the new teachings and the degree of assent they might deserve.

* * *

Traditional doctrine has always understood that the *Apocalypse* is a book of consolation. But consolation refers to sufferings and the people who endure them. Now, regarding the *Apocalypse*, who are the Christians to whom it intends to give courage and hope, and what are their sufferings that motivates the consolation?

Tradition has always thought, unanimously, that the book was addressed to the Community of the Primitive Church, which was already suffering terrible persecutions at that time. There is no doubt, therefore, about that point.

But here, too, important questions arise. First, because the *Apocalypse* being an eminently prophetic and inspired book, it can reasonably be assumed that its future projection goes beyond the temporal realm of the Primitive Church; and in fact the Book constantly refers to the End Times. On the other hand, the Church of modern times is suffering no fewer persecutions than the ones she had to suffer from the beginning. Even more, everything indicates that the current persecutions are more terrible than the former: in that they encompass much larger groups of Christians, and insofar as they use more refined and effective procedures. While those persecutions tried to *finish off the Christians*, the current ones, on the other hand, quite more powerful in means and techniques, try *to eradicate forever any idea that implies a trace of Christianity*. The first persecutions killed the body; and although it is true that the modern ones also do that, their objectives aim more at the destruction of minds and the annihilation of souls. The first persecutions produced martyrs and confessors of the faith, while the modern ones transform Christians into unbelievers, apostates, and deserters of their religion. Maybe this would be a good occasion to remember, in this regard, the words of the Lord: *Fear ye not them that kill the body, and are not able to kill the soul: but rather fear him that can destroy both soul and body in hell.*[34]

It is reasonable to think, therefore, that, although the *Apocalypse* is a book addressed to early Christians in need of consolation, since its scope extends to the consummation of the Times, its objectives must have full application in the current Church; perhaps much more in need than the old one. The problem complicates because while it is possible to mark the beginning of the *Novissima Tempora*, and assuming that current Christianity is already living in them, it is impossible however to pinpoint with exactitude the time of their consummation. Such Times encompass a *current development*, taking place in the present moment, and a definitive future

---

[34] Mt 10:28.

eclosion, whose precise fulfilment is impossible to determine despite the prophecies that point to the signs that are to precede it. The question, anyway, is not to be settled here.

It is indeed a Christian work of mercy to console those who mourn. *Blessed are they that mourn, for they shall be comforted.*[35] A twofold promise which includes in turn a double consolation: those who mourn will be comforted, and they shall be blessed.[36]

The persecutions and sufferings that the first Christians had to endure constituted the *first* of a number of tests to which the Church shall be subjected throughout her history. Later, many more came in the course of the centuries. After all, the disciples of Jesus Christ cannot but follow the path of their Master, the Innocent Lamb dead on the Cross for the sins of the world: *Whither I go you know, and the way you know... I am the way...*[37] *The disciple is not above the master, nor the servant above his lord. It is enough for the disciple that he be as his master, and the servant as his lord.*[38]

Something that Shepherds and theologians of the *Church* of Neo-Modernism tend to forget. The same one that intends to become a naturalistic and deistic religion, made by man and for man; the *Church* of social welfare, of human rights, of *solidarity* among men, and the one that hopes to achieve peace in the world apart from God. In short, the objective that Freemasonry has always pursued.

However, Christianity is the religion of the Innocent Lamb slain for the sins of men, whose triumph takes place precisely through His death on the Cross. After which, there is no other way for His

---

[35] Mt 5:5.

[36] Such beatitude does not refer primarily to the happiness of Heaven, obtained as a reward for those who suffered from injustice here on Earth. The promise of happiness contained in the beatitudes begins now in the present pilgrimage.

[37] Jn 14: 4.6.

[38] Mt 10: 24–25.

disciples by which they can reach the meaning and purpose of their existence: *For unto you it is given for Christ, not only to believe in him, but also to suffer for him* (Phil 1:29). Christianity is not the religion of welfare or social peace.[39]

The early Church had to suffer and cry for her members driven to martyrdom. Although, ultimately, it was a time of glory and a fertile seedbed for the golden stages that came later. The truth is that the Age of Martyrs underpinned the foundations of the Church.

What has happened in modern times, however, is very different. During the first half of the twentieth century, the Church continued to navigate the sea of this world. A stormy sea, of course, as it has always been and never ceases to be; but one which could not prevent Peter's Barque from crossing its waters with sufficient tranquility and in high spirits. The Church, despite confronting, as always, numerous obstacles and maneuvers of the Enemy, was able to live a flourishing period of profound and lively faith for the Christian People, along with a prestigious Hierarchy, vocations to consecrated life, and important and numerous conversions... Until at last Pope John XXIII decided to *open the windows of the Vatican* and announce later to the whole Christian world that, following an inspiration received from the Holy Spirit, he had decided with his Apostolic Authority to call a Universal Council. Any alert observer could have guessed that a profound change was coming.

---

[39] The claim (also supported by many Catholics) of a well-being and social peace *for this world*, is but one of the consequences of the rejection of the doctrine of original sin. The good man *by nature,* who in turn can give rise to a society that is also natural and definitively good, which does not exist anywhere, which is, for the same reason just a utopia, despite the Rousseau-type rationalist philosophy. The only reality is that of a fallen nature because of sin, although later repaired by grace (granted by Jesus Christ) with all the attendant consequences.

The windows of the Vatican did open, and probably a new air entered through them. The bad thing about the case is that *new* is not synonymous with *good*, so it is not possible to deduce from this fact that things would necessarily improve.[40] With all certainty, what was introduced into the Church, according to a later confession of Paul VI, was the *smoke of Satan*. And subsequent events seem to have confirmed it.

The Catholic world witnessed the rising of a large group of *Novelties*. Most of which have given plenty of reasons to cry and lament: *Here is the patience and the faith of the saints*.[41] And indeed all those novelties clearly manifested that the consolation of the *Apocalypse* was going to be more necessary than ever for the faithful of good will.

The Catholic Church, which until then had been the Church founded by Jesus Christ, seemed to have fallen in rank and lost her status as the *Only Church*. Single Church status. From now on, and according to the conciliar texts, the Church founded by Jesus Christ *subsisted* in the Catholic Church, now renamed the *Church of Christ*. It is obvious that, if words have meaning, the concept *subsist* displaces here the doctrine of the One True one, or the *Unam, Sanctam, Catholicam, et Apostolicam Ecclesiam*. If that is the case, was then accepted the doctrine that acknowledges that all churches are true, and, consequently, none of them can claim to be the only one founded by Jesus Christ? Or the doctrine which maintains that in any of them one can validly and lawfully seek the way of Salvation? Since an exhaustive and firm clarification on the

---

[40] It is painful to admit that the phrase of his successor is somewhat demeaning to and undeserved by Pope Pius XII, after all a great Pontiff, whatever his malicious detractors may say.

[41] Rev 13:10.

Introduction 31

subject was never made afterwards, it is obvious that the question has been left up for grabs.[42]

The fact is that the windows were opened. Or perhaps it was the door which was *left open* with an obvious ecumenical intention, whichever one chooses. The results were the same and quite surprising. Highly influential elements rushed in whose orthodoxy in doctrine was rather doubtful. Some of the most important elements were Maritain, Hans Küng, Schillebeeckx, Rahner, etc. The influence of the latter (what is known and what has not been sufficiently studied yet) was decisive in the deliberations of the last Council.(D)

* * *

(D) This is not the place to outline a history of the development and of the structures of the Second Vatican Council or the influence which, to a greater or lesser degree, certain theologians or *periti* may have had on it.

Suffice it to point out now, with regard to Maritain (whose inclusion on the list may surprise the less aware), that his alleged *Thomism* was more verbose than real. And since this is not about judging intentions of people, we will not call into question the faith of this convert who personally always appeared as an ardent Catholic. Doctrinally, however, his *humanism* was so excessively human as to be able to do without God. In his attempt at solving the problems of the Church and of the world, Maritain advocated for a certain *universal brotherhood* among all men of

---

[42]It is possible to discuss whether or not *subsist* includes other Churches, but it is quite obvious that *it does not exclude them*. Perhaps the solution to the problem needs to be found in *Ecumenical good will*. Nevertheless, it will always be weird not to present the Catholic Church as the only Church founded by Jesus Christ. It is easy to guess the intention: to leave the door open and see if those who are outside come in; not realizing, unfortunately, that an *open door* also allows the exit of those who are inside. The worst consequence of this issue is the enormous danger of leaving matters of such decisive importance mired in ambiguity.

good will, in which he included all who professed any religion, or even none. Within it, the Church would be in charge of exercising her salvific mission, but without trying to impose herself and be recognized as the only true Church. His excessive faith in what is human as such, the offshoot of an exaggerated optimism that put original sin in parentheses, impelled him to leave the divine in the shade, with the usual consequences: a religion more centered in man than in God. "The main defect of anthropocentric humanism (writes Maritain) was that it was centered on man, and not on humanism." However, it is obvious to everyone that humanism, by definition, is man centered! The adjective is completely superfluous; a simple tautology, only possible through the linguistic trap of using a Greek root that repeats the meaning of the noun of Latin origin.[43] His most important and decisive book, *Humanisme Intégral,* was the vade mecum of Pope Paul VI, an ardent enthusiast of Maritain's doctrines, who had them translated into Italian. Which doctrines, as it is easy to demonstrate, lie in the background of many of the Pope's decisions regarding the Council.

* * *

That was how the Catholics (and also the non-Catholics) of the years that followed the Second Vatican Council found themselves unexpectedly with a different Church than the one they had known before said Council:

Radical change in the Liturgy, with more than a Copernican turn.[44] The Mass (now the Eucharist) had been completely desecrated and left in the hands of the anarchic improvisation of one and all (Episcopal Conferences, Bishops, and of course, the simple

---

[43] Michael Davies, *o. c.* pg. 286.

[44] Would this turn be somewhat strange if the Liturgical Reform was directed by Archbishop Bugnini, head of the corresponding Commission and a known and recognized Freemason? It is true that the person was deposed by the Pope after being discovered. Nonetheless his work was left intact.

Presbyters acting creatively on their own). Gregorian chant had been replaced by the music and revelry of the nearby disco but of a worse quality. The Latin and the texts of the Liturgical Books were supplanted by the language of the *man in the street*. The Mass (Eucharist) has lost entirely its character of Sacrifice (the Sacrifice of the Cross), giving way to the concept of a mere meal that promotes solidarity among the faithful.[45] The faith of the faithful (and of much of the Hierarchy) in the Real Presence of Jesus Christ in the Eucharist is now past history. The sacraments, and especially that of penance, have been relegated to the attic where useless junk is kept. Consecrated life (secular and religious) has been reduced, in terms of number of vocations, by an eighty and ninety percent; meanwhile, desertions have increased in similar number (the seminaries and novitiates are closed at a rate similar to the closure of parishes). The spectacle of the temples during Sunday Mass is reminiscent of the photographs of deserted and uninhabited places. The cult and the devotion of the Christian people towards the saints has been dismissed by introducing hundreds and hundreds of new ones in the Book of Saints, thus depriving the old and the new ones alike of their status as *extraordinary figures* and turning them into pocket currency that everyone handles.

Young people (including those who, according to the *media*, are always with the Pope) are nowhere to be found; as busy as they are with sex, drugs, and other attractions offered by *progressive culture*. The Hierarchy and the Magisterium have been discredited. The *democratization* of the Church has reached the most humble and

---

[45]The sacrificial character of the Mass is *expressly denied* by Groups and increasing numbers of theologians within the Church; as, to cite just one patent example, the Neocatechumenal Communities (founded by Kiko Argüello and Carmen Hernández), today one of the largest and most powerful Groups within the Church.

remote parishes, where it has been discovered that the figure of the priest or the pastor is no longer necessary for anything. There is no need to continue.

In spite of which (and much more) it is a common opinion that the changes introduced cannot be cause for alarm, since, it is claimed, they are merely accidental or insubstantial; besides, they have been extremely beneficial for the Church (the so-called *Springtime of the Church*).

It is necessary to recognize that the behavior of human nature is often amazing. As it happens, for example, with its ability to ensure, naturally and without batting an eye, that white is black and that black is white. In the issue we are examining nothing has changed, and everything remains the same. Or the change seems substantial but, in reality, is merely accidental. Or the other way around; actually, it is quite a problem to figure out. Which brings to mind an old well-known. Certain stories or anecdotes, such as the one told below, alluding to human behavior, despite the fact that they just seem comical and funny, and sometimes even crazy, they contain in the background a deep philosophy that points to a more exhaustive knowledge of man:

Two presumed friends meet on the street and one of them says to the other:

—Hello, Pepe; but how changed you are...!

And the aforementioned answers:

—Listen, friend, I'm not Pepe...!

To which the first insists:

—Well, more in my favor, gosh, more in my favor...!

Where everything seems to indicate that here the Aristotelian logic has been ruined. Pepe has changed so much that he is no longer

Pepe (according to his own confession), in spite of which he is still Pepe for the friend, who only appreciates a profound (substantial?) change there. In short, without being Pepe, he is still Pepe. This reasoning seems unable (impossible for some) to follow the laws of Logic; nevertheless, it is a fact. It could even happen that what the laws of human Logic cannot admit is quite acceptable to divine Logic.

Of course, divine Logic may be above human reason, human all you want, but never against it. An explanation, therefore, must be found. And it is that the Church has changed so much that she no longer seems to be herself in any respect; hence it is difficult to believe in a mere accidental change. However, it is known, against all appearances, that she is still the Church since the very promise of her Divine Founder is at stake: *and the gates of hell shall not prevail against it.*[46]

So, the Church cannot be destroyed, according to the words of the Lord, which is therefore safe and incontrovertible. Although something can also happen which, although not contradicting that statement, is capable of posing serious problems: the Church is there and cannot disappear, according to the promise of Jesus Christ. But she can be so disfigured that it becomes difficult to recognize her with certainty and without danger of getting lost:

> *Shew me, O thou whom my soul loveth,*
> *Where thou feedest, where thou liest in the midday,*
> *Lest I begin to wander*
> *After the flocks of thy companions.*[47]

---

[46] Mt 16:18.
[47] Song 1:7.

Or it may even happen that the number of sheep becomes extremely small, to the point that it becomes difficult to locate the place where the authentic and diminished herd is to be found. It could happen that it would not be easy to find the flock with certainty, among other numerous ones that are not those of the true Shepherd (*the flocks of thy companions*). There is no exaggeration here, since Jesus Christ Himself had already announced it: *And because iniquity hath abounded, the charity of many shall grow cold.*[48] *But yet the Son of man, when he cometh, shall he find, think you, faith on earth?*[49] *For there shall arise false Christs and false prophets, and shall show great signs and wonders, insomuch as to deceive (if possible) even the elect.*[50] *For there shall be then great tribulation, such as hath not been from the beginning of the world until now, neither shall be. And unless those days had been shortened, no flesh should be saved: but for the sake of the elect those days shall be shortened.*[51] Of course it would be impossible to pinpoint the precise moment in which these words will come true, *although it is evident that the time for their fulfilment will certainly arrive*: it is an equally incontrovertible fact.

The time may come when things will not be easy, not even for the very elect. With a Hierarchy of authenticity and probity difficult to verify, a Theology diluted with elements imported from Protestantism and distorted by Modernism, an anarchic and desecrated Liturgy, consecrated life disappearing and becoming disbanded, an intentionally discredited clergy, a Morality questioned and questionable in all its parts..., would it be so strange if there were moments

---

[48] Mt 24:12.
[49] Lk 18:8.
[50] Mt 24:24.
[51] Mt 24: 21–22.

in which the sheep of the flock felt disoriented, even momentarily, and not knowing where to turn? They would feel so confused and disoriented, should they see themselves without a shepherd, that they would not know what to do or where to go: *They shall be afflicted, because they have no shepherd.*[52] *Strike the shepherd, and the sheep shall be scattered.*[53]

What could happen if the sheep found themselves without a shepherd? Or if the shepherd would not lead them to good pasture, or even would deprive them of grass. What then if he would desert them in the face of danger and falter before the duties of his office, or if his conduct would no longer deserve their trust? What would happen to Catholics of good will if they came to think that their Shepherds no longer believe in their job, that being the reason for their abandonment of the ancient beliefs and practices inherited from their ancestors? And what if, in addition to all this, the Shepherds were in favor of procedures and doctrines, strange or foreign, that would lead to nothing but confusion and the loss of faith on the part of the members of the flock?

Catholics of good will would stand firm in the faith. Remembering the promise of their Lord, they would know that the Church is still there, immovable and indestructible. They would insist on their conviction that one of the foundations of their faith is their bond with their Shepherds, constituted in Hierarchy: *Ubi Petrus, ibi Ecclesia.* And they would continue believing that breaking their ties with the Church would mean for them to abandon the only way of salvation. So it is and so it should be. However, how to associate such beliefs, true and certain as they are, with the reality of the facts that they are witnessing every day? With the acceptance of

---

[52] Zec 10:2.
[53] Zec 13:7. Cf Mt 26:31; Mk 14:27.

doctrines and practices that are being imposed on them since they are convinced that those doctrines are strange as well as harmful? How can the faithful believe in a Hierarchy that no longer believes in itself? And how can they live the fundamental principles of their faith when their own Shepherds consider them obsolete, inappropriate, and useless for the *new age* which the world is living?

How can they feel protected by a Magisterium that *expressly* recognizes that its mission is none other than to *cancel* the previous one? For it has been said and repeated, in an official or quasi-official manner by prominent members of the Hierarchy of the Church, that some of the Conciliar Documents aim directly against the *Syllabus* of Pope Pius IX.[54] How can they not feel strange and foreign in what always was (and still is) their House, which is the Church, if it is now extremely difficult for them to recognize her? And how are they not going to cry about it? As indeed it has already been said: *How shall we sing the song of the Lord in a strange land?*[55]

The *Apocalypse* is a Book of Consolation. A consolation very much needed by the Christians in the early days of the Church. However, even persecuted and martyred, they knew perfectly what to expect They firmly believed in Jesus Christ and joyfully gave their lives for Him. They felt within the Church, which they knew without hesitation where she was and where she was not. They were also aware of who their Shepherds were, and which were the sentiments by which they ruled themselves and governed the faithful; at the same time they saw their Shepherds march to martyrdom ahead of them and leading the way.

---

[54]Regarding the magisterial importance of this last Document, it suffices to refer to the treatises of Theology or of the History of the Church.

[55]Ps 137:4.

Introduction 39

The situation of the Christians of the last times is much more serious.[56] Now they are not only persecuted (although persecution exists, and with greater refinement and cruelty); they are confused and dispersed. Early Christians marched with joy towards martyrdom: in life and in death *they felt inside the Church*. The Christians of the last times, who are also persecuted and with greater intensity, are subjected to confusion, which is something still more serious. Is death really worse than the darkness that involves not knowing where you are, or where you are going, or what is the end of it all? *The fact is that now it is not so easy to know for sure where one is*. And there is something else: For early Christians, Paradise meant the possession of God; something they expected beyond, once they suffered martyrdom. The Christians of the last times, instead, are offered something else as their final destination: a better world, built on the basis of material well-being, human justice, and solidarity among men. And the tremendous thing about this situation, which carries with it an incredible tragedy, is that the human heart is incapable of being satiated with a horizontal perspective of *more of the same*; and hence his anguish: *If in this life only we have hope in Christ, we are of all men most miserable.*[57] On the other hand, when the human being has the courage to face himself, and includes honesty in the monologue of his intimate speech, he ends up knowing the falsehood of utopias (after all, a product for the exclusive use of the self-deluded) and *he feels utterly unable to believe in them*. The truth is that *more of the same but better* becomes in the end *nothing of what was promised*.

---

[56]To term the times under which the current life of Christians takes place as last times, or *novissima tempora*, is an original idea of Sacred Scripture.

[57]1 Cor 15:19.

In short, once admitted that the *Apocalypse* is a Book of Consolation, it is easy to see that it was written with a view to the recent times even more than for the first. Whence one can ask: In what sense and in what way can it serve as consolation to some Christians who are to be harassed and persecuted like vermin? *Behold, I am sending you out like sheep in the midst of wolves.*[58] For it is indeed true that harassment will give quarter neither from outside nor from inside. And it may even happen that there are times when persecution from within shall be more intense than that exercised from outside: *The brother also shall deliver up the brother to death, and the father the son: and the children shall rise up against their parents, and shall put them to death. And you shall be hated by all men for my name's sake: but he that shall persevere unto the end, he shall be saved... And as a man's enemies shall be they of his own household.*[59]

Since God does not do anything at random, it is evident that the *Apocalypse* had to be written with a well-determined intention. The intention, indeed, of consoling (with a view to the moment the Book was written and especially to the future) some disciples who would have to go through the trance of painful tests. After all, they have been called to participate in the existence and in the Cross of their Master.

Such consolation would have to be carried out considering the ways of human nature. Now the man who suffers needs to know *why* he suffers, and also *for which purpose* he suffers. It may happen that he never finds out, in which case he will be doomed inevitably to anguish, as happens with so many human beings. Which is still a situation *contra natura* because the human being, and even more

---

[58] Mt 10:16. Cf 7:15.
[59] Mt 10: 21–22.36.

so the Christian, has not been destined to despair or to emptiness. On the other hand, he does have to count on suffering as part of his existence, but never on anguish.

A *Christian* synonymous with *object of persecution*. Actually, one thing necessarily leads to the other: *Blessed are ye when they shall revile you, and persecute you, and speak all that is evil against you, untruly, for my sake: Be glad and rejoice.*[60] *If they have persecuted me, they will also persecute you.*[61] *If the world hate you, know ye, that it hath hated me before you.*[62] *Woe to you when men shall bless you: for according to these things did their fathers to the false prophets.*[63] That is why the Christian knows with certainty the cause and the meaning of his sufferings. And since he knows they are part of God's plan, integrated as something essential in the structure of his Christian existence, he cannot adopt an attitude other than *to rejoice in them and for them*. Being destined to a glorious and victorious end, his sufferings are marked necessarily with a tinge of joy. Once they have been announced by the Lord, they must become for the disciples an instrument that strengthens them in their faith and confirms them in their hope: *But these things I have told you, that when the hour shall come, you may remember that I told you of them.*[64]

That is the meaning of a consolation prophecy. It does announce persecutions and sufferings; nevertheless, since such sufferings are for the Christian a source of joy, advanced knowledge of them is a foretaste of that joy: *For as the sufferings of Christ abound in us:*

---

[60] Mt 5: 11–12.
[61] Jn 15:20.
[62] Jn 15:18.
[63] Lk 6:26.
[64] Jn 16:4.

so also by Christ doth our comfort abound.[65] The Apostle puts the two hemistiches in the present, since both ailments and consolation take place now.

But suffering does not have its reason for being in itself, unless one tries to explain it with absurd arguments, which actually happens outside the Christian view of reality. Its deepest reason for being cannot be any other, within the context of Christian existence, than love itself. As we have seen from the Apostle, the cause of the sufferings, as well as the consolation, of the Christian is none other than Christ: the abundance with which the Christian partakes in the sufferings of Christ corresponds to the abundance of his consolation in Christ. From the point of view of the prophetic framework, knowing that one suffers for the Beloved and with the Beloved is already sharing in the joy of the Beloved.

This is how a dualism of contradictory sentiments (suffering/joy) is produced in the Christian, that actually merge into only one, although with two apparently different faces (*sweet and sour*), namely: a suffering that causes joy.

Such a bittersweet feeling feeds off two others, which also are dependent on each other: the feeling of *absence* and the *nostalgic hope*. Now it is already lawful to speak of a true contrast: the sharp reality of absence is what gives rise to the adamantine strength of hope. In turn, the interregnum or interval between one feeling and the other paves the way for suffering. All these are expressed in the *Song of the Songs*, according to its poetic genre and precisely in that order: absence, nostalgia, and the interlude of suffering. All of this with respect to the Beloved, according to what is essential in Christian existence:

---

[65] 2 Cor 1:5.

> *I opened the bolt of my door to my beloved:*
> *But he had turned aside, and was gone.*
> *I sought him, and found him not:*
> *I called, and he did not answer me.*
>
> *The keepers that go about the city found me:*
> *They struck me: and wounded me:*
> *The keepers of the walls*
> *Took away my veil from me.*
>
> *I adjure you, O daughters of Jerusalem,*
> *If you find my beloved,*
> *That you tell him that I languish with love.*[66]

The very expression *not yet*, with which is designated, in the eschatological theological language, the situation of the Christian in the present eon while waiting to reach his ultimate end, already means both extreme terms (*absence/hope*) of the trinomial alluded to above. *Not* actually indicates absence. But the adverb *yet* has an eminently positive meaning: you do not have it, but there is the certainty that you will have it; where it is evident that the emphasis is placed on *what is to be had* rather than on *what you do not have*. The adverb *yet*, to the extent that it indicates a certainty about something that is going to happen (or that is going to be possessed) in a certain future, expresses hope, or anticipated possession. It seems, indeed, as if *not* was absorbed by *yet*.

According to which, if the term *not yet* is placed in relation to its apparently contrary *already*, it can happen that both indicators of the current and final situation of the still-itinerant Christian do not appear as antagonistic as one might think. Otherwise, as far as that, even the *still*, as has been seen, indicates in itself a true hope;

---

[66] Song 5: 6–8.

it is also already an anticipated possession. And it is that, in reality, the existence of the Christian *has already received the pledge of the Spirit* (2 Cor 1:22; Eph 1:14). Therefore, his existence, even if now an itinerant one, involves more possession than absence.

The first persecuted Christians had, however, the opportunity to see things clearly: from the militant Church on earth in which they found themselves, through suffering and martyrdom to Heaven. There was no room for hesitation: *And whither I go you know, and the way you know.*[67]

For the Christians of the *novissima tempora*, on the other hand, things are different, and the situation is much more painful. *Lord, to whom shall we go?* Like Saint Peter, they know that their true point of arrival, the one that unfailingly marks the end of the way, is Christ. He is also the only way for the Christian, since any other would be the wrong one —otherwise wide and comfortable, on which many walk— which leads to perdition (Mt 7:13). But it is not easy for them to *know* for sure if they are really at the right starting point, or if they really walk on the right path. Understand well that here we are not saying that it *is not possible for them know*, but merely *that it is not an easy task for them to know with certainty*. Such uncertainty of knowledge can but produce intense anguish, insofar as it is nothing less than Eternal Life which is at stake. It is true that such uncertainty is destined to become certainty; although, the Christians of the *novissima tempora* will not be able to reach that security if they do not strongly embrace the Cross, because the Church seems to have entered a situation of *kenosis* or concealment. They know that she is there and could not be destroyed, according to the guarantee granted by her Divine Founder that *the Gates of Hell*

---

[67] Jn 14:4.

will not prevail against her.[68] However, when they contemplate what is being offered to them as the Mother herself from which they were born into supernatural life, in whose lap they had always their Home and their refuge, they cannot fail to see something which, under all aspects, strikes them as different, as if that Mother had been spirited away from them and replaced by a different and spurious one.

And therein lies their tragedy. Because either they think they cannot find her, or they find it very difficult (perhaps impossible?) to recognize her. And yet they know that it is not lawful for them to set out on the road in search of another, since only One is the one founded by Jesus Christ, and only One is the True one. The same in which they were born to the life of grace and in whose womb they were welcomed to be led towards fullness in Christ; despite the fact that, not infrequently, more with gestures than with words, She herself seems to place herself on an equal footing with other different and even antagonistic options, as if she considered them equally valid. Of course, she cannot be the author of such a felony since she could not contradict herself. But a number of her members, even some high-ranking Hierarchs, could definitely be held responsible, hence the anguish and confusion of the sheep that make up the Flock of the One Shepherd: *And my sheep were scattered, because there was no shepherd: and they became the prey of all the beasts of the field, and were scattered. My sheep have wandered in every mountain, and in every high hill: and my flocks were scattered upon the face of the earth, and there was none that sought them, there was none, I say, that sought them.*[69] That the same Revealed Word be the one that denounces the existence of bad Shepherds (Jn 10) is the only thing capable of dissipating the wicked lethargy that has

---

[68] Mt 16:18.
[69] Ezek 34: 5–6; cf 34:8; Is 56: 9–12. Etc.

plunged the Flock into a dangerous dream, induced by an anesthetic propaganda, which has led us to believe that the existence of bad Shepherds is impossible. A dangerous dream which came about thanks to a certain indiscriminate cult of personality, without any possibility of questioning it, that someone has spread, and which ancient Christians never suffered.

Next to the tomb of the Risen One, the angels thus addressed Mary Magdalen:

—*Woman, why are you weeping?*

—*They have taken my Lord away,* she replied, *and I don't know where they have put him.*[70]

And how could true Christians not cry when everything seems to indicate that the Lord's Body has been stolen from them? And there are, indeed, moments in the life of the human being in which there is no room but for tears and pain: *Can the children of the bridegroom mourn, as long as the bridegroom is with them? But the days will come, when the bridegroom shall be taken away from them, and then they shall fast.*[71]

Is there greater pain than that of a wife in love who believes that she has lost her husband? Perhaps that of a mother who has lost her children? Perhaps. But surely there is still a most incomprehensible pain, which is that of the children who come to think that they have lost their mother or that they have been abandoned by her; and not because of an inescapable misfortune, but because she had reneged her own maternal condition, having given herself to some histrionics that makes her appear to her own children as something different, strange, and unknown to them.

---

[70] Jn 20:13.
[71] Mt 9:15.

Introduction 47

But is it possible that a situation could arise in which a mother abandons her children? It would seem so: *For my father and my mother have left me: but the Lord hath taken me up.*[72]

And yet..., not even in the face of this last and terrible situation, in the event that it happened, *would the good sons disown their mother*. And where would they go?

The Mother will never relinquish her condition as Mother and will always be there for her children (*portæ inferi non prævalebunt*), no matter how big an effort her children will have to make in looking for her and recognizing her. Which will by no means be an easy task, as evidenced by the words of Jesus Christ stating that the Bridegroom will be *taken away* from His friends.[73] Where it does not seem to allude to a state of mere kenosis or concealment, but to that of looting or dispossession. Be that as it may, one thing is certain: the situation which Christians will be forced to confront at some point in History, regarding the Body of Christ that is the Church (Col 1:24), will not be a joke at all. On the contrary, they will be distressing moments and a difficult ordeal in which the task of knowing where the Body of the Lord has been placed (Jn 20:13) will be beyond difficult.

However, all this will happen for the greater glory of the elect, *because to them that love God, all things work together unto good, to such as, according to his purpose, are called to be saints.*[74] And also for greater derision and ignominy of those who have embraced the paths of the Lie and opted for Evil. This is, in reality, the only reason that explains the passage of time: so that the human being, in the exercise of his freedom, become more perverse if he has

---

[72] Ps 27:10.

[73] The verb used here is ἀπ-αίρω, *aufero*, *tollo*.

[74] Rom 8:28.

so chosen; or for him to increase his maturity in Christ, if he has decided for Him. Definitely, God created time to manifest His glory before the creatures: *For the time is at hand. He that hurteth, let him hurt still: and he that is filthy, let him be filthy still: and he that is just, let him be justified still: and he that is holy, let him be sanctified still.*[75]

The sufferings and persecutions to which the elect are subjected point towards a single end: to widen and dilate their hearts so that they overflow with feelings of abandonment, absence, nostalgia, desire, and anxiety to be with their Lord. The greater the sense of absence, the greater anguish for the encounter. Faced with greater suffering and difficulties, the greater the growth of hope. The greater abundance of darkness, the greater the joy because of the certainty that the moment of light is approaching: *The night is nearly over, daylight is on the way.*[76] The *Apocalypse* is a Book of Consolation, written precisely to testify and endorse these realities. And hence the apotheosis of its gigantic culmination:

The Spirit and the Bride say, "Come!"
Let everyone who listens answer, "Come!"
...The one who attests these things says:
I am indeed coming soon.
Amen; come, Lord Jesus.[77]

Man was created as a person because he was made to love and to be loved, and in the manner of perfect love, that is: *usque in finem.*[78] In a way (*secundum quid*) for him to carry out his act of love to an even higher degree than that of the angels. For love is a

---

[75] Rev 22: 10–11.

[76] Rom 13:12.

[77] Rev 22: 17.20.

[78] Jn 13:1 according to the Vulgate; *in finem* in the Neovulgate.

relationship of equality in perfect reciprocity, or from a *thou* to an *I*: *My beloved is for me and I am for my beloved.*[79] And the Word became a man, and not an angel.

However, the way in which human existence has been structured in the History of Salvation (in the last, eternal, and unknown plans of God), set to carry out the preliminary test of itinerancy and militancy, an unlimited anguish of anxiety was necessary first. Or an infinite desire. Hence the need for the immense pains of absence, of nostalgia, and of so many kinds and species of sufferings. For only an infinite love (of a *thou* toward an *I*) can be called to fulfill an infinite longing (from an *I* toward a *thou*).

If the greatest sufferings are the gateway, for the human being, of the greatest love, such sufferings can only be blessed: *Beati qui lugent.*[80] And this is precisely what the Book of the *Apocalypse* announces. Once again, God has been the Victory. For Himself and for His own.

---

[79] Song 6:3; 2:16. Innumerable are the texts of the New Testament that could be quoted here, which express the identity or communion of lives between Jesus and His own.

[80] Mt 5:4.

*He who has an ear, let him hear what the Spirit says
to the churches*
(Rev 2:7)

LETTER TO THE CHURCH OF EPHESUS

To the angel of the church in Ephesus write:
The words of him who holds the seven stars in his right hand, who walks among the seven golden lampstands. "I know your works, your toil, and your patient endurance, and how you cannot bear evil men but have tested those who call themselves apostles but are not, and found them to be false; I know you are enduring patiently and bearing up for my name's sake, and you have not grown weary. But I have this against you, that you have abandoned the love you had at first. Remember then from what you have fallen, repent and do the works you did at first. If not, I will come to you and remove your lampstand from its place, unless you repent. Yet this you have, you hate the works of the Nicolaitans, which I also hate."

(Rev 2: 1–6)

I

THE VOICE OF THE SPIRIT

Since it is the Spirit Who is going to speak to the respective churches, it is important to be ready to listen: *He who has an ear, let him hear what the Spirit says to the churches.*[1] Of course, since we are dealing with the Spirit, to say that it is important to pay attention to His words is almost superfluous. It is indeed necessary to place the greatest possible emphasis on the warning, hence the opportunity to use an exhortation with a strong tone; one that is sufficiently capable of provoking an attitude of attention and extremely vigilant listening.

However, the challenges presented by the task must be taken into account. For language, as is well known, contains strange and exciting peculiarities: always insufficient to show completely the thought of the speaker and at the same time, as if by paradox, possessing infinite virtualities and possibilities. Hence, the exhortation to be ready to listen attentively to the words of the Spirit is no more than a minuscule warning, even if, at least for the moment, that is all that can be said. Just as it would be almost unimportant to insist that careful listening is a matter of life or death; for what is at stake here is something that goes beyond the one and beyond the other, if one

---

[1]Rev 2: 7.11.17; etc.

tries to signify by these two words what men ordinarily understand by them.

On the other hand, the fact that the exhortation is addressed *to those who have ears* is not an inconsequential or trivial matter. Obviously, only those who have ears will be able to hear the Spirit. Although anyone can immediately understand that no allusion is made here to the need to possess the pertinent sensory organ; which would be such a simplistic and naive way of understanding things as not to take them into account at all.

Possessing ears capable of hearing the Spirit is something more complex and complicated than it might seem. And since the bodily senses are not the normal means of hearing Him, there is reason to think that the biblical expression is nothing more than a metaphor.

We must keep in mind that the Spirit, if we can speak in this way, is extraordinarily versatile and absolutely unpredictable. Of course, It is Perfect and Absolute Freedom (2 Cor 3:17), and hence It is unfathomable and unpredictable for the human understanding and heart: *The wind (πνεῦμα) blows where it wills and you hear its voice, but you do not know where it comes from or where it goes.*[2] If He blows *where He wills*, it is also to be supposed that He blows *when He wills*. Man can certainly *hear His voice*, but this does not necessarily mean that he *listens* to it; still less that he understands it, for which he needs to possess a certain affinity with the Spirit (1 Cor 2:14), which will be discussed later.

The fact that the Spirit of God is unpredictable and absolutely transcendent to the human being, to the point that it is not possible to know where He comes from or where His breath leads, does not mean that His voice is unintelligible. On the contrary. The voice

---

[2] Jn 3:8 The Neovulgate translates thus: *Spiritus, ubi vult, spirat, etc.* The Greek term πνεῦμα, like its Hebrew equivalent, also means wind or spirit.

through which God has spoken to man is the Word itself, or the Word made Flesh, thus becoming for man Supreme Intelligibility. It is true that God had already spoken to him through the ages in many and various ways. But never so clearly until He became Man in Jesus Christ, in order to be seen, heard, and understood at last with the utmost clarity. From then on God no longer spoke from the cloud, nor through Moses or the other prophets, but directly and in a way we can hear: *In many and various ways God spoke of old to our fathers by the prophets; but in these last days he has spoken to us by a Son, whom he appointed the heir of all things, through whom also he created the world.*[3] After that, the Spirit would continue personally to exercise His functions, but only to *remind* and *make men understand* the words and deeds *(coepit facere et docere)* of the Word made Flesh (Jn 16: 13–14).

It is quite another thing that the hardness of the human heart does not want to hear the voice of God: *Utinam hodie vocem eius audiatis: Nolite obdurare corda vestra.*[4] If only the pure in heart will see God (Mt 5:8), the same can be said of those who are able to hear the voice of the Spirit. Who, being Love, never gives Himself except in sovereign and perfect freedom (2 Cor 3:17), which is the same as saying to the expectation of a reciprocal (loving) response that is also voluntary and absolutely free. Hence the Spirit does not seem willing to enter into dialogue with the fool who does not want to hear: *Do not speak in the hearing of a fool, for he will despise the wisdom of your words.*[5](A)

* * *

---

[3]Heb 1: 1–2.
[4]Ps 95:8; Heb 3: 7–8.15; 4:7.
[5]Prov 23:9.

(A) Never has there been so much talk of *Dialogue* and never has there been less understanding among men as now. The Catholic Church herself (now renamed the *Church of Christ*) has opted for this procedure as the best way to achieve a greater understanding of the *Separated Brethren*. Everything seems to indicate that men are convinced that any problem can be solved, including the most difficult ones, as long as there is an exchange (rapprochement) of opinions. The bad thing is that such an assumption has been given pride of place, forgetting other presuppositions no less fundamental and equally necessary.

In the first place, any Dialogue that intends to be fruitful must first count on the sincere and good will of the interlocutors. Good will, which, in turn, can only be based on mutual respect and on some sort of true love between the two. Since Dialogue that seeks an understanding, by definition, must be based on a series of *concessions*, it would become useless if there is no previous willingness to surrender (love) on both sides. If no one is willing to *give in* (in its original sense of giving, conceding, and renouncing), Dialogue has no meaning. And God being the only fount of all true love, if men do not drink from It, it is impossible for them to love one another. Or to put it another way: if men do not know how, or do not want to dialogue with God beforehand, they will never be able to do so among themselves. Of course, they will be able to deceive each other and themselves with intricate rhetoric and sophisticated verbiage (solidarity, fraternity, collaborationism, insistence on what unites in order to put in parentheses what separates, etc., etc.), disguised in turn in the form of brilliant and showy speeches, agreements, and joint communiqués. But it will all be in vain. In reality, the possibilities of human imagination for both mutual and self–deception are practically limitless.

As for the problems facing the Catholic Church (now *the Church of Christ*) with regard to the *Ecumenical Dialogue*, the least that can be said is that they are thorny and quite difficult. To explain this, and in order to simplify the question as much as possible, leaving aside complex distinctions and designations, let us imagine only two Churches or Interlocutors: the *Catholic Church*, on the one hand, and the *Separated Brethren*, on the other.

Prior to the beginning of the Dialogue, it is assumed that both *Churches* are convinced, each for its part and as a prerequisite, that they contain the truth and the totality of the truth. *If this were not the case, Dialogue would be meaningless.* For if either of them were to believe that it is in error, or that it does not possess the whole truth, what would be the purpose of dialogue? All that would be left would be to accept what the one recognized as being more correct defends in order to resolve the problem.

But in that case, if both the one and the other consider that they contain the truth and the whole truth, *Dialogue becomes impossible*, since it is not possible to renounce the truth and not even a part of it for the sake of error.

Although there is also the hypothesis that both *Churches* at the same time, each one for its part, are willing to recognize that they contain part truth and part error. This can in no way be admitted by anyone who wishes to stand on the ground of truth. For it is impossible for the One Church founded by Jesus Christ to err.[6]

Finally, there still remains the possibility that both *Churches* together recognize that neither of them contains the truth. This is even more aberrant, since such a thing would be tantamount to proclaiming that the Church founded by Jesus Christ *is nowhere to be found.*

From this we must conclude that the mere fact of positing the possibility of *mutually concessive* Dialogue is already an error. Although love presupposes surrender and renunciation, this has nothing to do with this case. For *one cannot give up at all, not even in the slightest part, when it is a question of truth.* To renounce the truth, whether in whole or in part, would be the greatest and most crude of errors. The truth, as well as the condition of being a person, *are the only things that cannot be renounced.* As far as the person is concerned, one cannot love to the point of surrendering the faculty of surrendering (one would cease to be a person); as far

---

[6]We refer, of course, to doctrinal errors; not in terms of discipline or procedural policies. As for the faithful as such, it is evident that they could fall into error or apostatize; many of them or even the great majority: remember the great apostasy (2 Thess 2:3) that will occur at the end of time. But it would be impossible for the Church as such to be subject to error.

as the truth is concerned, to renounce it would be to renounce *being* in order to submerge oneself into *nothingness.*

This is what explains, although it is not always acknowledged, the failure of the so-called *Mixed Commissions* or the *International Theological Commissions.* Their conclusions or joint agreements are perhaps in line with diplomacy and with the attempts at a misunderstood Ecumenism, but not always with the right orthodoxy or with the spiritual good of the Christian People.[7]

Should we believe, therefore, that any ecumenical attempt is doomed to failure? Surely not. It is important to realize that Jesus Christ Himself already recognized that there are sheep that are not within the Flock; at the same time He promised that a time will come when the Flock will be just one, guided in turn by a single Shepherd: *I have other sheep, that are not of this fold; I must bring them also, and they will heed my voice. So there shall be one flock, one shepherd.*[8] Unfortunately, He does not expressly indicate the way to achieve this. Perhaps because, according to His own words, it is only He Who can accomplish it: *it is necessary that I bring them, and they will hear my voice,* He says, speaking in the first person. Or perhaps because the solution could be deduced from an attentive and humble reading of the Gospel as a whole. And it may even be that the key to the problem is contained in the words of the following verse: *For this reason the Father loves me, because I lay down my life, that I may take it again.*[9] According to all this, once again and as always, when all is said and done, it seems that total immolation out of love is the only whistle that Christians could blow to summon them all into the same fold. What is certain, however, is that *the possibility of arriving at union,*

---

[7]Some years ago, some members of the Ecclesial Association *Legionaries of Christ* used to say that *if the Pope is wrong, we will be wrong with the Pope.* A slogan, however, as fervent as it is nonsensical. In the supposed hypothesis that the Pope were to err, being in favor of the error would not cease to be in turn a grave error.

[8]Jn 10:16.

[9]Jn 10:17.

on the basis of yielding to the truth, is absolutely foreign to the Master's thought.

On the other hand, the attempt to arrive at a common path with the *Separated Brethren*, unless they are given a different name, *is a semantically misguided pretension*. For if they are recognized as *separated* Brethren, and if words have any meaning at all, it is because it is admitted that they have separated or split from the common trunk or root of origin. Which implies, as the rules of elementary logic demand, that since they have been the ones who have been separated by their own will from the place of their birth, or only source of waters, *it is precisely for this reason that they are compelled to return.* Or if we go out in search of them, as the Good Shepherd does with the lost sheep, it is precisely to bring them back to the sheepfold (Lk 15:4).

If *Separated Brethren* were in times past considered heretics or schismatics, they are now given a new name. Undoubtedly with good and generous intention, although useless and in vain. For if they are recognized as *separated*, by the very fact of implicitly proclaiming the evident reality of their *voluntary departure*, one ends up at the same reality rendering useless the attempts to elaborate euphemisms. It is always dangerous to play with language.

* * *

It is impossible to imagine the *kenosis* of the Church without the previous *kenosis* of God.

But the *kenosis* of God means the *kenosis* of the Spirit and therefore the absence of His Voice. Precisely now, when it is more necessary than ever to listen to it.

As a consequence, or as a simultaneous (or perhaps previous) event, the Church is struggling in a terrible Darkness into which She has been plunged by a crisis such as She has never known in her history. A gigantic and planned Universal Conspiracy has been unleashed against her. The Enemy, having overcome the outer walls that defended it, has managed to get inside the Inner Sanctuary, where an all–out battle is now being waged... Or perhaps it is not so and there is no such fight, after the Enemy has so wisely managed his strategy that he hardly encounters any resistance. His *Intelligence Agency* has managed to make the inhabitants of the Citadel believe that there is no fighting and no danger in sight; quite the contrary, since they are at that same moment enjoying the most flourishing *Springtime*. It is logical, therefore, that the bastions and strong places of the Fortress have been abandoned, as well as that their courtyards and arcades appear adorned with garlands. Hence also, no one will be willing to admit the truth of what is being said here. Thus, while in what was once the Fortress there is a carefree and festive atmosphere everywhere, the Enemy can now act without hindrance; having cleared the field, he can at last strike the definitive blow at the Immaculate Bride of the Lamb.

As for the few who have survived the Great Deception and are still able to appreciate the reality of things, what can they do but cry out as in the *Apocalypse*, with all the anxiety of which their heart is capable:

—*Come, Lord Jesus*!?

Or else search anxiously everywhere to hear again the voice of the Bridegroom. Who seems to have disappeared, leaving them orphaned.

> *Tell me you, beloved of my soul*
> *Where do you shepherd, where do you rest at midday...*[10]

For they no longer hear in their land the songs of yesteryear. Those same ones that in other ages, singing the melodies of divine

---

[10] Song 1:7.

Love, made human love understandable and livable. Those were the times when love itself, not yet transformed into *solidarity* or *universal brotherhood*, was still simply *charity*: which was not ambitious and never sought its own; which was not irritated and took no account of evil; which did not rejoice in injustice and was always pleased with the truth; which endured all things, believed all things and hoped all things...[11] This was in that Golden Age when people did not speak so much of man–made God as of God made Man in Jesus Christ; when men thought less of *demanding* than of *giving*, or naively believed that *human rights* could only be realized by first considering *divine rights*. Those were the Happy Times when men were convinced that the Adventure of following Jesus Christ, in order to share His Life and Death, was the only goal that could give meaning to their lives and the only thing that could bring them Peace... Or in other words, true Peace, *not that which the world gives* (Jn 14:27); which truly quiets the heart and is capable of filling it with Perfect Joy...

Everything speaks now, however, as if the Great Darkness had definitively arrived. When Art itself seems to have lost the meaning of Beauty, which it used to work so hard to copy (as a mirror does, after contemplating it so profusely scattered throughout Nature), to replace it with the cult of Ugliness and Emptiness. And even Music, which used to captivate the ears of men with its sweet and delightful, almost celestial sounds, has now changed into unpleasant screeching and twisted dissonant noises... capable of finally upsetting human beings already alienated by madness. And what can we say about the way and manner in which men have profaned and perverted the concept of Love? But has the light which radiated in the World, from the very heart of Being, Goodness, Truth, and Beauty, vanished

---

[11] Cf. 1 Cor 13.

in order to give way to the Gloomy Darkness of Perversity and of Nothingness. . .?

If this is so, is it so strange that those who suffer for having refused to participate in what would seem to foreshadow the Apostasy already announced in the *Second Letter to the Thessalonians*, think that God has disappeared and wait in anguish to hear His Voice again? In spite of everything and beyond all that, they continue to be hopeful and believe, with the prophet Jeremiah, *that in these desolate places, in the cities of Judah and in the squares of Jerusalem, without men and without cattle, the voice of joy and the voice of gladness, the voice of the Bridegroom and the voice of the bride, will still be heard.*[12]

The voice of the Bridegroom and the voice of the bride... For the sheep need to hear the voice of the Shepherd, lest they feel forsaken and end up wandering in inhospitable places (Jn 10: 3–5).(B)

* * *

(B) It is noteworthy that the Good Shepherd calls each of the sheep *by name* (Jn 10:3). Indeed, because the name, insofar as it specifically and directly designates a *person*, possesses transcendental importance in the mutual and intimate relationship of the two who love each other, or of the Bridegroom and the Bride in this case.[13]

Hence the surprising observation of what happens in the *Song of Songs* love Poem, in which both the Bridegroom and the Bride never call each

---

[12] *Haec dicit Dominus: Adhuc audietur in loco isto, quem vos dicitis esse desertum, eo quod non sit homo et iumentum in civitatibus Iudæ et foris Ierusalem, quæ desolatæ sunt absque homine et absque habitatore et absque pecore, vox gaudii et vox lætitiæ, vox sponsi et vox sponsæ* (Jer 33: 10–11).

[13] The most peculiar love relationship is that of one to another, or *I* to *thou*. It is the divine–human love relationship.

other by name or use it when referring to the other (for example, to describe him). Instead, they appeal to locutions of love expressed in beautiful and passionate metaphors: *My bride, my sister, my beautiful one, my immaculate one...*, are some of the expressions addressed by the Bridegroom to the Bride throughout the Poem. As for the Bride, she also always speaks of the Bridegroom, or describes him, in the same way: *My beloved is for me a bundle of myrrh... a cluster of cypress... Like an apple tree among the wild trees is my beloved among the young men...*

Whence it is worth asking: Why does the *Song of Songs* use such terminology? Of course, as is logical, only more or less speculative hypotheses are possible here. Which is the only thing to do when delving into the unfathomable mysteries of Love.

That said, everything seems to indicate that the uttering of the name —*[Ego] vocavi te nomine tuo*—[14] is not yet the last stage, but the penultimate, in the relationship of love. It would seem that the relationship of intimacy reaches a moment in which the name is surpassed; as if it would then be more appropriate to substitute it with loving epithets, more capable of deepening and expressing the intimacy and overabundance of love than pronouncing the name of the beloved person would apparently do.

The narrative of the appearance of the Risen Jesus to Mary Magdalene could perhaps provide a hint to explain this. Useful simply to satisfy the curiosity of a scholar of love relationships.

Jesus said to her [Mary Magdalene]:
—Woman, why are you crying? Who is it you are looking for?
Thinking he was the gardener, she said,
—Sir, if you have carried him away, tell me where you have put him, and I will get him.
Jesus said to her,
—Mary.
She turned toward him and cried out in Aramaic,
—Rabboni! (which means "Teacher").
Jesus said,

---

[14] Is 43:1.

—*Do not hold on to me, for I have not yet ascended to the Father...*[15]

Where it is worthy to note the intensity and intimacy of love with which Jesus calls Magdalene by name:

—*Mary*

And yet, He rebukes her not to touch Him: *For He has not yet ascended to His Father.*

Mysterious words that could perhaps allude to the fact that the coming of the Spirit had not yet taken place. And without Him, the love that is manifested here does not yet possess the sufficient *super–natural* entity on which the divine–human loving relationship is based. The use of the personal name is fine; but the time has not yet come for epithets and loving gestures, which are those that most fully express a more intimate and superabundant relationship of love.

* * *

The Bride is filled with joy when she hears, still from afar, the voice of the Beloved:

> *Listen! My beloved! Look! Here he comes,*
> *Leaping across the mountains,*
> *Bounding over the hills.*[16]

The Bridegroom arrives as lovers usually do, hurriedly and impatiently: *leaping over the mountains, bounding over the hills*. And indeed: *leaping* and *bounding* refer to the impatience and speed with which the steps of the lover run; while *mountains* and *hills* has to do with the fact that love overcomes all obstacles, so as not to stop or delay.

---

[15] Jn 20: 15–17.
[16] Song 2:8.

For her part, the Bride feels even more joyful when she realizes the impatience of the Bridegroom. That is why she then says:

> *My beloved is like a gazelle or a young stag.*
> *Look! There he stands behind our wall,*
> *Gazing through the windows,*
> *Peering through the lattice.*[17]

Gazing through the windows implies the possibility of clearly and entirely observing the object contemplated. *Peering through the lattice* is equivalent to looking through in order to perceive what one wishes to see, even if only partially and with difficulty. But in one way or another, what is evident here is that the Bridegroom wishes to reach his bride as soon as possible, in order to contemplate her in any way possible and to express his love for her.

For her part, the Bride feels exhilarated and excited when she hears the voice of the Bridegroom:

> *The voice of the Bridegroom*
> *Like the elusive wake of a ship,*
> *Like the murmuring air,*
> *Like a soft whisper,*
> *Like the nocturnal flight of some bird.*

And since in love everything is mutual and reciprocal, the Bridegroom in turn feels no less eager to hear the voice of the bride. In fact, even more impatient than she is. Although here it could be said, taking advantage of the freedom granted by the subtle, obscure, and often metaphorical language of love, that both possess

---

[17]Song 2:9.

the same heart in a communion of feelings and in supposed unity and equality of anxieties; although without ceasing to be both *one* and the *other* who contemplate and give themselves to each other.

Consequently, the Bridegroom, consumed with anxiety, urges the bride with overtures of love:

> *My dove in the clefts of the rock,*
> *In the hiding places on the mountainside,*
> *Show me your face, let me hear your voice;*
> *For your voice is sweet, and your face is lovely.*[18]

The Bridegroom in love alludes here to the *sweetness* of the Bride's voice, which He wishes to perceive again and again. He likewise applies to the voice the delicate qualities He attributes to her face (*thy face is lovely*), or similar ones. Whence it is perhaps worth remembering here that sight and hearing are the two senses by which beauty is perceived:

> *It is the voice of my beloved*
> *Like a dove's sweet cooing,*
> *Like a rose dawn*
> *That takes on a thousand colors*
> *When the sun is already peeking through the mountains.*

Before proceeding any further, however, it should be noted that in the Church today there are two currents of thought, which are opposed to each other regarding the action of the Spirit;[19] more

---

[18] Song 2:14.

[19] The writing of this book took place during the first decade of the twenty-first century.

specifically, with regard to His Word addressed to mankind. Without being overly concerned with criteria, they could be referred to respectively as minimalist and maximalist.

The *maximalist* current, which could also be described as an *optimistic* position, is in fact another fruit of the so–called flourishing *Springtime of the Church* and defends an overabundant activity of the Spirit during the times that followed the closing of the Second Vatican Council, even more profuse than that which took place in the Early Church.

Indeed, because an overflowing action of the Spirit has coincided with the appearance, within the Church, of numerous and powerful groups that consider themselves in possession of many charisms; so abundant, that they far exceed what the Church experienced during the Apostolic Age. Among the gifts given to these groups, according to their own confession, are first and foremost the gifts of tongues (*glossolalia*) and that of prophecy, used profusely during the celebration of their assemblies,[20] which consist of festive and tumultuous events, generally celebrated outside churches, where the assistants feel enlightened and impelled by the Spirit to exhort, sing praises, give personal exclamations of impetuous sincerity (referring to themselves or to others, and even to the circumstances of the present moment in which one lives), etc. The *inspirations* and *impulses* coming from the Spirit cover a multitude of aspects, including providing a foundation for assertions used as a justification for the convocation of Councils, etc., etc., etc. *The Spirit blows where He wills*, as it was said; although now He does it in such a way that, rather than a gentle breeze, it resembles the gusts of an impetuous hurricane.

---

[20]The names of these groups are usually quite expressive: Charismatics, Catechumenal, etc. *Communities* (a generic term which is ever–present).

The *maximalist* current is not concerned with justifying the authenticity and supernatural basis of such manifestations. The facts are there, and their mere presence is sufficient demonstration of their legitimacy. Or someone solemnly proclaims it (*I have received a motion of the Spirit*, or something similar) without bothering to give proof that would otherwise be impossible to provide.[21] After all, it is a question of being in tune with modern fads. The heralds of freedom of speech and thought merely present the facts as established, so that from now on it only remains for them to see to it that no one contradicts them.[22] It is clear that modern generations are eager to be deceived; for what really prevails in the modern world is not merely the passive attitude of being seduced by deception,

---

[21] The very act of asking for what might justify, even in some way, the legitimacy of such *motions* (which would be tantamount, according to some, to calling them into question), would be an annoying scandal for the large crowd of enthusiastic followers. Those who, by not allowing themselves to be too influenced by feelings, appear to be demanding, often forgetting that the idols of crowds are exempt (as if by mandate) from the burden of proof: their testimony suffices.

[22] The author of this writing had the opportunity to witness this kind of performance, organized by Protestants, during his pastoral stay in various countries of Latin America in the 1960s. Signs were posted in the streets, as is done in Spain to advertise Bullfights, summoning people, especially the sick and disabled, on a specific day and time, to attend the *Services of Worship and Miracles*, also sometimes called *Services of Worship and Healing*. Needless to say, miracles were anticipated as surely to be present, and all the *Services*, of course, ended in buffoonery. This writer did not witness or hear any reference to the performance of a single miracle during the five years he spent in Hispanic America. This was never an obstacle for the assemblies to continue to be repeated *ad infinitum*, and if miracles did not take place, it was always blamed on the lack of sufficient faith.

It was evident that the love of God was being replaced by pure *entertainment*, with no other object than the pursuit of purely human selfish interests. A religion of *entertainment* had made its appearance, which a few years later, would burst into the Catholic Church.

but that of vehement rejection of Truth, which in turn leads to an unconditional surrender into the arms of Falsehood.

The *minimalist* position, on the contrary, maintains the belief in the *kenosis* or concealment, perhaps even the *absence*, of the Spirit. It bases its conviction on the state of desolation in which the Church finds herself at the present time; a subject already discussed in the Introduction to this book, albeit in a cursory manner.

This school of thought is convinced that the Spirit, precisely because *He blows where He wills and we do not know where He comes from or where He goes*, acts in sovereign freedom and in a way that is entirely unpredictable by the creature; and hence He does not go about submitting Himself to the whims of anyone who wants to invoke Him. Presumably, the activity of the Spirit is something more serious than certain assemblies of *glossolalia*, so similar in some respects to the invocations that take place in seances. The charisms of the Primitive Church knew their moment until they definitively ceased, without there being any possibility of certifying their presence again throughout history, unless the Church officially says otherwise, which does not seem to have happened.

True, the Spirit lives and works continually in the bosom of the Church, whose Liturgy invokes Him continually and in a special way in the Eucharistic Sacrifice or Holy Mass. Beautiful antiphons such as *Veni, Sancte Spiritus*, or majestic hymns such as *Veni, Creator Spiritus*, used by the Church in her Liturgy and which also appear in the private prayers of the faithful, testify to His presence. After all, the Spirit is the Soul of the Church, its Dynamic Principle, the Caretaker–Guarantor of its Infallibility and Promoter of all the work of sanctification in the faithful who are part of it. Hence, it seems almost blasphemous to try to reduce His role to that of a Theater Performer or an Entertainer of Parties and Feasts.

No one should claim, without fear or trembling, that he speaks *inspired by the Spirit*. No matter how prominent his position in the ecclesiastical estate may be, unless he does so *ex officio*, in the circumstances and under the conditions indicated by the Church herself. Apart from that, anyone who boldly and with pretended certainty claims for himself the presumption that he speaks prompted or moved by the Spirit, runs the grave risk of falling victim to the deception of the Evil One... as well as endangering his own salvation. *Do not quench the Spirit.*[23] But neither make a game of Him or of His name, for *whoever speaks against the Holy Spirit will not be forgiven, neither in this age nor in the age to come.*[24] For practical purposes, someone speaking against the Spirit, or claiming, with imprudent boldness and certainty, to be His spokesman or to be moved by Him, amounts to the same thing.

As for the prophecy contained in Acts 2: 16–20, taken in turn from the prophet Joel (3: 1–5), the most that can be said is that it would be foolhardy for anyone to pretend to apply it to himself and acting in the present moment. The prophecy, although it refers to the Last Times (*in novissimis diebus*), corresponds in reality to the peculiar charisms with which the Early Church was graced, as Saint Peter expressly recognizes (v. 16). It is true that Saint Peter seems to extend it to the culmination of the Last Times or moments of the Parousia (vv. 19–20). But in any case, no one can affirm with certainty, based on the text, that it also refers to the *present time*, and even less that it is being realized in his own person. It should also be noted that it is applicable only to the servants and handmaids of the Spirit (*super servos meos et super ancillas meas*),

---

[23] 1 Thess 5:19.
[24] Mt 12:32; Lk 12:10.

and thus the fact that he who dares to arrogate to himself such a condition would show a high degree of arrogance.

The way in which the glossolalia of the early Church were conducted is not known in a concrete way. Contrary to the modern ones, where the abundance of nonsense and superficialities that are heard in the assemblies of these groups are no secret.[25] Saint Paul tried to moderate and regulate the use of the charisms and especially that of the glossolalia, as can be seen in Chapter 14 of his *First Letter to the Corinthians*, where he is not too enthusiastic about these gifts or give them excessive importance: *Now I want you all to speak in tongues, but even more to prophesy... I thank God that I speak in tongues more than you all; nevertheless, in church I would rather speak five words with my mind, in order to instruct others, than ten thousand words in a tongue...But earnestly desire the higher gifts. And I will show you a still more excellent way.*[26]

This last observation about the importance given to the phenomenon reveals the notable contrast between the practice of the Primitive Church and that of the modern *Charismatic* Movements in general. It is evident that for the Apostolic Church and subsequent times, charisms were not the neuralgic point of piety. You do not need to know too much about the history of the Church to know that the importance given to these gifts, inside or outside the liturgical functions, was merely incidental until they practically disappeared. Just the opposite of what happens in the *Eucharistic celebrations* (a name that has replaced the *Sacrifice of the Mass*) of the modern Charismatic Movements, in which the practice of *glossolalia*, with the usual soliloquies and speeches of the laity, occupy the

---

[25]Although it is not always easy to provide proof of the fact. For, as required by the esotericism that has always been practiced in the sects, attendance at such assemblies is not usually permitted to the uninitiated.

[26]1 Cor 14: 5.18–19;12:31.

greater part of an otherwise excessively long session. It is curious, however, that it is precisely the priest (now called *President*) who speaks the least and to whom the least attention is paid; a logical thing if one considers that he is only considered as a Representative of the Community, besides the fact that in such *Eucharists* the idea of Sacrifice has been obviated and replaced by that of a festive meal of solidarity.

Perhaps someone might be tempted to think, in view of all this, that Catholic theology has been banished to make way for that of the Protestant Reformers.

In any case, we have not yet reached the most important point of the problem. However widespread it may be and in spite of the fact that the subject is considered incontrovertible, it is difficult to believe that the Spirit goes around, being invoked on a whim and speaking trivialities through the mouths of the illuminati of the moment. In no way does it follow from Revelation, from the teaching of the Magisterium, or from the Doctrine of the Church throughout its history, that this is what the mission of the Spirit consists of.

The true and specific mission of the Spirit is to speak of Jesus Christ. Everything He says and does *always has Jesus Christ as its point of reference.* He never speaks of Himself or by Himself, but merely of what He hears (from Those from Whom He proceeds), in order to make it known: *When He, the Spirit of Truth, comes, He will guide you into all truth,*[27] *for He will not speak of Himself, but whatever He hears He will speak, and He will declare to you what is to come. He will glorify me, for he will receive of mine and declare it to you.*[28] The reference to the whole truth, and even to the things that are to come to pass, can have no other object and no other

---

[27]For Jesus Christ, the fullness of Truth is He Himself: *I am the Truth* (Jn 14:6).
[28]Jn 16: 13–14.

end than Jesus Christ. An attentive and dispassionate reading of these verses, reinforced in turn by the context, indicates this. And the final words confirm it conclusively: *He shall receive of mine and shall declare it unto you.* It is easily forgotten that what is peculiar and proper to the Third Divine Person consists *in being a Reference to the other Two.*[29]

Other words of Jesus Christ also contained in the Last Supper Discourse confirm what has been said so far: *These things I have spoken to you, while I am still with you. But the Counselor, the Holy Spirit, whom the Father will send in my name, he will teach you all things, and bring to your remembrance all that I have said to you.*[30] From which it follows that it is the mission of the Spirit to remind and make the disciples understand all that the Master had said to them: *all things that I have said to you.* And further on He adds: *But when the Counselor comes, whom I shall send to you from the Father, even the Spirit of truth, who proceeds from the Father, "he will bear witness to me."*[31]

As for the three condemnations that the Spirit will pronounce against the world, they all have Jesus Christ as the final point of reference and the basis of their motivation: *And when he* [The Paraclete] *comes, he will convince the world of sin and of righteousness and of judgment: of sin, because they do not believe in me; of righteousness, because I go to the Father, and you will see me no more.*[32] Accordingly, the Spirit will accuse the world of sin, because it has not believed in Jesus Christ; of righteousness, because Jesus Christ, after having been rejected as Messiah and Savior, abandons it and

---

[29] It goes without saying that this refers to what is peculiar and proper that constitutes Him as a Person, and not to His true identity with the Divine Essence.

[30] Jn 14: 25–26.

[31] Jn 15:26.

[32] Jn 16: 8–11.

will no longer be seen; of judgment, because the Prince of this world has already been judged and of course by Jesus Christ: *And then the lawless one will be revealed, and the Lord Jesus will slay him with the breath of his mouth and destroy him by his appearing and his coming.*[33] The destruction of the last Instrument of Perversion wielded by the Evil One, of his most powerful Ally in the seduction and deception of men, supposes unfailingly the defeat of Satan. The Apostle insists elsewhere on the final triumph against Evil, already definitively judged: *For as in Adam all die, so also in Christ shall all be made alive. But each in his own order: Christ the firstfruits, then at his coming those who belong to Christ. Then comes the end, when he delivers the kingdom to God the Father after destroying every rule and every authority and power. For he must reign until he has put all his enemies under his feet.*[34]

In the *Charismatic Eucharistic celebrations*, the voice of the Spirit is no longer heard through the preaching of the priest, whose role has been annulled and not merely minimized.[35] He is just admitted as a mere *President* of the Congregation, not being even recognized as a moderator. His role being reduced to listening to the spontaneous interventions of the participants. In this way, the voice of the Spirit, once *authenticated* by the hierarchical Church through preaching framed in the Magisterium, has now been replaced by the

---

[33] 2 Thess 2:8.

[34] 1 Cor 15: 22–25.

[35] The Voice of the Spirit cannot be recognized as such with certainty if it is not endorsed by the Church and framed within the parameters of the Magisterium. Otherwise, its authenticity or untruth would not be even an issue. As for the spiritual life of the faithful, the sanctifying action of the Spirit in souls must always be ascertained through the Church, hence the need for spiritual direction and the sacrament of Penance. The mystical paths that claim to act autonomously always end up showing their falsehood, as demonstrated by the numerous mystifications of this kind that the Church has known throughout her history.

voice of men, with no other *confirmation* of its veracity than that which they themselves attribute to it. In summary: The Catholic Church has yielded her place to the Churches of the Reformation, while the worship formerly rendered to God by man has given way to the worship rendered to man by man himself.

It has been repeatedly said that *The Apocalypse* is a book of Consolation. Nothing could be more logical if one assumes that it is proper for a prophetic book to be a vehicle of the Voice of the Spirit, also called the *Paraclete*, or Comforting Spirit. Hence its Voice is consolation for those who suffer, who in times of tribulation, such as those of today, are confused and troubled in many ways and forms: *Beati qui lugent, quoniam ipsi consolabuntur.*[36]

Evidently, the consolation spoken of here does not refer to a mere *mitigation* or softening of suffering, but to a state of happiness or *beatitude* promised to those who mourn. Although destined to be realized *now* and not later in another aeon, since it is now that weeping takes place; without the need for the troubled to wait for the time when *the Lamb, who is in the midst of the throne, will be their Shepherd, who will lead them to the fountains of the waters of life, and God will wipe away every tear from their eyes;*[37] when the hour has sounded when *He will wipe away every tear from their eyes; and there will be no more death, nor weeping, nor mourning, nor pain, because all that was before has passed away.*[38]

It is important to note that Christian existence has nothing to do with sadness. Nor is it sufficient to say that such an existence is compatible with suffering, since both, like what the Psalm says about justice and peace, also kiss each other (*osculatæ sunt*). It

---

[36] Mt 5:4.
[37] Rev 7:17.
[38] Rev 21:4.

can even be said that Christian existence and suffering are mutually necessary, as Christian tradition has always understood: *Desiderans te videre, memor lacrimarum tuarum, ut gaudio implear.*[39]

> *The Friend said to his Beloved:*
> *—Thou who fillest the Sun with radiance,*
> *Fill my heart with love.*
> *The Beloved replied:*
> *—Unless you were full of love*
> *Your eyes would not shed tears,*
> *Nor would you have come to this place to see your Beloved.*[40]

It is necessary to recognize a relationship of affinity between friendship (love), joy, and, strange as it may seem..., tears. And it is striking that both the bond that unites the three, as well as the place to which they refer, is precisely the Voice of the Spirit, or of the Bridegroom. And concretely, with respect to tears, it can be said with certainty that they are always the expression of a feeling of love.

There are, of course, tears of rage and despair, which are nothing but a perversion of authentic pain and a caricature of real tears, just as hatred is the perversion of love. This imitation of a corrupt reality has nothing to do with the true feeling of tears (or *gift of tears*, as it has been called by mystics and spiritual authors), undoubtedly one of the most delicate that man has received from God.

Everyone agrees, however, that the tears that flow at the loss of a loved one, for example, are tears of love. Or those that come from a repentant heart that has offended the loved one. And let the same

---

[39] 2 Tim 1:4.
[40] Ramon Llull, *Book of the Friend and the Beloved*, 5.

be said of those which arise from a heart unable to contain its joy at having finally found the loved one for whom it has long pined.

Sometimes this fact has gone unnoticed by some literary geniuses. But this is not the case of Tolkien, whose Gandalf, one of the characters of his *The Lord of the Rings*, addresses his friends at the time of parting: *I will not say: do not weep; for not all tears are an evil.*[41] Tagore seems to perceive something else in his Poetry: *If you weep because the sun is setting, tears will prevent you from seeing the stars.*[42] When in fact tears, or at least true tears, are *never* evil inasmuch as they are a manifestation of love. And likewise, the Spirit, just as He produces charity as the first of His fruits, *also gives rise to joy as the second of them* (Gal 5:22). As for Tagore's admonition, it is true that it seems to sound like a repudiation of tears; but the truth is quite different. For tears of love, though they may momentarily render vision veiled, misty, and vague, are only to give way afterwards to a clearer and brighter contemplation of the wonders of heaven. Unless the poet, as seems most likely in this case, wanted to use a kind of synecdoche and identify tears with sadness.

Hence, when the angels and Jesus Christ Himself (Jn 20: 13.15) ask Mary Magdalene for the reason for her weeping, they do not intend to recriminate her attitude. It is rather the desire to transform her anxious, nostalgic, and impatient feeling into one of overflowing love and lacking any connotation of pain.

It is not strange that it is precisely the Baptist who provides the most profound information about this. According to his own words, *the Bridegroom is the one who has the bride; the friend of the Bridegroom, who is present and hears him, rejoices greatly at*

---

[41] J.R.R. Tolkien, *The Return of the King*.
[42] Tagore, *Stray Birds*.

the voice of the Bridegroom. Therefore, my joy is complete. It is necessary for Him to increase and for me to decrease.[43](C)

* * *

(C) It is interesting that the Baptist does not here equate himself to the level of the love of the bride regarding the Bridegroom. He limits himself to recognizing himself as a *friend of the Bridegroom*, taking good care to point out that *the one who has a bride is the Bridegroom*, which is the same as saying that it is the bride who has the Bridegroom. The Forerunner thus establishes an important distinction, which is the basis for a scale in the degrees and ways of love. As he himself acknowledges, he is but a friend who accompanies the Bridegroom; with the consequent possibility of hearing His Voice and of rejoicing in it. Nothing more.

The precision is significant insofar as the Baptist recognizes himself in a state of *not yet*, thus outlining an important doctrine regarding the degrees or states of love.

The clarifications the Baptist makes concerning his person —which, on the other hand, transcend him completely— complement the content of the other New Testament texts that refer to him. While Jesus Christ recognizes him as the greatest of those born to woman, he adds that *the least in the Kingdom of Heaven is greater than he.*[44] The Forerunner himself is careful to insist repeatedly and humbly on the idea of his annihilation: *He must increase, and I must decrease.*

The figure of the Baptist is an eloquent demonstration of one of the most important aspects of Christian life, namely: being provisional, precarious, and *the state of "not yet"* in which it takes place. It is also clear, through its trajectory, that the love of friendship is not yet conjugal love. Divine–human love, which logically begins in the present time, does not reach its culmination immediately, but develops gradually: from the less to the more, from the superficial to the intimate, from the initial attempts

---

[43] Jn 3: 29–30.
[44] Mt 11:11.

to the ultimate nuptials that entail totality and finality, from the state of joyful hope to that of definitive possession. The Christian life is a continuous progress along a path, a journey on an itinerary that someone has traced before us, a *quest* that seeks its goal, a risky adventure that hopes to reach a happy ending, a steep and abrupt path that many do not dare to walk (Mt 7:14)... Mystics and spiritual authors usually speak of a certain *Itinerarium Mentis in Deum* (Saint Bonaventure), of various and different *Dwellings in an Interior Castle* (Saint Teresa of Avila), or of *Three Ages of the Interior Life* (Garrigou–Lagrange) to cite some of the best known examples.[45] The Christian life is a difficult wandering in constant pursuit of Someone Who walks ahead (Jn 10:4) and Who compels His followers to force a hurried pace: *I do not run aimlessly, I do not box as one beating the air.*[46]

However, this *kenotic* aspect of the Christian life described here is only the tip of the iceberg. The reality is that it becomes deep enough to be referred to as a tragedy. There is nothing strange about this, if one considers that the life of every Christian, from the moment he has been called to *complete* the Passion of Christ (Col 1:24), must necessarily face a degree of suffering whose consummation is crucifixion; about which it would be inconsequential to ask whether it is exterior or only interior.

In this sense, the life of the Baptist reaches almost inaccessible heights. Anguish, anxiety, fear, and uncertainty are present in his soul with an intensity and strength rarely mentioned in the works of the biographers of the saints. The group that he sends to Jesus Christ (Mt 11 and Lk 7) during his stay in prison, when his death was near, is the clear exponent of a torn existence that seems to waver at decisive moments. His question is sufficiently revealing: *Are you the one who is to come, or are we waiting for someone else?* For a better understanding of its scope and depth, we must bear in mind that the Baptist had previously proclaimed, on several occasions, his *solemn testimony* of the messiahship of Jesus Christ. It is

---

[45] The mystics and writers on spirituality provide abundant doctrine about the *Purifications, Nights of the Sense and of the Spirit*, etc., although they tend to stay within the life of prayer in general.

[46] 1 Cor 9:26; cf. Heb 4:11.

possible to get an idea, though only approximate, of the terrible *Night* that flooded his soul at that moment with darkness, not even oblivious to the fact it was near scandal, if we listen to the response he received from Jesus Christ. To the consoling words, destined to testify to the messianic signs, the Master adds an admonition whose depth impresses those who ponder it: *Blessed is he that shall not be scandalized in me...* How can anyone find these words disconcerting when one considers that the suffering of the Baptist, overflowing with anguish in these moments of total darkness, is along the same line as the sentiments of Jesus on the Cross: *My God, my God, why have you forsaken me?*[47] After all, no Christian can forget that the *scandal of the Cross* (Gal 5:11) has as its precedent the one caused by the very Person of Jesus Christ, a stumbling block and a rock of scandal, according to Saint Peter.[48]

We should bear in mind that it is not always advisable to *soften* the content of Sacred Scripture with euphemisms, paraphrasing, or circumlocutions. If the Word of God attributes to Jesus Christ the condition of a *stone or stumbling block and rock of scandal,* without further attenuation, we should take this expression seriously. Hence, when we speak of the *scandal* caused by the figure of Jesus Christ, together with the scandal produced by the Cross on which He gave His life, this expression must be considered entirely free of metaphors or incitements to piety.

What we see, therefore, is a true *scandal,* both for those who receive and for those who reject Jesus Christ. Therefore, the *encounter* that takes place with Him, which occurs for every man at some point in his life and on which his eternal salvation or damnation depends, must necessarily be shocking and, in some way, heartbreaking. The result of which is the fact that every man must be forced, whether he wants to or not, to decide between two extreme options, without the possibility of any other in between: *He who is not with me is against me, and he who does not gather with me, scatters.*[49] It is evident that the *shock* produced by such an encounter, which moreover lasts forever without excluding eternity, leaves

---

[47] Mt 27:46; Mk 15:34.
[48] 1 Pet 2:8; cf. Lk 2:34.
[49] Lk 11:23

The Voice of the Spirit

a deep imprint on man from which he can never recover. This is not to be confused with the profound feeling of acceptance or rejection, of love or hatred, experienced in the presence of Jesus. Here we are dealing with something different and more transcendent.

But even for those who accept it, this feeling is not reduced to the rapture and fascination produced by the contemplation of Beauty, Goodness, or both at the same time. This would be too simplistic and incomplete an explanation of a deeper and more complex event. It must be considered that the *aura* that surrounds the figure of Jesus Christ, once it has been perceived by man, has an ambivalent character; due in part also to the multitude of apparent contradictions the one who approaches the Mystery of Christ has to face.

First of all, some of the messianic prophecies of the Old Testament highlight the ineffable figure and appearance of Jesus Christ:

> *You are the fairest of the sons of men;*
> *Grace is poured upon your lips;*
> *Therefore, God has blessed you forever.*[50]

As for the impression that His figure produced on the people, the Gospels simply describe Him as a *seducer* (Mt 27:63). It is neither necessary nor possible to say more. For no human artist has been entrusted with the task that the Holy Spirit has reserved for Himself, which is to engrave, through the veil of Faith, the face and figure of Jesus Christ in every human soul. The resulting image, a *unique* stamp by the Divine Artist in each man, is transcendent to all his possibilities of perception and expression, which makes the task of communicating it to others impossible. Apart from that, whether it is perceived with more or less clarity by others depends only on the purity of each heart (Mt 5:8).

The ambivalence is caused by the surprising fact that other texts of Scripture seem to speak in the opposite sense. But in reality, it is superfluous to insist on apparent contradictions of texts that easily disappear

---

[50] Ps 45:3.

once they have been examined more carefully. Nor is it necessary to consider them as complementary, since they are but different aspects of the same reality. As can be seen when the text cited above is compared with another of Psalm 22, also messianic:

> *But I am a worm, and no man;*
> *Scorned by men, and*
> *Despised by the people.*[51]

This is a clear indication that the reference to the Passion, the Cross, and the Death of the Messiah, through which and by which humanity was redeemed, is neither banal nor figurative. When Scripture speaks of the scandal of the Cross, far from using figurative language or alluding to metaphors, it actually refers, as in the case of the Baptist, to a peculiar state of mind in which uncertainty, confusion, discouragement, despair, distrust, and even the apparent option for nihilism all come together. The scandal of the Cross has become a true scandal for too many people; and as for the account of the sufferings of the Passion, both in the Old and the New Testament, the least that can be said is that it is far from being a simple piece of tragic literature:

> *O all ye that pass by the way,*
> *Attend, and see*
> *If there be any sorrow like to my sorrow.*[52]

But the scandal of the Passion and the Cross is not so much the application of Justice as punishment for sin, as it is the demonstration of the definitive defeat and destruction of Evil through love. For *no one has greater love than to lay down one's life for one's friends.*[53] What really redeems sinful humanity is the Act of infinite value carried out by Jesus

---

[51] Ps 22:7.
[52] Lam 1:12.
[53] Jn 15:13.

Christ (infinite because He is true God; sacrificial because He is true Man) in offering His life freely for Love. As Saint Bernard said, it was not His death that pleased God, but the free and voluntary offering of Himself unto death.[54] Thus the hideousness of the *mysterium iniquitatis* (according to the Pauline expression in 2 Thessalonians 2:7, which Scheeben also applies to sin) has been overcome and eliminated forever through the beauty of the *sacrifice for love,* for not in vain has it been written that the *foolishness of God is wiser than men, and the weakness of God is stronger than men.*[55] Thus it is that stench became beauty, weakness became strength, and folly became wisdom, for just as *in the wisdom of God, the world did not know God through wisdom, it pleased God through the folly of what we preach to save those who believe.*[56] The figure of the anguished and tormented Christ on the Cross could have no other meaning, so that nowhere else could the beauty, goodness, wisdom, and glory of God have shone more clearly. Since the Death of Christ on the Cross is the greatest act of Love, impossible even to have been imagined either in Heaven by the angels or on Earth by men, it is for this very reason and at the same time the greatest dawn of Beauty ever dreamed of or contemplated by one or the other.

There remains, however, the unshakable fact that Jesus Christ came into the world to redeem men by giving His life for them. Hence a Christology without Sacrifice and without the Cross has nothing to do with Jesus Christ or with the reality of the Redemption, since *sine sanguinis effusione non fit remissio.*[57] The only purpose of such a false *Christology* would surely be to make the Apostle's fear come true, since, as he himself says, *the scandal of the Cross would have disappeared.*[58] Hence the care he takes not to preach with wisdom of words (eloquence or verbosity?) *ut non evacuetur crux Christi.*[59]

---

[54] *Non mors, sed voluntas placuit sponte morientis,* Saint Bernard, *De erroribus Abaelardi,* n. 21, PL, 182, 1070A.

[55] 1 Cor 1:25.

[56] 1 Cor 1:21.

[57] Heb 9:22.

[58] Gal 5:11.

[59] 1 Cor 1:17.

As anyone who wants to see it can easily understand, the Christianity without the Cross that both Protestant theology and the Neo–modernist heresy want to impose on the Church, is entirely foreign to Gospel Teaching. It is something like transvestite Christianity. Foreign to the Gospel Message are therefore the religion of noise, of the feast, of the Spirit served à la carte at party meetings, of the Gospel Message, abolition of the Sacrifice of the Cross and consequent secularization of the Mass, of the denial (explicit or tacit) of the Real Presence, of the annihilation of the Christian Priesthood, etc., no matter how much it pursues the objective (not always recognized) of an alleged *Ecumenism*.

If Jesus Christ is the only Master (Mt 23:8) and the only Way (Jn 14:6); if he who does not take up his cross and follow Him cannot be His disciple (Lk 14:27);[60] if the only Path that leads to Life is arduous, narrow, and steep (Mt 7:14)... it is impossible to admit that the Spirit acts on the members of the Mystical Body by the easy ways of the suppression of Sacrifice and Immolation, of the Mass secularized and converted into a meal of solidarity, or of the noisy meetings in which the Paraclete speaks profusely through the mouths of one or another, *at will*. The Apostle Paul, who undoubtedly fixed his attention on more important and loftier things than alleged and boisterous *charisms*, warned us clearly and forcefully when he said: *But I want to show you a better way...*[61]

* * *

Man is unable to hear the voice of God except through the Voice of the Spirit. Both are the same Voice, although it is the Person of the Spirit Who makes it reach the hearts of men. He is responsible for its being remembered by them and finally understood. Even the Voice of the Word made Man, whose name is precisely the Word of God (Rev 19:13) or simply the Word (Jn 1), cannot be heard and understood except through the Spirit (Jn 14:26). Without His work and cooperation, the Voice of the Word made Flesh (Jn 1:14) would

---

[60] Mt 10:38; 16:24; Mk 8:34; etc.
[61] 1 Cor 12:31.

be nothing more to men than the *sound of many waters*,[62] namely, a completely incomprehensible Voice, quite capable of being *heard* but impossible to be *listened to*.

In turn, the Voice of the Spirit cannot be listened to unless certain conditions are met. These were precisely pointed out by the Forerunner in the text quoted above from John 3:29. In which it is clearly stated that he hears the Voice of the Bridegroom Who, being his *friend*, is *close to him* and therefore in a position to *hear him*.

So it is a matter, first of all, of being the Bridegroom's friend; then of being with Him and next to Him; and finally, of listening to Him.

It is easy to understand that the three conditions come together in one, which is none other than the relationship of intimacy or relationship of love. If one is a friend of the Bridegroom, one necessarily seeks to be close to Him, and with greater passion the more intense the love relationship. In turn, the love relationship is inconceivable without loving dialogue, inasmuch as those who love each other need to tell and express their mutual love:

> *Arise, my love, my fair one,*
> *And come away.*
> *O my dove, in the clefts of the rock,*
> *In the covert of the cliff,*
> *Let me see your face,*
> *Let me hear your voice,*
> *For your voice is sweet,*
> *And your face is comely.*
>
> ....
>
> *I slept, but my heart was awake.*
> *Hark! my beloved is knocking.*[63]

---

[62]Rev 1:15.

[63]Song 2: 13–14; 5:2.

The Bridegroom is dying of anxiety to hear the voice of the bride: *Let me hear your voice...for your voice is soft...* While the bride, even in sleep, keeps her heart in a state of wakefulness longing to hear the voice of the Bridegroom: *I sleep, but my heart is awake...* Before she heard that Voice, the bride was relegated to living *in the clefts of rocks and in the covert of the cliff.* And how else could she face the possibility of living in the absence of the Bridegroom? Only Love can provide the strength to cope with an otherwise extremely precarious existence when the loved one is absent... In such an absence, life passes as if between rocks and cliffs, in the most desolate of desserts or in the loneliest of wastelands. A profound mystery whose reality only those in love are capable of understanding.[64]

One thing is sufficiently clear: there must be a friendship with the Bridegroom as a prerequisite for hearing the voice of the Spirit. It has already been seen that, according to the Forerunner, the friend who accompanies and is close to the Bridegroom is the one who hears His voice. And is there any dialogue between strangers that is not merely superficial or purely formal? Is it possible for those who are not present to each other to engage in dialogue, in any way whatsoever? Moreover, the Spirit never speaks of Himself, but only of what He hears from Those from whom He proceeds (Jn 16:13); which means that the object of His conversation is always Jesus Christ. In fact, not only does the Spirit refuse to initiate any dialogue with those who do not believe in the Person of the Son, but He will even accuse them of sin for their lack of faith (Jn 16:9). In other words, it is clear that the absence of friendship with Jesus Christ, which

---

[64]The punishment for guilt in hell is nothing other than this same anxiety, although turned upside down, which reaches its infinite intensity, expressed among other ways in its unending duration.

precludes any nearness, makes it impossible to hear the voice of the Spirit.

It is in this way, and only in this way, that the bride is able to speak of the Bridegroom to anyone who asks her. When, by being in contact with Him, she enjoys the possibility of hearing His voice:

> *What is your beloved more than another beloved,*
> *O fairest among women?*
> *My beloved is all radiant and ruddy,*
> *Distinguished among ten thousand.*
> *His head is the finest gold;*
> *His locks are wavy,*
> *Black as a raven.*
> *His eyes are like doves...*[65]

This explains the ineffectiveness of many pastoral activities, especially preaching. It is impossible to be a witness of Jesus Christ if it is not through the voice of the Spirit and under His influence. Otherwise, one always ends up speaking of the world and the things of the world, in an empty discourse without supernatural content or projection: *They are of the world; therefore, they speak according*

---

[65]Song 5: 9–12. It is noteworthy that metaphor is one of the last resources of language —poor resource, after all— to which poetry resorts when man is the other term in the love relationship. Poetry itself is already a resource, when simple prose proves inadequate to account for the twists and turns and depths of love. An insufficient resource in any case, forced in turn to use different and more varied ones... which remain equally insufficient. In any case, it is important to realize the necessity of language as a vehicle of dialogue in every love relationship, not excluding the divine–human one. The encounter of the divine *Word* with human *word*, or the richness of infinite expressiveness with the penury of meager babbling, is the event to which Love grants the possibility of the culmination of the divine–human love–dialogue.

*to the world, and the world listens to them.*⁶⁶ A strange verse that admirably summarizes the situation of a good part of the current Catholic Pastoral Ministry and that contains, in a brief and compendious way, three resounding statements of enormous transcendence:

1) They are of the world.

2) Which explains why they always speak according to the world.

3) And that is why the world listens to them.

The Bible is the most excellent and accurate Book of Diagnoses of human behavior that there is in the entire world. Its language, precise and at the same time forceful, does not depend on circumstances or considerations that could soften, blur, or palliate its meaning: *The word of God is living and active, sharper than any two-edged sword.*⁶⁷ According to the Bible, *the sword of the Spirit is the word of God.*⁶⁸ And it adds that this word *is not fettered,*⁶⁹ no matter how much the world tries to keep it under its control. Hence, the true witnesses of Jesus Christ, acting courageously and free from bonds and complexes, preach it in the way Saint Paul says he did: *not proceeding with cunning or to tamper with God's word.*⁷⁰ The Apostle of the Gentiles is careful to warn that, as far as the tasks of evangelization are concerned, *we do not preach of ourselves, but Jesus Christ as Lord.*⁷¹ Which should be a warning to be heeded by the modern Pastoral Care focused on *appearance*, so frequent and ubiquitous today. Those who preach or act with appearance in mind should not forget another admonition of the Apostle no less timely: *Am I now seeking the favor of men, or of God? Or am I*

---

[66] 1 Jn 4:5.

[67] Heb 4:12.

[68] Eph 6:17.

[69] 2 Tim 2:9.

[70] 2 Cor 4:2.

[71] 2 Cor 4:5.

trying to please men? If I were still pleasing men, I should not be a servant of Christ.[72] In short, the texts make an accurate diagnosis of the situation of the Church today. She is in the midst of the greatest crisis in her history, and in order to confront it, if it is a question of confronting it, there are many who only use those means that can *in no way disturb the world*. It is clear, for those who want to see it, that all too often, rather than attending to the good of the souls and their needs, modern Pastoral Care is more concerned with having political or local interests in mind, with its eyes fixed on the *media*, and always trying to anticipate the possible negative reactions of the world, in order to avoid them. Everything seems to indicate that the Church, rather than striving to appear as the *Church founded by Jesus Christ*, the Immaculate Bride of the Lamb, prefers to appear as the *Modern Church*, so convergent with the criteria of the World as to be accepted by it. And no one will be able to doubt, in view of the facts, that those within the Church who follow this path —Hierarchy or simple faithful— *always speak like the World*.

The situation of those who act in this way could be explained by criteria that serve to minimize the problem. Methods, however mistaken, or motives animated by a certain fear of the world, etc. Which would not solve the problem, inasmuch as they seemingly proceed in this way because they are of the world. As it used to be said in the *Perennial Philosophy*, acting follows being.

On the other hand, they are enthusiastically welcomed by a world which, in its turn, has chosen Falsehood. Which is preached and spread by the System which uses media in an abundance never seen before, under the approval of a society that welcomes everything that contributes to keeping it in error. No wonder that those who

---

[72] Gal 1:10.

endeavor to uphold the integrity of Truth and Justice are rejected and persecuted, while the seducers and deceivers are applauded and listened to. Once the World has fully committed itself to rejecting God, it is only logical that it should enthusiastically embrace the manipulators and propagators of error. After all, it cannot but love what is its own: *If you were of the world, the world would love its own; but because you are not of the world, but I chose you out of the world, therefore the world hates you.*[73] And so it is that the applause and good reception on the part of the world is a sign, even for those who insist on appearing as *true witnesses*, that they are going astray (Lk 6:26). As far as certain circles of modern Catholicism, perhaps it would be prudent to be wary of a certain type of *holiness*; for it is well known that he whom the world welcomes with enthusiasm *is because it recognizes him as its own*. And it is evident that the Devil learned how to act long ago and does not hesitate to use the sacred as a suitable instrument of disguise.

Regarding hearing the Voice of the Spirit, whether it is heard by the Church as the Mystical Body or privately by a member of the faithful, much has been written and spoken over the centuries. Everything revolves around paying attention to that Voice, the conditions required to be able to hear it, the guarantees as to recognize its authenticity, the way and manner of hearing it, etc., etc., etc. Although speculations have not always been developed with the desirable clarity in such a transcendental matter. It is known, for example, with all certainty, that the Spirit speaks through the

---

[73] Jn 15:19.

Magisterium of the Church, provided that it is the authentic Magisterium and meets the conditions required to give it firm assent.[74] Apart from that, however, we must recognize that this subject is apt to cause great confusion.

The mystics, for example, have focused mainly on the life of prayer. The complex world of Mysticism, with the multitude of phenomena that can accompany relationships of divine–human love, necessarily presupposes constant communication with the Spirit. After all, it is the union of the human being with God, carried out above all through prayer in its highest degrees, which manifests itself in the divine–human loving dialogue and therefore in communication, thus making room for the mysterious and complicated subject of revelations, apparitions, locutions, inspirations, etc., coming from on High. A subject which is certainly not the most important chapter of Mysticism, contrary to what is usually believed, but which evidently enjoys sufficient importance to be mentioned here, although with no pretension of going deeper into a question that does not correspond to this place.

Regarding this, there are mainly two very different Schools: one that could be called the *Strict Observance* and the other that could be known as the *Liberal School*. Led —as is now said in barbaric language— respectively by Saint John of the Cross and by Saint

---

[74]The problem is extraordinarily complicated today. Not infrequently, what is offered to the faithful as the Magisterium of the Church is far from being so. As if that were not enough, the criteria for recognizing it are not easily understood by many of the faithful, due to the ignorance that prevails among most Christian people in this as in so many other issues, which brings about dishonest manipulations and falsifications in this most delicate field of ecclesial activity.

Teresa of Avila.[75] The former considers all kinds of phenomena of this nature: revelations, locutions, or anything of the sort, to be entirely proscribed. Accordingly, there is no need to consider the problem of ascertaining whether they come from the good or the evil Spirit, since everything must be eliminated in view of the need to suppress anything that hinders *pure* communication with God. The Saint from Avila, however, delights her devotees and readers of her works with detailed narrations of locutions, revelations, apparitions, communications, amorous dialogues with the Divine Spouse, etc.

Which of the two schools should one choose...?[76] The problem has an easy solution, assuming that there is one, however thorny it may seem. Since the Church has considered both as equally legitimate, and the two authors who elaborated them as worthy of the glory of being declared Doctors, it is clear, therefore, that the answer to the question is whichever school one chooses or, from a different point of view, the one which the Spirit inspires in each person.

The practical aspect of the problem does not exist, as has already been said, since both paths are equally licit. As for the speculative aspect, however, the question would be very different, since it would lend itself to all the inquiries, investigations, analyses, researches, theories, and hypotheses that can be imagined..., and perhaps some others. So it is not surprising that no solution acceptable to everyone has been found so far; assuming that it exists and that the question

---

[75]The reader should not be misled by these designations. It is simply an *amusement* which, apart from an affectionate irony, in no way excludes the greatest respect. Both saints are extraordinary luminaries in the firmament of the Church, recognized by Her as Doctors and as two of Her greatest mystics. *The Mansions* or *The Interior Castle*, of Saint Teresa of Jesus, for example, is perhaps the best treatise on prayer of any that swell the treasure of Christian spiritual literature.

[76]The issue had already been pointed out, though not solved, by Hans Urs von Balthasar in his *Herrlichkeit. Eine Theologische Ästhetik.*

is relevant. When all is said and done, the fact is that the writings of the two Saints are available to anyone who sincerely wishes to take advantage of them.

Some think that deciding for one or the other of the two Schools is a trivial and unimportant question. Both are part of the immeasurable spiritual treasure of the Church, while their doctrines *are simply there*, for whoever wants to take advantage of them and according to the way the Spirit inspires him. Bearing in mind, however, that the expression *they are simply there* is not said on a whim, nor unintentionally. For both doctrines, in spite of the large number of details and multitude of specifications they contain, of the varied and complex schematic structure of their contents, of their numerous and complex explanations, of the abundant apparatus of Scriptural authorities (especially in Saint John of the Cross) so generously lavished, etc., *in reality the intention of the authors does not seem to pursue the practical ends that many readers may have imagined.* We are not aware of many people, for example, who have been able to know with certainty, after an attentive reading of the *Interior Castle,* the exact place their soul finds itself in the tortuous itinerary of the encounter with God. Whether they are in the first Abode, in the Second, or in any other; whether they are advancing in the spiritual life, or stopped perhaps by this obstacle or that, etc. As for the Saint of Fontiveros, one cannot even dream of the possibility of deducing with certainty, from a meticulous reading of his works, the exact moment one passes from prayer to contemplation, from the Night of the Sense to that of the Spirit, from active contemplation to passive contemplation, etc. But does this mean that such sublime and elevated doctrines, sprung from the fire of hearts in love with God, are a product without any practical use, relegated at most to the sphere of mystical literature? Mystical, of course, but *literature* after all? In no way, and it has already been said above that they are precious jewels of the incalculable spiritual treasure of the Church, known only to God. No one will be able to deny that the life and works of these two giants of Mysticism will have sanctified a multitude of souls. As well as that such treatises, with their contents so far unimproved by anyone, have justly merited for their authors the name of Doctors of the Church.[77] It is probable that the proper way and manner by which their works act in souls that sincerely seek God will never be known. We are also convinced that the various guides, norms, counsels, and *recipes* elaborated by them with the purpose of walking and traversing the paths and twists and turns of divine–human love, will never lead to the *concrete* result that they pursue; but this aspect of the problem is unimportant. The works of both saints are a reality owned by the Church as an imperishable monument, in the certainty that they fulfill the task dreamed by their authors in lavishing the ineffable secrets of their heart. As for the rest of the intricacies, it is probable that the Spirit has reserved them for Himself; whose work and operation, after all, is what maintains the fabric of their content.

But perhaps it would be convenient to abandon here the digression in the field of Mystical Theology and leave the matter in the hands of the specialists. And the same regarding the complex and meticulous debates raised by the various Schools of Spirituality.

---

[77] The treatises of Saint John of the Cross, such as *Dark Night of the Soul*, *Ascent of Mount Carmel*, or *Spiritual Canticle*, have enjoyed enormous diffusion and transcendent importance in Christian Spirituality. His orthodoxy, like that of Saint Teresa, has never been questioned, which cannot be affirmed with the same certainty of the mystics who, from the fourteenth century onwards, appear in Europe (especially in Germany) and whose mention is not for this place either.

The Voice of the Spirit

Apart from that, there is something here that is all too evident and does not admit of dispute: the absolute necessity of listening to the voice of God, or the voice of the Spirit, in the divine–human loving relationship. For if man has been destined to maintain a loving relationship with God, and if such a relationship cannot exist without dialogue, the conclusion must be made that man *needs* to hear the voice of God.[78]

The *Song of Song* expresses the bride's anxiety, emotion, and agitation at the impression that she has heard —at last— the voice of the Beloved:

> *The voice of my beloved!...*
> *My beloved speaks and says to me...*[79]

A superficial reading of the Holy Book would consider such excitement of the bride as mere exclamations of joy. And, of course, they are, although in reality they respond to a much deeper feeling.[80] The bride expresses her anxiety and eagerness to hear the voice of her beloved as soon as possible. And since her feelings now spring from the unfathomable and mysterious abyss of love, which

---

[78] We are not referring here to the creature's need to listen to its Creator, insofar as it is absolutely dependent on Him as a means to attain its salvation, once elevated to the supernatural order. The issue developed here belongs to another, higher level, even if both are ultimately reduced to the same thing, since it is now a question of delving into the study of the divine–human love relationship.

[79] Song 2: 8.10.

[80] The common practice, often unconscious, of reading the Bible quickly and superficially, without considering it in the light of prayer, leads to the disconsolate consequence of not perceiving the unfathomable riches contained in the Word of God Who, because He comes from God, *is living and active, sharper than any two-edged sword* (Heb 4:12).

here is as intense as it is eager and avid, they escape description for the moment.

However, those who have been truly in love are capable of some understanding, for they have also been equally anxious and impatient to hear the voice of the loved one. Bearing in mind —and this is not the least important thing— the infinite distance between mere human love, however pure and authentic it may be, and divine–human love. The latter, as the mystics would say, is a love which, once experienced, makes impossible any moderately satisfying explanation.

It would also be a mistake to pretend to see in these exclamations an *overabundant* feeling of joy on the part of the bride. It is no longer a question here of the intensity of the bride's joy. Rather, we have here, even if it is not possible to express it beyond the limitations of human language, an immense cry of longing and anxiety of the bride. The Bridegroom is no longer someone whose presence rejoices the bride to the point of filling her with happiness, for *He is, in reality, the life of the bride.* The distance between this exclamation of love of the bride and that which springs from a merely human love is the same as that between Heaven and Earth: between that which does not reach beyond what is human love, on the one hand, and the depths of the unfathomable abyss of divine–human intimacy, on the other. One can ardently *desire* the presence of a loved one for the joy of being at his side; or one can *need* that presence as no one can live without that which constitutes his own life (Gal 2:20).

Unfortunately, fundamental realities of the Christian life are often treated as secondary. In any case, they are relegated to the world of mystical experience, or considered as belonging to more perfect stages of the Christian life, ordinarily reserved for the chosen or select (the so–called *consecrated souls*). And yet, the fact that Jesus

Christ represents for Christians the possibility of becoming *His own life* is something so transcendental as to cause either the success or perhaps the failure of a human existence; in an absolute and eternal way: *Just as the Father who sent me lives and I live because of the Father, so he who eats me will live because of me.*[81] It is often forgotten that man was created to love and to be loved, and that love knows no measure. And yet all these realities are often regarded as something like a bonus, reserved as an extra for those who wish to perform certain services.

The vehement longing and anxiety produced in the bride upon hearing the voice of the Beloved are described in the Song of Songs, albeit in a very special way, as befits a reality that is very far from ordinary:

> *I slept, but my heart was awake.*
> *Hark! my beloved is knocking.*[82]

Which happens, as can be seen, both day and night, in the waking state and during sleep; for love knows no intermittency. This exclamation of the *Song of Songs* is another proof of a double character that confirms what we have been saying. First of all, because it is an allusion to a mystery, that of love, which surpasses everything that human beings have been able to imagine. And secondly, because it is one more evidence of the anguish experienced by human language, which cannot but feel distressed when it realizes its own insufficiency.

Insufficiency in terms of being exhaustive, but not in terms of its (relative) effectiveness. The reality of love is ineffable but not

---

[81] Jn 6:57.
[82] Song 5:2.

impossible to know, and even less incapable of manifesting itself. The problem lies in the fact that Love is God Himself, and hence the more He is known, the greater is the perception of a final place and goal... which have no end.

The incredible thing about human language is its capacity to not be daunted by its inadequacy. At the same time that it laments what it cannot express, it rejoices in the attempt to reveal in its own way —with words— something of what it perceives of that Infinite Beauty that compels the creature to Love. Hence, among the juggling and pirouettes it is forced to perform, trying at the same time to conceal and overcome its own impotence while singing of Beauty and Love, it appears before itself transformed into something like a bouquet of strange flowers, of incredible charm, and sublime splendor. Such an anguished and happy attempt to overcome the insurmountable is known to many by the name of *Poetry*. And so we can see, as an example, the uncontainable emotion of the bride at the possibility of hearing again, from the lips of the beloved, the disturbing *I love you (Amo te)*. Which is not surprising when one considers that the one who now pronounces it (the conjunction of the two most beautiful and sublime words that Heaven and Earth could have invented) is the One who considers the bride:

> *Who is she that comes forth like the dawn,*
> *Fair as the moon, bright as the sun,*
> *Terrible as an army with banners?*[83]

Why is it so surprising, according to this, that the bride feels *frightened* (there are also pangs and torments of love) at the possibility of knowing that she might die of excitement if she were to hear

---

[83] Song 6: 4.10.

that pair of *divine words*(D) again from the Bridegroom? Something like this:

> *If you should see me again,*
> *Down in the glen where the singing blackbirds fly,*
> *Do not say you love me then*
> *For, were you ever to repeat that sweet sigh,*
> *On hearing it, I may die.*

* * *

(D) Indeed, the two words of the statement *I love you* form a whole that seems to contain the depths of the divine. Whatever it may be, this is not an exaggeration. After all, that phrase contains the most passionate and direct way of expressing love: the love that an *I* feels for a *thou*, waiting to be reciprocated and to hear the same from that *thou* who in turn is also an *I*. And the language of love is the language of the heart. And the language of love —language as an expression of love— is precisely what most intimately unites man with God, Who is Love. Moreover, the Bridegroom is for the bride *her life* (Col 3:4).[84] And as for the Bridegroom Himself, unable on His part to express in human language what He feels for the bride and what she means to Him, He calls her *terrible as an army ordered for battle*. Here again is the unusual language of lovers... It is necessary to recognize that the complex web of tropes, metaphors, allegories, epithets, etc. —all the lavish abundance of figurative language— is one of the most disconcerting, strange, and mysteriously beautiful realities that form part of the enchanted world of Poetry. Fascinating is the extent to which Love and Beauty, constrained as they are to give themselves only partially to the creature, can go when they try to break in a thousand ways the bonds that gag them. And though such an effort bears fruit only in a very small way, both never cease to try again and again, always with their

---

[84]Cf. Phil 1:21; Rom 14: 7–8; Jn 6:57; 1 Jn 4:9; etc.

eyes fixed on the happy outcome of an enterprise which they well know will only culminate... at the definitive arrival of the lovers to the Homeland.

Now, what exactly does the expression *I love you* mean? The only possible answer to that question is that nobody knows. Despite the fact that millions of human beings have been uttering it for centuries and centuries, no one has ever been able to provide an entirely satisfactory explanation. Nor does it seem very likely that anyone will be able to do so in the future.

And yet —and this is truly surprising— no one doubts what he means when he pronounces these words. Whoever does feels sure about what his heart is experiencing, although he will never be able to precisely explain the content of his feelings.

What does the person who pronounces these words really feel in his heart? Of course, the easy and prompt answer that comes to mind is known to all: love, evidently. What that phrase expresses is the feeling of love for the person to whom it is addressed. Although this is really no answer... because what exactly is love and what does it consist of?

Created love, generously bestowed on the creature as a participation in Infinite Love,[85] is always a *mysterium fascinosum*. To simplify, it could be qualified as a feeling of attraction, on the part of the creature, toward Someone in Whom it perceives the good and the beautiful; although perhaps it would be better to consider it as a *set of feelings*. Needless to say, love, as the ontological reality that it is, is far from being reduced merely to feelings.

In the face of which, it is still possible to ask: What kind of feelings? And here something happens similar to what would be experienced by someone who finds himself suddenly in some unknown place in complete darkness: not knowing where he is, or why he is there, or what is around him, or what is the direction in which he should move. And yet he would understand the need to start walking somewhere until he stumbles upon something, in an effortful attempt to get out of such a situation any way he can.

---

[85] Here we do not intend to speak of Perfect or Infinite Love, which is God. The ideas presented here refer exclusively to created love, as a simple approach to the subject, without pretending to delve theologically into the mystery.

And perhaps that is the best thing to do here. To start taking steps even without any predetermined direction, perhaps going around in a circle, in the hope of finding something and getting as close as possible to the core of the mystery.

The expression *I love you*, addressed to the loved one, actually responds to a number of feelings: surprise, astonishment, admiration, joy, tenderness, and more; but most of all, and above all of them, that of attraction towards the loved one. In any case, since the feelings involved in love are more intricate and profound than can be said here, any attempt to explain them is in advance a task doomed to fail.

The declaration *I love you* is a declaration of unconditional surrender to the loved one. The one who pronounces it is recognizing the desire to *belong* to the other, which cannot be done except by means of *surrender* or donation. A first approach to the subject would discover that surrender to the beloved is subsequent to the desire to belong to that person.

Love offers itself to the consideration of the created being as a series of feelings, one of which is that of submission to the beloved.

An illustrative episode in this respect is contained in the narration of the events of the Last Supper. When Jesus prepares to wash the feet of His disciples, Saint Peter refuses to accept such a humiliation before him on the part of his Master:

—*You shall never wash my feet.*

—Jesus answered him, *If I do not wash you, you have no part with me.*[86]

It is evident that Jesus' attitude obeys the demands and intricacies of love, even if Saint Peter cannot understand it at that moment: Jesus answered him, *"What I am doing you do not know now, but afterward you will understand."*[87]

At least at first sight, such an attitude of submission leads to the recognition of a certain level of *inferiority*, on the part of the one who loves, with respect to the beloved. This brings to light another of the

---

[86] Jn 13:8.

[87] Jn 13:7.

apparent contradictions and mysteries of love that demand explanation. If it is possible or as far as it is possible.

But, at the same time, it must be taken into account, with respect to this inferiority, that the love relationship is always based on a situation of *bilaterality* and *reciprocity*. Thus love, rather than creating different levels (of superiority or inferiority), establishes a plane of *equality*. Love tends to equalize, in the same way that those who love each other wish to be together and that everything that belongs to one also belongs to the other. The bride manifests this clearly in the *Song of Songs*: *My beloved is mine and I am his... I am my beloved's and my beloved is mine... I am my beloved's, and his desire is for me.*[88]

The New Testament texts also seem to state it clearly: *No longer do I call you servants, for the servant does not know what his master is doing; but I have called you friends,...*[89] *And when I go and prepare a place for you, I will come again and will take you to myself, that where I am you may be also*[90] And the Apostle Paul likewise points to the same thing, in a text at once as mysterious as it is apparently bold: *For now we see in a mirror dimly, but then face to face. Now I know in part; then I shall understand fully, even as I have been fully understood.*[91]

Secondly, it should be noted that such a situation of *equality* does not indicate fusion or mixture. Neither of nature nor person. In divine–human love, the Creator is always the Creator, and the creature is always the creature. Any misunderstanding on this subject would be an aberration, nullifying the concept and possibility of love. Only in the Perfect and Infinite Love of the Divine Trinity are the Persons identified in one and the same nature (numerically one), which does not prevent *them from remaining really distinct as Persons*. In created love, on the contrary, which is but a participation and an analogy to divine love, the distinction and differentiation of the Persons is absolute and does not imply oneness of nature. Intimacy, equality, and mutual reciprocity have nothing to do

---

[88] Song 2:16; 6:3; 7:10.
[89] Jn 15:15.
[90] Jn 14:3.
[91] 1 Cor 13:12.

with a fusion (*con–fusion*) which, as has been said above, would destroy love. Pantheistic doctrines, like certain misunderstood mystical theories, are poles apart from true love.

But then, where are the submission and belonging to the beloved, we mentioned before? Is there in love what could be called a leveling of rank and dignity, or is there nothing here but a mere poetic wandering through the literary terrain of metaphors and allegorizing illusions...? Human understanding, however, confined to develop in the terrain of its limitations, proper, moreover, to a created being even if endowed with rationality, tends unfailingly, either to confuse perspectives, or to believe that it knows in its totality something which he has only apprehended, in reality, only partially and often very partially. Thus, it becomes possible, for example, that *self–abasement*, which is but the fruit of a loving humility —and is there any humility that is not loving? — is often considered by many as a kind of *lowliness*, or as a voluntary diminution of one's own dignity. And yet, would anyone think that the *semetipsum exinanivit formam servi accipiens*, of the *Letter to the Philippians*,[92] could have meant for God a humiliation or even a diminution of His glory? Does greatness, when it extends a loving hand to lowliness, lose some of its magnificence or see its own excellence reduced? Is it not rather that the majesty and splendor of nobility becomes more effulgent and brilliant with glory? Jesus Christ Himself, after having washed the feet of His disciples, clearly solved the problem: *Do you know what I have done to you? You call me Teacher and Lord; and you are right, for so I am. If I then, your Lord and Teacher, have washed your feet...*[93] The Baptist, too, was completely perplexed: *Jesus came from Galilee to the Jordan to John, to be baptized by him. John would have prevented him, saying, "I need to be baptized by you, and do you come to me"? But Jesus answered him, "Let it be so now; for thus it is fitting for us to fulfill all righteousness."*[94] And after all, was it not Jesus Himself Who said that everyone who exalts himself will be humbled, and he who humbles himself will be exalted (Mt 23:12; Lk 14:11;

---

[92] Phil 2: 7–8.
[93] Jn 13: 12–14.
[94] Mt 3: 13–15.

18:14)? But perhaps a text from Isaiah is most eloquent and the paradox becomes most forceful: *He was despised and rejected by men; a man of sorrows, and acquainted with grief; and as one from whom men hide their faces he was despised, and we esteemed him not. Surely, he has borne our griefs and carried our sorrows; yet we esteemed him stricken, smitten by God, and afflicted.*[95] Note, however, that it is precisely love which creates these strange and incomprehensible paradoxes!

The subject has particular relevance and application in the modern world regarding married life. Modern theories, in which it is necessary to include numerous Catholic theologians, are reluctant to admit the authority of the husband over the wife. Because such a prerogative, they say, supposes a reduction of the dignity of the woman. Hence the almost unanimous tendency to reject a well–known text of Saint Paul: *Wives, be subject to your husbands, as to the Lord. For the husband is the head of the wife as Christ is the head of the church, his body, and is himself its Savior. As the church is subject to Christ, so let wives also be subject in everything to their husbands.*[96] Such opponents often overlook the fact that the Apostle then adds that *husbands should love their wives as their own bodies. He who loves his wife loves himself.*[97] They also omit the Apostle's statement that *woman is the glory of the man.*[98] The twisted intention of feminist doctrines is clearly manifested in their habit of forgetting too many things. For example, the absolute necessity that in every kind of society, large or small —including the family—, there must be an authority; unless one desires anarchy and the consequent disappearance of such a society.[99] And since necessity is dictated by the very nature of things, no one can claim any reason to feel *humiliated* or diminished by the fact of not being constituted in authority. Such nonsense would be similar to the absurdity of man feeling humiliated because he is merely a creature

---

[95] Is 53: 3–4.

[96] Eph 5: 22–24.

[97] Eph 5:28.

[98] 1 Cor 11:7.

[99] The persistence in not recognizing such an obvious truth is another cause of the destruction of the family in modern society.

and not God. But humiliation can only exist when one fails to recognize, in whatever way, the dignity *due* to a person: And how can anyone feel offended, in his personal dignity, when his position is honorably recognized, as well as the *irreplaceable* and dignified work that he is carrying out in it? Feminist doctrines insist on confusing the distinction of functions with a difference of dignity that sound doctrine has never taught. How is it possible to honestly accuse of being ignorant of the dignity of women those who say, as we have seen above, that he who loves his wife, loves himself? Adding, a little further on, that, *in the Lord woman is not independent of man nor man of woman; for as woman was made from man, so man is now born of woman. And all things are from God.*[100] It is clear, therefore, to anyone who wishes to see things honestly and without prejudice, that the Apostle firmly proclaims the essential equality in the dignity of both sexes.[101]

And therefore, the possibility of equality, of bilaterality and reciprocity, in the love relationship, notwithstanding the existence of hierarchies and degrees that love is pleased to *disregard*. Had it not been so, the inspired Book known as *The Song of Songs* would never have existed. If greatness had not had the opportunity to lower itself to the level of insignificance, how could it have been recognized as such greatness, outside of itself?

* * *

That God has spoken and continues to speak to men is a reality. The Spirit has spoken to the churches, both in the Angel of each

---

[100] 1 Cor 11: 11–12.

[101] As if this were not enough, it is worth remembering that the refusal of women to accept certain attitudes, of *submission* and of *belonging*— means the refusal to recognize essential qualities proper to love. This means the absolute rejection of love itself. And if we consider that the function of loving —with the consequent and reciprocal function of being loved— is a fundamental constituent of human nature, the consequences of this refusal are self-evident: in short, man is placed on a lower level in the scale of living beings, exactly that of the irrational animal.

one and in the individuals who compose them. The Voice of God has resounded over men and the Breath of the Spirit has been diffused over each one of them. Indeed, the Spirit has been speaking constantly to the Church, which is the Body of Christ, and to each of her members. This is the same as saying that God addresses His Word to men in an official or public manner, without excluding private communication.

However, it is one thing for God to speak to men and another thing for them to *listen* to Him. Either because they do not want to hear it, or because they do not understand it, or even because they remain ignorant of the fact that God speaks to them.

Since divine–human dialogue must take place in freedom (*Ubi Spiritus ibi libertas*), the Voice uttered with free will expects in turn to be heard also in freedom. Of course, it is impossible to think of the possibility of dialogue, and even more so if it is a matter of loving dialogue, if both parties do not carry it out in freedom. Although in reality, to speak of freedom in dialogue, or of loving dialogue, is a kind of redundancy or tautology. Dialogue is not feasible when it ceases to be one of the (essential) ways of expressing love; and love is only realized in pure freedom. Hence, the pretense of carrying out a dialogue, simply out of a mere will to dialogue, or without the prior existence of a sincere will of loving understanding in those who undertake it, is a pure attempt to waste time or to engage in exercises of verbiage. And even worse; since if it is practiced in a selfish spirit by either party, or by both at the same time (of seeing, for example, who yields less and who gets more), then it loses all meaning.

The Spirit of the Lord is an expert on human nature, and He knows a great deal about this approach. It is not surprising that it is He Himself Who gives the warning: *He who has an ear, let him hear what the Spirit says to the churches.*[102] Where it is beyond doubt that the expression, *he who has ears* signifies that what is to be said immediately after is addressed to *those who want to hear.* Or, to put it better, to those who want to hear and to those who are able to hear; for the possible difficulties and obstacles to hear or to understand are not always sufficient to exempt the listener from all guilt.

In the account of the disciples traveling to the village of Emmaus, for example, it says that Jesus joined them on the way, *but their eyes were kept from recognizing him.*[103] The text does not expressly attribute any fault to the absolute lack of insight of the disciples, although it does not take much to divine in the narrator a certain gentle reproof of the wayfarers. Even the tender emotion they felt while He spoke to them was not enough to make them recognize the Master (v. 32), to the point that His identity only became evident to them at the moment of the *breaking of the bread* (v. 35).(E)

* * *

(E) That the Voice of God, or the Voice of the Spirit, is heard but not recognized, is something that can happen normally, as we have just seen. In the Old Testament there is also a notable case of this type, like that of the insistent and fruitless calls of God to Samuel (1 Sam 3: 1 ff.). In any case, it does not seem most important to insist now on the subject of the listener's responsibility, or on the greater or lesser degree of guilt on his part, if any.

More interesting is the case, truly admirable in spite of the frequency with which it happens, of those who feel themselves impelled by the inspiration of the Spirit... and proceed accordingly. Usually this *inspiration* has

---

[102] Rev 3:6; *passim.*
[103] Lk 24:16.

no other foundation than that of the simplicity or pedantry of the *enlightened* person, although it almost always turns out to be the consequence of a lack of humility. In any case, even in the case of simple stupidity or foolishness, as is usually the case, such *inspired* people tend to end up being dangerous. With no other basis than that of their own presumption and personal conceit, they always find listeners willing to believe them in spite of everything. When, in reality, the very firmness of their presumption would be sufficient proof that the Spirit has not intervened at all.[104] In short, here is another of the remarkable and curious qualities of human nature, being more inclined to listen to nonsense and foolishness than to the truth. Hence, in general, it is always a sign of sanity to flee from those who are convinced that they speak and act *moved by the Spirit*. The capacity for action (or destruction) of such enlightened ones is unlimited. They can prophesy the imminent end of the world, discover and proclaim the uselessness of Ecclesiastical Magisterium, impose norms of conduct as original as they are unusual, found a new sect of fanatics..., in addition to a set of multiform and varied possibilities, known only to God, which can vary from attributing to themselves portentous charismas to intending to convoke a Council, etc.

And even more. For we must also consider the role played by some revolutionary theories, recently appeared, held by a large group of experts and advanced theologians. All in all, this is a rare species of scholars, albeit one that is now very widespread and in power, which arose in the wake of the Second Vatican Council and is proving to be very influential. As a result of their erudite research, they claim to have discovered, among other things, the uselessness of the Hierarchy within the Church. The hierarchy, these erudite maintain, hitherto regarded as a fundamental part of the organism founded by Jesus Christ, has nevertheless been proving its ineffectiveness throughout history; consequently, it has become clear that the Holy Spirit is the Soul of the Church and the true and only Authority

---

[104]The Spirit of God *is usually humble*. While, on the contrary, the fanciful trumpery of those who, not content with attributing to themselves the influence of the Spirit, pretend to impose such a belief on others, is convincing proof of banality and stupidity. Here again it could be said that *ubi Spiritus Domini, ibi humilitas.*

capable of governing it. As for the way to exercise such government, the interpretation of the content of the laws or motions emanating from the Spirit, to make them known to the Christian People, etc., is a task that falls exclusively to such masters, as was to be expected. And so, by a strange sleight of hand, a Hierarchy, hitherto shown to be inept by the aforementioned experts, has been replaced by another Hierarchy which is now entirely (self) qualified.[105]

After what has been said, being able to listen to the Spirit with guaranteed authenticity will seem rather problematic. We can only answer that it is impossible to think that God cannot communicate with men, clearly and freely, when He wants to.

As far as the public or official Voice of the Spirit is concerned, there is no difficulty whatsoever. The Authentic Magisterium of the Church, meeting the due conditions, more than guarantees the authenticity of the Word of God as well as its interpretation.

As for private inspirations, there are also means capable of assuring their authenticity. Mystics and spiritual authors have always advised the practice of spiritual direction. Since one's own spirit is a poor counselor for itself, it is necessary to seek the advice of knowledgeable and discreet men, skilled in prayer and in the interior life. To regard such a practice as unnecessary would lead only to the ruin of those who consider themselves self–sufficient. And here again the Church has the last word and the final judgment.

Besides that, there is an instrument that can be considered definitive; very appropriate to assure the authenticity of the inspirations coming from the Spirit. Its fundamental value derives from the fact that it is based on the teachings of Jesus Christ, which refer to the knowledge of men, but which are equally applicable in this case: *A fructibus eorum*

---

[105] As a brief explanatory appendix, we must recognize that, at least in some cases, the attribution of incompetence to some part of the Hierarchy, on the part of such advanced scholars and doctors, does not lack completely a certain basis in reality. This, however, does not pretend to justify such qualified and competent connoisseurs of Theology.

cognoscetis eos.[106] Indeed, sound doctrine has always been in agreement in using results to help in the discernment of spirits. If the effects produced lead to confusion, loss of interior peace, wavering in faith, temptations and increase of concupiscence, etc., there can be no doubt that the supposed inspirations come from the evil spirit. As for the effects produced by the Spirit of the Lord, they are set forth by the Apostle, albeit in a non–exhaustive way, in his *Letter to the Galatians*, where he enumerates *love, joy, peace, long–suffering, kindness, goodness, faith, meekness, continence.*[107]

For both the one and the other, we need only consider them in order to find clues that lead to the clarification of the truth. Hence their usefulness is invaluable, since, although many false prophets have always existed in the bosom of the Church, their number, power, and influence will reach the greatest heights towards the End Times (Mt 7:15; 24: 11.24; 2 Pet 2: 1–3).

Undoubtedly, this is another thing that makes us think that the ecclesial world is a kind of *Wonderland*, in which the multitude of Alices that populate it live happily as if everything were magnificent. It is surprising what little value humans give to the criteria for the discernment of spirits. For example, there are undeniably new currents of doctrinal orientation that have arisen in the Church; led by *experts*, whose influence is powerful enough to make it risky to resist them. Too many members of the Hierarchy, who have allowed themselves to be dominated by fear, have been overruled in their functions. Those who, having practically renounced the exercise of their duties, have been limiting themselves to a decaffeinated resistance, both in their words and in their actions, whose main aim is not to appear as strangers to the modern world. Hence the emptiness of some speeches, which lack the will to fight while only being concerned with moderation, which renders them inoperative and incapable of combating the evil that reigns supreme: *a Cat with gloves on does not catch mice.*

A determined love for the truth and the good of the Church would lead both Hierarchy and faithful to take into account norms of discernment,

---

[106] Mt 7: 16–20.
[107] Gal 5: 22–23.

whose neglect could mean the destruction of the Church. If some so–called visionary, to use an example that may seem out of place to many, were to undertake a new *Crusade*, feeling inspired and moved by the Spirit..., perhaps it would be good to wait for the definitive results before deciding on the authenticity of the alleged *inspirations*. Here again is another of the noteworthy marvels of the behavior of human nature: how little it uses, and how seldom it puts into practice, common sense, to which it should normally resort.

* * *

A human being who has never heard the Voice of God (under the auspices of the Spirit), has never felt flooded by Joy. And since it is not possible to know what it consists of without having experienced it, it can happen, as in fact it does, that millions of human beings have seen their existence pass without hearing it.

—*Did not our hearts burn within us while he talked to us on the road, while he opened to us the scriptures?*[108]

Chesterton said that Joy is the gigantic secret of Christians, although the phrase needs certain nuances to be accepted. First of all, because not all Christians come to know Joy, or at least not all those who bear that name. Presumably Chesterton was referring to *true Christians*, who, as everyone knows, are not very abundant. This confirms that the English writer's expression, taken literally, contradicts itself: secrets —and even more so when it is a *gigantic secret*— are by definition never in the general domain; they always belong to a very few, or to a closed circle.

And we should apply even more restrictions to the beautiful thought attributed to Escriva de Balaguer, according to which *God*

---

[108]Lk 24:32.

has reserved the joy of Heaven for those who have known how to be joyful on Earth. Beautiful words; and truthful from a certain point of view, since they are inadequate if only taken literally. Indeed, given that few Christians (in fact, very few) have known how to be joyful on earth, we must conclude that Heaven would be practically empty.[109]

Of course, too many will reject these thoughts as exaggerated or false. Without realizing in doing so that *they too have never known Joy.* So, by the very words with which they reject them, they are proving the truth of what is said here.

Though there is no reason to put too much effort into incriminating them. Since Joy has been known to so few, it is not strange that people speak about it, and that some even believe that they have experienced it, without having the slightest idea of what it is or what it consists of. An absolute lack of knowledge in which millions of human beings live and die. Because the fact, it is worth repeating, is unquestionable: without having heard the Words of God, through the Spirit, *it is impossible to have known Joy.*

Once again, as is so often the case, the words of Jesus Christ are taken as mere exhortations. Hopeful, pious, and consoling, perhaps; but exhortations, nonetheless. And yet they are absolutely normative, statutory, and *ontological.* In the sense that there is no other way to know Joy. And as for what the world considers as joy, or

---

[109]The words of Léon Bloy (The Woman Who Was Poor) are well known and worthy of attention: The only sadness is that of not being a saint. For his part, Bernanos also said (Diary of a Country Priest) that the Church cannot teach Joy to her faithful in a measly half hour a week. A meager and insignificant amount of time that nowadays cannot even be counted on, since we only have to consult the statistics of Mass attendance (Bernanos wrote his novel before the Second Vatican Council). And there is yet another more painful reason, since everything seems to indicate that the Church is no longer so interested in teaching Joy.

joys in the plural,[110] Jesus Christ absolutely does not know them...,
and neither do men (except as pure concepts, entirely empty of content): *You will be sorrowful, but your sorrow will turn into joy... I will see you again and your hearts will rejoice, and no one will take your joy from you... Hitherto you have asked nothing in my name; ask, and you will receive, that your joy may be full.*[111] It would be a grave error for a Christian to pretend to see in these words of the Master a mere promise of consolation.

Starting from the premise that Joy is a fundamental element of Christian existence (*Gaudete in Domino semper. Iterum dico: Gaudete!*[112]), a problem of capital importance arises here. It has been said above that the Church has given up on preaching Joy. However, as is often the case when a statement is made that affects many, there is a danger of overgeneralizing. Of course, the Church as such cannot renounce its duty to preach Joy. This would be the equivalent of ceasing to proclaim the Gospel (*the Good News*). But the Church, being the Body of Christ and possessing as its Soul the Holy Spirit, is made up of men capable of making better or worse use of their freedom; and hence the multitude of varied vicissitudes through which it has passed in the course of her history. There was a time, for example, when it was on the point of becoming entirely Arian; and now, at the present time, it is quite impregnated with modernism.

The culminating moment of this particular crisis came with the appearance of the Protestant Reformation. One of the tenets of Protestantism is that human nature, intrinsically and irreparably

---

[110]There is a parallelism between the peace of the world and the peace that comes from Him, entirely different and even antithetical, on the one hand; and the Joy that He promises to His own and the merely worldly, on the other.

[111]Jn 16: 20.22.24.

[112]Phil 4:4; cf 3:1. Incidentally, even Nietzsche himself recognized this.

damaged by sin and incapable of good deeds, had no other way of salvation than *sola fides*. And so it was that man suddenly found himself entirely naked before God, as in the first moments of Eden, but now without innocence. From then on, the problem of salvation ceased to be something which, by a free and generous divine decision, through Grace, was to be accomplished between the two —God and man, cooperating hand in hand— and was now left solely in the hands of God. From that moment on, man had nothing left but to *trust* in Divine Mercy, without recognizing that he had been granted the gift of cooperating in such a sublime operation. In other words, the moment had come when everything depended on the Bridegroom, without the bride in turn being able to reciprocate. Bilaterality, or the relationship between two, had been replaced by the sad and (as if arbitrarily) unilaterality of only one. The (love) relationship of reciprocity and bilaterality, of giving and receiving, was destroyed. . ., and with it also any possibility of access to Joy. The relationship of mutual donation, of intimacy and friendship between husband and wife, was reduced to the strict and icy one of Lord-servant. The enamored cooing of the nightingale, through which could be heard the sweet words of *No longer do I call you servants; but I have called you friends*,[113] had been silenced forever. The bride now found herself unable to *respond and correspond* to the Bridegroom, to meet Him on the plane of the same place (*that where I am you may be also...I will not leave you desolate; I will come to you*).[114] Those almost heavenly words that the bride addressed to the Bridegroom would no longer have any meaning:

---

[113] Jn 15:15.
[114] Jn 14: 3.18.

> *Come, my beloved, let us go forth into the fields,*
> *And lodge in the villages...,*
> *There I will give you my love.*
> *The mandrakes give forth fragrance,*
> *And over our doors are all choice fruits,*
> *New as well as old,*
> *Which I have laid up for you, O my beloved.*[115]

How could the bride now invite the Bridegroom to go with her *into the fields*? And even worse: How could she please the Bridegroom by assuring Him —as lovers do— that she had *laid up for Him the old fruits as well as the new*?

It would no longer be possible to hear again the sweet words with which, through centuries and centuries, the bride invited and flooded with happiness the Bridegroom:

> *Draw me after you, let us make haste.*
> *The king has brought me into his chambers.*
> *We will exult and rejoice in you;*
> *We will extol your love more than wine;*
> *Rightly do they love you.*[116]

There can be no *relationships* of joy and rejoicing where there is no *relationship* of love. Which is always a matter of two who correspond to each other: they speak and listen to each other, they look at each other and contemplate each other, they give and receive, they treat each other as a *thou* and an *I* where everything of the one is of the other and everything of the other is of the one, and where if

---

[115] Song 7: 11–13.
[116] Song 1:4.

one cannot or does not want *to give*, the other neither wants nor can *receive*. In a word, there is no longer any possibility of *giving*. But if we ponder that there is *more joy in "giving" than in receiving...*[117] where is the Joy then?

The modernist heresy, or Neo–modernism, which seems to have taken its toll on Catholicism today, leads to the same consequence. After all, as Saint Pius X said, *Modernism is the compendium of all heresies*.[118] It has been demonstrated that all the main postulates of the post-Vatican II theological, liturgical, and pastoral *revolution* are an exact reproduction, almost one by one, of the principles condemned in the Decree *Lamentabili* and the Encyclical *Pascendi*. The problem is meticulously detailed and amply demonstrated in the brief but important book by Rudolf Graber (consecrated as Bishop of Regensburg by Pope John XXIII in 1962).[119]

In a purely horizontalist and this–worldly religion in which the cult of God has been replaced by the cult of man; in which an attempt has been made to reopen the Paradise of Eden, this time forever, after having believed to discover that it is not possible to hope for another, beyond the earth; in which human reason has decided that there is nothing that can transcend it; in which the notion of a God offended by sin has been made to disappear and consequently, therefore, the idea of mercy and redemption have been banished forever; in which every possibility of a relationship of divine–human intimacy and love has been eliminated; in which the ideas of sacrifice and death, as the supreme demonstration of love, have been

---

[117] Acts 20:35.

[118] Saint Pius X, *Pascendi*.

[119] There is an English translation of the book: *Athanasius and the Church of our Time;* Van Duren Contract Publications, England 1974.

erased and prevented from any possibility of their reappearance on the horizon of human thought...

In such an environment, all the Joy that a religion of *Love* and *Salvation* for man carried with it has disappeared. Is human existence still worthwhile if it can hope for nothing else beyond this earth? Can an existence still have meaning when the relationship of divine–human love has been replaced, it is not clear why, by material well–being, by peace understood in a worldly sense, by so–called human *rights* on the content of which no one can agree,[120] or by a religion in which Truth matters less than the *tranquility* of an otherwise dead, mismatched understanding that is very much reminiscent of the silence of cemeteries?

Fortunately, the songs of the Ancient Times are still heard. There are still those who think that human existence, far from remaining stagnant in a pool of still water with no way out, is a continuous *journey* towards a better world. For them, the Church is itinerant, migratory, and even nomadic, if you will, and by no means sedentary. For them too, knowing that the bride remains in the *not yet*, but nourished with hope, she seeks the Bridegroom, the beloved of her soul, with courage and without pause. And does not the anxious search make the final encounter even more exciting?

> *Tell me, you whom my soul loves,*
> *Where you pasture your flock,*
> *Where you make it lie down at noon;*
> *For why should I be like one who wanders*
> *Beside the flocks of your companions.*[121]

---

[120]It is foolish to pretend to pursue human rights that are either not based on *anything*, or at most try to be based *on themselves*. The ancients were right when they said that the gods drove men mad when they wished to destroy them.

[121]Song 1:7.

And how could the bride fail to hear the voice of the Bridegroom calling her to come quickly?

> *The voice of my beloved!*
> *Arise, my love, my fair one,*
> *And come away.*
> *O my dove, in the clefts of the rock,*
> *In the covert of the cliff,*
> *Let me see your face, let me hear your voice...*[122]

He that has ears, let him hear what the Spirit says unto the churches... Yes, because there is as much that he has to say to them as the Bridegroom would like to exchange lullabies and sayings of love with the bride:

> *My Bridegroom's voice is for me,*
> *Like the wake of a ship deeply furrowing*
> *Like winds that stir so lightly*
> *Like a gentle whispering,*
> *Like the solemn moves of a night bird on wing.*

In the meantime, the Spirit, who flows where and when He wants, continues to speak to His Church. In reality, we do not know where He comes from or where He is going, but there is the certainty that He is there, even though at times it may seem that His voice is not heard. It would be a grave error, however, to confuse *kenosis* with *absence*. For the Bridegroom has never ceased at any time to watch over the Bride or to express to her His sayings and yearnings of love.

---

[122] Song 2: 8.10.13–14.

Hence, in the present situation of the Church and of the World, it is important to be ready to listen attentively to what the Spirit has to say *to each of the seven churches*. For seven indicates fullness. Which is the same as saying that the Spirit wants to speak *to His whole Church*, which is Holy and Immaculate, the Bride of the Lamb, the One True Church. The Church of Christ, which is none other than that which has always been known as the *Catholic Church* from the beginning of all beginnings.

...But I have this against you, that you have abandoned the love you had at first.
(Rev 2:4)

II

LOST LOVE

...*But I have this against you: that you have lost the passion of your first love,*¹ as some translate it less literally, although also in accordance with the tradition of the text.²

However, can Love be lost or disappear? According to Saint Paul, *love never ends.*³ As for the *Song of Songs*, it also seems to understand it this way:

> *For love is strong as death,*
> *Jealousy is cruel as the grave.*
> *Many waters cannot quench love,*
> *Neither can floods drown it.*⁴

Indeed, there is not the slightest hint in the Sacred Poem that the love between the Bridegroom and the bride could be destined to fade away. Even when it comes to created or participated love,

---

[1] Rev 2:4.

[2] *Sed habeo adversus te quod caritatem tuam primam reliquisti*, says the Neo-Vulgate.

[3] *Caritas nunquam excidit* (1 Cor 13:8).

[4] Song 8: 6–7.

to which these texts refer, it is difficult to imagine that love could ever be lost once it has emerged as a relationship of intimacy and mutual surrender between a *thou* and an *I*.

According to this, is perpetuity one of love's essential notes — *forever*—, as the texts and the most common sentiment seem to suppose? Or should we rather admit the possibility that it may disappear, in spite of everything?

Saint Thomas openly rejects the error of some heretics who maintained that man, once he has received the grace of the Holy Spirit, cannot sin; and if he sins, they said, it is because he never had that grace. For the Saint the doctrine is sufficiently clear, inasmuch as it is evident that charity can be lost.[5]

The *Song of Songs*, as it could not be otherwise, also seems to admit in other texts the possibility of losing Love. This is accomplished by the Sacred Book through some expressions that even sound harsh:

> *If a man offered for love all his wealth,*
> *He would be utterly scorned.*[6]

Here it can be interpreted that perhaps someone would be capable of pretending to acquire Love in exchange for other goods; and, consequently, also to offer it in order to obtain them. Accordingly, Love could be acquired or lost and even be the object of transactions.[7]

---

[5] *Contra Gentiles*, lib. 4, Chapter 70. Cf. also, for example, *De virtutibus* q. 2, a. 12.

[6] Song 8:7.

[7] *Your silver perishes with you, because you thought you could obtain the gift of God with money*: Saint Peter to Simon (Acts 8:20).

Moreover, the Lord clearly states it with words referring to the events of the End Times: *and because wickedness is multiplied, most men's love will grow cold.*[8]

However, the text from Revelation to which we refer here, even at first glance, does not seem to say that Love has been lost, but rather the impetus of the *first* Love (*primam caritatem*). The use of the adjective seems to give a peculiar meaning to the expression: if what has been lost is the *first love*, it is because it would not be Love; and the same is the meaning of the expression about the *impetus* of the first love, if this interpretation of the text is admitted. The initial fire or ardor would have vanished to give way to a state of lukewarmness or mediocrity, which could be described as diminished or degraded love.

Summarizing therefore, and if what has been said is true, Love could be lost entirely, as well as increase or decrease.

However, with regard to its *decrease*, a serious difficulty arises. Considering the problem theologically, it seems entirely impossible that the virtue of charity is susceptible to decrease.[9] It can be increased or lost, but in no case diminished.

Saint Thomas clearly poses the question and gives a negative response.[10] The Saint only admits the decrease in charity speaking improperly, or at any rate indirectly: *Hence, strictly speaking, charity can in no way diminish; however, improperly speaking, we can*

---

[8] *Et quoniam abundavit iniquitas, refrigescet caritas multorum* (Mt 24:12).

[9] Here we will not enter into the lengthy problems that arise in Theology, both with respect to terminology and to the different concepts which, in one way or another, refer to love. Saint Thomas clearly explains the distinction between *amor, dilectio, caritas,* and *amicitia* in *Sum. Theol.* I^a–II^æ, q. 26, a. 3, *Respondeo*, where he says that *quator nomina inveniuntur ad idem quodamææ modo pertinentia.* Cf. also, among many other texts, *Sum. Theol.*, II^a–II^æ, q. 25, a. 2.

[10] *Sum. Theol.*, II^a–II^æ, q. 24, a. 10.

say decrease of charity referring to the disposition to its corruption, which venial sins cause; or also not exercising the works of charity.[11] In another place he says that *venial sin delays the act of charity by its excessive attachment to the created good.*[12] And he still further clarifies that *daily we lose something in the spiritual by the heat of concupiscence of venial sins, which diminish the fervor of charity.*[13]

It is evident that, if one cannot admit theologically an ontological diminution of charity as a virtue, it is at least possible to speak of a *diminutio fervoris caritatis*, according to the expression of Saint Thomas himself. And such has been the constant sentiment in Christianity, where it has always been taken for granted, in Christian life, both the possibility of an increase in Love and also of its loss; as well as a possible cooling of the loving sentiment of the heart, which leads first to lukewarmness and then to the total loss of charity. Saint Francis de Sales, commenting in his *Treatise on the Love of God* (4:22), on the reproach addressed by the Spirit to the Angel of the Church of Ephesus says that *he did not accuse him of lack of charity, but that he was not as he was at the beginning, so*

---

[11] *Unde consequens est quod caritas nullo modo diminui possit, directe loquendo. Potest tamen indirecte dici diminutio caritatis dispositio ad corruptionem ipsius: quæ fit vel per peccata venialia; vel etiam per cessationem ab exercitio operum caritatis* (II^a–II^æ, q. 24, a. 10, Respondeo).

[12] *Peccatum autem veniale non contrariatur habituali gratiæ vel caritati, sed retardat actum eius, in quantum nimis hæret homo bono creato* (III^a, q. 87, a. 2, Respondeo).

[13] *Spiritualiter autem quotidie in nobis aliquid deperditur ex calore concupiscentiæ per peccata venialia, quæ diminuunt fervorem caritatis* (q. 79, a. 4, Respondeo). The Saint adds (II^a–II^æ, q. 54, a. 3, Respondeo) that *ad primum ergo dicendum quod minor amor Dei intelligi dupliciter. Uno modo, per defectum fervoris caritatis: et sic causatur negligentia quæ est peccatum veniale. Alio modo, per defectum ipsius caritatis: sicut dicitur minor amor Dei quando aliquis diligit Deum solum amore naturali.*

fervent, so willing, so fruitful, just as we usually say of a man who from courageous, jovial, and gallant has become dejected, sad, and decayed.[14] Matthew 24:12 seems to reinforce this sense when, referring to the End Times, it says: *Because wickedness is multiplied, most men's love will grow cold.* Translated by the Neo-Vulgate as *quoniam abundavit iniquitas, refrigescet caritas multorum*. But the original Greek of *refrigescere* is the verb ψύχω, which in the present tense is equivalent to *spiro, refrigero, exsicco,* and whose passive would lead to *refrigesco* or *exaresco*,[15] the meanings of which are quite clear. Only the verb *spirare* could offer some difficulty, one of whose meanings is to blow, to make the wind flow, to breathe, etc., pointed out by Bailly in his Dictionary as *souffler très légèrement, rejeter por le souffle, exhaler*, in addition to those proper to *refraîchir*, etc., all of which come to confirm what has been said above.[16]

The text of Apocalypse 2:4 is as disconcerting as it is disturbing: *Sed habeo adversus te quod caritatem tuam primam reliquisti.* For centuries, Christians have seen in it, even if not fully aware, a direct stab to the heart, of course; but also a painful recrimination born of a disappointed Love, a defiant rebuke, a lament of immense pain coming to them from the dawn of Christianity... and, even above all that, an unfathomable mystery. It is easy to say that the Spirit accuses the Angel of Ephesus of lukewarmness and then goes on to something else, as if the fact of a *Love that has become less intense* was something easy to understand. Is it a question of a *complete disappearance* of Love or, simply and without going any further, of

---

[14] Quoted in the *Biblia de la Universidad de Navarra*, New Testament, Commentary on Apocalypse 2,4.

[15] Zerwick, *Analysis Philologica Novi Testamenti Græci*.

[16] Bailly, *Dictionnaire Grec-Français*, verbo ψύχω. We will soon see that, even leaving intact the possibility of the cooling of Love, we cannot exclude from the text of Matthew 24:12 the meaning of a complete disappearance of charity.

a *decrease of the feeling of love*? In the end, how can we explain a decrease of the feeling of Love in a being who was made to love, by feeling this love more and more strongly, until he himself becomes a burning ember, by participation in the Life that is Infinite Fire? *I came that they may have life, and may have it more abundantly.*[17] Hence the reproach addressed by Jesus Himself to the Jews: *you refuse to come to me that you may have life.*[18] And even the Apostle saw here the whole meaning of the existence of the disciples: *so that the life of Jesus may also be manifested in our bodies.*[19]

Although it is not often noticed, lukewarmness is one of the greatest mysteries of the Christian life. The chilling reproach that the Spirit addresses to the Angel of the Church of Laodicea is as disturbing as it is difficult to understand: *I know thy works, that thou art neither cold, nor hot. I would thou wert cold, or hot. But because thou art lukewarm, and neither cold, nor hot, I will begin to vomit thee out of my mouth.*[20] According to the Spirit, any of the extreme positions, even that of total coldness, is preferable to that of a neutral choice between good and evil: *Utinam frigidus esses aut calidus*! However, how is it possible that the position that opts for evil could be better than another possible intermediate one —neither bad, nor good—, which is even capable of provoking vomiting? To explain this —to the extent that it is possible— it would be necessary to understand the meaning of an *indifferent* posture that has decided neither for good nor for evil. Or perhaps to delve into the mystery of the possibility that something, made for totality and fullness, can be reduced to the realm of the partial,

---

[17] Jn 10:10.
[18] Jn 5:40.
[19] 2 Cor 4:10.
[20] Rev 3: 15–16.

the measurable and the conditioned. In short, or to put it another way, it is evident that in order to explain lukewarmness, it would be necessary to understand the mystery of Love that has been reduced to nothing. Something that no one has yet done.[21]

Our text of Apocalypse 2:4: S*ed habeo adversus te quod caritatem tuam primam reliquisti*, must necessarily refer to a diminution or cooling of Love, and by no means to its total loss. It is enough to read its context (2: 1–6) to be convinced of this and dispel any doubt. Everything in it is praising the Angel of the Church of Ephesus, which would not make any sense if he had disowned charity, which would mean that he had lost it entirely.

If this interpretation is accepted, it would give way to the alternative interpretation: *But I have this against you, that you have lost the impetus of your first love.* Two things are to be noted here:

First, that it may be the case that a love may be the *first* in a series of other different or distinct ones. Secondly, that the text seems to term as *impetuous* precisely the first love; perhaps as something proper and constitutive and probably exclusive to it.

As for the former —a series of various loves—, it is evident that the case would exclusively affect the creature. About Infinite or Substantial Love, it is interesting to note that Dante, in his *Divine Comedy*, in the inscription that appears on the façade of the gates of Hell, calls it *First Love*:

---

[21]Man is surrounded and immersed in realities that *are simply there*. About some of which it has been agreed to assign a meaning, more or less complete or true, but about which any attempt at discussion is excluded in advance. No doubt this is done for a merely reassuring reason. The attempt to delve into the abysmal mystery of certain realities, besides being beyond the capabilities of the creature, would be too disturbing for it. And one of these realities is precisely lukewarmness.

> *Giustizia mosse il mio alto fattore;*
> *Fecemi la divina potestate,*
> *La somma sapienza e'l primo amore.*[22]

The meaning here is very clear and evident. The *First Love* is Infinite Love, the First and the Last, the Beginning and the End (Rev 1:17; 2:8; 22:13), the origin and cause of all things and especially of all other love, which, precisely because it is created, always arises through participation.

Creatures are not capable of an infinite act of love.[23] Infinitude for them can only mean totality. As Saint Thomas says, *quando aliquis secundum totum suum posse diligit.*[24]

The proof that we are dealing here with nothing other than *totality* is in the precept itself: *The first* [commandment] *is, 'Hear, O Israel: The Lord our God, the Lord is one; and you shall love the*

---

[22] *Justice moved my supreme Author; //I was made by the divine power,//the supreme wisdom and first love* (Dante, *The Divine Comedy*, Inferno, Canto III).

[23] On whether the virtue of charity can be made perfect in this life cf. Saint Thomas, *Sum. Theol.*, II^a–II^{ae}, q. 24, a. 8. According to the Saint, the perfect act of charity can be understood in two ways: *ex parte diligibilis*, on the one hand, and *ex parte diligentis*, on the other. He affirms that God, the Supreme Good, is Himself capable of being loved *infinitely*. However, he goes on to say, *nulla autem creatura potest eum diligere infinite: cum quælibet virtus creata sit finita*. On the other hand, on the part of the one who loves, *caritas dicitur perfecta quando aliquis secundum totum suum posse diligit*. This can happen, according to him, in three different ways.

[24] In Heaven it also takes the form of infinity in *duration*; namely, of a *succession* in which there is no duration and no end. However, in such absence of a *final* term, there is the proof that it can always go beyond: hence it is not infinite, therefore. Unless Love, in this case, is considered as *ratione termini* or *objecti* but never *in itself*. With which we come to the same conclusion, without forgetting also that infinity is not the same as eternity.

Lord your God with all your heart, and with all your soul, and with all your mind, and with all your strength'.[25]

A precept that refers more to a goal to be reached than to a reality already achieved. This becomes clear when we consider that in this life the Christian only comes to possess the Spirit as a foretaste or first fruits (Rom 8:23; 2 Cor 1:22). The Apostle even uses heart–rending expressions at this point: *For in this also we groan, desiring to be clothed upon with our habitation that is from heaven. Yet so that we be found clothed, not naked. For we also, who are in this tabernacle, do groan, being burthened; because we would not be unclothed, but clothed upon, that that which is mortal may be swallowed up by life. Now he that maketh us for this very thing, is God, who hath given us the pledge of the Spirit.*[26] Indeed, as we have seen above following Saint Thomas, one can only speak of perfect Love in this life *quando aliquis secundum totum suum posse diligit*. However, who would be able to say that he loves God with all his being, with all his heart, and with all his strength? And even if this were so, and given that the ultimate goal of Love has been set too high (Mt 5:48; cf. Phil 3:12), would anyone dare to say that he could not fly higher?

The great tragedy of man in this life is that he cannot yet love in perfect totality. Yet he was made for the total and absolute, and not for the partial and transient. The tremendous condition of the Christian, with respect to the full realization of his being, starts from the fact that he finds himself in the situation of the *not yet*, unable to reach the definitive of the *already* until he finds himself in Heaven. Is it strange that Saint Paul felt himself pierced with anxiety to the point of saying that *my desire is to be dissolved and*

---

[25] Mk 12: 29–30; Deut 6: 4–5.
[26] 2 Cor 5: 2–5.

to be with Christ, a thing by far the better.[27] And hence death, far from being seen as a loss, or even as something that goes far beyond a simple completion of the journey —*cursum consumavi*—,[28] is for him the highest of all gains (Phil 1:21). Something similar to what Saint Teresa of Jesus also felt when she said that *I die because I do not die*. And the same thing came to say, in perfect parallelism, the other great Doctor of Mysticism:

> *But how, O life, dost thou persevere,*
> *Since thou livest not where thou livest,*
> *And since the arrows make thee to die which thou receivest*
> *From the conception of the Beloved*
> *Which thou formest within thee?*[29]

The transitory situation of the Christian, according to the imperative of the *not yet*, is what makes him live in hope: *But hope that is seen, is not hope. For what a man seeth, why doth he hope for? But if we hope for that which we see not, we wait for it with patience.*[30] The disciple lives in anxiety, as well as in the certainty that at last the moment of his definitive encounter with the Lord will come. On the other hand, the absence of hope leads to the emptiness of sadness and the anguish of despair (1 Thess 4:13); for he who hopes for nothing will receive nothing. Such a situation requires the Christian to be always prepared, in a constant state of vigilance and watchfulness: *Estote parati, quia, qua nescitis hora,*

---

[27] Phil 1:23.
[28] 2 Tim 4:7.
[29] Saint John of the Cross, *Spiritual Canticle* VIII.
[30] Rom 8: 24–25.

*Filius hominis venturus est.*³¹ At the hour you do not know, of course. Which is usually always during the Night, whichever way this Scripture is interpreted; but which undoubtedly always refers to some crucial moment of life wrapped in uncertainty, in darkness, and even in an anguish caused by the Night. Which will ordinarily happen around midnight, which is the same as saying at its peak, at the moment of deepest shadow: *Media autem nocte clamor factus est: "Ecce Sponsus! Exite obviam ei."*³² And indeed, because *hoc autem scitote quia, si sciret paterfamilias qua hora fur veniret...*³³ And hence the need for intensive vigilance and a permanent state of tension:

> *Watchman, what of the night?*
> *Watchman, what of the night?*³⁴

It should be noted that the Christian's anxious and watchful waiting has nothing to do with anguish or fear; rather, the opposite is true. For it is precisely the Bridegroom Who arrives: *Ecce Sponsus*! And how could the bride await Him except with the most intense longing and the greatest impatience? Since it is the Bridegroom Who comes, the impatient waiting of the bride can only be loving: *Qui diligunt adventum eius.*³⁵ The servants watch attentively for the arrival of their master; to open the door to him at once (*confestim*). For he returns precisely from the nuptials, and

---

[31] Mt 24:44.
[32] Mt 25:6.
[33] Lk 12:39; cf. Mk 13:35.
[34] Is 21:11.
[35] 2 Tim 4:8.

the first thing he will do the instant he arrives, is to seat them at table and *serve them himself*.[36]

Hope is indeed the business of love. For it should not be forgotten that all the virtues acquire their value through charity and finally identify with it. Hope, or the virtue of Waiting, is born precisely of Love (he who loves waits), at the same time as it contributes to the increase and true meaning of Love (the definitive meeting and embrace of the Lovers is all the more real and intense the more eager the waiting has been). Hence it can be said that the virtue of hope is born of Love, on whose fire it feeds and in turn fuels. And since Love *never ends* (1 Cor 13:8), it is found at the beginning and at the end of the journey, sustained in turn by a hope that will never be *disappointed* (Rom 5:5): for to discover the meaninglessness of the virtue of Hope would be tantamount, no more and no less, to revealing the meaninglessness of Love.

Since hope is a faithful transcript of Love, it cannot lack the quality of *reciprocity*, even though this aspect tends to go unnoticed. This leads to the affirmation (which may sound strange) that hope, or the virtue of anxious waiting, *affects both lovers equally*, and not only the one who awaits the arrival of the one who is absent. And it is present even more intensely in the one who loves more strongly. This leads to the surprising but logical conclusion that in

---

[36] Lk 12: 36–38. The express allusion to the *wedding*, as in the parable of the virgins who awaited the arrival of the Bridegroom, is an indication of the nuptial character of this moment; in clear reference, therefore, to the definitive union of the Bridegroom and the bride. And not only that. For, as is always in the affairs of Love, the episode carries with it the seal of total reciprocity. Therefore, better still than to say that the Bridegroom returns from the nuptials, would be to say that in reality he returns to carry them out; and if he was previously absent, it was precisely to prepare for them: *And if I shall go, and prepare a place for you, I will come again, and will take you to myself; that where I am, you also may be* (Jn 14:3).

the divine–human Love relationship, it is the Bridegroom who *waits* most anxiously for the bride. It would be unimaginable, and even more so given the way in which this love relationship takes place, for God not to await, with *loving anxiety*, the definitive embrace and consummation of the reciprocal possession with His creature: *Desiderio desideravi hoc Pascha manducare vobiscum...* [37]

It is often forgotten that God loves man with a love that is both divine and human. For that reason the Word became Man. Indeed, it is precisely through the human love that Jesus Christ has felt for him, that man also becomes aware of divine love. A love that would otherwise be *quite difficult* for him to perceive. To understand the infinitely mysterious reality of Love would be for man a more than arduous task; unless he were able to reach the very frontier of the depths of divine Love; even if through the immeasurable tenderness and depth of human love. Which happens for him in Jesus Christ. Since human love becomes divine precisely in the human Heart of Jesus Christ: but now perceived, felt, and lived by the man who is grafted and intimately united with Him. And this is how God and His creature, in sublime and mysterious union, come to live one and the same Love; as Scripture affirms and God also demands a perfect relationship of love: *that the love with which thou hast loved me* [O Father] *may be in them, and I in them.*[38]

---

[37]Lk 22:15. It is evident that this *desiring with great desire* refers to the human will of Jesus Christ; but without excluding in any way His divine will, given the perfect identification of both, even though they are distinct. If it is possible to put it this way, it is a way of *translating into the human* (or of making it more accessible and comprehensible to man, in order to give more capacity for authenticity and depth to his response, which is moreover expected) the Love of God for man. Once again, man's inability to reach the Father except through Jesus Christ is evident (Jn 14:6).

[38]Jn 17:26.

But we must return to *reciprocity* in the virtue of hope. And, as a consequence, to the mutual anxiety that both the bride and the Bridegroom feel to meet and reunite:

> *My Love, I have walked anew*
> *On your orchard path where lemon blooms have burst.*
> *There I hid myself from you*
> *Behind lemon trees from view*
> *Just to see, My Love, if I could kiss you first.*
>
> *Beloved, I searched to see,*
> *In my orchard, the path where lemon blooms burst,*
> *There I stayed in wait for thee,*
> *Out behind my lemon tree,*
> *To see if, My Beloved, I found you first.*

Although it often goes unnoticed, some Bible texts provide indications on this point that may confirm, once again, such an essential quality of Love as reciprocity: *Behold, I stand at the gate, and knock. If any man shall hear my voice, and open to me the door, I will come in to him, and will sup with him, and he with me.*[39] It is noteworthy that the one who now knocks and waits is the Bridegroom: patiently and humbly, appealing to the generous will of the bride: *if anyone shall hear my voice, and open to me the door...* The conditional *if* has a special value here, as an invitation to a spontaneous response on the part of the other; since, after all, it is an act of Love, in which freedom is essential. And the same seems to be

---

[39] Rev 3:20. Some bible scholars and translators simplify the text and translate here *and we will dine together*. They forget that, while simplification is sometimes useful to make things simpler, at other times, as in this case, it only serves to distort and confuse. Modifying the inspired text, even with the best intentions, can ruin much of the richness of its content. One cannot be a theologian without knowing Scripture, just as no one can presume to be an exegete if he does not have sufficient knowledge of theology.

confirmed by certain texts of the *Song of Songs*. In some of them, the Bridegroom appears to be driven by an impatience bordering on nervousness, which seems to reach an anxious restlessness; or even, perhaps, imprudence:

> *Behold, he comes,*
> *Leaping upon the mountains,*
> *Bounding over the hills.*
> *My beloved is like a gazelle, or a young stag.*
> *Behold, there he stands*
> *Behind our wall,*
> *Gazing in at the windows,*
> *Looking through the lattice.*[40]

In other cases, He also seems to be waiting at the door, likewise in an imploring attitude:

> *Open to me, my sister, my love,*
> *My dove, my perfect one;*
> *For my head is wet with dew,*
> *My locks with the drops of the night...*[41]

The accumulation of compliments and endearments addressed to the bride, some of which seem incompatible (*my sister, my bride, my dove, my immaculate one...*), do not appear to have a merely literary-metaphorical-poetic character. Rather, they seem to express the desire of the Bridegroom to help the bride understand that the Love with which He loves her is a *perfect* Love: in which, therefore, all forms of love (conjugal, fraternal, paternal-filial, etc., etc.) are included, which is another characteristic of divine Love and, by extension and by certain participation, also of divine–human Love.

---

[40] Song 2: 8–9.
[41] Song 5:2.

However, too much emphasis is usually placed on the poetic literary genre of the *Song of Songs*. Hence the inclination to think of it as merely love poetry or epithalamic poetry, with the inspired character of the book occupying second or third place. To which must be added the mysterious and profound condition with which poetry is endowed. Poetry, if it is authentic, contains much more than what is apparent from the mere meaning of the words to the point that, not infrequently, it seems to escape the perception and control even of its author.

Now, since hope is a matter of Love, it cannot be a virtue of mere consolation, but as something that has to do fundamentally with salvation (Rom 8:24).[42] How can those who hope for nothing, love? Man having been made by Love and for Love, and since he is in a *not yet* stage, it is evident that the attitude of *waiting* is connatural to his being. We wait as intensely as we love, and to this end all human existence is oriented. Since both the Old Law and the Prophets, and even more so the New Law, are reduced to Love (for God and, by extension, for one's neighbor),[43] hence the necessity of the attitude of (longing) waiting for salvation.

---

[42] Cf. Heb 11: 6.13–16.

[43] Mt 22:40; Jn 15:12. According to Saint Thomas, *the precept to love is said to be a general precept because all the other precepts refer to it as their end, as stated in 1 Timothy 1:5: "Finis præcepti caritas es"* (II^a–II^æ, q. 23, a. 4, *ad tertium*). The Apostle adds, following that same text, that *From which things some going astray, are turned aside unto vain babbling: Desiring to be teachers of the law, understanding neither the things they say, nor whereof they affirm* (vv. 6–7). This explains much of modern theology and pastoral work. Such an excessive concern for peace (understood in a purely human way), for understanding among men (respecting everyone's beliefs since they are all valid), for human rights, and even for the conservation of the environment and a long etcetera, has led to forgetting what is fundamental: that Theology is the science whose object is God and whose end is the salvation of man. No one should be surprised that the Apostle, also acting as a prophet in this case, announced the arrival of a time abounding in charlatans and lacking in Shepherds.

And what does the Christian really hope for, or for whom does he really wait? It should be kept in mind that hope, far from referring merely to the definitive condition in Heaven, has to do also, and to a great extent, with the Christian's present pilgrim status. He also hopes, *for this life*, for the reality of a greater love and a greater intimacy toward and with the Lord: *Desiderium habens dissolvi et cum Christo esse.*[44] So the only thing that the Christian eagerly awaits is Jesus Christ, Who is his life and his everything: *For to me, to live is Christ, and to die is gain.*[45] On the other hand, it is already known that love is totality; as strong as death and with its darts like flaming arrows (Song 8:6). Hence the attitude of waiting is most natural for the Christian, so that his existence has no other meaning than a vehement restlessness to attain something that he does not yet possess, according to the saying of Saint Augustine: *You made us, Lord, for yourself, and therefore our heart is restless...*That is what makes him become, throughout his life, a man of desires (Dan 9:23; 10:11; 10:19). Saint Paul expressed it by saying that *none of us lives to himself, and none of us dies to himself. For whether we live, we live unto the Lord; or whether we die, we die unto the Lord. Therefore, whether we live, or whether we die, we are the Lord's.*[46]

Of course, this attitude of waiting on the part of the Christian who awaits his Lord, however yearning and impatient it may be, takes place in this world. Exactly as long as the journey lasts that leads, through a tiring path, to the Father's house. And where, therefore, there is room for the ups and downs of weakness, the limitations of weariness, and the contingencies imposed by the danger

---

[44]Phil 1:23.
[45]Phil 1:21.
[46]Rom 14: 7–8.

of a constant struggle. In the parable of the virgins who awaited the coming of the Bridegroom, some wise and others foolish (Mt 25: 1–13), there is a detail expressed as if in passing: because of the delay of the bridegroom, *they all slumbered and slept*. Something quite normal, after all, given human nature. Although the fact that all were careless during the vigil tends to go unnoticed: both the foolish and the prudent.

Pointing out that, in fact, *they all* fell asleep is perhaps of no great importance and is probably even required for the greater fluidity of the narrative. But, important or not, it is curious that the prudent women also fell asleep; a circumstantial incident, however, which seems to have had no influence at all on the final outcome, inasmuch as they were prepared anyway, and hence they entered the wedding hall with the Bridegroom. However, such an insignificant and minor detail lends itself to some consideration which, though perhaps trivial, seems intriguing.

The waiting for the Spouse, together with the Love that nourishes it, takes place, as we have already said, during the present stage of itinerancy or *not yet*. Therefore, we can expect possible hesitations, a decrease of impetus or fervor (*You have lost the impetus of your first Love*), and even the total loss of the feeling that nourished the confident and longing vigilance. In other words, both hope and love are subject to different and contrary vicissitudes. For even prudent virgins can fall asleep, as in fact happened. Hence the Lord's repeated remarks and warnings to all concerning the need for vigilance, as well as Saint Paul's pressing warning that it is time to awaken from sleep (Rom 13:11).

Such vicissitudes and eventualities are a natural part of the great adventure of Love to which man has been called. Its culmination is the prize of a crown that is supposed to be well earned, and not something given as compassionate alms or an undeserved gift (1 Tim 6:12; 2 Tim 2:5; 1 Cor 9: 24–26; Heb 10:32). At the same time, the combat that the bride has to fight, the merits for which she is worthy of the crown received from the Bridegroom, are also the work of grace. This in turn serves to highlight even more the greatness of divine Love, which endowed man with freedom and the capability of attaining merits that are now his own: *his own and deserved*, as well as *received and granted*. An unfathomable mystery of divine Love whose depth escapes human understanding in this life. And yet *it had to be so*, from the moment that God wanted to be loved by man with a true love; and therefore reciprocated, willed, free, shared, and bilateral: since Love is *always reciprocal and a matter of two*. The two, being separate, decide to give themselves to each other because they wish to do so in absolute freedom.[47] Love places the two lovers on an equal plane, as demanded by the intimate dialogue of *face-to-face* communication.[48]

As expected, the *Song of Songs* echoes the painful experiences of the bride as she waits, which impels the tender and loving compassion of the Bridegroom to console her and encourage her hope, so close to its fulfillment

> *Arise, my love, my fair one,*
> *And come away;*
> *For lo, the winter is past,*
> *The rain is over and gone...*[49]

---

[47] Saint Augustine said that *no one knows himself unless he is tempted; nor can he be crowned unless he is victorious; nor overcome unless he fights; nor fights if he lacks enemies and temptations. Enarrationes in Psalmos*, 60,3. Cf. Rom 7: 19–23.

[48] Cf. Mt 10: 24–25; Lk 6:40; Jn 13:16; 15:20. *And if I shall go, and prepare a place for you, I will come again, and will take you to myself; that where I am, you also may be* (Jn 14:3).

[49] Sg 2: 10–11.

It has already been said that the journey to the Father's house, or the wait (or the search) for the Bridegroom, is subject to eventualities, since we are in the *not yet*. These can be positive or negative: advancement, *regression*, triumph, and even defeat. Sleep affected *all* the virgins in the parable equally, whether prudent or foolish. A possibility that became a reality; for they were all equally in a situation of waiting and suffering in uncertainty. The *Song of Songs* deals with this issue, and therefore describes an unexpected stubbornness on the part of the bride. She, after having been requested by the Bridegroom with ineffable tenderness,

> *Open to me, my sister, my love,*
> *My dove, my perfect one;*
> *For my head is wet with dew...*

to some extent inexplicably, responds negatively:

> *I had put off my garment,*
> *How could I put it on?*
> *I had bathed my feet,*
> *How could I soil them?*[50]

We are thus faced with the vagaries and ups and downs of the itinerant situation, in which there is a constant interaction of the *already*, which is still not finished, with a *not yet*, which is not entirely in the future. Where the *already* is a reality, although in no way in fullness and perfection; and where the *not yet* is also not in its entirety, insofar as the Christian already enjoys the first fruits

---

[50]Song 5: 2–3.

of the Spirit, as well as the Joy that was granted to him by Jesus Christ in anticipation of the encounter in Heaven. Isaiah's oracle about Edom, in the way that is peculiar to prophecy, also points to the ambiguity that affects the Christian's itinerant reality:

> *Watchman, what of the night?*
> *Watchman, what of the night?*
> *The watchman says: Morning comes, and also the night...*[51]

The repetition of the first verse cannot be accidental. The need for vigilance is fundamental for a Christian; as a matter not of life or death, but of salvation or condemnation (1 Pet 5:8). The same can be said of the constant and grave exhortations contained in the Gospel. As for the watchman's response, perhaps it has to do with the intended allusion to the ambiguity of the situation that the Christian has to face: Morning comes, *and also the night.* The dawn and the light of day have not yet left behind the night of suffering and bitter struggle. In a certain sense, this is the logical requirement of participation in the cross of Christ, as well as of the need for purification, which every Christian has to face, and which the mystics explained at length through their *Nights* of the Soul.[52] But Christ has merited for His own the virtue of hope. The meaning of which is trust, joy, and salvation. It is true that the itinerant reality has to face the chiaroscuro of night and day, in a strange mystification and in a situation of possible ups and downs of change. However, in the end, hope will not disappoint (Rom 5:5);

---

[51] Is 21: 11–12.

[52] Remember the extensive doctrine of the Nights of the *Sense* and of the *Spirit* in Saint John of the Cross. Or that of the ways and paths of purification so beautifully explained by Saint Teresa of Avila in her book *Interior Castle*.

and as for the darkness that envelops the present stage, it is also consoling to know that, according to the Apostle, *the night is already advanced, while the day is drawing near.*[53]

During this transitory stage of the *not yet*, there are situations that are perhaps at first sight easy to understand but which, due to their complexity, would actually require a profound knowledge of the mysteries of Love. The *Song of Songs* shows one of these situations: the bride, after having been slow to receive the Bridegroom, feels compunction and begins her search again, now more longing than ever:

> *I adjure you, O daughters of Jerusalem,*
> *If you find my beloved,*
> *That you tell him*
> *I am sick with love.*[54]

According to the bride, therefore, the absence of the Bridegroom makes her faint with love (*quia amore langueo*). As for the longing of Saint Paul (*desiderium habens dissolvi et cum Christo esse*[55]), or the *I die because I do not die* of the Saint of Avila, although they are expressions that essentially coincide with the yearning of the bride in the *Song of Songs*, they also have their own nuances. What the bride really says in the Book of Solomon is that she *languishes* for love. Which is equivalent to proclaiming that she feels sick and weak, that she is losing vigor, that she is dying little by little, that she is exhausted and fatigued..., and all that, in short, could lead one to believe (if the sayings were always taken literally), in a certain diminution of strength and life because of Love. But what the

---

[53]Rom 13:12.
[54]Song 5:8. Cf. 2:5.
[55]Phil 1:23.

expression means in this case (*to die of love*) is an increase without measure of the fire and flame of life, because of Love. What the bride really means is that she loves now more than ever. With such an intense feeling... that it makes her feel that she lacks strength; or with a fire that burns her in such a way that it seems to be ending her existence. Love, being the greatest of all the mysteries that exist in the Universe, once poured out and placed in the heart of man (Rom 5:5), can do nothing else, if it wants to express itself in any way, but to resort to metaphor, allegory, and even aporia and paradox. The longing for Life is what makes the bride feel that she is living more fully than ever; although in such a way and to such a degree that it could cause her death... if the delay of the Bridegroom in appearing is prolonged. Well understood that *death*, in this case could have no other meaning but that which the New Testament so often attributes to it: to die to oneself, or to lose one's own life, but to find and live the life of the other. Apparent paradoxes...? Perhaps. In short, poor and insufficient instruments to which the penury of human language has to resort; but which in turn do nothing but highlight this incapacity while *pointing* to a distant horizon where the feelings reside that are, for now, impossible to describe.

* * *

Modern Pastoral work, on the other hand, seems to have forgotten that the Christian's main task is to run after Christ, craving to reach him (1 Cor 9:26; Gal 2:2; Phil 2:16; 3:12).

The bride in the *Song of Songs* has a very different attitude, finding the meaning of her life in running after the Beloved of her soul:

Draw me after you, let us make haste.
The king has brought me into his chambers...[56]

But modern Christians have changed the object of their search, replacing the race to attain Jesus Christ with the race to attain man. Thus, it is that Catholic theology, especially under the influence of Maritain, has come to discover that man cannot be limited to being a mere creature of God, but must be valued *in himself*, as a being who enjoys his own autonomy (*Integral Humanism*). But there is a catch here: the difficulty of explaining the scope of *a self* which, without claiming to dispense with God, proclaims that his own nature has a capacity for self-determination, which looks a lot like an emancipation. And along with man, things. After *Gaudium et Spes* came the great discovery of the *autonomy of temporal realities*; the intrinsic reality of which, considered in itself and without the need for extrinsic connotations, had not been taken into account for centuries because, so it seemed, of the old theology's *contemptus mundi*. Thanks to this, Christians suddenly felt themselves affected by a profound complex that made them feel inferior to the world: for, lo and behold, they had neglected the value of temporal things as they are in themselves and *for themselves*!

Fortunately, there are solutions for everything. In this case, you can resort to one of those strange forms of behavior to which human beings are so prone. Hiding an issue when its conclusions oppose, or at least seem to get in the way of, one's own elaborated ideas. How can one claim that the autonomy of temporal realities and their condition as created things are compatible...? The solution, which might perhaps seem to some to be difficult or even impossible, is nevertheless simple: just set aside the problem. Certain words are

---

[56]Song 1:4.

emphasized, with the help of elaborate literature, whereas delving into concepts is avoided at all costs. In this way, serious literature is transformed into ornate prose, re*sonant* (insofar as it *sounds* good) and not exempt from the esotericism necessary to deceive and seduce modern man, already accustomed to dispensing with reality for the benefit of appearances. What *sounds good* is written and accepted; its content is taken for granted and beyond debate according to the law of *Magister dixit,* while the *truth* of the content is disregarded. In the background of the Second Vatican Council, many ideas were accepted for the sole reason that they came from Karl Rahner. Regarding Maritain's books (to cite an isolated but influential case), they deal with innumerable questions that are treated as *definitive*, without providing any proof or clarifying explanations; and even contradictions are accepted in a much greater number than desirable.

Saint Paul's grave warning to Timothy, *According to their own desires, they will heap to themselves teachers, having itching ears. And will indeed turn away their hearing from the truth, but will be turned unto fables,*[57] which is never considered to be up to date and is always looked at with future perspectives (as if it had never been pronounced for *today*), this warning should be considered at this time with much more attention. Especially with regard to *prurientes auribus*. Since modern man pays much more attention to appearances, paraphernalia, and circus-like literary verbiage than to reality, there has sprung up everywhere a flood of writings, with *grandiose* style, riddled with neologisms pretending to be erudite, incomprehensible, and mysterious but flattering to the ear, which have turned the field of philosophy-theology into something quite close to science-fiction; though with little science and much fiction, as one can surmise. But these writings are pleasant to read and provide, on top of it, an

---

[57] *Ad sua desideria coacervabunt sibi magistros prurientes auribus, et a veritate quidem auditum avertent, ad fabulas autem convertentur* (2 Tim 4: 3–4).

air of great erudition for their authors and for those who read them. To which we must add the most important thing of all: *they do not challenge our existence or take issue with absolutely anything.* Where it is necessary to recognize their perfect adaptation to the desires of today's man of being the *only* rule by which he must be governed. This kind of *literature*, always presented as science, and which also attributes to itself the privilege of not needing to be demonstrated, is what prevails today within Catholic Philosophy and Theology, with the consequent derivations and ramifications in the field of Pastoral Care. The millenary Theology of the Fathers, together with the monolithic Philosophy of the great Catholic Masters so recommended by the Popes until the Second Vatican Council, have given way to the crypto-grammatical and esoteric (and very striking) elaborations put into circulation (and to their own great advantage) by the *Violet Scholars.*[58]

This whole set of ideas, which could fall under the Maritainian denomination of *Integral Humanism* (at least this once), had not taken into account, to the disgrace of the world and particularly of the Church, that what man really is had already been proclaimed, long before, by a person of such little philosophical entity as Pilate. For it was he who, pointing to Jesus Christ, pronounced before the Jews and before the world his famous *Ecce homo*! A transcendental historical fact before which the Jews, speaking also on behalf of so many others (Jews and non-Jews) who would second them through the ages, were quick to shout: *Tolle, tolle*! The claim that man had not discovered himself until the time of the Renaissance, means forgetting that God had already become Man in Jesus Christ. Or, to put it another way, it is nonsense that amounts to burying more than twenty centuries of history as if they had never existed.

---

[58] Allusion to the work *Los Eruditos a la Violeta*, by José Cadalso, one of the great Spanish satirists (1741-1782). The work seems to still be very relevant today.

Thus, we have reached a point where it is appropriate to ask what is going to happen now. Neo-Modernist Catholic theology has preferred to hide Jesus Christ, no doubt in order to increase and widen the sphere of purely human autonomy. However, it is important not to forget that such autonomy is understood as pure self-sufficiency. The winds seem to be blowing in a predetermined and precise direction: the recognition of a universal Religion in which there is only one God for all men (whoever or whatever he may be), but capable of uniting and satisfying them all. It could be accepted indistinctly as the God that Christians have always adored, as Jehovah, as Allah, as the Great Architect of the Universe, as one of the oriental deities, as the First Immobile Mover and, in short, with any denomination that could be universally accepted. Ultimately, an Entity valid for all, not different or belonging exclusively to any one group. In an absolute turn from what had been believed until now, man is no longer a being (created) who depends on God, but rather God is an exclusive product (elaborated) by man. Of course, it is no longer necessary to imagine God as a *personal Being*; still less as transcendent to human understanding. But as the masterpiece of such understanding, elaborated within the mold and limits of its own parameters. But ultimately accepted by all and, as a consequence, made manifest as the only one capable of establishing the hitherto so long sought after, and never achieved, *fraternity* among men. Or to put it more briefly and succinctly: as the God Freemasonry had always advocated and fought so hard for.

Now that the Person of Jesus Christ has finally disappeared and His presence has been banished from theology, pastoral work, and the life of the Christian People, the attitude of Mary Magdalene, when she was asked by the angels who were at the tomb, becomes relevant again (for the faithful who are still faithful):

—Woman, why are you weeping?

—Because they have taken away my Lord, and I do not know where they have laid him.[59]

But now the weeping of Mary Magdalene has a greater justification. In the new Babel the Devil has worked intensely to prevent any kind of communication and understanding among men; achieved by the corruption of language and the inversion of its meaning. That is why the icy winter that spreads its mantle of desolation throughout the Church is now pompously called the *Ecclesial Springtime* as if with intentional irony when, in reality, present times could only be called the *Age of Sadness and Emptiness.* Indeed, true Joy, or the Joy proper to Jesus Christ which He had promised on a certain occasion to His own (Jn 15:11; 16: 20.22.24), has disappeared from the life and the horizon of the Christian People.[60]

* * *

But before going any further, we must insist on an important clarification that affects everything that has been said, regarding both this and our other writings, in which we have always maintained that love is proper and exclusive to the *person*, and only to the person. However, that the perfection to which the human creature is called can only be attained through love is not to maintain that his constitution as a *person* depends on a relationship (loving or

---

[59] Jn 20:13.

[60] This is not the place to point out some of the many unmistakable symptoms that demonstrate this assertion. We have already done so, albeit partially and scattered in some of our books. But it is now that Nietzsche could rightly say that the Christian People are a sad People. That this phenomenon goes unnoticed by most people does not prevent it from being a fact and, actually, such inadvertence is nothing more than another proof of its tremendous gravity.

less loving) with others.[61] What we maintain has nothing to do with the ramblings of the personalist theories of Martin Buber, Gabriel Marcel, Max Scheler, Emmanuel Mounier, or Jacques Maritain; the same theories that provoked such deep enthusiasm in a good part of the works of Popes Paul VI and John Paul II.

Paul VI was a passionate disciple of Maritain. As for John Paul II, his thought was influenced by the ideas of Buber, Marcel, Mounier, and, above all, Max Scheler, to whom he dedicated one of his two doctoral theses. It is known that the views of these two Popes had a considerable influence, both on the preceding deliberations and the final contents of the Documents of the Second Vatican Council. It is also known that the subsequent application of some of these doctrines, through the Commissions created for this purpose, has been producing intense uneasiness in post–conciliar Catholicism. The *personalism* of these French and German thinkers, of such undeniable influence in the Church since the middle of the last century, has managed to displace the metaphysical meaning of *person*. With a result that now, with the passage of time and with complete justice, can be termed as catastrophic.

The objective of the new personalisms? John Paul II himself admitted that defining man as a *rational animal* is not enough. It is necessary to add emotions and feelings to the essential constituent of the human being, whose location is undoubtedly the *heart of man*.

In one way or another, *personalism* leads to admitting feelings and emotions, the situations experienced at each moment, and the personal circumstances (always different for each individual) as constitutive elements of the human composite. All this within a

---

[61]The only relationship that is a constitutive part of the human person is the one ensued from the fact of being created and the Creator. Although this relationship is not accidental, but transcendental. Cf. my book *Waiting for Don Quixote*, Shoreless Lake Press, USA, 2022, pp. 338-340.

sphere of absolute personal autonomy, devoid of *external* interference. Trower rightly says that the *centrality of the "human subject" in Catholic philosophy and theology has been one of the most risky operations ever undertaken by the Church*.[62] When in reality feelings and emotions (including love) are the product of the person as such, and not its constituent principles.

The centralism of the *human subject* and the false concepts of person, so often accepted by relevant modern representatives of Catholic philosophy and theology, have given rise to the grave crisis (in Dogma, and then in Liturgy and Morals) that has affected the Church since the time of Vatican II, and which still persists.

For Buber, for example, the supreme reality *is the person in his relationship with other beings*. Thus, for him, the *relational situation* is the focal point of reality, and not the person constituted as such by his act of being by participation.

But in created beings the active relationship with others is an accident and cannot therefore be considered as a constituent of the human person, but rather as something that derives from it and to which the person gives rise. In the biblical narrative, for example, Adam would not have been a person until the appearance of Eve (assuming an otherwise unknown time between the creation of the two).

But then, according to Buber, once the individuals have made themselves mutually present —the *I* and the *Thou*— and are thus constituted as persons, both fulfill their relationship through *Dialogue*.

It is well understood, however, that Dialogue, for Buber, in no way means what it has always meant for the Church, for Philosophy

---

[62] Philip Trower, *The Catholic Church and the Counter-Faith*, Family Publications, Oxford, 2006, pg. 114.

(perennial or not perennial)..., and for the common sense of men. Dialogue, according to our thinker, only serves for each party to affirm *the truth* of the other, or *the right* to be as he or she is. To try to influence the other party, or to modify his points of view, would be to lower the level of the *I–Thou* relationship (personal) to a lower one called by Buber that of the *I–It* relationship (objective), which would turn the former into a relational situation that is no longer subjective.

The result has been none other than that this strange type of relationism and this novel form of *dialogism* have taken root in modern society. And they have even penetrated, with no small repercussions, into Catholic Theology and Liturgy.

According to this, the important thing about *Dialogue* is to speak with many people. Even if merely to exchange points of view, to share situations and life experiences, and to lead above all to relational situations. It does not matter at all that each one continues to maintain his or her own point of view; and it is even necessary that this be so, so that the nature of the *Dialogue* is not distorted.

In recent times, some documents and actions of the Catholic ecclesiastical hierarchy have caused confusion and even division among the faithful. This has been the case, for example, with the publication of Pope Benedict XVI's Motu Proprio *Summorum Pontificum* on July 7, 2007. The Document authorizes the celebration of the Mass of Saint Pius V (better known as the Tridentine Mass), as an Extraordinary Rite and under certain conditions. It has been considered by some as the beginning of a return to the Traditional Liturgy, as a certain recognition of its superiority over the post–conciliar Liturgy (specifically over the Mass of Pope Paul VI), and as a triumph, albeit minimal, of the conservative faction of the Church over the *progressives*. Others, who represent the larger and more aggressive faction of the ecclesial world, have branded it as a *regres-*

sion and a step backwards from the new tendencies and achievements of post–conciliar Catholicism.

As a result, just as some have considered Benedict XVI as the savior of Catholic Tradition and Faith, others have labeled the Pope as little less than a traitor to the advances achieved by the Second Vatican Council.

Curiously, however, there is something on which both seem to agree. In the light of events, the Pope has come to be seen as contradictory and inconsistent.

Accordingly, in view of the rather progressive ideology of Pope Benedict XVI (as it seems to be clear from his writings and speeches, and even more so from his actions), the regression implied by *Summorum Pontificum* means for the Progressive Movement a regrettable step backwards as well as a painful concession to the Traditionalist Movements, branded by progressivism as schismatics (an accusation mainly directed against the followers of Archbishop Marcel Lefebvre).

In turn, those who consider themselves as defenders of the authentic Tradition of the Church also come to the same consideration of inconsistency on the part of the Pope. In short, is the Pope willing to return to the traditional Church, turning back the clock on his actions up to this point in his pontificate?[63] Does the intention of *Summorum Pontificum*, however moderate it may be, signify a return to the conservative character that is evident in some of the writings of the former Cardinal Ratzinger? Or is it another sign of the Pope's good will and his desire to attract certain dissidents and avoid possible schisms?

The question has given rise to confusion, and a certain irritation among the majority. While the Motu Proprio has seemed to some a timid retreat (advance) towards tradition, others consider it regressive and a sign of weakness towards the traditionalists. In one way or another, all end up agreeing on the inconsistency of the Pope's decision.

Everyone agrees that Benedict XVI is a man of high intelligence, endowed with a deep culture, and that he has always demonstrated firmness

---

[63]Those who think this way direct their attention to a certain series of actions, such as, for example, the appointments made by the Pope; especially with regard to positions of importance and serious responsibility in the Church.

Lost Love   155

of character. It is therefore difficult to label him as inconsistent, contradictory, or weak. There is nothing in his conduct, either as Cardinal or as Pope, that could be the object of the accusation of inconsistency.

As for the writings of Cardinal Ratzinger, recognized, at least in their majority, as *conservative* in character, they must be examined in the light of *global* or overall consideration as is always the case with any human action. Since it is impossible to know men by their intentions, one can only look at their deeds and the fruits of their actions as a whole (Mt 7:16; *passim*). And there is no doubt that a careful study of *all* the Cardinal's writings, as well as a dispassionate consideration of his actions, make difficult the task, intended and desired by almost all traditionalists, of considering Ratzinger simply as a conservative.

There can be no objection to the favorable opinion of a serious intellectual like Christopher Ferrara, a man scarcely suspected on this point and not a friend of the progressive current.[64] According to the American writer, by means of this *counter-revolutionary* Document, the Pope has put an end to the debate and has courageously put things in their place, recognizing the juridical validity of the ancient rite, which was never abrogated.

It is not easy to suppose, however, that the controversy has been settled with the Document. Nor can other points of view be ruled out.

Benedict XVI was formed in the same philosophical school as his two immediate predecessors, Paul VI and John Paul II. It is not surprising, therefore, that his thought seems to have the same influences which affected these two Popes, even if the fact goes unnoticed by most. It cannot be ruled out, therefore, that the Pope's desire to avoid confrontation also extends to fostering Dialogue. An explanation of this situation could include a desire to give to each his own, in order to procure respect for all. Why not allow the adherents of Tradition to abide by it, even in part, and thus give legitimacy to the so–called Tridentine rite? Throughout History, various rites have concurred in the Church, in chronological succession or together: the Mozarabic, the Ambrosian, the Milanese, the Benedictine, the Eastern

---

[64]Cristopher A. Ferrara, *The Motu Proprio and the "Polity of Death, The Latin Mass* magazine, Fall 2007, NJ (USA), pg. 20.

Orthodox rites, etc. In support of which Benedict XVI has demonstrated, through his ecumenical policy, that he is in favor of recognizing a certain legal *status* of various religions, and especially of Christian confessions.

If the latter is true, it could undoubtedly give rise to serious risks. In short, given the turbulent times that have followed the Second Vatican Council, no one would have thought that the pontificate of Benedict XVI was going to be a bed of roses.

The possibility of serious dangers lurking in the background is not to be taken lightly.

In spite of the principle formulated by Saint Paul, according to which *there is nothing unclean in itself*,[65] which some misunderstand, in the sense of *omnia munda mundi*, or that *everyone is good*,[66] it may become clear that these were not merely tendencies within a common doctrine, but rather contrary positions...not easily reconcilable. And trying to reach an agreement between contradictory positions can engender confusion, and even lead the more fainthearted spirits to think that none of this matters.

As for absolute respect, once Dialogue has been established, for everyone's ideas, without differences mattering too much, one can already understand what this can mean for current doctrines for the Church such as *Ecumenism*. This also sheds light on the insistence on the Dialogue-Ecumenism dichotomy. The conclusion is that it is *not necessary* to expect that any group may change its tenets. The only thing that can be anticipated, in any case, is the confluence of one and the other in a *common place*. A mysterious meeting point

---

[65] *Nihil immundum per seipsum* (Rom 14:14).

[66] As unbelievable as it may seem, this idea is very fashionable, in a more or less surreptitious way, in modern theology. It is the one that has given rise to the denial (more or less disguised) of the existence of Hell, or to postulates such as that of the *anonymous Christian*. For our part, we have already spoken at length elsewhere of what we have agreed to call *Theologies of Goodness* (Cf. Alfonso Galvez, *The Importunate Friend*, Shoreless Lake Press, New Jersey, 2020).

Lost Love   157

whose consistency can be described in advance as something more or less precarious.

A common place that can be both disturbing and intriguing, especially due to two reasons:

First, because it is rather difficult to explain how to arrive at the aforementioned common place *without anyone abandoning their own positions*.

Secondly, because it would be no less difficult to explain the possibility of meeting in a *common place* where all discrepancies would have been eliminated. On the other hand, it would be equally difficult to explain how to arrive at such a miracle. Would such a common place be something other than a neutral void? If not, what would be the content of this alleged *deposit* of resolutions everyone would agree on?[67]

This makes it easier to explain the meaning of *Dialogue as an end in itself* and the extraordinary frequency of its use in modern society. *Dialogue* is always welcomed, if it is nothing more than *talking for the sake of talking*, to build relationships which are always beneficial even if they do not involve any kind of commitment. At least that is what is usually said. It would be a good time to recall here Churchill's phrase during the Second World War: *Useless talk is better than going to war*. For the proponents of modern Ecumenism, it is not merely a matter of talking for the sake of talking (something like making time, entertaining people, or creating a smokescreen to hide other intentions), but of talking to reach the

---

[67]Something common to all utopias is to create *bombastic* literature, with apparently magical and infallible formulas...without ever giving reasons or necessary explanations. It is as if the sea were nothing more than the water that can be seen on the surface, with no further need to ask what may be underneath. As is well known, bombastic literature considers itself exempt from the need to provide evidence or face possible objections.

so-longed-for *Common Place*: Perhaps the Religion of Universal Fraternity, purely naturalistic which recognizes no other worship than to Man...? Perhaps something akin to what Freemasonry has always advocated...? Churchill was too intelligent to believe that it was worth talking for the sake of talking, for no other purpose than to avoid war. It is well known how often these expressions conceal their intentions. And this is always the case with those who insist on Dialogue as an end in itself, without excluding, of course, many other trends that work in favor of an alleged Ecumenism.

The famous *Assisi Meetings*, organized by Pope John Paul II, took place in 1986, 1993, and 2002, as well as another one promoted by Pope Benedict XVI in 2006. And there is no reason to doubt the good faith of these Popes in advocating this type of activity. All *religions* were invited to take part in the Meetings, including those who do not believe in any religion, and the proposed objective was none other than to *pray together for peace*. However, no one is unaware of the ecumenical intention that lay at the heart of these meetings.

As for the spiritual effectiveness of this *common prayer*, it is known only to God and therefore nothing need be said about it. Although, it is impossible to deny the legitimacy of offering some reservations. The main one comes from the fact that almost none of the participants believed in the divinity of Jesus Christ; and some of them not even in God.

It is difficult not to see here another example of what was said above. For everything seems to point to the fact that the key to these convocations revolved around the possibility of *dialogue*; without the slightest pretension on the part of anyone to impose their own beliefs, or the absence of them, on others. The same applies (in fact it is the same thing) to the fact that the meetings were organized in such a way that each one should pray *according to his own faith*, without delving in any way into the content and viability of such *faith*. And as it has been said before, it does not make much sense to talk about the effectiveness of such prayers, since only God knows the value and the result of man's *prayers (For who has known the mind of the Lord so as to instruct him?*[68]). Although, on the other hand and as already stated also, it is legitimate to question the event as such, in terms of its practical usefulness at least, as well as in terms of a fair evaluation of the pros and cons.

One might ask, for example, the following question: What can be expected from *group prayer* when most of the people do not believe in God? Someone will rightly say that only God could give the answer. Nor is there now, as in Ancient times, the possibility of consulting the Oracles; or else, as in the Old Law, the prophets, or the sibyls. But this is not the case here. For the event is of such transcendence, both for believers and non-believers all over the world, that it must but be analyzed, and even questioned, if apparently there are sufficient motives to do so; as has been done by a multitude of believers, in whom it is impossible to suppose ill will or lack of fidelity to the Church.

It is evident, as has been repeatedly said, that no one can judge the mind of the Lord with regard to the actions of men, unless He has expressly spoken on the subject. This must be extended *a fortiori* to those actions to which, with a certain amount of good will, even an ambiguous or perhaps doubtful value can be attributed. Nevertheless, it should be noted that the Apostle concludes the text quoted above by saying that *we have the mind of Christ*.[69] A bold affirmation that the disciple of Jesus Christ has the right, and even

---

[68] 1 Cor 2:16, quoting Is 40:13; Rom 11: 33–34.

[69] *Nos autem sensum Christi habemus* (1 Cor 2:16).

the duty, to examine events in the light of the Gospel; not, of course, according to a personal and arbitrary interpretation, in the Protestant style, but as the Good News has always been understood by the Church. If a Christian, through a communion of lives (between him and Jesus Christ) that originates a true participation of each one in the existence of the other, has made his own the mind or the *thought* of his Master, it would be normal for him to think and judge according to gospel criteria. In view of this, we cannot but admit that, applying the consequences that derive from the teachings of the New Testament, there are sufficient reasons to *question* such encounters. The Apostle affirms, in effect, that *The things also that are of God no man knoweth, but the Spirit of God,*[70] although he then adds, in the following verse, that *Now we have received not the spirit of this world, but the Spirit that is of God.* Here it would also be possible to take into consideration what the Apostle says in the same *First Letter to the Corinthians*: *But the sensual man perceiveth not these things that are of the Spirit of God; for it is foolishness to him, and he cannot understand, because their value can be assessed only in the Spirit.*[71] Nor would it be out of place to heed the serious warning of the Apostle John: *For many seducers are gone out into the world, who confess not that Jesus Christ is come in the flesh: this is a seducer and an antichrist... Whosoever revolteth, and continueth not in the doctrine of Christ, hath not God. He that continueth in the doctrine, the same hath both the Father and the Son. If any man come to you, and bring not this doctrine, receive him not into the house nor say to him, God speed you. For he that saith unto him, God speed you, communicateth with his wicked works.*[72] The Lord,

---

[70] 1 Cor 2:11.
[71] 1 Cor 2: 14–15.
[72] 2 Jn 7–11.

for his part, does not seem too complacent with those who refuse to follow his teachings: *And whosoever shall not receive you, nor hear your words: going forth out of that house or city shake off the dust from your feet. Amen I say to you, it shall be more tolerable for the land of Sodom and Gomorrha in the day of judgment, than for that city.*[73] It must not be forgotten that the Church, and not theologians, has the right and the duty to interpret *authentically*[74] the content of Revelation, and specifically the words of Jesus Christ. Bearing this in mind, it is difficult to attribute an ecumenical meaning to certain words of Jesus Christ: *He who believes and is baptized will be saved; but he who does not believe will be condemned.*[75] At least as certain theologians understand ecumenism: authors of theories such as anonymous Christianity, universal salvation, hell as a mere real possibility, that the Catholic Church cannot claim to be the *One* Church founded by Jesus Christ, etc., etc. Among them we must count the great Patriarchs of Catholic Theology today, headed by Karl Rahner; although we must not forget the huge and enthusiastic multitude of his followers..., among which we can find many important members of the Hierarchy of the Church.

It is interesting to note that Jesus Christ spoke on one occasion about *group prayer*, precisely to commend it. In a text contained in Saint Matthew, the Lord says: *Again I say to you, that if two of you shall consent upon earth, concerning anything whatsoever they shall ask, it shall be done to them by my Father who is in heaven. For*

---

[73] Mt 10: 14–15.

[74] In legal doctrine, the *authentic interpretation* of a Law is the one carried out by the Legislator himself; hence, it cannot be questioned. It can already be assumed that the concept is used here in a broad, although legitimate, context.

[75] Mk 16:16; Cf Jn 3:18.

where there are two or three gathered together in my name, there am I in the midst of them.[76]

The problem here lies in the fact that the texts of the Bible must be read within their *complete* content (without separating them from their context) and according to their *proper meaning*. And here, the words of the Lord refer to those who gather to *pray together*, expressly *in nomine meo*. Yet how can it be supposed that those who do not believe in the Lord, and even those who openly deny Him, are gathered together in the name of the Lord...?

The problem faced by *personalist* doctrines is precisely the same problem faced by all false doctrines: the lack of metaphysics and absence of Logic. Human reason is made to know the truth, and not to *invent it*.[77] Logic is the science that regulates the right functioning of reason, and hence its disregard inevitably leads to contradiction and absurdity. It has been rightly said that the postulates of the French Revolution are by-products of Christian truths, now converted into heresies: ideas such as liberty, fraternity, etc., as understood by the revolutionaries and the children of the Enlightenment, are nothing but by-products of the worst kind that originally belonged to the Gospel Message.

According to personalism, the relational situation (the person in his relationship with others) is the supreme reality, rather than the individual person on which this relationship is based. Hence, persons are not fully human, but are constituted as such through a *Thou* with whom they enter into relationship. This explains why for Martin Buber, and for Gabriel Marcel, communities are the only place where men become *perfectly themselves*. On the other hand,

---

[76] Mt 18: 19–20.

[77] Or perhaps it would be better to say that its proper function is not to *create* it; if we want to take into account the Latin etymology of the word. The Latin verb *invenire* means to find or to encounter.

however, personalism asserts that it is not necessary for the members of such communities to think alike; for it is important that each person asserts his right to be as he is.

As anyone who reasons calmly can see, there is nothing here but a hodgepodge of ideas which, if taken seriously, can lead anyone to mental chaos or perhaps worse. The human person was created as such in the likeness of God and with an immortal destiny. The commandment of charity or brotherly love is the *New Commandment* of the Gospel; with the admonition, on the part of Jesus Christ, that His disciples would be recognized by the intimate relationship of love that unites them. But the *personalists* have believed that they have found a truth beyond the evangelical teaching; with which they have rediscovered the Mediterranean Sea, except they didn't.

What exactly is the meaning of the statement that the relational situation is the authentic reality, beyond the individual as such? Unless common sense is forced to the point of violence, at the created level it is the persons who constitute the relationships, and not the relationships that make the persons. And how can it be claimed that the person is only constituted as such in the community and in the elaboration of the community, while at the same time it is said that it is the person who builds the community? On the other hand, individuals, neither through Dialogue nor in any other way, can try to influence others... since each one must maintain his own truth, or his *own identity*. But if the Dialogue, or the relational situation, does not seek to influence the other, then what is its meaning...? If people are only constituted as such within the community, each one maintaining his own truth and without influencing others, what is the content of the community and how can its structure be explained...? All these questions remain unanswered and without any other basis than that of the *Magister dixit*.

A practical example of what *communities* would be, as understood by the personalists, could be a colony of penguins. In which each individual of the species needs the community (colony) to *be fulfilled* (although in reality the *fulfillment* here is a problem of survival). And where, on the other hand, each of the members composing the whole is not at all concerned with influencing the *individuality* of the others: apart from the need of the colony (community) to subsist, it is licit to suppose that each penguin does not care about the *truth* of the others. There are therefore two elements required here: the need of the community (colony) to subsist (fulfill itself) on the one hand, and the total respect for the truth or point of view of each of the other penguins that compose it, on the other.

Both in modern Catholic Pastoral Care and in its Liturgy, the emphasis placed on the idea of *community* has reached the point of considering such a reality as something, in Philip Trower's words, quasi-sacramental.[78] In such a way that the worship of God has given way to the worship of man, through what is described as the *edification and realization of the community*. And furthermore, it remains there; since no one knows what lies beyond, once the community is constituted. Is it a community in which, as it was said of those formed by the first Christians, there is only one body and one soul? Of course not since there is no mention at all of the necessity of charity as a Christian virtue. These doctrines affirm that the human being feels fulfilled when, within the community, he is capable of treating the other as a *You*, and not as an *It*; but no one has so far explained what the essence and the ultimate content of this relationship consist of. The constitution of the community, without the need to invoke Christian charity (which is not expressly rejected, but simply ignored), seems to lack consistency. According to the

---

[78]Philip Trower, *Op. cit.*

Apostle Saint Paul, it is charity alone that builds up;[79] so one might ask what is going to happen once the community is constituted. Unfortunately, no explanation is ever given for this. So, in the end, it is difficult to avoid the impression that there is nothing here apart from logomachy and verbiage: talk and talk and dazzling literature; appealing above all to those who are not accustomed to in-depth analysis and are prone to feelings of admiration. It is a type of literature that sounds good, produces an impression of erudition and brilliant intellectual flashes... and does not require any commitment. No evidence is adduced, since the word of the *Masters* seems more than enough.[80]

Now, how can a relational situation be understood from which all kinds of relations are excluded, on principle? Undoubtedly, in every relationship there must be a certain intercommunication or some form of exchange, of whatever kind, but exchange. In the paternal-filial relation, for example, the son receives existence from the father, in addition to the source of filiation; while the father, in turn, receives from the son the source of paternity; there must always necessarily be a *giving* and a *receiving*, from which reciprocity cannot be excluded. Considering this, if the fact of giving, and the consequent receiving, should not and cannot be considered as the *influence of one party on the other* (intruding into the being of the

---

[79] *Scientia inflat, caritas vero ædificat* (1 Cor 8:1).

[80] This brings to mind the vain attempts made by many members of the clergy to show to the world (and convince themselves) that they live fraternal charity (the secular clergy in particular usually use the formula *always in the Presbytery and with the Presbytery*). The way to do this is usually praying together, in meetings and assemblies more especially, reciting a Canonical Hour which is ordinarily one of the Lesser Hours (perhaps in order not to overburden); after which each one goes off, without worrying too much about the *truth* or the *individuality* of the others.

other), in what then does the relational situation consist and what is the object of the Dialogue...? Could someone explain how it is possible to think of a giving and a receiving, carried out at least between two, without *affecting*, in any way whatsoever, the being of the other? As for the use of expressions such as *the truth of the other*, in order to allude to the sacred and inviolable respect due to the other person, it is nothing more than a way of displaying (or so it seems) verbiage capable of convincing those who are too prone to admiration.

On the other hand, and this is undoubtedly the most important point, the personalist doctrines attack the concept and the reality of love. The human being, created as a person for the primary purpose of loving and being loved, which is the same as saying to give oneself to others and at the same time to depend on them, now turns out to be, as is clear from the logic of personalism, *the most individualistic and solitary entity in creation*.

They talk of treating the other as a *You* (as a person, and not as an object) and of respecting *his truth*, or his individuality. But to treat the other as a *Thou* for personalists means not pretending to modify (by any action with the intention of influencing) the personality of the other. And yet they do not explain how it is possible to respect the *Thou* of the other without influencing his personality, or his *truth*: yet another concept among the many that remain unclarified. For example, to continue with the list, at least briefly: In what exactly does *the truth* of the other consist? How are the *truth* and the *personality* of a being identified and what exactly is the relation existing between these two concepts...? On the other hand, it is taken for granted, without proof, that any influence to be exerted on another is necessarily negative; in spite of the fact that it has always been believed, by common sense and according to the most universal belief, that there are equally good and bad influences.

Since man has been created as a social being, to live in communion with others (with all that this implies), being elevated to the supernatural order and destined to love them both naturally and supernaturally, we cannot understand how such a thing is possible if you exclude any kind of influence between people. We realize that in the personalist approach respect due to *the other* requires considering the individuality of his personality, so as not to modify in any way the *truth* of his being, but this establishes an aberrant and distorted concept of the person and the individuality of the human being. A human being cannot develop as such, nor enrich himself in a fuller maturity throughout his life, both natural and supernatural, without depending on others and a certain reciprocity. The same reciprocity in which a mutual exchange of ideas, affinities, feelings, and all kinds of possessions must take place; and which even culminates in what can properly be called an *exchange of lives.*

If the concepts of *giving* and *receiving* are eliminated in the relational situation, in order to suppress all possible influence and to leave entirely safe the *truth* or the *Thou* of the other, it becomes impossible to explain the relational situation itself in the first place. Besides —and this is the most serious thing— a basic and fundamental component of the concept of love is destroyed, since it *cannot* even be imagined without the existence of mutual giving and receiving.

Unless the intention is to engage in pure logomachy, to deprive words of their most common meaning, or simply to speak in a high-flown manner for the admiration of fools, etc., if one sticks to what the *new discoveries* proclaim, one arrives at surprising conclusions. The philosophy of being and of precision in truth has been replaced by the phraseology of appearance and bombastic verbiage.[81] It is well understood that such verbiage neither pretends nor needs to be understood, since what is important in it is not so much the precision of the concepts as the way it sounds.

That *giving* and *receiving* are fundamental in human existence, to the point that without them there cannot be any kind of relational situation, is something that Jesus Christ Himself expressly affirms. He is careful to add that in every loving relationship (every relational situation between humans is called to become loving) there is more blessedness in giving than in receiving: *Beatius est magis dare quam accipere*.[82] Of course, it would not be licit to restrict here the meaning of both concepts of giving and receiving as they would be understood, for example, in human juridical language relative to contracts (*do ut des; facio ut facias*). It is evident that here we are dealing with intercommunication that affects both parties to the relational situation, both internally and externally.

Respect for *the truth* of the other, while taking care to avoid any attempt to influence in any way his person, as personalisms understand the problem, not only subverts the concept of respect, but destroys the most fundamental bases of Christian existence, and even of human life.

---

[81] To abide by the meaning of the words as universally understood is what makes understanding between men possible. However, one of the most successful procedures employed by today's theologizing progressivism (Neo–modernism) is to use commonly used words, whose definition is never questioned, with a meaning different from the usual one. People accept them as good (they should not have to stop doing so), when in reality they are receiving something very different from what they imagined. The medicine labeled as a healing balm actually contains corrosive acid.

[82] Acts 20:35.

If *respect* for others means anything, it is precisely the decision to treat them with love, which is the same as seeking their good. Of course, to try to approximate the concepts of respect and love as synonyms will cause a serious scandal among personalists, not to mention many others who will hasten to label as ignorant those who do such a thing. And so, in retaliation and also as an instrument of defense, there will always be those who will resort to name calling, which, as everyone knows, does not need proof: it is enough to assign them to a group. But the most serious aspect of all this is that this world of so-called modern scholars, determined, moreover, to arrogate to themselves the office of new designers of human nature, stopped believing in love a long time ago.

Where did the personalists get the doctrine that everyone has the right to shape his own personality (*autonomy*) and that no one can pretend to interfere with it? What we have here, in short, is man as the definer of his own existence, which is precisely something in which they cannot claim any originality: *Dixit autem serpens ad mulierem: "Nequaquam morte moriemini! Scit enim Deus quod in quocumque die comederitis ex eo, aperientur oculi vestri, et eritis sicut Deus scientes bonum et malum."* [83]

The words of Jesus Christ contained in the Gospel have nothing to do with mere spiritual exhortations —or better said, spiritualistic ones— uttered perhaps for the comfort and consolation of devout people: *The words that I have spoken to you, are spirit and life. But there are some of you that believe not.*[84] God has addressed man and spoken to him in words. But no longer to make them the object of research as food for curiosity, whether by exegetes, scholars, or

---

[83] Gen 3: 4–5 We should pay special attention to the final words: *Aperientur oculi vestri, et eritis sicut Deus scientes bonum et malum.*

[84] Jn 6: 63–64; cf. Heb 4:12.

mere students; nor even for the simple consolation of troubled or perplexed souls. The word of God is indispensable food for the soul, just as bread is necessary food for the body: It is written: *Not in bread alone doth man live, but in every word that proceedeth from the mouth of God.*[85] Hence, there is no possibility of reconciling the teachings of Jesus Christ with personalist dogmas (not to interfere with *the truth* of the other), even without adding the following: *Then Jesus said to them: Amen, amen I say unto you: Except you eat the flesh of the Son of man, and drink his blood, you shall not have life in you. He that eateth my flesh, and drinketh my blood, hath everlasting life: and I will raise him up in the last day. For my flesh is meat indeed: and my blood is drink indeed. He that eateth my flesh, and drinketh my blood, abideth in me, and I in him. As the living Father hath sent me, and I live by the Father; so he that eateth me, the same also shall live by me.*[86] So *he that eateth my flesh, and drinketh my blood, abideth in me, and I in him*; a statement difficult to reconcile with many of the findings of personalism. And something even more serious. For just as He, Jesus Christ, lives for the Father, so he who eats Him will live for Him. Where there is something more than *interference* or *respect for the truth of the other*: here we speak of a true intercommunion and exchange of lives, in which each one, precisely because of this and through this, continues to be himself despite the fact that he gives everything *to the other*. For the only way for man to *find* his own life is *to lose it* in Jesus Christ (Mt 10:39).

There is in all this something more incredible, if possible, than the incongruence between the personalist musings and the doctrine of the Gospels. It is the curious phenomenon that, after more than

---

[85] Mt 4:4.
[86] Jn 6: 53–57.

twenty centuries of History, a mass of fantastic daydreams have been able to arouse more admiration than the words of Jesus Christ; although, in this particular topic, the enthusiasm has also contaminated a number of important members of the Hierarchy of the Church. It is not, however, a new development in the History of the Institution, which has a proper explanation. Contrary to the above-mentioned dictates, many will say that the personalist doctrines have not been understood by those who wield them. This may be true, at least in part. But there is always, in any case, a way to believe Buber: it is enough to decide to disregard *being* in favor of *appearance*, to prefer *subjectivity* to *objectivity*, to opt for the *truth of man* in order to forget the *truth of God*.

Since this work is not a philosophical, theological, or historical essay, it can leave aside other personalist thinkers mentioned above, or the followers of the phenomenological method. This would be a task for specialists and does not correspond to this place. However, it does seem important to add a quick, albeit summary, reference to Max Scheller and his disciple Pope John Paul II. Although Pope Wojtyla was not in fact a direct disciple of Scheller, he was nevertheless greatly influenced by him. Apart from dedicating one of his doctoral theses to him, both his thought and his actions are quite reminiscent of the German thinker; and according to some authoritative people, also of Maurice Blondel.

Perhaps Scheller's most characteristic trait is the priority he gives to feelings over reason in human nature; namely, emotional perception in preference to intellectual perception. For the founder of *axiology* (theory of values), even values are perceived and qualified (recognized for what they are) through feelings. However, in the doctoral thesis of the future Pope John Paul II, he denies the possibility of elaborating a system of Catholic ethics on something as subjective as *values* (which Scheller nevertheless considers objective), and which in any case are only grasped through feelings. In fact, if it is admitted that values (following David Hume) cannot be grasped except through feeling and experience, nor can they be universally and compulsorily imposed, since they depend on *one's subjective appreciation and taking into account one's personal situation*, it is evident that subjectivist idealism is knocking at the door and demanding entry.

Nevertheless, it seems clear that it was Scheller's influence that induced the Pope to prefer the phenomenological method of analysis. And hence the danger of exposing himself to many of the criticisms that Edmund Husserl's thought had already merited. For John Paul II, man is a rational animal, but endowed with feelings (all kinds of feelings), which are what, ultimately and from the heart, complement and fulfill his personality.

And to conclude this rudimentary sketch of philosophical ideologies, perhaps it is sufficient to point out what Trower, a great admirer of Pope John Paul II, says. According to this author, the Pope was chosen, providentially according to him, because he was the only one who could have overcome the labyrinth of German subjectivism: *without a total surrender to it*.[87] But if this is so, what does Trower mean by his indirect allusion to a possible *total* surrender? If this is not merely a figure of speech, is he implying that there was such a surrender, at least partially...?

The answer belongs to the experts and to history. Here I can only suggest some considerations (also in an excessively summary way and without pretending to judge intentions) about the consequences the Pope's personalism and *emotionalism* have brought to

---

[87]Philip Trower, *op. cit.* pg. 114.

the Church, both with regard to the Second Vatican Council and to the post–conciliar period.

The Pope of sentiments and emotions was the Pope of great crowds, populous shows, and sensational gestures before packed multitudes.[88] It is impossible not to see that the Church had chosen to magnify human sentiments and to base on them, in some way, the worship that man owes to God. Although with the evident danger of subjectivism and of ending up in something quite similar to a cult of man.

It goes without saying that Christian Spirituality has always considered feelings, without which there can be no devotion or even a minimally human conduct. Saint Paul advised the Christians in Philippi to make Jesus' own feelings their own: *Have this mind among yourselves, which was in Christ Jesus.*[89] It should be noted, however, that although feelings *come from* man, they do not constitute him as such; although they imprint on him a distinctive stamp, they add nothing to the person *as person*. The *capacity* to love, for example, is a constitutive part of the human person, but not the acts of loving or hating, which are nothing more than the free exercise of this capacity in a positive or negative sense. The same could be said of the other feelings, which, besides being indifferent in some cases, can also be focused towards good or evil, determining the *character* of the person and qualifying him as good or bad; but without influencing at all his constitution or the degrees of personality (greater or lesser) of which Scheller speaks: for the expression referring to a

---

[88]The intention here is not to judge the philosophical or theological ideas of Pope John Paul II, but merely the consequences they may have had on Catholic Theology and Pastoral Care. Without judging the intentions. Or in any case, taking for granted that John Paul II only wanted what was best for the Flock that Christ, as Supreme Shepherd, had entrusted to him.

[89]*Hoc sentite in vobis, quod et in Christo Jesu* (Phil 2:5).

greater or lesser personality always has a psychological sense, and in no way ontological.

The great danger that can appear has to do with the blurring of the issue. Religion, worship, or liturgy, do not have as their primary object the promotion of sentiments in man, however good they may be; *but the worship of God, carried out by the creature in the most dignified way possible to honor his Creator.* When the objective of worship, or of liturgy, is encouraging feelings in man, religion becomes *psychology*. If this happens, the supernatural motives pass to the background at first, to be definitively forgotten afterwards. Christian asceticism (with its arsenal of pious practices, such as prayer, penance, etc.) is inevitably replaced by psychological procedures that end up hiding the supernatural. Today it is common to consider as apodictic, demonstrated, and indisputable, certain postulates that are in no way so; namely, and merely to cite a few examples: that *pop* music or profane songs are more fervor-inducing than Gregorian chant or merely religious chant; that noise and excitement are more useful for worship than silence; that dances and other ethnic ceremonies, however extravagant, are superior to a liturgy that is more than a thousand years old and full of supernatural gravitas..., etc.[90]

This loss of the sense of the supernatural has reached the point of turning the cult of God into a cult of man, because of the forgetfulness of the supernatural motives and foundations on which man's relations with God are based, as well as the way in which they are to be carried out. Love for God, for example, or the increase of

---

[90]There are photographs of a group of Catholic Bishops, dressed in all the ornaments proper to the office (such as the crosier and miter) dancing the *dance of the Crane*. It is a way, like any other, to confuse the right sense of the integration of cultures with *theatrical performances* and at the same time, as if in passing, ridicule.

charity in the human soul, *cannot* be the result of listening to *pop music*, nor of attending a *Eucharist show* with Hawaiian dances; *but it is only the Holy Spirit who infuses them into the heart of man.* As Saint Paul, for example, expressly says in his *Letter to the Romans*: *The charity of God is poured forth in our hearts, by the Holy Ghost, who is given to us.*[91] Someone might say that, while this is certainly so, such practices better predispose man to an increase in fervor. However, that is *precisely what remains to be shown.* For up to now, no such proof has ever appeared anywhere; whereas the facts proving the opposite are everywhere.

The great tragedy of the post–conciliar Catholic Liturgy has happened because of the shift in its objectives. The purpose of worshiping God has been *replaced* by that of the encouraging human feelings. To what end? Many have insisted on the desirability that modern man should attend a worship ceremony feeling comfortable, without being besieged with unpleasant or disturbing feelings; and hence any reference to perturbing lifestyles should be carefully omitted. In short, the artifice put into practice by the modern Liturgy, whose objective is none other than to encourage *purely human* feelings, is still extremely serious; the same feelings that have the virtue of converting a theocentric cult into a purely anthropocentric one.

As is logical, and many reasons have been given to justify such a change of course. They have insisted on the need for the Christian of this age to participate more intensely in the Liturgy; or on the importance of adapting worship to the needs of our time, of a modern mentality, whose rhythm of life is much faster. It is accepted as undisputed, even if it is not always clearly stated, that man today is more dependent on his own reason, even in the Kantian sense, than in times past; he is therefore only willing to accept what his reason is

---

[91] Rom 5:5.

capable of understanding and to question, at least, everything that is outside of it or beyond its reach.[92] An irreversible reality to which today's Church and the modern Liturgy must necessarily adapt.

However, the proponents of these new trends know very well that their reasoning *is false*. The new doctrine (theoretical and above all when put into practice) about participation in the Sacrifice of the Mass (now called the Eucharist, with special care to avoid any reference to the Sacrifice of Calvary), has nothing to do with the doctrine that has always been held and practiced by the Church. To believe that participation in the Liturgy consists of such things as distributing the Eucharist, practicing the office of lector, assuming roles and functions proper and exclusive to clerics, dancing and adding fanfare and extravagances based on profane and theatrical gestures and attitudes, etc., etc., is a complete mistake. And those responsible and the spreaders of these beliefs know well that their teaching is outside of and against Catholic Doctrine.

Perhaps it would be opportune to bring up here the words of Jesus Christ (quoting Isaiah) concerning false cults, filled with hypocrisy: *This people honors me with their lips, but their heart is far from me; in vain do they worship me, teaching as doctrines the precepts of men.*[93] Although it is true that, taken literally, the text does not have an exact and complete application here. First of all because this new Liturgy does not usually propose to honor Jesus Christ with its lips; inasmuch as its point of view is not precisely the worship of His Person (and it is enough to attend them to lose any doubt about this). Nor does it attempt to replace the divine teachings contained

---

[92]Which is the same as saying *everything*, inasmuch as it is impossible to prove the reality of what is outside the mind of man. The only principle of certainty, true certainty, is universal doubt. Although it is not always said so crudely, modern man is more Kantian than he realizes.

[93]Mt 15: 8–9.

in the Gospels with purely human precepts; since, in fact, the divine teachings hardly appear and are often not even alluded to. From which it is clear that it is no longer a question of merely *changing* such teachings, but of *uprooting* them completely. Even some valid and perfectly legitimate elements of the modern Liturgy (such as the Mass of Paul VI, now official in the whole Church), hardly avoid the impression of being a *decaffeinated* liturgy, in which the supernatural element and the idea of *Sacrifice* have been reduced to a minimum.

These tendencies would be more likely to be accused of containing hints of Pelagianism. For, while seeming to forget the necessity of grace, they emphasize purely human activity and human potentialities. Here again, however, it would be necessary to clarify. Because Modern Pastoral practice no longer tries to put in the background the absolute necessity of grace, the undoubted reality of original sin, or the impotence of purely human acts to achieve a supernatural goal; rather, they seem to try to *dispense with grace altogether*. And even if they generally do not want to acknowledge this, it is enough to examine the question thoroughly and dispassionately for suspicion to become certainty.

This is where the effort to emphasize man's feelings and emotions to the point of considering them as a *constitutive* element of his person leads to. Therefore, the new Liturgies, whose main action seems to be to stimulate man's feelings, have ended up reducing their horizon to *man as a subject–capable–of–feelings*.

Thus, theocentrism has become anthropocentrism. For Protagoras, in the fifth century B.C., man was the measure of all things; while for Petrarch, already at the dawn of the Renaissance, man was also the center of the created universe. But modern theologies and their consequent progressive liturgies have gone further; they seem to look upon the human being as the center of the visible and only universe that exists. Is it affirming with this process, which is supposed to be a progressive ascent, that human nature has finally reached the peak of its being and its possibilities...? Or is it perhaps rather the final point of its descent into degradation and nothingness?

As for the consequences on Catholicism today (embodied above all in the Liturgy), and of the influence suffered by the doctrine that sees *building community* as proper and constitutive of man, it is enough to realize something obvious and public that has spread throughout the Church. The Sacrifice of the Mass, now called the *Eucharist*, has been reduced, in many places, to a purely social meal or act, in which any element of a supernatural character has disappeared, as well as any reference to the Cross as the Redeeming and Expiatory instrument through the death of Christ. It is a matter of building and fostering community, and not of participating in an alleged Sacrifice of Christ Whose existence is often denied. Such is the doctrine that underlies, for example, the *theology* of two of the most important and influential groups that today make up Catholicism: the *Catechumenal Way* and *Base Communities*.

The new concept of *Dialogue* has also had consequences: it no longer has as its object the sincere common search for truth in charity, but rather that of achieving mutual tolerance, each respecting *the truth* or the identity of the other. Its results are visible in the new ecumenical policy of the Catholic Church. As Trower says, *the notion of "Dialogue" is susceptible to misunderstanding. And of course, as expressed by Buber, it does not coincide with that of the Church. For the Church, Dialogue is nothing other than an apostolic method that consists in speaking about certain subjects within an atmosphere of charity and good will. Its main purpose is to achieve agreement on an objective truth. For Buber, on the other hand, its primary aim is to promote mutual respect within a community of feeling; or the universal tolerance of all points of view which, whether physically or otherwise perceptible, cannot harm man. In this way it is possible, as far as Christians are concerned, to find a pretext for avoiding difficult questions, relegating unpopular truths to the realm of the irrelevant or the impossible to know.*[94] A dialogue that is absolutely impossible, both in theory and in practice, as the results have made clear.

First of all because, as far as the Separated Brethren (Protestants, schismatic Orthodox, etc.) are concerned, there is not the least willingness on their part to concede absolutely anything. This has been demonstrated in the many years that have passed since the Church initiated the new policy of rapprochement after the Second Vatican Council. It is true, however, that Catholicism, despite the numerous concessions made (many of them questionable), cannot give in on the truths of the Faith without denying itself.[95]

Nevertheless, there are many who continue to believe in the possibility of the fusion of the various Christian Churches into a so-called Church of Christ, in which Catholicism would renounce its claim to be the only Church that came from the hands of her Divine Founder.

It happens, however, that the doctrine according to which all religions possess truth, even partially but to a sufficient degree to legitimize them (and therefore to accept them), openly contradicts the words of Jesus Christ: *And other sheep I have, that are not of this fold: them also I must bring, and they shall hear my voice, and there shall be one fold and one shepherd.*[96] The possibility of

---

[94] Philip Trower, *op. cit.*, pg. 108.

[95] If the Magisterium admits the possibility of denying or questioning any of its teachings, present or past, it puts itself in danger of destroying itself. And without a legitimate Magisterium, the Church founded by Jesus Christ cannot exist.

[96] Jn 10:16.

thinking that religions professing different dogmas, and even quite often contradictory ones, can be gathered into a single Church is nothing less than an aberration. There is nothing more *absolutely contrary* to the doctrine of the New Testament than the belief that Christ had the will to found a Church, gregarious and heterogeneous, in which there would be room for beliefs, not only disparate and foreign to the essence of Christianity, but contradictory to dogmas that the Church has defended as such for many centuries since her foundation. Christ laid as the foundation of His Church a Rock (Mt 16:18; Lk 22:32) as an unshakable Stone: justly and precisely to preserve unity in Faith and charity.

* * *

From what has been said up to this point, two questions arise whose relationship raises new questions. On the one hand, the doctrine of the universal and general extension of the *great apostasy* in the Church is certainly true. Which will take place, according to the texts, in the times immediately preceding *Parousia*. On the other hand, every Christian is aware that *radicalism*, or a posture of authentic seriousness, is a quality that is part of Christian existence. This leads one to ask about the possible interaction between these two issues and the consequences that may follow.

That the great apostasy will have a universal character, within the Church itself, is beyond doubt. The words of the Lord are so categorical that they admit of no reply or euphemism: *Verumtamen Filius hominis veniens, putas, inveniet fidem in terra?*[97] The System, or the progressive Theology prevailing in the Church since the

---

[97] Lk 18:8.

death of Pope Pius XII, tends to forget the problem and to hide and conceal it from the faithful; in spite of the fact that the words of the Lord are unshakable: *Verba autem mea non transibunt.*[98] Indeed, it is a peculiar feature of progressive theology, borrowed in turn from rationalist philosophy, the disinterest in the evidence of the facts. The System affirms or denies what it sees fit, without admitting discussion. If someone pretends to call it to debate, he will be blacklisted, a situation from which he will not be able to free himself. And it is evident that the System knows how to exploit the universal fear of such punishment.

Fear is a phenomenon that in recent times seems to have deeply affected the universal Church, and in a special way the Hierarchy. It extends to all areas: fear to the ideologies that have been imposed on the world, to the advances of technology, to political power, to the media, to world opinion (and especially to the accusation of inflexibility or intolerance), to being branded as conservative or enemies of progress, to being regarded as anti-democratic, to the loss of influence, to the loss of subsidies... and so on and so forth. This is what has given rise, for example, to the fact that in Preaching, as well as in numerous Documents emanating from the Hierarchy, it is common to avoid any reference to topics that may seem unpleasant or disturbing; or to the fact that it is all too noticeable that we want to appear as being in line at all times.

As for the explanation of the phenomenon, it was given long ago by the Apostle Saint John: *There is no fear in love, but perfect love casts out fear.*[99] The statement of the Disciple Evangelist could not be more forceful: as charity diminishes, fear appears. And that Love, or the fervor of charity, has grown cold in the Church is obvious; although Jesus Christ had already announced that this would reach its culmination in the end times of History: *And with the increase of lawlessness, love in most people*

---

[98] Mk 13:31; Lk 21:33; cf. Mt 24:35.
[99] 1 Jn 4:18.

will grow cold (refrigescet).[100] The same Apostle Saint John adds, in the verse just quoted, that *he who fears is not perfect in love.* This can be completed with the affirmation he makes in another place, according to which *He who does not love does not know God; for God is love.*[101]

But the fear of progressive Catholicism, however painful it may be to admit it, is nothing more than the degradation, carried to the extreme, of a weakness that man has carried with him since the Fall. For fear became his constant companion after the expulsion from Paradise. Although in a less coarse and crude form than the present one, which has a somewhat different character. The present fear induces Catholicism to feel cornered by the world and to blush when it is accused of still believing in the historicity of the Gospels, in the figure of Jesus, or in the viability of the Beatitudes; it urges Catholics, and sometimes succeeds, to turn their face to man and their back to God. That is why it tries to take refuge in safer places; once it is convinced that the figure of man is gaining prominence, at the same time as that of God is gradually but surely fading away in the mist of myths already surpassed by humanity.

Some would label the fear of today's Catholicism as cowardice. No doubt this is what Jesus Christ meant when He said that *Whoever is ashamed of me and of my words, of him will the Son of man be ashamed when he comes in his glory.*[102] This is why Saint Paul openly confessed his attitude with regard to the teachings of the Lord: *I am not ashamed of the Gospel.*[103]

The History of Christian Spirituality has recognized that fear has been present, on some occasions, in the very structure of Christian life.

It is also true that fear is also a feeling of safeguarding human life in special circumstances; a kind of sixth sense, granted by God to man, to protect him against particular dangers. When this happens, and if it is assumed with a supernatural spirit, it can even become sanctifying. The fear of death, so connatural to the human being, was accepted by Jesus

---

[100] Mt 24:12.

[101] 1 Jn 4:8.

[102] Lk 9:26.

[103] *Non enim erubesco evangelium* (Rom 1:16).

Christ Himself and since then exalted: *Pretiosa in conspectu Domini mors santorum eius.*[104] Without forgetting either the reverential and justified fear that the author of the Book of Proverbs so wisely recognized: *Timor Domini principium scientiæ.*[105] However, when it leads to surrender before evil or error, motivated by pusillanimity or unforgivable ignorance, it can only be considered as cowardice.

Manichaeism left its mark on Christianity, however, in the form of fear of matter and more specifically of the body. A fear that is reflected in the Platonism of some Fathers, who came to consider the body as a burden or impediment to the soul. Saint Augustine, for example, thought of the human body as a *prison* for the soul. A strange belief which, in one way or another, has survived to the present day and was even sometimes shared by great mystics. To the point of considering the Humanity of Jesus Christ... *as an impediment to be dispensed with*, once we have reached the highest degrees of contemplative life, or union with God. Which approach, fortunately, already belongs to History, after the favorable advances made by healthy Christian Anthropology.

However, the fear that affects the ecclesial world today, although now in the context of the modernist heresy, has more the character of the *kneeling before the world* that Maritain spoke of. There are many who have embraced the attitudes of the world, which have seemed to them firmer and more secure than those offered by what is for them the *refuge* of Faith. This has led to doctrinal conclusions that are strange and even contrary to Christian principles.

One of the most clamorous chapters of the policy of surrender of the new Catholic Morality, elaborated on the basis of concessions, took place with respect to the possibility of legitimizing contraception. Since the first third of the last century, something that was hailed as a great practical discovery in the field of morality was spoken of with enthusiasm, and even considered by some as a triumphal discovery: *the natural method of abstinence during the fertile days of women*. It definitively solved the problem for those who, wishing to avoid the procreation of children, did not wish

---

[104] Ps 116:15.
[105] Prov 1:7.

to use clearly sinful contraceptive methods. With the discovery of such a happy solution, Morality was finally reconciled with the practical reality of life; or so it was thought.

Up to this point, it would have been fine..., if the approach to the problem had not overlooked a fundamental detail. The precepts of Christian morality, as an application of the principles of the Gospel, have not been given for a *practical* life. Especially if by practical life we mean a comfortable, convenient, and trouble–free life. The Gospel is a Book of conflict (Mt 10:16; Jn 16:33; 2 Tim 3:12), and its methods must take into account the famous *narrow and hard path*, followed by few (Mt 7:14). Attempts to reconcile the authenticity of evangelical existence with an easy life have never succeeded. Because of this, and the fact that Nature does not seem inclined to be mocked, the *natural method of abstinence, etc.*, ended in failure. Certainly, it cannot be affirmed that the method as such was sinful. The Apostle Saint Paul himself recommended abstinence for a time if there was agreement between the spouses; although the problem, apparently simple, becomes more complicated if one takes into account that the Apostle understood that the agreement was made *in order to devote oneself to prayer* (1 Cor 7:5); by which he excluded in fact any practical intention. On the other hand, as has already been said, while it cannot be said that *the natural method of abstention, etc.* is contrary to the Natural Law, nor therefore sinful, the same cannot be held (something that was not usually taken into account) with regard to setting aside the evangelical principles; and specifically the fundamental one of trust in Divine Providence (Mt 6: 25–32; 7: 7–11; Lk 12: 27–30).[106]

---

[106] Something similar happened with another finding of the new Morality that acquired legitimacy in the middle of the last century. We are referring to *mental reservation*, which was nothing more than an attempt to legitimize certain circumstances in which it would be licit to lie. And as it could not be otherwise, the principle also ended in failure. Given the irrefutable logic of things, a lie is always a lie; and if someone defends the contrary, he is only adding another lie. Evidently it is difficult to pretend to elaborate morality based on platitudes. As for the difference between the clear denial of the evangelical principles, on the one hand, or merely putting them in parentheses, on the other, it is a difficult task that can only be left to the experts.

In view of which all seemed lost... until another new discovery took place. Which also enjoyed great popularity during the last half century, and even part of the second: *responsible parenting*. The method and terminology were coined to indoctrinate parents fearful (and not fearful) of the possible increase of their offspring. It was intended to encourage them to consider whether they had what was necessary for the obligations that were to ensue: housing, food, education, etc.; with no other intention than to induce them to practice abstention if they did not.[107] And as could not be otherwise, the final result was not flattering either. Responsible parenthood immediately turned into irresponsible behavior. This is not very difficult to understand, since it is well known that, once a spillway has been opened to let the waters flow, it is not uncommon for them to burst into an overflow. After all, one cannot expect too much from human nature. The truth is that the *discovery* suffered from the same defects as the previous one: it ignored trust in Providence, it forgot the context of the Gospel teachings and, as always happens when a new cloth is put on an old garment (Mt 9:16), in the end nothing was left but the tear. Today hardly anyone remembers *irresponsible parenting*, once the use of contraceptives has become widespread.

The case of *divorce* is peculiar and most alarming. Throughout its history, the Church has never doubted that the indissolubility of Christian marriage belongs to Divine Law. This is clearly confirmed by Scripture, as well as by Tradition and the uninterrupted Magisterium of twenty centuries. However, after two thousand years, divorce has been legitimized. For which the simple procedure of substituting the name has sufficed: so that now it is known as the *declaration of nullity of the bond*. Something similar to the procedure used for abortion, nowadays disguised under the euphemism of *interruption of pregnancy*.

---

[107]And it can be assumed that the opposite was always the case, since human beings usually behave in no other way. The invention also came about at the time of the fever for *social justice*, when the problems of economic welfare seemed to take priority among Catholic theologians, moralists, and pastoralists. In short, the same as always: material well-being versus the evangelical principle of trust in Providence.

However, the legitimization of divorce by the Church has given rise to three disturbing facts:

First of all, when one consents to wordplay and manipulation of language, as is now the widespread custom, such attitude can become an instrument of confusion and lead to serious and unforeseeable consequences.

Secondly, this course of action has been carried out without any symptoms of general alarm among the people, which seems to indicate that the *sensus fidei* of the Christian People is dormant; or that it has been effectively annulled.

Finally, the consequences of ignoring Divine Law are foreseeable. They can only lead to the subsequent disappearance of human Law, as is well demonstrated by History. And in the absence of Law, inevitably the specter of anarchy appears. And who will dare to doubt that the rule of Law will cease to exist in the Church once Divine Law has been willfully ignored? *If they do this when the wood is green...* (Lk 23:31).

But what is most painful and hardest to suffer, within the climate of submission that currently affects an important part of Catholicism, is the general loss of faith in the Eucharistic presence. And where could a Church that has been left without the Eucharist go? Such capitulations to the principles of the world, even more than an attitude of fear, what they really show is that Charity has been lost. If the indissolubility of marriage is no longer considered an inalienable value (a principle now considered obsolete and impractical, according to the criteria of the world), it is because Love is no longer considered total, unconditional, and eternal. In short, because we have stopped believing in Love, which is the only thing that could frighten Christians and bring them to tears. Once again, someone has taken away the Body of the Lord and we do not know where they have put it:

> *Upon my bed by night*
> *I sought him whom my soul loves;*
> *I sought him, but found him not.*[108]

---

[108] Song 3:1.

It is worth noting that the bride's loss of the Bridegroom takes place at night, while in bed and in her sleep. Which sounds like a distant reference to the *dum dormirent homines* of the parable of the good seed and the weeds. As if someone had been careless, forgetting Saint Peter's warning (1 Pet 5:8), and by his lack of vigilance allowed the *smoke of Satan to penetrate the Church*, in the words of Pope Paul VI.

The present crisis of the Church is due to the fact that many of its members have lost the Faith... because they had previously ceased to love. This is something that today's heralds of the *Springtime of the Church* will refuse to acknowledge, in spite of all the evidence. This has led many Shepherds to abandon their sheep or lead them astray on evil and erroneous paths. Jesus Christ had already warned: the bad Shepherd, or mercenary, abandons the sheep in the face of danger precisely *because they are not his own* (Jn 10:12). This is an allusion, albeit an indirect one, to the fact that the Shepherd *does not love* his sheep. For it must not be forgotten that possession, as a consequence of the mutual self–giving of those who love each other, is the main characteristic of Love.

The bride in the *Song of Songs* was well aware that her wanderings could cause her to lose her Bridegroom, which would be tantamount to losing her life and the meaning of her life, that is, Love and the object of her Love. That is why she tries to ask the Bridegroom where she can find him. As if foreseeing the possibility of getting lost and the difficulty of finding Him again, should she suffer such a misfortune:

> *Tell me, you whom my soul loves,*
> *Where you pasture your flock, where you make it lie down at noon;*
> *For why should I be like one who wanders*
> *Beside the flocks of your companions?*[109]

Something to keep in mind, but which usually goes unnoticed, with respect to the great apostasy, is that it will also affect the Hierarchy of the Church.

---

[109] Song 1:7.

Which is not difficult to understand. For how would the dispersion of the flock be possible if the Shepherds, conscious of their responsibility, acted responsibly...? Is a scattering of the flock imaginable when there is a firm and decisive stance on the part of the Shepherds? The New Testament theology of the Good Shepherd (Jn 10) only admits, as an explanation, the possibility that the Shepherds have become mercenaries: *I will strike the shepherd, and the sheep of the flock will be scattered.*[110] With the particularity that the infidelity of the Shepherds is much more serious than that of the sheep, even disregarding the cause–effect relationship that may be present.

One could question if the infidelity of the Shepherds is perhaps due to the loss of faith to the circumstance that, as the Bible says, *initium superbiæ hominis apostatare a Deo.*[111] Although it is more likely that the situation of which Saint Paul spoke applies here: *For Demas, in love with this present world, has deserted me.*[112] It would undoubtedly be interesting to study the causes of the defection of so many Shepherds. Even if the problem does not correspond to this place, and the difficulty it would entail is extraordinary.

In any case, it is perhaps worthwhile to point out the influence of the policy followed for years by the Nunciatures, the Episcopal Conferences, and even by the Vatican itself concerning the election of Bishops. Too often the political ideology of the candidates has been taken too much into account, while their qualities as Shepherds and the intensity of their faith have been relegated to second place.

On the other hand, if it is admitted that the apostasy will have a universal character, it is not possible to limit it to a determined

---

[110] Mt 26:31.
[111] Eccl 10:14.
[112] 2 Tim 4:10.

number of Shepherds; more or less extensive. For the general defection of the sheep would not be possible without the general infidelity of the Shepherds.

Demas has forsaken me for love of this world, exclaimed Saint Paul in a lament that is already twenty centuries old. Since then there have been many throughout the ages who have also abandoned, for love of this world, a way of life that appeared to them as too radical or too demanding: *This is a hard saying; who can listen to it?*[113] But we must recognize that such a *desertion* as the present one, which moreover has affected even the Hierarchical Estate, had hardly been known before in the history of the Church, except for the case of Arianism in the fourth century.

And here it would be appropriate to ask whether it is love for this world that has had a negative influence on the Hierarchy of the Church. It would be difficult to deny that there must be something of this at the root of the problem; although it is probable that fear also be one of the main factors: in the face of the advances of technology and the strength of ideologies, all of which, it seems, are ready to shape a world that no longer needs God. With regard to Marxism, it is well known that during the time of the Second Vatican Council many members of the ecclesiastical hierarchy were convinced that it would end up imposing itself on the entire planet. We must also include the lack of generosity in the face of the *radical* practical consequences of gospel teachings. And we should also add, as one of the most important driving forces, the extraordinary growth and influence that Freemasonry has acquired in many areas of the Church.

Of course, the ultimate reason for all of them is eminently supernatural: the great power of Evil. Hence the indecision and hesitation

---

[113] Jn 6:60.

of so many Shepherds. As if they were afraid of openly proclaiming the Faith that a paganized and post–Christian world is no longer willing to admit.

It is not surprising, therefore, that certain *condemnations* of the Hierarchy against actions or persons are not based on supernatural motives, or on specific reasons derived from the Church's own mission. Rather, they are based on criteria and logic that the world would be willing to admit, and only on them. After the dogmatism that establishes *Dialogue* as the sole and determining element in any attempt at agreement, many in the Church have accepted the method; besides showing themselves convinced, it seems, that it is impossible to convince the world except by using its own principles and taking for granted that it would not be willing to admit others. As if it did not matter that the world is pagan and an enemy of Christianity.

All things considered, it is most likely that it is indeed fear that motivates these actions, accompanied as always by the consequent inferiority complexes. However, it has been demonstrated that easy explanations do not usually exhaust the truth; therefore, it may be possible to go deeper.

The way in which the Hierarchy of the Church, with the corresponding Pastoral care and Theology, proceeds and confronts today the challenges posed by Modernity, shows that the defensive strategy used responds to parameters based on a rationalist philosophy, not always in accordance with the Faith. As has been said above, not only is the language of the World adopted, but also its philosophy and ideas are accepted in order to carry out the *Dialogue*. It is convenient to insist on this last statement, since it is merely a matter of dialogue, and not of anything else; since the most innocent pretense of arguing or confronting the World is rejected beforehand, if not condemned. It is not difficult to guess, although no one dares to admit it, that Freemasonry is not far from all this.

The strategy used as just described —if it is still a strategy— would be enough to grant victory to the enemy in advance, and it also would provide reasonable doubt about the existence of a firm and serious will to defend the Faith.

* * *

In the Old Law it had been said that *the Lord your God is a devouring fire*.[114] It is not strange, therefore, that the Forerunner announced that Jesus Christ had come to administer a *baptism of fire*;[115] something that was later confirmed by the Lord's own words: *I came to cast fire upon the earth; and would that it were already kindled.*[116] Indeed, because once in the divine–human Love relationship Love has reached its state of perfection, *when the perfect comes, the imperfect will pass away*,[117] a change takes place like an ineffable metamorphosis. When the human part of the relation, as combustible material, has been entirely consumed by the fire and is no longer capable of nourishing any flame, it becomes a burning ember. Its work done, the fire seems to identify itself with a combustible material which is now nothing but incandescent embers. And while neither of them has lost its identity (the fire as such continues to nourish a material that has now become a burning ember, sharing the nature of fire), it is evident that a transformation has taken place: at least on the part of the creature, which has now

---

[114] Deut 4:24.
[115] Mt 3:11.
[116] Lk 12:49.
[117] 1 Cor 13:10.

passed, in the form of a flaming ember, to share the nature of fire (2 Pet 1:4). That the creature, in spite of everything, continues to be such a creature is proved by the fact that it is now a *burning ember*, even without having been transformed into fire; as the Apostle said: *Vivo autem iam non ego, vivit vero in me Christus*,[118] in an expression that seems to break all ways of understanding according to purely human logic: so that, according to his statement, *vivo ego* and yet, however contradictory it may seem, *iam non ego*; for it is Christ who lives *in me*.[119]

Yet a Catholic today, or someone sincerely seeking the truth and considers such things, would find an astonishing contrast.

For evidently, divine–human Love, along with the Revelation contained in New Testament Revelation as its foundation, and all that Christian existence entails, are too far removed from the humble remains of the Gospel that the modern *thinkers-evangelizers* of the twentieth century have bequeathed to Catholicism. And it is not unfair to describe them as garbage since they are nothing less. If *integral humanisms*, the *rights of man*, the so–called *democracies* (especially the self-styled Christian ones, in an expression that seems even laughable), the discovery of so numerous *freedoms* of man, together with not a few *temporal autonomies*, etc., if they intended to exalt and elevate the human condition, what they have done is nothing short of destroy it; they did not hesitate to reduce a flourishing Christianity to nothing in order to implant in its place strange doctrines, justly qualified as sequels of the modernist heresy; although in reality, in the end, they are nothing but the proof that the millenary and never–dead

---

[118] Gal 2:20.

[119] The apparent contradiction or paradox, however much it may seem to go against the demands of logic, simply overcomes the framework according to which human understanding functions. The revelation of the Word, which is but the manifestation of the divine mysteries and the work of God, sometimes comes up against the fact that it too is not capable of breaking through the limits of human understanding; at least for the time being. The mystery has been expressed, and for now it remains there; until one day it will be entirely unveiled in Heaven.

heresy of Gnosticism is more alive than ever. A gamble in favor of man, undertaken as in a dice game by modern Catholicism, without hesitating to risk God's part in the divine–human relationship, has been lost. And as usually happens in failed bets, the loser is left with nothing: on this occasion without God and, of course, also without man. There are wagers in which the mere fact of accepting them presupposes beforehand the determined will to lose them.[120]

The human being, once he has reached perfection in Love, finds himself in a certain state of repose or rest. An expression which, as can easily be understood, is nothing more than a figure of speech and somehow inexact, although valid as an introduction to the matter. It is a peace that contemplates past longings that now are finally calmed; and intense desires of Happiness at last fulfilled. When the fire no longer finds material to consume, the whole is transformed into a burning ember capable of giving off blinding light and scorching heat. This completes a final stage of human existence which also is the opposite of any form of *quietism*.

Such a situation of rest or consummation is already a reality in this life, in the form of a foretaste or first fruits. For both the Bridegroom and the bride are anxious to meet each other. The Bridegroom ardently desires to present the bride with a pledge of His Love; which, He longs to see soon become totality. It is well

---

[120] To attribute to temporal things an alleged *autonomy* (which had never been denied or forgotten by Christianity), pretending to recognize them as a *value in themselves*, is nothing else in the end, whether it is recognized or not, than removing their condition as created things: in short, an attempt to *reconcile oneself* with the world by forgetting God. As if such a vain endeavor would achieve anything positive for the world.

The true *autonomy* of any created thing is always based on the fact that it has its *consistency* in Christ, and not in anything else: *For all things were created through him and for him. He is before all things, and in him all things hold together* (Col 1: 16–17).

understood, however, that such a pledge or first gift is not mainly a demonstration: rather than the desire to convince the bride, there is an eruption of a Heart that feels itself seized by an uncontainable Love.

As for the bride, she too is aware that she has finally attained the (one) thing her soul so longed for:

> *My soul has employed itself,*
> *And all my possessions in his service;*
> *Now I guard no flock,*
> *Nor have I now any other office,*
> *For now my exercise is in loving alone.*[121]

> ....
>
> *I remained, lost in oblivion;*
> *My face I reclined on the Beloved.*
> *All ceased and I abandoned myself,*
> *Leaving my cares*
> *Forgotten among the lilies.*[122]

Everything seems to indicate that the *not yet* has finally disappeared and given way to the *already*. A stage of searching and hard journeying has been consummated, finally reaching a state of stillness, peace, serenity, and absolute happiness. The narrow door through which it was necessary to pass, and the steep and narrow road that had to be traveled, have finally led to Life (Mt 7:14) desired so intensely and for so long.

It is important to note that the situation of Love already consummated is not reduced to a state of mere stillness; at least in the

---

[121] Saint John of the Cross, *Spiritual Canticle.* 28.

[122] Saint John of the Cross, *Dark Night of the Soul.*

Lost Love   195

sense in which this word is ordinarily used. The *more abundant Life*, promised by Jesus to His own (Jn 10:10),[123] has nothing to do with *stillness*. For Life in Fullness is equivalent to Abundant *Activity*. Of course, taking into account, once again, the limitations of language. Which are the same as those imposed on human understanding, in this particular case, by the idea of *activity*; for lack of a better one. When in reality, in order to find the most adequate concept, it would be necessary to know the deep mysteries of true Life. We must keep in mind that God being Pure Act, and precisely because He is so, He is Infinite Activity; although without any shadow of change existing in Him. It is Infinite Life in all its Fullness, with all its infinite virtualities made reality. An Infinite Life that also flows —another portentous *discovery* of the New Testament Revelation— in the form of a Pure Dialogue of Love between Persons; namely: Two who love each other and a Third as a Bond of Love that unites them. With all this in the absolute Unity and Simplicity of a single Nature.

But divine–human Love —especially that which has reached a certain state of perfection— is but an analogue of divine Love. The *serene stillness* of the human heart, raptured by divine Love, is also, therefore, another analogous concept, with respect to true Life as it flows in God; where, therefore, there is also everything, with the exception of stillness as it is commonly understood.

All heresies, in spite of their content of (apparent) truth (necessary, moreover, for their subsistence), are absolutely unreasonable. *Quietism*, for example, sustains the enormous nonsense of supposing stillness and passivity where there exists only that *maximum* activity which is proper, on the other hand, to the passion of love; namely, the absolute, constant, and reciprocal surrender of

---

[123]Cf. Jn 5:40.

the lovers which takes place in divine–human Love; which cannot be understood except as Life carried to Its highest degree, as in an exacerbation of activity or fullness. For Love, in its most original source, is nothing but the Infinite Life of Pure Act; Who is also Infinite Fire. A Fire which, moreover, by Its very nature, never says *Enough!* (Prov 30:16).

But if the Infinite Life in God —*Ipsa Vita*— takes place in the form of a Loving Dialogue between Divine Persons —the Two Who mutually give themselves to each other and the Bond that unites them, which is also a Divine Person—, and the divine–human Love being a true analogue with respect to divine Love, it is logical that it will also have to take place in the form of a dialogue. However, it is a dialogue between lovers that is far from being reduced to mere dialogue. At least as dialogue is usually understood by human understanding.

Dialogue, in its normal form and as it is understood by man, is a communication between people by means of words. And words, as is well known, are nothing but vehicles that contain and transport ideas or concepts. But none of them —neither words nor concepts— are capable of expressing exhaustively the feelings they are trying to convey. Their storage capacity —of the words with respect to the respective ideas, and of the ideas with respect to the realities they attempt to express— is extremely limited and insufficient. Hence the need for the human being to multiply indefinitely his language —his words— in order to try to communicate with his fellow human beings that which is never perfect or complete.

But Dialogue, taken to the apex of the utmost perfection, does not use words. Such is the one that takes place in the bosom of the Trinity, in which the use of words would have no meaning whatsoever. Inasmuch as, as has just been said, words are always insufficient and limited in their capacity of expression; and hence the need to accumulate and multiply, although without ever reaching a perfect form of communication. But in the Trinitarian life, the Father does not have to communicate any new idea to the Son, since He has said and delivered it *all* to Him in one Word; which is precisely the Word, or the second Person of the Trinity. Since everything has been given to the Son by the Father, and since the Son has also responded to the Father with the same totality, there is nothing else to communicate or to say: *All things have been delivered to me by the Father... and all that the Father has is mine* (Mt 11:27; Jn 16:15). *Perfect dialogue*, having reached its culminating point, has become a form of communication in which there are no words, or at least only one: the *Word*. Which, together with the One Who has pronounced it and the Bond that unites them, forms the one and only Divine Essence.

This does not mean that the dialogue between human beings ceases to be analogous to that which is consummated in the bosom of the Trinity. The distance of the former from the latter should be measured according to its distance from perfection. But all in all, human dialogue being true dialogue —a communication by means of words— is always insufficient but fulfills its purpose.

What is really incredible about this is the fact that *personalist* philosophers have managed to distort and turn the concept of dialogue into nonsense. According to them, it no longer has as its object communicating ideas and feelings between human persons: And what could that object be when it can only pretend to respect *the truth of the other*, without trying in any way, far from it, to influence his way of thinking, his mood, and even less his conduct...? And hence, if dialogue must, always and in any case, respect the truth of the other, without any shadow of an attempt at *communication* (which would be nothing more than a *transmission* of ideas or feelings), then dialogue has become mere words; namely, talking for the sake of talking. A way of speaking in which each one possesses *and keeps* his own truth; and where there is, therefore, no objective and universal truth valid for all.

The dialogue of the French and German *personalists* is nothing but a return to the Tower of Babel but with pretensions of modernity and being a luminous invention. Its consequences in Theology, in the Liturgy and Preaching of the Church, and in Ecumenical politics, among other areas, are so obvious and so visible to all that they do not require any further detailing. Their influence has even reached modern Poetry and Art (painting and sculpture), which, as a rule, *do not claim to say anything* (and of course they do not), leaving each one to his own feelings (again the subjectivity of *one's own truth*).

And to sum up; what has taken place here is nothing other than a transition: from *perfect dialogue*, which does not use words because it says *everything*, to the *personalist dialogue*, which takes great care not to transmit *anything* (neither ideas nor feelings). Perhaps because it is completely devoid of them; despite the theatrics of a brilliant and cultural development, in reality it is nothing but nihilism.

The solitude and stillness sought by both —the Bridegroom and the bride— to achieve the best realization of their Love, is a leitmotif in the *Song of Songs* and, in general, everywhere divine–human Love is spoken of:

> *The king has brought me into his chambers.*
> *We will exult and rejoice in you...*[124]

Always in search of solitude and in flight from everything else. That is why the Bridegroom exhorts the other creatures not to disturb the bride:

> *I adjure you, O daughters of Jerusalem,*
> *By the gazelles or the hinds of the field,*
> *That you stir not up nor awaken love*
> *Until it please...*[125]

> *Come, my beloved, let us go forth into the fields,*
> *And lodge in the villages...*
> *There I will give you my love.*[126]

---

[124] Song 1:4.

[125] Song 2:7; 3:5; 8:4.

[126] Song 7: 11–12.

Since the essential note of love is *reciprocity*, it is difficult to understand points of doctrine of certain mystics. Although they have always been admitted as true doctrines, and the passing of the centuries has given them the character of consecrated tradition. Venerable doctrines, endorsed by the genius of saints and illustrious Doctors of the Church, have been held in great esteem by the Church, and rightly so. This should not constitute an obstacle to the posing of a question on the subject, which, in a certain way, may perhaps contribute to a better understanding of the problem:

If reciprocity (*My Beloved is for me and I am for my Beloved*)[127] is recognized as a quality of Love, how can it be admitted that in so-called passive contemplation all activity must be merely divine, with hardly any other option recognized for the human creature than that of disposing himself to passively receiving grace?[128] The torrential rain that falls from heaven, without any effort or activity on the part of the creature, is often contrasted with the activity involved in the water laboriously drawn from the well. Absolute *passivity* of the creature is proposed, without any intervention on his part, before the torrent of special and singular graces that come down from Heaven. *Everything is grace*, Bernanos said with complete justification, although speaking in a different context. And such has been the doctrine of Catholic theology from the beginning; which has never prevented it, however, from recognizing the necessity of

---

[127] A commonplace in the *Song of Songs*, to which could be added the *I will no longer call you servants, but friends*, of the Sermon on the Last Supper, as well as many other texts.

[128] Of course, everything depends on grace, and even more so in an area in which especially high supernatural graces are supposed to be at work. But that is not the point here. In divine–human relations, once the priority and absolute necessity of grace is recognized, human cooperation is not excluded, at least in Catholic theology. Why should it be so when it is a question of Love?

the creature's cooperation. How, moreover, is it possible to imagine that God, in granting the human being the character of a privileged sharer in His own Life, as a friend and not as a servant, admitted to the dialogue and the tenderness of the intimate relationship of Love of a *thou* and an *I*, would leave him in the role of a mere spectator or passive recipient? *Say what you will, if there is no relationship in Love from an "I" to a "thou," there is no Love at all.* That the human *I* is capable of becoming a *thou* for the divine *I is the greatest, the most mysterious, and the most admirable miracle of Grace.* True, everything is grace, to the point that we must exclude any merit on the part of the creature that does not originate in grace; but it is equally true that it is not possible to deny the fact that, in the relationship of divine–human Love, the role of the creature reaches heights of intimate and profound *activity* —of intense Life— that escape any attempt at human measurement. Ultimately, it is Grace that accomplishes the miracle of making the human being truly an *I* in his relationship with God... and, therefore, also with other men. It is only when God treats him as a *thou* that man begins to be *himself*. This is possible from the moment when the mutual dialogue of Love of the I and the thou has begun.[129] From which it seems possible to conclude that every Dialogue is either a loving dialogue or it is not a dialogue at all. And this is how modern Pastoral Care is not always on the right track: man is *himself* only when he *has lost himself*; which is what the teaching of the Master says: *He who loses his life for my sake will find it.*[130] For man, in fact, has no other way of

---

[129]Such a dialogue, in the relationship of divine–human Love, begins at the moment of the reception of baptism. Initiated in the dark unconsciousness of faith, its destiny is none other than that of maturing until it reaches the clarity of the *face-to-face* encounter in Heaven.

[130]Mt 10:39.

finding himself —or of being himself— except through Love. And this is why Saint John of the Cross said:

> *If, then, on the common land,*
> *From henceforth I am neither seen nor found,*
> *You will say that I am lost;*
> *That, wandering love-stricken,*
> *I made myself lost, and was found.*[131]

To suppose that in contemplative prayer man has no other role than to dispose himself to *passively* receive the flow of Grace that comes from on High, without acting as an *I*, an indispensable condition, moreover, for such passive contemplation to be truly a loving *Dialogue*...[132], would be in danger of recalling the teaching of Miguel de Molinos.

The love relationship is entirely peculiar and unique in a certain sense. First of all, the condition of the lovers as such remains the same within the relationship; since each of them retains his own individuality and differentiation, as is normal in any relationship. In this one, however, the note of *differentiation*, not only deepens and becomes *opposition*, it is also demanded by the very condition of the relationship of Love.[133] Since the loving relationship that constitutes

---

[131] Saint John of the Cross, *Spiritual Canticle*.

[132] It has been said above that any self-respecting Dialogue tends to be amorous, just as no Love can be conceived that is not Dialogue. The faculty of communicating was not granted to man only as an instrument for the transmission of ideas, but also of feelings. In any human *communication* it is not the brain that speaks, but *man*: brain and heart. Man was created for Love: to love and to be loved. Hence the Master's counsel: *Love one another*, would be especially forceful, going far beyond merely religious content and being a veritable institutional ingredient that derives from the constitution of human nature.

[133] *Opposition* in created beings is in turn an analogy —another one— with respect to the divine relations in the Trinity.

the Lovers as such can only be established between *different persons*. It could not be otherwise since Love consists in the *departure* of one *to go towards* the other; or in the *giving* of one *to be received* by the other. And all this in turn in a reciprocal way. It follows that, in the play of Love, the *distinction* between persons and the condition of *reciprocity* are essential elements.

However, as we have already seen above, God is a *devouring fire*. As such, being Infinite Love, He scorches and *consumes* His creature to the extent that it is able to withstand the intensity of a Fire of Infinite Love. In this case, the *Infinitudo originis* acts on the *finitudo recipientis* to give rise to the divine Love participated in and received as a gift by the creature. There is thus a place of origin *a quo*, another place of destination *ad quem*, and the link that is established between one and the other to constitute the whole which the loving relationship consists of. This can be better understood by analyzing the Apostle's text in its various parts: *The love of God* (a) *has been poured forth in our hearts* (b) by (c) *the Holy Spirit who has been given to us.*[134] It can therefore be said, with regard to the divine–human Love relationship, that the human being is *devoured* by the Fire of Love that descends from God and *consumes* His creature:

> *Its flashes are flashes of fire,*
> *A flame of Yahweh himself.*[135]

But then, one may ask, where is the reciprocity to be found here? Could it be said that the fire of the bride's heart is capable of affecting the heart of the Bridegroom? Would the fire of a human

---

[134] Rom 5:5.
[135] Song 8:6.

heart, seared by Love, be able to *wound* the Heart of God in its desire to make it His own and possess it?

And the answer, of course, is affirmative.

To bring a possible explanation to this issue, some interesting texts from the *Song of Songs* may be helpful:

> *I would lead you and bring you*
> *Into the house of my mother,*
> *And into the chamber of her that conceived me.*
> *I would give you spiced wine to drink,*
> *The juice of my pomegranates.*[136]

It is evident that there is a kind of restrained desire, on the part of the bride, *to take possession of* the Bridegroom. She seeks to lead him to a solitary and safe place, by choice or by force, to entertain him to the point of drunkenness. After all, what she desires is to be alone with her Bridegroom in order to rejoice in their mutual Love. It is necessary to recognize that the madness and foolishness, sometimes capable of becoming true madness, that either of the Lovers is capable of realizing with respect to the other, can only seem such to those who have never known Love.

What is admirable in this case is that the enamored Heart of God can actually be wounded, and also in a human way, if one wants to speak in this way (in bold but true language), *through the Love experienced by the Heart of flesh of Jesus Christ.* Or by the human Heart of Jesus Christ, if one wants to speak with all propriety.

In order to understand this in some way, it is necessary to keep in mind that God wanted to make human love His own, *experienced*

---

[136] Song 8:2.

in a human way.[137] For God wanted man to be able to love Him freely and openly, in his own way, according to his human nature and way of loving. That is why Jesus eats before His disciples after the resurrection in order to convince them that He is not a spirit (Lk 24: 36–44). And that God was interested in demonstrating His love to man is evident from the fact that He gives His own life precisely for this purpose (Jn 15:13). The demands of Love reach such craziness, together with the desire to feel equal in status and to be at the side of the beloved Person: *I will no longer call you servants...* And once again what was said in the last note applies here. God does not need *to feel* He is at man's side, since in fact He *is*, and in a more transcendent way: *More intimate to me than I myself*, said Saint Augustine.[138] But man does need, in order for his love to be authentic and true, to feel God at his side and to be able to love Him in his own way.

And it is now that the conditions demanded by true Love are fulfilled. Once what seemed impossible, reciprocity, has been made possible. Now, at last, *felt and perceived* by man.[139]

---

[137] It can already be understood that such an *experience* looks more towards man than towards God. God does not need to experience anything. Man, on the other hand, does need to know that God loves him *in his own human way*. After all, this is the only way of loving that man knows for the time being. And Love, or at least a Love called to be perfect, could hardly be such if there are no common feelings involved. Equality, both of levels and of situations, so characteristic of Love, takes again its pride of place: it is enough for the disciple to be like his Master, and the servant like his Lord (Mt 10:24; Lk 6:40).

[138] *Intimior intimo meo et superior summo meo* (Saint Augustine, *Confesiones*, III, 6.)

[139] Love is not merely a product of knowledge, but also of the will: *Nihil volitum quin præcognitum*. The good and the beautiful are desired once they have been perceived. It would not be enough for man to know that God loves him, but he needs to *feel* such Love; and as always, in reciprocity. Therefore, it seems insufficient to make *Beatitudo* consist in the satiating contemplation of Truth.

Lost Love

Now it has become possible for the human Heart of Jesus Christ to be pierced by the fiery darts of His creature's Love. The same darts that come from an ardent Love that desires to correspond to His own. While the creature, for his part, can perceive that the Word made Flesh also lives the *sufferings and anguish* that, for the time being, usually accompany Love; that is to say, during the time when the sweetness of Love is full when tasted in sight of the Cross. Only in this way is man capable of living true Love: in totality and in his own way. And God, for His part, also wanted to live it as His creature did and together with His creature. Thus, we can better understand the tender words of the bride in the *Song of Songs*, without the need to resort to poetic metaphor:

> *O that his left hand were under my head,*
> *And that his right hand embraced me!*[140]

At last divine Love, reciprocated by the creature, has become divine–human Love. Now God loves as God and as Man. While man, elevated by grace, can now love with a divinized, or quasi–divine Love; while sharing the same Life and the same Love of the Infinite God: *So that the love with which thou hast loved me may be in them, and I in them.*[141]

Jesus Christ is the expert witness whose Heart, flooded with desires to demonstrate His Love (Jn 15:13), lives in anguish until the moment of giving up his life: *I have a baptism to be baptized with;*

---

[140] Song 8:3.

[141] Jn 17:26. One of the things that have been missing in Catholic theology is a more serious and profound doctrine about devotion to the Heart of Jesus. Up to now it has been reduced practically to pious practices for devout persons, when not to theories with little foundation in dogma.

and how I am constrained until it is accomplished![142] Too important a text, transferred by the Neovulgata from the original Greek as: *Baptisma autem habeo baptizari et quomodo coartor, usque dum perficiatur.* Where it is to be noted that the verbal form συνέχομαι, here in passive form, means *contineor* (to hold together or bind, enclose, embrace; in passive, to be encircled or surrounded, etc.); or *coarctor* (to tighten, squeeze, compress, etc.); or *affigor* (to affix, nail, drive, drive in, etc.); or *animo angor*.

Driven by his natural desire to know, man is given to formulating hypotheses and theories that later may become proven truths. On the other hand, he is less inclined to deduce relevant consequences, even if they have sometimes proved to be convenient or even necessary. This explains, for example, that in divine–human Love (the loving relationship between God and man), not much stress has been laid on the fact that it is both a divine and a human love at the same time. And since it affects both terms of the relationship, the Love of man for his God is as much Human as Divine; or at least quasi divine. And the same can be stated about the Love of God for His creature, which is both *divine and human at the same time*. Thus, just as God is loved by man with a human love, even if divinized or elevated by Grace, so God loves man with human Love through the heart of Christ. Therefore, if it is possible to think here of a kind of *communicatio idiomatum* between the Love of the one and the other, then identical or similar qualities could be applied to both. Man suffers the impact of the fire of divine Love, just as God is also affected by that which proceeds from the Love of His creature. In this regard, the consequences derived from reciprocity in Love, as well as the profound meaning of the sacred texts, may go unnoticed. It is not infrequent that more attention is paid to their literary,

---

[142]Lk 12:50.

metaphorical, or poetic character than to their profound content. As can be seen in one of the most impressive exclamations which, put in mouth of the bride, appears in the *Song of Songs*:

My beloved is for me and I am for my beloved.

* * *

When we speak of the relationship of Love between God and man, we usually insist more on the Love of man *for God* than on the Love of God *for man*; and it is evident that pastoral reasons, or those that have man's salvation at heart, are the determining factors here. The relevance of the precept according to which *Thou shalt love the Lord thy God with all thy heart*, etc., is more than justified if one considers the condition of the creature with respect to its Creator. It would be quite another thing if the precept were considered as a *commandment* rather than as an act of true Love; which, as is well known, is essentially free. But for obvious reasons, the timeliness of such a *command* cannot be the subject of discussion, although a more thorough and detailed study of the problem would not be without interest. Nevertheless, both terms of the relationship (the Love of God for man and the Love of man for God) appear in the Bible with a similar predicament, although, as might be expected, with a preponderance of the former.[143]

---

[143] With regard to this priority, we could mention texts such as *God so loved the world that He gave His only begotten Son* (Jn 3:16), or *We love because He first loved us* (1 Jn 4:19), etc.

In any case, it is important to underline the condition of reciprocity in the divine–human Love relationship. In it, God is always God, while man remains man. But God willed to be loved by man with perfect and authentic Love insofar as the creature is capable of attaining such perfection. Which man can do at a high level granted by Grace. Which love, nevertheless, remains human, or rather superhuman. Grace does not suppress nature. It is logical to think that God became Man *for a purpose*. To redeem man, of course; although everything suggests that it was additionally for something else. Undoubtedly to actualize a good number of virtualities derived from the fact of the Incarnation. Much more difficult for man to discover, both in their depth and in their abundance, than the possibility of knowing the exact number of stars in the firmament.

Therefore, as has already been said above, it is to be expected that the Heart of God, through the Person of the Word made Man, will also be affected, and even wounded, by the Love He receives from His creature. In this way we understand the meaning of the representations that are usually made, both in painting and sculpture, of the image of the Heart of Jesus: wounded, bleeding, and surrounded by thorns. It is regrettable that this Devotion has found in the Church more support from *devotion* than from authentic *theology*. In this regard, it is worth remembering that no one is attracted by the love of which he is the object, but by the *Person* who professes it.

Once again, as always, the *Song of Songs* abounds in the matter by putting sublime expressions on the lips of the Bridegroom:

> *Turn away your eyes from me,*
> *For they take me by assault.*[144]
>
> ....

---

[144] Song 6:5.

Lost Love 209

> *You have ravished my heart, my sister, my bride,*
> *You have ravished my heart with a glance of your eyes...*[145]

That the human Heart of Jesus Christ has been affected by passions so proper to human nature, as suffering and love can be, is something that emerges quite clearly from the Gospel, as Saint John affirms on the occasion of the resurrection of Lazarus:

Now Jesus had not yet come to the village, but was still in the place where Martha had met him. When the Jews who were with her in the house, consoling her, saw Mary rise quickly and go out, they followed her, supposing that she was going to the tomb to weep there. Then Mary, when she came where Jesus was and saw him, fell at his feet, saying to him, "Lord, if you had been here, my brother would not have died."

When Jesus saw her weeping, and the Jews who came with her also weeping, he was deeply moved in spirit and troubled, and he said,

"Where have you laid him?"

They said to him,

"Lord, come and see."

Jesus wept.[146]

It is frequent in Christian Spirituality, as well as in the common feeling of the faithful, to place more emphasis on the divine will of Jesus Christ than on His human will. It is as if the reality that He is *also* true Man were left in the shadows, to the point of giving the impression, sometimes, that vestiges of Monothelitism live on.

And yet the contemplation of Jesus Christ as true Man is essential for spirituality and Christian life in general. Otherwise, man

---

[145] Song 4:9.
[146] Jn 11: 30–35.

would not be able to love God in a *perfect* way —human–divine— as God wishes to be loved by him. It is not well understood how man could do so without passing through the Heart of Jesus Christ, recognized by him as also truly human. The adverb *also*, however strange it may sound, is of fundamental importance here. When man perceives the Heart of Christ as authentically human, he would not be able to feel a mad love for Him if he did not at the same time recognize it as the Heart of his God. The same God who became man in order to give His life out of love for man, and to make him able to reciprocate Him in totality: *No one comes to the Father except through me...*[147] *Without me you can do nothing.*[148] That is why the Bride said:

> *At my Love's side I lingered,*
> *In the silence of Love's mutual sweet word,*
> *While still at his side I heard*
> *Soft in my ear he whispered*
> *That he too, wounded by my love, has suffered.*

* * *

...But I have it against you that you have lost the impetus of your first love.

It is therefore possible that Love may at some time become distorted and be deprived of Its dynamism and strength. In which case It would be deprived of that passion that It had in the beginning and that usually marks the beginning of every love story: Cupid's

---

[147] Jn 14:6.
[148] Jn 15:5.

arrow. The instant in which someone feels sweetly wounded by a force that induces him or her to surrender, totally and unconditionally, to another person. That moment of high intensity is destined, by its very nature, to become an immense bonfire capable of burning all things.

Is it not true that Love both enslaves and at the same time grants freedom?[149] *Nexus dourum*, as the Fathers called the Holy Spirit. And a nexus is what binds and unites, although this one in particular is the only thing that grants true freedom: *Ubi Spiritus Domini, ibi libertas.*[150]

However, the lover wants nothing more than to feel bound and imprisoned by the person he loves. Diego de San Pedro wrote in the fifteenth century his *Castell of Love*, framed in the environment that later historians would call *Courtly Love*, and according to a theme that has always been considered as a basic element of the love relationship. Everything seems to indicate that lovers of all times have desired nothing more than to feel imprisoned, and even put in prison by (or because of) the loved one. Only in this way, and not in any other way, could they imagine themselves free:

---

[149] Jesus Christ establishes an intimate relationship between the practice of His teachings, the knowledge of truth, and freedom (Jn 8: 31–32). Likewise, between fidelity to His words and love (Jn 14: 15.23).

[150] We see an important difference here. For liberalism (so often condemned by the Church) freedom is based on the absence of coercion: freedom of thought, freedom of expression, freedom of association, freedom of commerce, freedom of action... and, in short, freedom to do whatever one wishes. This is how it is understood by those who see in democracy the supreme and only good... and in the totalitarian state the only and supreme evil. For Jesus Christ, however, freedom can only be based on and be a consequence of *truth* (Jn 8:32).

> *Draw me after you, let us make haste.*
> *The king has brought me into his chambers.*[151]

Of course, it is not the same thing to love as to be in love. For to love would perhaps be something that could be within the reach of anyone; while to fall in love would correspond, as an exclusive privilege, to those who really know how to love.

But can a Love that has lost its impetus, its strength, and its dynamism still be considered Love? Judging from the text of Apocalypse 2:4, taken literally, it would seem so.[152] If so, we would then be dealing with a Love *reduced* in quality and price; and now, at last, within the reach of everyone.

The enigmas posed by the complex phenomenon of Love are very complicated. What has been said about It here, as anyone can see, is no more than a mere superficial sketch. What refers to Its intensity and Its possible diminution, or to whether the character of totality belongs essence of Love, are but a few of the many questions susceptible of further investigation. And it is worth stressing the word "investigation" since it is not possible to aspire to anything else. After all, Love is identified with God, the Infinite Mystery. Therefore, even created love, as the participation that it is of Infinite Love, contains many things that man will never be able to unveil entirely in this life.

Nevertheless, it seems tempting to make a quick foray into some of these problems, without pretending to go beyond what can be expected from a mere spirit of curiosity.

It may be helpful to devote a little attention to the aforementioned novel by Diego de San Pedro. Bearing in mind the almost

---

[151] Song 1:4.

[152] For the purposes of this analysis, it is indifferent to speak of the loss of *first love* or of the loss of the *impetus of first love*; inasmuch as the meaning is the same.

total agreement among critics, according to which the *Love Prison* is an emblematic work of the so–called *Courtly Love*, as it was understood and sung by the Provençal minstrels and poets of the late Middle Ages.

Precisely one of the issues which, in relation to Courtly *Love*, has led scholars to criticize its exaggeration has been the alleged *divinization* of the beloved by the lover. Hence the objections, and even the rejection, on the part of quite a few moral theologians; to the point that the *Prison of Love* was forbidden by the Inquisition.

However, if one examines today, in a more benign and unprejudiced mood, this type of literature that flourished in the autumn of the Middle Ages, it is easy to discover the scant foundation of such accusations. At least as far as the *Prison of Love* is concerned, the epithets and expressions addressed in it to women in general are there to extol them. Although the same cannot always be said of other literary creations; as is the case, for example, with the *Tragicomedy of Calisto and Melibea*, whose eminently pagan character and high concupiscence is impossible to deny. On the other hand, at least on this point, Diego de San Pedro writes emphasizing Christian virtues; with exaggerated expressions if you will, and even more so those directed at the heroine, but which do not go beyond those typically used by those who are *madly* in love. Once they have been serenely considered, the author's intention cannot be supposed/thought to have gone beyond the desire to make use of metaphor; after all, an almost obligatory language in writers and poets who speak of love.

The *exaggerated* epithets addressed to the beloved, ordinarily ardent and fiery, are such a common constant in the world of lovers that even the *Song of Songs* uses them in almost excessive abundance. The Sacred Book goes so far as to compare the beloved to the beasts of Pharaoh's chariot (Song 1:9): a strange trope, to be sure; difficult to understand for the modern mentality, but containing a detonating poetic charge, as well as a highly evocative value according to the mentality of the ancients.

Perhaps the problem lies in the fact that passion has often been identified with concupiscence. And many have understood Love as necessarily carnal. To all this we should add the resistance of many Christian moralists (in the Ancient and Middle Ages, but also in later times) to not consider sinful the conjugal act carried out with passion; which would make it at least a venial sin or a corrupt act.

The truth is that the problem, already quite complex, requires a careful use of terminology. If passion is identified with concupiscence, conjugal carnal acts could be considered flawed.[153] But it seems obvious that Christian moralists (especially medieval ones) sometimes went to extremes in their requirements on this point. To demand, for example, that the husband, in order to carry out his duty to his wife, must always and in every case consider her as his wife, and never as a mere woman, may seem to be too extreme; as well as to demand that certain acts or moments of intimate conjugal life must be carried out at all times *cum moderatione* etc.

Whatever the case may be, it is evident that passion, or being passionate, understood here in the strong sense, is inherent to Love. The accusation that the Spirit addresses to the Angel of the Church of Ephesus is based precisely on this point: because he has lost the *impetus* of his first love or, which is the same thing, the piercing and wounding fire of his *first* love:

---

[153] The only one we are talking about here, because the carnal act outside of marriage is always sinful.

Lost Love

> *For love is strong as death,*
> *Jealousy is cruel as the grave.*
> *Its flashes are flashes of fire,*
> *A flame of Yahweh himself.*[154]

And when we speak of the love that Jesus professed to His own, we say that it was love *to the end* (Jn 13:1). This expression does indeed contain a certain ambiguity, but it always leaves the door open to a deeper understanding of its possible meanings. On the other hand, when Jesus Himself speaks of the way and manner in which man is to love God, He does not mince words or use euphemisms: *You shall love the Lord your God with all your heart and with all your soul and with all your strength.*[155] And the fact is that Love supposes an overflowing surrender to the loved one, in the expectation, of course, of an equal response. The relationship that is thus established —the flow of love— cannot be expressed in words. Inasmuch as language is not capable of expressing the almost infinite volcano of feelings that nests in the heart of man (*You made us, Lord, for you and our heart will be restless until it rests in you*).[156] It can only do so in a partial and stammering way, by resorting to all the resources of language: literary figures in all their forms and the varied use of words and their diverse senses. Procedures that are always insufficient. Human love, in its created condition and analogous to divine Love, transcends the intellect of the creature. In the bosom of the Trinity, the Father *says* to Himself what He is in the completeness of a single Word, since both of them —the Father and His Word— are identical in the same Essence. But man is incapable of expressing to himself the fullness of his being: what he is or what

---

[154] Song 8:6.

[155] Mk 12:30.

[156] Saint Augustine, *Confessions*.

he feels; at least during the present eon, *for now I know imperfectly, but then I shall know as I am known.*[157] For His part, when God speaks to man, and since He wishes to be understood, He uses human language. If, moreover, in view of the difficulty of the problem, He intends to communicate with regard to the mystery of Love and of the relationship He wishes to establish with His creature, He cannot but use the procedures proper to human forms of expression. Note, for example, the metaphor, transcendent to all capacity for human apprehension in its content and beauty, as it appears in the following verses of the *Song of Songs*. What might appear to be a mere poetic composition is in reality an attempt to reach the depths of the human heart by making it sense the superabundance of Love. And with what words, and by means of what figures of speech could such realities be expressed...? Hence it becomes clear, once again, what always happens with true Poetry: what is *insinuated* (by the speaker), and also what is *sensed* (by the listener), means much more than what the mere meaning of the words encompasses:

> *I come to my garden, my sister, my bride,*
> *I gather my myrrh with my spice,*
> *I eat my honeycomb with my honey,*
> *I drink my wine with my milk.*
> *Eat, O friends, and drink:*
> *Drink deeply, O lovers!*[158]

It is the voice of the Bridegroom, expressing His desire to go to His bride. He says it and repeats it with impatience: I am coming, *I am going to my garden...* For the bride's longings to welcome

---

[157] 1 Cor 13:12.
[158] Song 5:1.

Him, *Come, Lord Jesus*,[159] is preceded and reciprocated by the even greater yearning of the Bridegroom to meet her: *Surely, I am coming soon...*[160]

And He compares the bride to a garden. It is a garden of abundance and beauty, where myrrh, balsam, virgin honey, wine, and milk abound... What can the one who loves do but compare the beloved —since it is a matter of expressing her beauty and also His own love— according to the best that human understanding can imagine and words are capable of expressing?

> *A garden locked is my sister, my bride,*
> *A garden locked, a fountain sealed.*[161]

It would have been a cause of despair for the Bridegroom to be unable to describe either the beauty of His bride or the love He feels for her. He is not saddened, however. He knows well that He will never be able to describe her to strangers..., or to do anything but reserve for Himself the depth of His feelings. He could never really go beyond that, nor would He ever be understood; which does not matter to either of the lovers, determined after all, to seek solitude:

> *Come, my beloved, let us go forth into the fields,*
> *And lodge in the villages;*[162]

It is interesting that the Bridegroom addresses the bride with passionate, seemingly incompatible loving epithets: *My sister, bride...* Which he sometimes accumulates in abundance:

---

[159] Rev 22:20.
[160] Rev 22:20.
[161] Song 4:12.
[162] Song 7:11.

> *Open to me, my sister, my love,*
> *My dove, my perfect one;*[163]

As if He wanted to imply that what He feels for His spouse embraces all possible forms of Love.[164] It is but a new attempt at expressing, as far as is possible and in the best way it is possible, the totality and the absolute character of a love that embraces all forms and modalities. Jesus Christ Himself seems to allude on some occasion to this way of qualifying divine Love for His creature: *And one said unto him: Behold thy mother and thy brethren stand without, seeking thee. But he answering him that told him, said: Who is my mother, and who are my brethren? And stretching forth his hand towards his disciples, he said: Behold my mother and my brethren. For whosoever shall do the will of my Father, that is in heaven, he is my brother, and sister, and mother.* [165]

This leads us to consider one of the most difficult and delicate problems of the mystery of Love, that of *total love*.

What is the meaning of the expression *total love*, apparently so simple and easy to explain? Everything leads us to think that *totality*, as something consubstantial to the phenomenon of Love, is a definitively acquired truth.[166] Difficulties arise when we consider

---

[163] Song 5:2.

[164] Created love, which is but a reflection of or participation in Infinite Love, is expressed in the human being in various and distinct forms, which only have the essence is common: paternal–filial love, conjugal love, fraternal love, friendship... In each of which the analogy is reflected in a different way, in degrees of greater or lesser perfection.

[165] Mt 12: 47–50.

[166] This has been stated in all our writings. And it seems that the problem does not give rise to major concerns... as long as we do not try to go more deeply into it. When an attempt is made to do this, all its complexity and acrimony is immediately revealed.

that the love bestowed by God on man, as is always the case with created things, is realized according to different modes of analogy; which is the same as saying in varying degrees of perfection. Conjugal love, fraternal love, or the love of friendship, for example, seem irreducible to a univocal meaning.

Nevertheless, it seems that, at least in principle, it should be normal and even necessary to consider *totality* as an ingredient of all forms of love. Although not in the same way or to the same degree. Therefore, it will be necessary to use totality in the broad sense, or improper, and in the strict sense, or proper. This will lead us to the conclusion that it is in divine–human Love that the quality of *totality* clearly appears, which is not the case in purely human love (conjugal, paternal-filial, fraternal...), even in love elevated by grace.

Jesus Christ Himself establishes the distinction between one love and the other. Questioned by one of the doctors of the Law, the following dialogue took place between them: *Master, which is the greatest commandment in the law? Jesus said to him: Thou shalt love the Lord thy God with thy whole heart, and with thy whole soul, and with thy whole mind. This is the greatest and the first commandment. And the second is like to this* [simile est huic]: *Thou shalt love thy neighbor as thyself.*[167]

Where it can clearly be seen that the first commandment imposes on man to love God *with his whole being*; while the second, on the other hand, which is only similar to the first, commands to love one's neighbor *as oneself.* The difference goes far beyond mere nuance and must therefore be important. For the qualities of the one and the other love are quite distinct: the *dissimilarity* contained in the analogy of created love with respect to Infinite Love from which it

---

[167] Mt 22: 36–39.

proceeds is much greater in the purely human than in the divine–human.

This does not mean that the so–called totality in the improper sense, which corresponds to purely human love, is ultimately incomplete. However, if the analogy is with respect to Substantial Love, its degree of perfection is much lower than that of divine–human Love. Therefore, it can only exist as an intention which, although it looks to totality as its end, is always reduced to attempts that do not reach their goal. After all, purely human love is contained within the sphere of the second commandment, unlike divine–human Love, whose sphere of realization is properly that of the first: *with all your might*, commands the first of the commandments; *as yourself*, prescribes the second of them.

However, a more detailed examination of things is desirable in order to clarify what has been said.

Purely human love, as in all kinds of love, translates into the reciprocal self-giving of those who love each other. However, even in the case of a perfect love, the *totality* implied in such self-giving is nothing more than an attempt destined to fail, or else an ideal that will never be realized, even in the case of a love elevated by grace. To understand this, it is enough to examine conjugal love, after all, the most characteristic and typical of them all.

It is true that the *Song of Songs* uses conjugal love as the most adequate means, in spite of its limitations, to refer to divine–human Love and to describe its development. It does so because it is the form of love best suited to accomplish such a difficult task. It is the closest to divine–human Love, despite its remoteness, and the one that can best illustrate the mystery of the divine–human Love relationship. God must use language, with the whole mechanism of man's communication, if He wants to be understood by him.

However, the mutual self-giving that conjugal love entails, however loving and perfect it may be, is far removed from the divine–human Love relationship. The exchange of affections, feelings, ideas, and wills..., whose culmination is somehow consummated in the conjugal act, has little or nothing to do with the complete exchange of lives that takes place in divine–human Love. It is true that the conjugal act makes both spouses become *una caro* —one flesh—, within the highest and most possible expression of their mutual love, destined also to be confirmed by the fruit of children. Something so sublime that Saint Paul had no qualms about likening it, even in the form of a distant analogy, to Christ's self-giving and love for His Church (Eph 5:32). But how can that love be compared to what the Apostle also said: *I have been crucified with Christ; it is no longer I who live, but Christ who lives in me*?[168]

The carnal union of the spouses, honestly carried out within a legitimate marriage, is both glory and misery for man.

The most sublime aspect of this union is that it signifies and consummates the love of the spouses in the highest form of expression of which human nature is capable. And something even more important: it is the instrument with which man collaborates with God in the highest of creations, namely, that of other human beings, constituted as persons and destined to be children of God and to eternal beatitude.

At the same time, it also signifies the misery of human insufficiency. It is a loving relationship in which man *would like* to carry out, at the same time, both a total giving and a total receiving with respect to the beloved. After all, totality corresponds to the essence of true Love. However, man knows well, from his own experience and from the analysis of his feelings, that it remains an attempt

---

[168] Gal 2: 19–20.

that does not go beyond the limited possibilities of human nature. There is a mutual communication of ardent affections, of feelings, of wills, of love... but *in no way does an exchange of lives take place there*. On the other hand, that conjugal love falls within the scope of the second commandment is clearly shown by the teaching of Saint Paul: *Husbands should love their wives as their own bodies. He who loves his wife loves himself...*[169] *In any case, let each one of you love his wife as himself, and let the wife see that she respects her husband.*[170] As the Apostle insists, establishing a difference with respect to the degree of totality (and therefore of perfection), between purely human love and divine–human Love: *The unmarried man is anxious about the affairs of the Lord, how to please the Lord; but the married man is anxious about worldly affairs, how to please his wife, and his interests are divided.*[171]

The founder of *Opus Dei*, Saint Josemaría Escrivá, wrote in the first half of the last century, in the emblematic book of his spirituality and referring to the consecrated life, that *marriage is for the common people, and not for the High-Ranking Staff of Christ.*[172] With the passage of time, the expression has been the cause of deep controversy; and, strange as it may seem, even of confusion for his own disciples and spiritual children. They often seem to be trying to hide it and to prefer that it had not been written.

The reasons for such a situation are well known. The exaggerated exaltation of the laity with the consequent deterioration of the idea of the ministerial priesthood, the discredit and even contempt for consecrated life, the inferiority complex before the world and new ideologies, the influence of Neo–modernism, and the diffusion of doctrines on the superiority of marriage over celibacy, etc. The ideological absurdity of the so–called

---

[169] Eph 5:28

[170] Eph 5:33.

[171] 1 Cor 7: 32–34.

[172] Josemaría Escrivá, *Camino*, 28.

promotion of the laity, for example, uses as its battle standard the bizarre idea of the despotism and abuse with which the clergy has handled the laity for many centuries.

This fact, which can only be cited here as an isolated anecdote, albeit a regrettable one, is but one more example of the crisis of faith that is gripping Catholicism today. On the other hand, and even if it is typical of its time, the expression is absolutely correct; and we experience the deepest perplexity when contemplating the confusion of those who are ashamed of it.

But the main difference has already been mentioned above. The perfection to which man is raised by grace, in which a true exchange of lives takes place, is only found in human–divine love: *He who eats my flesh and drinks my blood abides in me, and I in him. As the living Father sent me, and I live because of the Father, so he who eats me will live because of me...*[173] *He who finds his life will lose it, and he who loses his life for my sake will find it.*[174]

On the other hand, however close the loving relationship in the conjugal bond may be, and as long as it is intended to keep such a union within the bounds of what is natural and normal, there is one element that must always remain; namely, the relationship of authority. After all, conjugal life functions as a society, and hence the need for a governing head, as occurs in any group. According to the Bible, which is the Word of God, and according to natural law, this role corresponds to the man. Unless one wants to denaturalize the institution: *For the husband is the head of the wife as Christ is the head of the church, his body, and is himself its Savior. As the church is subject to Christ, so let wives also be subject in everything to their husbands.*[175] Of course, the Feminist Movements, backed

---

[173] Jn 6: 56–57.

[174] Mt 10:39.

[175] Eph 5: 23–24.

by all the ideologies that have arisen in a world that was once, but no longer, Christian, will here bring their accusations of sexism, of discrimination against women, of ignorance of fundamental rights, etc. All of which, apart from *not being able to change the reality of things, except to subvert it*, only highlights the crisis of a pagan society in full decomposition.

In divine–human Love, however, the idea of *authority* is blurred, while the idea of *mutual and reciprocal possession* is emphasized. Unlike in conjugal love, where the character of possession also acquires an aspect of exclusivity: *my* wife, in a unilateral sense; *my* husband, also in a unilateral sense. In divine–human Love, on the contrary, possession is always mutual and reciprocal, in a kind of relationship of equality in which all that is mine is yours and all that is yours is mine (Jn 16:15; Mt 11:27; Jn 15:11; 17:10):[176]

> *My beloved is mine and I am his.*[177]
>
> *I am my beloved's and my beloved is mine.*[178]
>
> *I am my beloved's, and his desire is for me.*[179]

Indeed, the degree of perfection contained in divine–human Love is impossible to attain in mere human love. Divine love establishes a relationship between God and His creature that places both on a certain plane of equality, which is characteristic of the highest

---

[176] In the lower forms of love in the hierarchical order, such as the love of simple friendship, the concept of *authority* does not appear. But the concept of *possession* is also absent in them, both in the unilateral and in the reciprocal sense.

[177] Song 2:16.

[178] Song 6:3.

[179] Song 7:11.

degrees of love: *And when I go and prepare a place for you, I will come again and will take you to myself, that where I am you may be also...*[180] *I will come in to him and eat with him, and he with me.*[181]

The *Song of Songs* speaks of divine–human Love presenting it as conjugal love. But with a curious peculiarity in this case, which seems to be contrary to what was said above with respect to conjugal love, since here the idea of authority is entirely absent. Since the Book revolves around divine–human Love, it is rather the assumption of a level of equality that is taken for granted throughout the Poem. That is why certain exclamations of the Bridegroom, addressed to the bride, which have a marked tinge of humble and begging pleading, seem normal:

> *Open to me, my sister, my love,*
> *My dove, my perfect one;*
> *For my head is wet with dew,*
> *My locks with the drops of the night.*[182]

Having this in mind, there is reason to think that the Inquisition could have spared itself the trouble of proscribing *Castell of Love*. If the issue of the divinization of the Beloved was what concerned the guardians of the Faith, such concerns were excessive and unnecessary. If they refer to this idea, as it appears in Diego de San Pedro's novel, they target the whole philosophy of Courtly Love.

For if the divinization of the Beloved does not go beyond the category of literary metaphor, there is no reason for concern. Especially if the metaphor is not very fortunate in this case, according to what has been said here.

---

[180] Jn 14:3.
[181] Rev 3:20.
[182] Song 5:2.

If, on the other hand, such dithyrambic expressions were to be taken seriously, the reasons for alarm would be even more unfounded. For if the divinization of the Beloved is understood as it sounds, *Courtly Love* is senseless and absurd; for such a category of love is even further removed from the notion of true love. Insofar as it is impoverished and blurred, by ignoring two essential qualities of love that tend to be perfect, which are equality and reciprocity. *Courtly Love* thus departs from the notion of true love and approaches that of purely human love, which is nothing more than a caricature of Love. In short, if it were to be taken seriously, *Courtly Love* would be closer to a nonsensical idolatrous worship than to true love.

Needless to say, with respect to divine–human Love, God remains God and the creature remains a creature. In fact, the creature would desire nothing else but to recognize the divinity of the Bridegroom, with the ardent desire that it should be so and not otherwise. Or to put it in the only possible way, however insufficient, in which one can express the inexpressible: the bride *desires* the Bridegroom as He is; simply because it is He, and no other. And that is why the saints expressed the sentiment that burned in their hearts by joyfully exclaiming: *God is!*

Curiously, however, no trace of divinization is found in the *Song of Songs*, either on the part of the Bridegroom with respect to the bride, or even on the part of the bride in her recognition of the Bridegroom. So, it could well be said in this sense that the *Song of Songs* is an atheistic book; and hence there have been more than a few who have thought that it is nothing but an epithalamic poem. Conclusions that would lead to nothing but a complete distortion of reality.

Lost Love 227

The Poem only wants to sing the ineffable glory of divine–human Love. But the reality of the betrothal of God with His creature — *mysterium tremendum*— is something *excessive*; at least in the sense that it far exceeds the possibilities of the human understanding and heart. Hence, to affirm that the event surprises man as entirely *unexpected* is always saying something, though not much.

That is precisely the reason for the peculiar literary style of the *Song of Songs*. And since the Book is not a catechetical treatise for the enlightenment and formation of neophytes, hence its apparent lack of didacticism. There is no reason here to insist on the obligation (*ob–ligare*), on the part of the creature, to recognize his relation of dependence with respect to his Creator and to act accordingly. Nor to proclaim, on the part of the Creator, the bond by which the creature remains entirely subject and linked to Him (*re–ligare*, from which comes *religio*). As if it were just another biblical book. Here it is a matter of singing the excellencies of divine–human Love, which, precisely because it is Love and in Its highest degree, is a voluntary, mutual, and reciprocal surrender in absolute freedom. Here the rights and prerogatives of the master and the obligations and duties of the servant are set aside, since Love places the lovers on equal terms and conditions: *No longer do I call you servants... but I have called you friends.*[183] The divinization of the beloved, as understood by *Courtly Love*, is further removed from the concept of true Love the more it is taken literally.[184] The book attempts to

---

[183] Jn 15:15.

[184] Within this same context, it is the kind of love that Don Quixote professed for Dulcinea; recall the heading of the famous Letter that was to be carried by Sancho Panza: *Sovereign and high lady...* (*Don Quixote*, I, 25). Cervantes ironically criticizes the expressions of love of the Knights Errant, exaggerated to the point of silliness but very typical of the time (direct or indirect references to *Amadís de Gaula, Florisel de Aniquea, Caballero de la Cruz, Don Olivante de Laura*, etc.).

sing of the most wonderful love relationship that has ever existed: the highest that could have been created by God and the highest that could never have been imagined by man. That is why it does not speak of lords and servants, of authorities or servitude, of rights and obligations... For in love all that is yours is mine, and all that is mine is yours; each of the lovers exchanges his life for that of the other; both engage in a loving competition to give more to the other; and if that were not enough, the victory in the struggle is not assured beforehand either for the one or for the other: *And he who had received the five talents came forward, bringing five talents more, saying, 'Master, you delivered to me five talents; here I have made five talents more.'*[185] True Love does not take place in a servant-lord relationship, but in a thou–I relationship: *I will no longer call you servants, but friends...* Once again, the divinization of the Beloved in *Courtly Love*, where the lovers appear on such different levels, leads to a relationship more similar to that of master and servant than to anything else. Of this kind, and following this same philosophy, is woven the love of Don Quixote for his idealized Dulcinea: *High and sovereign lady...* The true nature of Love has been obscured.

In any case, within this concept of true Love, the aforementioned equalizing takes place from the top down, rather than from the bottom up. As the genesis of the divine–human loving relationship demands, and even more so if we take into account that the initiative must necessarily come from God (1 Jn 4: 10.19). Nevertheless, the equalizing between those who love each other is real,

---

[185] Mt 25:20. The possibility of returning to the owner twice the talents received indicates the truth and reality of human cooperation. Everything ultimately depends on grace; even the fact that the freedom granted by God to man is not an illusion, and that the *game* of love is so real that either side can win the victory in the struggle (Gen 32: 25–33; Song 2:4).

even if here the concept must be taken in a rather ambiguous sense. Or in other words, insofar as it affects not so much the persons as such, but the state or situation in which Love places them (cf. Mt 10:24; 20:28; Mk 10:45; Lk 12:37; Jn 13:16; 15:20; Phil 2:6–8; as well as the episode of the washing of the feet at the Last Supper, in Jn 13: 2–16).

According to the texts, it could seem that the divine lover is placed, because of the love relationship, in a situation of *service*, which is the same as saying of inferiority, with respect to the human lover. This interpretation, taken in its extreme significance, would end up distorting the content of revelation.

The meaning of the texts must be considered as a whole, if a correct interpretation is to be obtained from them, taking into account, moreover, the sense in which they have been read by Tradition and the perennial ecclesial Magisterium. According to all this, the Word did not take a human nature of His own in order to be constituted as inferior or superior to man: *the Word became flesh*, which is the same as saying *true man*, no more and no less. The letter to the Philippians says indeed that He became low and took the form of a servant: *formam servi accipiens* (v. 7).[186] Then it adds that he became like men and equal to other men: *in similitudinem hominum factus; et habitu inventus ut homo*.

The attitude of service, according to the concept of true Love, is light years away from the attitude of servitude characteristic of *Courtly Love*. In the latter, the lover surrenders his freedom and renounces his free will: a concept incompatible with that of true Love, in which free will would be the last thing the lover would renounce, since such a renunciation would absolutely entail the disappearance

---

[186]The word *form* must be understood here in the philosophical sense, and not in the sense of *appearance*, unless one wishes to incur in the heresy of Docetism.

of Love. But the poets and courtiers of the late Middle Ages, Christian though they were, failed to grasp the depths of the mystery of the Incarnation: according to which, although it is true that the Word became Man to redeem humanity, it is no less true that He also made possible the true relationship of love between God and man. If the texts speak of an attitude of service on the part of the Incarnate Word, it is precisely to underline the infinite leap that, impelled by Love, He had to make in order to take a human nature for Himself: *semetipsum exinanivit*. And hence the texts themselves insist on the paradox: *You call me Teacher and Lord; and you are right, for so I am. If I then, your Lord and Teacher, have washed your feet, you also ought to wash one another's feet.*[187]

The attitude of service toward the beloved, determined by Love, in no way places the lover in a situation of inferiority: *A disciple is not above his teacher, nor a servant above his master.*[188] Such attitude does not respond to any obligation (*ob-ligatio*), but is the exclusive consequence of Love. Which is essentially freedom: the lover loves because he loves, and serves because he wants to, with nothing to impel him to do so apart from Love: *For this reason the Father loves me, because I lay down my life, that I may take it again. No one takes it from me, but I lay it down of my own accord.*[189] If the lover, as in *Courtly Love*, were to renounce his free will, he would cease to love at that very moment; since without free will there is no love: one loves because one loves. In fact, this attitude of service is nothing but the manifestation of a current of thought, apparently absurdly contradictory, which runs as a substratum through the whole Gospel: *Whoever would be first among you must be slave of*

---

[187] Jn 13: 13–14.
[188] Mt 10:24.
[189] Jn 10: 17–18.

all.[190] This current of thought is nothing but the consequence of the fact that God became man. This made it possible for man to learn to look at others before himself. To practice forgetting one's own self and to relegate oneself to the last place, in order to place others first and to prefer them, which is the essence of Love. Of course, after the lesson of humility implied in the Incarnation of the Word, the fruit of Love, any attitude of submission on the part of the creature is justified, while any posture of pride is destined beforehand to condemnation.

The divinization and excessive idealization of the beloved in *Courtly Love* leads to the conclusion that it is impossible to obtain her. In fact, the position of the beloved as something unattainable is considered essential in the courtly poets of the late Middle Ages, in the Provençal singers of *Courtly Love* and, in general, in a line of thought that reaches practically up to the Romantic Era. Hence the feeling of extreme dissatisfaction and sadness of the lover who knows he will never obtain the object of his desire: *The most unfortunate of all*, confesses of himself the character of the *Castell of Love*. With such premises the end of a Love, convinced that he will never see his desire satiated, can only be tragic; according to a forced outcome that places him at the antipodes of the true concept of Love.

The Christian concept of Love —which in divine–human Love reaches the maximum perfection that is attainable to the creature— is diametrically opposed to this.

In any case, it is interesting that the human mind has been able to incorporate the ideas of *sadness* and *dissatisfaction* in the most sublime of human passions. Since they are feelings so opposed to the essence of Love, it is difficult to explain, even though it is evident as a fact, the enormous state of confusion and distortion man's thought

---

[190] Mk 10:44. Cf. 10:31; Mt 19:30; 20:16; Lk 13:30.

is capable of reaching. When in reality Happiness, or Perfect Joy, is the only thing that satisfies man and the only thing that is sought by him, whether he recognizes it or not. Perfect Joy or Joy is the first result of Love; and since both are the fruit of the presence of the Holy Spirit, we must recognize them as the only reality capable of satiating man, whether on Earth or in Heaven: *You made us, Lord, for yourself, and therefore our heart will be restless until...*

According to the Apostle Paul, one of the first fruits of the Spirit is to provoke deep groans of longing, experienced by the human soul as it awaits the consummation of redemption and the consequent adoption: *We ourselves, who have the first fruits of the Spirit, groan inwardly as we wait for adoption as sons, the redemption of our bodies.*[191] But anyone who interprets such groans as feelings of sadness would be making the greatest mistake. Since their cause or origin is the Holy Spirit, they are outbursts of joy; although of such intensity and delight that the Apostle himself describes them, two verses later, as ineffable: *gemitibus inenarrabilibus.*[192] Moreover, to suppose that the presence of the Holy Spirit in the soul is capable of causing sadness would be absolutely unthinkable, as well as incompatible with the most elementary Christian teaching.

When the bride in the *Song of Songs* speaks of her anxiety over the absence of the Bridegroom, she does so alluding to feelings far removed from sadness or bitterness:

> *Sustain me with raisins, refresh me with apples;*
> *for I languish with love.*[193]

---

[191] Rom 8:23.
[192] Rom 8:26.
[193] Song 2:5.

Lost Love

In fact, the expression to *die of love* has passed into the common language of lovers to signify the sweetest and most beautiful of deaths; or better still, as the most sublime way in which human language can express the feeling of love, itself so deep and delightful as to be capable of *piercing* the heart. This would be the moment to recall the case of the mystical phenomenon of the *transverberation* of Saint Teresa of Avila, as well as her well-known expression *I die because I do not die*. Here the poets have the last word. For it is poetry, as has so often been said here, that can glimpse or foresee, even better than prose, something of the great Mystery by which (and for which) man was created and which, in the end, is what *moves the sun and the other stars*. Certainly the words flow here halfway between the world of metaphor and that of reality, without it being easy to be sure where one ends and the other begins:

> *If you should see me again,*
> *Down in the glen where the singing blackbirds fly,*
> *Do not say you love me then*
> *For, were you ever to repeat that sweet sigh,*
> *On hearing it, I may die.*

For of Love it can truly be said, according to the *Song of Songs*, that:

> *Its flashes are flashes of fire,*
> *A flame of Yahweh himself.*[194]

In the sermon of the Last Supper, Jesus Christ contrasts Christian Joy with the sadness and suffering caused by the world. And in

---

[194] Song 8:6.

the Gospel, the paradox of Christian life arises again: for it seems to indicate that Joy always follows the other two feelings, as if it were a result, an effect following its cause: *Truly, truly, I say to you, you will weep and lament, but the world will rejoice; you will be sorrowful, but your sorrow will turn into joy... So you have sorrow now, but I will see you again and your hearts will rejoice, and no one will take your joy from you.*[195] As if all this were a distant echo of some words spoken in the Sermon on the Mount: *Blessed are those who mourn...* And where it is also to be noted that Christian Joy, promised by Jesus Christ to His own, has its source and foundation in that they will see Him again: *I will see you again and no one will take away your joy.*

And can there be any other source of Joy than the loving contemplation of the reciprocal gaze of the loved one...? So much so that the eyes of the bride, which are *like doves through your veil* as the Bridegroom says,[196] are also capable of killing Him with love. That is why it is He who anxiously addresses the bride:

> *You have ravished my heart, my sister, my bride,*
> *You have ravished my heart with a glance of your eyes,*
> *With one jewel of your necklace.*[197]
>
> ....
>
> *Turn away your eyes from me,*
> *For they take me by assault.*[198]

---

[195] Jn 16: 20.22.
[196] Song 4:1.
[197] Song 4:9.
[198] Song 6:5.

Lost Love

For in Love everything is reciprocity and mutual self–giving: you for me, I for you: *I am my beloved's, and his desire is for me.*[199] But beware! For if the Master promises His disciples that no one will be able to take away their joy, it is because He is *speaking for this life*, and not making promises of an eschatological future.

Far away are the unhappiness and bitterness, with an almost always tragic ending, which the impossibility of obtaining the object so desired causes in the person in love. For this is how things happen in *Courtly Love* and, in general, in the sphere of worldly love. Once one has lost sight, not only of the *impetus of the first love*, but of the very object of true Love, there remains only the sinking into nothingness of the best human feeling. It is painful to think that men always had the light that could have illuminated their way within their reach. For *The light shines in the darkness, and the darkness did not comprehend it.*[200]

In an entirely opposite attitude, Saint Peter exhorted Christians by showing them the way that leads to true Joy. Which, according to the Apostle, is none other than Jesus Christ: *Without having seen him you love him; though you do not now see him you believe in him and rejoice with unutterable and exalted joy.*[201]

*   *   *

But I have it against you that you have lost the impetus of your first love... Words as surprising as they are mysterious in their content. For what can a Love that has lost its impetus mean, and to what extent is it still true Love? It is difficult, if not impossible,

---

[199] Song 7:11.
[200] Jn 1:5.
[201] 1 Pet 1:8.

to believe in the authenticity of a lukewarm Love; for it seems that the Spirit also abhors attitudes of apathy or idleness: *I know your works: you are neither cold nor hot. Would that you were cold or hot! So, because you are lukewarm, and neither cold nor hot, I will spew you out of my mouth.*[202]

The Letter to the Angel of the Church of Ephesus contains both praise and reproach. Which gives way to a question that seems logical: Does this statement amount to a reproach or not? Is it merely a warning?

According to the text the phrase seems to be a real accusation. The expression *I have against you* contained in the verse is sufficiently indicative. And it is further supported by what the Spirit warns next: *Remember then from what you have fallen, repent and do the works you did at first. If not...*[203]

Be that as it may, the loss of impetus in Love, or the diminution of the fervor of charity, is an immense misfortune. Maybe the greatest of all. And since true Love carries with it the note of *totality*, the evanescence of the initial fire is practically equivalent to the loss of Love; or at least, to running the risk of Its disappearing.

Also, having established that Love is essentially freedom, Its loss must necessarily be the fruit of a free choice of the will. This supposes the voluntary renunciation of the meaning of one's own existence; nothing more and nothing less.

For man was created to love, and that is the end to which he is destined. Therefore, and since Love signifies the meaning and the framework of his own existence, it is necessary to recognize that he was born to find his true life... by renouncing that which he considers as his own; since Love demands going out of himself, by forgetting

---

[202] Rev 3: 15–16.
[203] Rev 2:5.

and renouncing himself, in order to find and give himself to the *other*.

But it is worth adding an important detail. For the existential maturity of which we speak here, and which man is destined to attain, refers to the supernatural plane. In order to *realize* himself as a truly complete human being, man does not need an encounter with the *other*, despite what the *personalist* doctrines may say. The reference here is to the experience of true Love, which only reaches its authentic perfection to the extent that it can be shared by the creature in divine–human Love.

It is important to remember that Christian life is a process of *losing-to-find*, to the point that only in it is it possible for the disciple to attain maturity in Christ: *He who finds his life will lose it, and he who loses his life for my sake will find it.*[204]

This is because man is made for Happiness. Though not merely for an abundant happiness, nor for all the great happiness that it is possible to imagine; but for that which responds to a capacity of reception that is infinite (*You made us, Lord, for you; and therefore our heart will be restless until it rests in you*). And since man is a created being, which is as much as to say finite or limited, he will never be able to find such infinity in himself..., so that necessarily — whether he wants to or not— he will be driven to go *outside himself* to find what he lacks; otherwise he will never be able to feel satiated. Only God, Who is the Infinite Being, is absolutely self-sufficient and does not need to go out of Himself to find something that He might lack. So the conclusion is clear: man has been created to go

---

[204]Mt 10:39. Cf. Mt 16:25; Mk 8:35; Lk 9:24. *Truly, truly, I say to you, unless a grain of wheat falls into the earth and dies, it remains alone; but if it dies, it bears much fruit. He who loves his life loses it, and he who hates his life in this world will keep it for eternal life* (Jn 12: 24–25).

outside himself in order to fulfill his infinite longing for Happiness in something else.

But as we have already noted above, this makes sense when we consider the *supernatural* or ultimate end of man. This, since it is not due to him, cannot be considered indispensable insofar as it constitutes human nature as such. It is quite another thing that man, if he wants to attain the ultimate end for which he has been gratuitously and definitively destined, must orient himself toward the supernatural order.

But *personalist* doctrines completely disregard the supernatural order in their conception of the human being. And yet they consider the going out of oneself towards *the other* as an integral and indispensable component of the human being in the natural order. A departure from oneself which, on the other hand, is meaningless, inasmuch as each person is always obliged to respect the *truth* of the other. In short, what does seem to be clearly deduced from this whole set of theories is an enormous confusion about the concepts of human nature and love.

However, in man's quest for Happiness, the object he searches for cannot consist in *another thing*. For there is no creature in the Universe that can satisfy the human heart, since a capacity for infinity cannot be filled by finite things, however numerous they may be. Hence it follows that such an object capable of satiating cannot in reality consist in *a thing*, but only ultimately *a person*. And Love, by its very nature, can only exist as a *personal relation*.

Renouncing true Love implies the renunciation of attaining perfection and the meaning of one's own existence. Since Love consists in forgetting oneself, together with the impulse to *go outward* and *give oneself* to the other, its disappearance causes one to remain enclosed in his own self. A kind of solitary confinement is produced, like a cell where selfishness is held, and which in turn prevents any relationship with another. The one who is imprisoned is a true *self*, of course; a complete human being. It had been destined to reach a perfection —natural at first, and ultimately supernatural— through surrender to a *thou* that would have been made possible through Love; although now the subject in question is nothing more than a failed project, whose destiny is none other than the garbage can.[205]

The doctrine is best understood by turning to the parables of the talents (Mt 25: 14–30) and of the mines (Lk 19: 11–27). It often goes unnoticed that the command given to his servants, after distributing his goods among them, by the man who went away to a distant land, —*trade with these until I come again*— defines the meaning of Christian life. This was not a friendly suggestion, but an absolutely compulsive command. The result is well known. Both the servant who buried his talent and the one who hid his mine suddenly found themselves surprised, without having produced any fruit and in the most complete barrenness. And the fate of trees that produce nothing is well known: *every tree therefore that does not bear good fruit is cut down and thrown into the fire.*[206] Neither of them wanted to take the risk of working with them. Which is the same as saying that they refused to face the great Adventure that every man who comes into this world is obliged to undertake; traveling the narrow path that leads to Life, with all the consequent

---

[205] Natural perfection, or that which man was destined to attain through Love, is ultimately reduced to questions of detail; like the side dish prepared by the *chef*. In this sense, even the reprobate in Hell remain their own *selves*. Supernatural perfection, on the other hand, which belongs to another order, elevates man to a condition that was not due to him; although here too the *self* remains the same; for grace does not change nature, but perfects it.

[206] Lk 3:9.

obstacles along the way which one must overcome. They preferred to live their *own* existence, fearing to assume the risk of the battle that Love presents (Song 2:4): the same one that leads one to go out of oneself to give oneself to the *other* in a mysterious struggle of *who-surrenders-more*. In addition, there is a set of imponderables, accepted by Love, in which the only thing certain beforehand is giving up control of the course and meaning of one's own existence.

Precisely in this lies one of the strong points of both parables. In the recognition of the existence of such imponderables and in the way they are dealt with. Which boil down to two:

For, either the goods received can be returned to their owner, though increased, after they have been traded and made to produce; or else strictly what has been received can be returned to him, without more, when the force of what is necessary and unavoidable imposes itself.

The first supposes a voluntarily assumed risk. But which ends in a victory over the owner of the goods, since *more is returned to him than what had been received*. Is it a triumph of the creature, in a good fight in the contest of love with its divine antagonist? There is no doubt that this victory of grace, in which it would seem to indicate that grace itself has been overcome, is one of the mysteries contained in both parables and, ultimately, of divine generosity and Love. This is a consequence of the fact that divine–human Love is, among all the possible forms of created Love, the most perfect analogue of Divine Love. That is why God wanted this loving relationship to be absolutely real, unlike the other forms of human love, in which the fundamental ingredient is a mere endeavor which remains just an *attempt*.[207] And therefore, in order to make the human component (which is, after all, an integral part of a relationship that is bilateral and

---

[207] The way the spouses express their mutual love to each other is nothing more than a vain attempt to achieve a complete communion or a true exchange of lives; all things to which the *una caro* can never accomplish. The same happens with all the expressions of human Love: it is necessary to resort constantly to metaphor: *my love*, *my* life, *all* for you and *forever*, etc. It is true that metaphor always responds to a certain reality; although in this case it is meager and far from fullness.

reciprocal) clear, it must also remain open to every event: failure, of course; but more commonly and as a more normal thing, triumph... of either party. The only way for the creature to perceive it, from his point of view at least, is as a true and authentic relationship of Love.[208]

The second denotes a clear position of cowardice, to the extent that someone refuses to face the risk of the great Adventure of existence or the one who was destined to receive the *corona iustitiæ* after having fought the good fight (2 Tim 4: 7–8). And there is an additional consequence: the attempt to ridicule God, by means of a smugness that implies that His gifts and His gesture of Love are useless.

It is worth noting that both parables underline another of the fundamental notes of Love: bilaterality or reciprocity. Matthew's text expresses it by saying that *For to every one who has will more be given, and he will have abundance; but from him who has not, even what he has will be taken away* (v. 29; parallel text in Luke 19:26). Hence abundant giving, on the part of one of the lovers, is to be reciprocated with another giving no less abundant, in clear reciprocity: *give, and it will be given to you; good measure, pressed down, shaken together, running over, will be put into your lap. For the measure you give will be the measure you get back.*[209] The term abundance in this case is synonymous with *totality* in the human lover, namely: with his whole being (*a quo* term and *ad quem* term); on the part of the divine Lover (a quo term), His Infinitude is also affected... albeit to the extent that a created (finite) vessel such as the human heart can be filled (*ad quem* term).[210]

---

[208] It is true that divine–human Love is also reduced to an *attempt*. Although it must not be forgotten, after all, that it is an analogized Love and therefore created, although the most perfect; for there is only one Substantial or Uncreated Love.

[209] Lk 6:38; cf. 7:47.

[210] On the part of man, the terms *a quo* and *ad quem* are to be taken in the strict sense; whereas, as far as divine Love for His creature is concerned, the term *ad quem* would have only a relative sense.

On the other hand, a small, stingy, or cheap gift is not answered with another of the same kind, but with pure *nothingness*. In which the notes of bilaterality and reciprocity in the relationship are also saved: for the simple reason that a Love that is calculated, measured, and sparing is equivalent to pure nothingness. Love is always totality, as the Apostle taught: *Love bears all things, believes all things, hopes all things, endures all things. Love never ends.*[211] And to the rich young man, who assured Him that he had already fulfilled all the commandments, Jesus replied: *You lack one thing; go, sell what you have, and give to the poor, and you will have treasure in heaven; and come, follow me.*[212]

Indeed, because a Love that lacks the force of totality is no longer the *first Love*, the one which was once received in the form of an impetuous torrent, like a *spring of water welling up to eternal life.*[213]

* * *

When one reaches the zenith of his life, and especially in the time of its twilight, it can be scary to look back. One can fall into the deepest of depressions... if one discovers that he has missed the opportunity to live by Love and for Love: the only purpose for which he had received existence and the only thing that would have given it meaning. Moreover, the opportunity was unique and unrepeatable since he will never have another. Hence it has been rightly said that the only sadness is realizing you are not a saint.

Of course, modern man, after having clamed time after time — or so it seems— that the ideal was unattainable, has preferred to

---

[211] 1 Cor 13: 7–8.
[212] Mk 10:21.
[213] Jn 4:14.

abandon it. Actually, he has simulated to forget it. Even worse, he has not hesitated to destroy it, to expose it to ridicule and contempt, and even to persecute the few who still believe in it.

The Church itself seems to have been affected, in some way at least, by a sense of impotence. After more than twenty centuries of Christianity, the world finds itself more and more immersed in error, while the Gospel, on the other hand, is in retreat. Atheistic ideologies and the advances of an agnostic and skeptical, if not disbelieving, science are imposing themselves as prominent realities. Moreover, desertions of believers are increasing everywhere, while other religions are gaining new impetus. At the same time, faith in the Message of the Nazarene is waning in the very heart of the Church. It is not surprising, therefore, that today's Church seems to have *lowered the bar* for modern Christians, seemingly less athletic and robust, than the old ones. Hence, when one contemplates —for example— new beatifications and canonizations, it is difficult to avoid the idea that the modern Canon of Saints is no more than a draft awaiting its definitive editing, which will only take place in Heaven. Valid and legitimate, of course, but a draft after all.

However, this very thing —and many others— is proof that the world and the Church are more in need than ever of authentic holiness. It is in moments of darkness that light is most needed. And it is only when it seems to flee, in shameful retreat, that Faith becomes capable of overcoming the World (1 Jn 5:4). Like Hope, which is only effective when it has to act against itself: *spes contra spem* (Rom 4:18). And it is not lawful for a Christian to look back, much less to sin against Hope.

The most difficult test that the Church has to face does not consist in some kind of struggle against the World, which, in reality, can do nothing against her. The most delicate and dangerous test she has to face... is precisely against Herself. And, of course, she will also be victorious: *Portæ inferi non prævalebunt...* Even if the strongest enemies are not those who are outside, but those who have already managed to overcome the walls of the fortress and have entered inside.

Inimicus homo hoc fecit.[214] They will not be successful, however. For, while for the moment the Enemy will be able to diminish the intensity of His flames —*the impetus of the first Love*—, he will never be able to extinguish in the Church the Fire of what has always been true Love: *Caritas numquam excidit.*[215] For

> *For love is strong as death...*
> *Its flashes are flashes of fire,*
> *A flame of Yahweh himself.*
> *Many waters cannot quench love,*
> *Neither can floods drown it.*[216]

---

[214] Mt 13:28.
[215] 1 Cor 13:8.
[216] Song 8: 6–7.

*...Et oves vocem eius audiunt,
et proprias oves vocat nominatim et educit eas.
Cum proprias omnes emiserit, ante eas vadit,
et oves illum sequuntur, quia sciunt vocem eius*

(Jn 10: 3–4)

*Prædica verbum, insta opportune, importune,
argue, increpa, obsecra
in omni longanimitate et doctrina*

(2 Tim 4:2)

Quis enim filius, quem non corripit pater?

(Heb 12:7)

III

GOD CORRECTS THOSE HE LOVES

The Letter of the Spirit to the Angel of the Church of Ephesus is a discourse that contains (1) Simple doctrinal instructions: *He that has ears, let him hear what the Spirit says to the churches. To the one who is victorious, I will give the right to eat from the tree of life, which is in the paradise of God.* (2) Praises: *I know your deeds, your hard work, and your perseverance. I know that you cannot tolerate wicked people, that you have tested those who claim to be apostles but are not and have found them false. You have persevered and have endured hardships for my name, and have not grown weary... you hate the works of the Nicolaites, which I also hate.* (3) Admonitions: *But I have this against you, that you have abandoned the love you had at first.* (4) And even Threats: *Remember then from what you have fallen, repent and do the works you did at first. If not, I will come to you and remove your lampstand from its place, unless you repent.*

Well examined, the Letters of the Apostles in the New Testament are of the same style.

This is because human nature is a composite of virtues and weaknesses in which one or another may prevail depending on the individual or the moment. Unless you opt for a continued and resounding decision in favor of good (holiness), or maybe in favor of bad (evil or treachery), though it would be difficult to find any of them in a pure state. That is why it may be considered normal that the exhortations of the Shepherd to the flock might contain, according to the moment and circumstances, either simple announcements or praise or condemnations; with the probability that the latter may sometimes become threats.

The Exhortation to the Spirit of the Angel of the Church of Ephesus is doubly emblematic.

First, because it deals with a Statement that comes from the Spirit, it requires an attitude of docility on the part of those to whom it is addressed. Which demands, at the same time, certain conditions for the hearing to be effective; or, if you want to say it another way, so that the words of the Spirit may produce the desired effect.

Second, and in a different sense, since the Angel to whom the Exhortation is directed is also a Shepherd in charge of sheep, once he has been called to become an intermediary (*pontifex*) who transmits the Words received, he should perform that function according to the way and means the Spirit desires them to be carried out. We must keep in mind that the *Angels* of the seven Churches in Revelation are Shepherds in their turn, on whom rests the grave responsibility of assuming the role of *Vicars* in regard to the Great Shepherd of the sheep (Heb 13:20).[1] In such a way that their mission is none other than the continuation of the one that belongs to the Supreme Shepherd: *Sicut misit me Pater, et ego mitto vos.*[2]

Both in one and the other sense, every *Shepherd* of the Church, whatever his degree of responsibility may be, must take on obliga-

---

[1] Cf 1 Pet 2:25; 5:4.
[2] Jn 20:21.

tions regarding the Instructions received from the Spirit. First and foremost, to *listen* to them scrupulously, to dismiss any danger of error; and then to transmit them with fidelity to the sheep that have been commended to him. Here we see the trajectory followed by the Words from on High whose destination is none other than the members of the Mystical Body. In the first instance, the Supreme Shepherd, through the Spirit, to the Shepherd who received the mission of intermediary; then, in a second moment, from him to the sheep to whom he has received the charge of pasturing: *Go, then, and make disciples of all nations... teaching them to observe all that I have commanded you.*[3]

In other words, it is evident that there must be a double disposition on the part of the Angel of a Church with respect to the Words received from the Spirit. One that looks up, in order to listen to such Words, and then acting accordingly; and another that points downwards, regarding the best way to pass the pertinent teachings on to the rest of the sheep. All this is a logical consequence of the fact that the Angel of a Church is both, a member of the Flock belonging to the Great Shepherd of the sheep and, at the same time, Shepherd of the members of the Flock that has been entrusted to him.

Before continuing, and as a parenthesis, two points must be made for a better understanding of the issue at hand.

The first refers to the title of this chapter: *God corrects those He loves*. At first sight, this phrase could justly be interpreted as an admonition; but here it is taken in a more general sense of God teaching His own, which includes, as indicated above, both praise and reprimand as well as mere instructions for the journey.

The second has to do with the two texts chosen as a heading for this chapter: John 10: 3–4 and 2 Timothy 4:2. It is easily understood, regard-

---

[3]Mt 28: 19–20.

ing the dispositions of the *Angel* of the Church regarding the Words of the Spirit (referring one to the hearing and the other to the transmitting), that both texts concern better and more correctly the latter; though, in a broader context, both contain aspects that may apply in both senses. Regarding the text of Saint Paul, it seems to contain at the same time, both the notion of admonition (*argue, rebuke*), in the sense of Proverbs 3:12 (*Quem enim diligit, Dominus corripit et quasi pater in filio complacet sibi*), as well as the notion of patience and care that a loving Shepherd must show for his sheep (*in Omni longanimitate et doctrina*).

It is unnecessary to point out that the second moment (transmitting) depends on the first (hearing). You cannot *transmit* someone's words if you haven't heard and *listened* to them first. Having in mind also that, since the Shepherd or apostle is a mere *envoy* or messenger, *he has nothing of his own to say*; for there is no other way to fulfill a task that must be limited to conveying someone else's words (Mt 28: 19–20). If Christ had personally said, speaking of Himself, that *My teaching is not mine, but his who sent me*,[4] it is easy to infer the appropriate behavior of His apostles and envoys.

In the framework of Christian existence no one, except the Father, seems called to speak for Himself. Jesus Christ is but the Word of the Father (Jn 14:24). And regarding the Holy Spirit, Who never speaks of Himself but only of what He has heard (Jn 16:13), His role regarding Christ's flock consists of transmitting to it what He has heard and guiding it to *all the truth* (Jn 16:13, 1 Jn 2:27); which is none other than Jesus Christ Himself (Jn 14:6), at the same time the only and required Path to the Father.

It is worth mentioning the way Christians have generally understood the expression *all the truth*, transmitted by the Holy Spirit and only by Him. The *deducet vos "in omnem veritatem,"* of John 16:13, and the *docet*

---

[4] Jn 7:16; cf Jn 14: 10.24; etc.

vos "de omnibus," of 1 John 2:27, are usually interpreted in a minimalist way as *He will lead you to the truth.* When the truth is that the text speaks of *all the truth*, in such a way that the adjective often goes unnoticed; or at least is not read with its content's true strength.

Everyday experience shows that it is very difficult to find *pure and total truth* often. In the speech and writing of too many people —including, of course, well intended people— it is absolutely normal to find truth mixed with error. Ordinary language usually affirms this with the expression *give and take*: even in good books and speeches, it is not rare for the reader or audience to recognize that, even among multiple and profound truths (entirely admissible), errors or at least some inaccuracies may be found (which may not be acceptable). Or also it may happen that such true affirmations stop half way, in the sense that, for lack of profound erudition, not all is said (half or incomplete truths). The Church herself —Master of Truth, and always so prudent—, for example, reserves the attribute of papal infallibility only when it fulfills strict and specific conditions.[5]

All the truth is the exclusive purview of the Holy Spirit and is only possessed by those to whom it has been communicated; that is, by those who are entirely under the influence of the Spirit: *Animalis* autem *homo non percipit, ea quae sunt Spiritus Dei, stultitia enim sunt illi, et non potest intellegere, quia spiritaliter examinantur; spiritalis autem iudicat omnia, et ipse a nemine iudicatur.*[6] It would probably be an error to interpret the *animalis homo* necessarily as a bad man, but more as someone who is not fully guided by the Spirit. Even though what they say may not be understood as *stultitia*, it is evident that in it will not be found the most profound content, *quia spiritaliter examinantur*. That is how to explain that some exegeses of Sacred Scripture, overflowing with erudition, are lacking in spirit; by which they may facilitate without a doubt, regarding its scholarship, to the *cultural* growth of others, but in no way to the spiritual enrichment of souls.

---

[5] We do not enter here into the topic of obedience due to the Magisterium, in general, which presents itself in degrees that require obligatory acceptance.

[6] 1 Cor 2: 14–15.

The fidelity of the Shepherd of any Church[7] regarding his office as conveyor of the Word received, is not merely reduced to a matter of fulfilling an obligation, as normally might be believed, but becomes an authentic image of the Trinitarian Life. In this, the Father and the Son are the same entity (Jn 10:30), while the Holy Spirit, Who proceeds from both —*Qui ex Patre Filioque procedit*—, identifies Himself with Them in the reality of the same Essence. The *Word* lacks all sense without reference to *Him* Who pronounces it: which is a valid statement of universal character. But in the case of the Trinity, the identification (likeness) of the Word pronounced is so perfect regarding the Origin from where (from Whom) It proceeds, that both, along with the *Love Relation* that binds Them, are really identical in the infinite perfection of one same Essence. In the Universe of created things, on the other hand, things exist according to a certain parallelism (or more correctly, analogy) regarding its origin. But also in that Universe the fidelity of the Shepherd to the Word received is something more than fidelity, since it requires the Shepherd to identify with that Word; though the identification must be considered here as analogical regarding the Trinity. Even so, we cannot expect from here more than a resemblance tending to perfection: *He who hears you, hears me.*[8] And, if this were not enough, the Angel of a Church cannot forget either that his fidelity does not refer to a mere received *Word*, but to a real *Person*. In such a way that, as we will see later, the fact that the hearers don't

---

[7] It is easily understood that the term Church must be interpreted in each case according to its context, while sometimes, as in this case, applies to what today is known as an ecclesiastical district equivalent to a *Diocese*, at other times it includes the whole Body of the Church in general. Regarding the word *Shepherd*, it is superfluous to mention that it is always considered here in a New Testament sense, unrelated to any Protestant connotation.

[8] Lk 10:16.

perceive discontinuity between the Words received and the one who transmits them, depends on the effectiveness of Preaching. In this sense, the testimony of the Shepherd is not a mere *echo* of the Words received, but an element capable of making present among the listeners *that same Person* from Whom they proceed as its original source. Accordingly, the office of intermediation requires the virtue of converting the Shepherd to an *Alter Christus* as referred to in Galatians 2:20.

Nevertheless, the expression *alter Christus* must be taken in a strict literal sense, and not in a mere moral sense as it is usually understood. In this way, the faithful transmitting of the received Word, beyond making the Shepherd himself an *alter Christus,* what it truly does is blur his own figure before the Community, allowing Christ to be more easily perceived: *He must increase, but I must decrease*, as the Baptist said.[9] And it is even probable that the words of the Precursor also must be taken in a very strict sense. Since, more than decreasing or waning, the mission of the Apostle is to personally *disappear.* According to Christ, His disciples must renounce all their goods, including their very life (Lk 14: 26.33). And on many occasions the Master speaks of the willingness to *lose life itself* for love of Him. Insisting that it is referring to an attitude that those who desire to become His disciples must make their own,[10] which leads to think that such a quality must refer, with greater reason, to the Shepherds of His Church.

From here we may conclude that renouncing all *prominence* is an indispensable condition for the exercise of the office of Shepherd, so that the Word may be transmitted faithfully and produce fruit.

---

[9] Jn 3:30.

[10] Mk 8:35; Lk 9:24; Jn 12:25; Mt 10:39. It is evident that the expression *losing one's life* also refers here to bodily life.

We may say, referring to the Pastoral activity of the Shepherds, that the amount of harvest collected is usually in inverse proportion to the prominence exercised by the sower. To the extent of greater relief acquired by the person sent, the more dissipates the figure of Him Who sends him. In Christian Existence, only Jesus Christ has the legitimacy to use appropriately the *I am* (Jn 8:58; 13:19) as the First and Last point of reference, as the Alpha and Omega in the end (Rev 1:8; 21:6; 22:13). Regarding those designated by Him for the job of shepherding, only those willing to disappear can offer a guarantee of effectiveness. This is why the cult of personality, either expressly sought or merely accepted, leads always in Pastoral work to attitudes far from the essence of the Evangelical Message. In reality, neither the simple messengers nor the ambassadors need to use their creative skills; since regarding the first it is enough to deliver the message that has been entrusted to him and, regarding the second, it is sufficient to strictly abide by the instructions received from his Government. Nevertheless, the job of the *dispensers* of the mysteries of God is much more important and sensitive than that of these offices; from which it is essential to expect from it a strict and absolute *fidelity* (1 Cor 4: 1–2).

The issue is transcendent enough to merit being treated later and more extensively. For now, it is sufficient to emphasize that the topic of prominence has acquired relief in the Church, with ever growing intensity, beginning most of all in the last third of the twentieth century. The necessity for the *office* to be accomplished by a human being who is a *person*, makes the cult of personality an unavoidable danger. Realizing well that in speaking of inevitable, we refer not so much to the effect already produced as to the danger of its happening. But, since all humans are subject to the effects of original sin, the confusion of the office with the person, including the possibility of transferring the emphasis from one to the other, is a risk hard to dissipate.

As we may easily understand, placed fully in the realm of Pastoral work, the responsibility of the consequences —in the case where the danger becomes a reality— falls on the Shepherd with more intensity than on the members of the fold. First and foremost, it corresponds to him the job of *channeling* the devotion to his person, comprehensible and even desirable (even more so if we have in mind that humans act according to the *per visibilia ad invisibilia,* toward the final object to Whom it should be directed, which is none other than Jesus Christ. Not doing this will cause an inevitable deviation of cult from its proper object toward paths that have nothing to do with the framework of Christian Existence.

The cult attributed to the person of the human Shepherd, abstracting from the fact of its being done consciously or unconsciously by the sheep, may lead to a decrease in the cult owed to the Divine Person of Jesus Christ. Remember what was said about the figure of the human Shepherd needing to decrease so that the Supreme Shepherd may increase (Jn 3:30). Once again, the subtlety of the Enemy unfolds here by means of a refined sophistry that contains, as always, a mortal lie. For it seems logical that the enthusiasm for the person must lead, as a normal consequence, to devotion for the office; or at least that is what we may suppose. Nevertheless, the painful reality is something else, to the point that, in the end and whatever may be said, unbridled enthusiasm for the *human person* ends up becoming very like a mere human *fanaticism.*

The problem is related to the devotion to the saints. Both because of the enthusiasm they have generated during their life as well as the devotion they are the object of afterwards.

But the cult of personality has nothing to do with the devotion to the saints. The fervor towards saints has a certain centrifugal reality, to describe it in some way: oriented beyond the subject that provokes it, it always refers to Jesus Christ, where it reaches its fullness and receives its meaning. The fervor produced by theatrics, on the other hand, is always centripetal; namely: oriented towards itself, as the true object to whom it is directed. The faithful do not usually realize this fact, even though it deals with a very evident reality that is right in front of them; in such a way that a simple reflection should suffice for everyone to understand. And this would happen, but for the well–organized propaganda montage that is carefully impeding it.

The cult of personality of the idol, which has acquired so much prominence in the modern Pastoral work inside the Church, is nothing more than the result of accepting worldly standards. That is how theocentrism has been blurred, giving rise to anthropocentrism. In such a way that the quest for success and acceptance of the masses has taken the place of devotion to the Cross (in the end scandal for the Jews and folly for the Gentiles),[11] while Exhortation has become reduced to Psychology lessons... In short and to summarize, all this leads to the replacement of a supernatural religion with a rationalistic one, more in tune with the appetites of a world that no longer believes in God. Everything seems to indicate now that Catholic worship no longer proposes honoring God as its proper object, nor providing the faithful with the means that lead to salvation; but pretends more to arouse feelings of a psychological tinge, of a purely human content and finality..., whose main feature is the lack of supernatural substance.

Regarding Spain in particular, some bishops have decided to impose the use of regional languages in the Liturgy, even though they are known

---

[11] 1 Cor 1: 18–28.

and used by a very small minority, deferring in this way the use of the common Castilian language. Regarding the reasons that have led them to do this, it seems difficult to dismiss a certain desire for keeping a leading role, materialized here in the desire to ingratiate themselves with the System or the Power of the moment, whose progressive and antichristian ideology is well known.[12]

The damage thus caused to the faithful's religious sentiment is irreparable. Of course, other causes exist; though, in either way, the reality is that in regions such as Catalonia, the affair has led to the *abandonment* of churches (attendance at Sunday worship has become reduced to almost nothing) and, in general, the practical disappearance of Catholicism.

What is remarkable is that this imposition comes from the same people who prohibit the celebration of the Mass of Saint Pius V, claiming that Latin is an obstacle for the participation of the faithful in the liturgy and their *comprehension* of the text.

That is how Shepherds, forgetting their duty to protect and feed the sheep, take sides in favor of the enemies of the fold who desire nothing other than to devour it. This would be hard to believe if it were not for the obvious reality of the almost total disappearance of Catholicism in vast regions like Catalonia and the Basque Country.

Nevertheless, the Shepherds' desire to *receive the approval* of worldly Powers, accepting for this reason ideologies that are totally alien, not to mention enemies, of Christianity, is not only unknown to the gospel but also opposed to it: *Woe to you when all men speak well of you...!*[13] The Church, who has never considered attaining the applause of the world as her own mission, always has been convinced that her destiny winds through paths of opposition: *We preach of Christ crucified, scandal for the Jews and folly for gentiles.*[14]

---

[12]The imposition of regional languages, deferring the common language, does not comply to any trivial reality or the desire to procure an alleged *patriotism*. It is evident that it attempts to dissociate itself from a country— that had until now a sense of Homeland where Christian values and ideals dwelt— to introduce Marxist-Masonic ideology without opposition.

[13]Lk 6:26.

[14]1 Cor 1:23.

The urge to be in the limelight, striving to achieve *approval* from world Powers at all cost, contains a strange error of vision which, as may be expected, ends up being fatal. Evil, by its own nature, cannot pact with Good: if it did, it would include something good, which is so contradictory that it would lead to its ceasing to be Evil. The only applause that Shepherds could achieve in this way is nothing but contempt on the part of Evil..., and the most complete indifference, in addition to the loss of prestige, by the faithful.

And if it seems strange that something so obvious could go unnoticed, there may be an explanation. A Shepherd of the Church stops *having his feet on the ground* when he has lost contact with Heaven. We should not forget that every priest of Jesus Christ is a *pontifex ex hominibus assumptus pro hominibus constituitur*;[15] from where, if he fulfills the role of *pontifex* (bridge), he has been established as an element of union between God and men, by which the loss of contact with one of the ends supposes a disconnection with regard to the other. The lack of prayer and interior life incapacitates Shepherds from knowing the surrounding reality in which they must act; and of which they must be responsible in regard to the salvation of souls.

According to what has been said, before the *Angel* of the Church directs himself to the sheep, it is necessary to hear and listen. For how else is he going to transmit a Message that he is supposed to have received, if not in this way? Any Message of a Shepherd to his faithful loses its validity if it pretends to be original and not a mere transmission. Saint Vincent of Lerins said *Nihil innovetur, nisi quod traditum est.*[16] The Shepherd in the Church is none other

---

[15] Heb 5:1.

[16] The original phrase is from Pope Saint Stephen (254-257), but Saint Vincent of Lerins seems to have propagated it. He was a fifth century monk famous for his important work *Commonitorium* (the only one of his that has been conserved). Though he defended semi–Pelagianism in good faith when this doctrine was not condemned by the Church, his holiness and sense of Catholicity are beyond all doubt.

than a minister of Christ and administrator of the mysteries of God, subject to the strict obligation to guard the fidelity of his office (1 Cor 4: 1–2). If Jesus Christ said that *the words that I speak to you I do not speak on my own authority...; the word that you hear is not mine, but the Father's who sent me,*[17] any attempt to invent doctrine, by a Shepherd of the Church, is preliminarily disqualified: *Go and make disciples of all nations... teaching them to observe all that I have commanded you.*[18]

Therefore, before delivering any message to men, as something that proceeds from God, it is necessary that the Shepherd of the faithful take charge, in the most trustworthy way possible, of the content and meaning of that Message. Or, in other words, it is essential that the Shepherd hear and listen to God before addressing men. Even though this may seem an obvious truth, the cause for the innocuousness we have come to expect from the exhortations of our Shepherds is usually the indolence they show regarding prayer. If they do not speak with God, it is useless for the Shepherds to attempt to make themselves heard by men, and even more so to reach their hearts. Neither less or more.[19]

A prayer life, therefore, is an essential necessity for every Shepherd of the Church... if he truly desires that the sheep that have

---

[17] Jn 14: 10.24.

[18] Mt 28:20

[19] The almost total ineffectiveness of exhortations of Shepherds (homilies, discourses, exhortations, higher or lower ranking documents, etc.), is something that, since it is well known and universally admitted, does not require any demonstration. The empty temples, liturgical functions with sparse attendance by the faithful (including the total absence of the youth), and the general indifference, when not outright contempt, for the Hierarchy (high and low), which is observed everywhere, speak for themselves.

been entrusted to him may hear his voice. In one way or another, before talking to them he needs to hear and listen to God.

But hearing God also means talking with Him. For prayer is not a monologue; it is a dialogue, and even more than a dialogue. If even in the Old Testament, *the Lord used to speak to Moses face to face, as a man speaks to his friend*,[20] what can we say about the New, in which God has desired to establish a greater and more intimate relationship of friendship and love with man (Jn 15:15)?

Hence, we have been led by unexpected paths to the *need for dialogue*, though this time in a very different sense than the one used by *progressive* theology. Now we are dealing with God as an interlocutor, convinced that the effort of men to understand each other, without previous dialogue with Him, is mere futility. Even if Modern Ecumenical Pastoral Work, explicitly or implicitly, suggests the contrary.

The modern fever of *dialogue at any price* has been introduced in the Church thanks to *progressive* theology through initiatives and procedures whose main feature is excluding God.

But we are not dealing with simple carelessness. The misrepresentation of Revelation's content, along with the oblivion (or putting in parenthesis) of the Magisterium of the Church, is frequently utilized by certain ecumenical Pastoral work, according to which, the objective allegedly pursued is an effort to establish bridges with the *separated brothers*. And also with those who are not brothers, like unbelievers, atheists of any sign, members of esoteric cults, *Fraternal* Societies, more or less secret, and declared enemies of religion (see Masonry).

It is one of the most laughable endeavors by modern Pastoral Theory, but a very dangerous one. It seems to take for granted that dialogue possesses the virtue of acting *ex opere operato*: it is enough to put it into

---

[20] Ex 33:11.

practice for problems to automatically lead to viable solutions.[21] Medieval alchemists devoted their efforts to searching for the philosopher's stone and the potion for eternal youth..., with the subsequent failure that was to be expected. But modern theologians and pastoralists do not seem to be bothered by the facts that show the evidence of the uselessness of their endeavors.

Having mentioned in passing the *contempt for facts*, it may be worthwhile it to make an observation.

Contempt for facts, as a result of the option for an ideology, is one of the principles of Marxist praxis, as it is well known; as Lenin used to say: *And if the facts are against us... too bad for the facts!* Which is a clear option for Lies and contempt for the Truth.

What is not so well known is the undoubted reality that Marxist philosophy is still alive, more or less hidden, and influencing life in the West. And even less noticed is the fact that its praxis, after having influenced Catholicism for a long time,[22] is still enjoying relevance in the life of the Church, in its doctrine and in its practices. The fact, among others, that falsehood has been used, sometimes shamelessly, as an instrument in the field of doctrine proves this.

In the Faculty of Theology of an ecclesiastical University, considered for a long time as a model Institution and dependable bulwark of Catholicism, students are indoctrinated with theories that, besides turning away from truth, raise prejudices and negative attitudes against rightful dispositions of the Hierarchy. According to their teachings, for example, the sacrificial sense of the Mass, which had been distorted by the Council of Trent, had

---

[21] One of the most notable features of Utopias (the same could be said of ideologies) is their recourse to magic. Using a magic wand would be sufficient for pulling the rabbit out of the top hat. The same occurs with class struggle or cleaning up of structures by Marxism or with dialogue for *progressive* theology: applied in convenient doses all problems may be solved, as with the Balm of Fierabrás, in whose healing properties Don Quixote believed so blindly. After so many years of accusing classic theology of turning sacraments into objects (that produce magical effects), in the end these same detractors have ended up believing in the magic of spells.

[22] Mainly through *Liberation Theology*, though not exclusively.

to be put in its place by the Second Vatican Council.[23] They take this opportunity to hurl vitriol against Trent on the basis of doctrine from the Second Vatican Council.

The falsehood of the manipulation is so clear that it is not worth refuting. Though, in any case, there is something more here than a mere ignorance of reality. The truth is just the opposite. It is well known that the sacrificial aspect of the Mass, so brilliant and clearly highlighted in the Mass of Saint Pius V, becomes more diluted in the new Rite of Paul VI. There is an almost universal agreement that the latter (an attempt done apparently with ecumenical intentions) is more in accordance with Protestant theology; which, as everyone knows, denies the true sacrificial Character of the Mass. There is serious and abundant bibliography that demonstrates this.[24]

One Council cannot be discredited based on the doctrines of another. This approach is extremely dangerous, for it would be hurting the one who attempts it, like a double-edged weapon or a kind of *boomerang*. It is too evident that the argument turns against itself, insofar as, for the same reason, *one could argue against the Second Vatican Council starting from Trent*. And more so if we consider that the latter is a dogmatic Council, while Vatican II is purely pastoral, according to its own assertion. Furthermore, the Church does not use as a reference the doctrine of only one Council, but that of *all its Councils*. Keep in mind that all Ecumenical Councils, legitimately presided over and approved by the Pope, deserve the same level of acceptance by the faithful. Attacking any of them using another is an extremely dangerous and delicate maneuver, for it would

---

[23] University of Navarre Faculty of Theology. *Institutions of Sacred Liturgy.* 2007–2008 academic year. The information was given to the author by trustworthy students. Unfortunately, we do not believe that we are dealing with an isolated incident.

[24] There are numerous and well–founded studies on the topic. Though maybe the most important is the trilogy by Michael Davies: *Liturgical Revolution.* Three volumes: *Cranmer's Godly Order*, Roman Catholic Books, Fort Collins, Colorado, 1995; *Pope John's Council*, Angelus Press, Kansas City, Missouri, 1992; *Pope Paul's New Mass*, Angelus Press, Dickinson, Texas, 1980. Though this isn't the most serious part of the problem.

endanger the authority of all the Magisterium of the Church. Today's frequent practice, popularized by *progressives* since the Second Vatican Council, of brandishing the *spirit of the Council*, is nothing more than a crude manipulation. The only magisterial support the Church has always used is not the *spirit* of only one Council, but that which is derived from and based on *all the Councils*.

The Marxist principle of contempt for facts, regarding an ideology or preconceived ideas, reaches today a much greater importance than is ordinarily believed. This practice has even penetrated the Church.

Facing the grave crisis the Institution has suffered since the time of the Second Vatican Council, many have imagined, as the best way of combating it, to hide it or, even better, to completely ignore it. But *Progressive* theology and neo-Modernist Movements have gone even further: having in mind the adage that *the best defense is a good offense*, they have carefully worked to convince popular opinion that there is no crisis at all; to which the *media* and modern technological capabilities have effectively contributed to manipulating the masses. According to this new theology, the Church finds herself in a period of triumphalism like she has never known before: it is the *Springtime* of the Church, a period of flourishing and splendor never before seen in her History. It is futile arguing with facts that are there for everybody to see: empty seminaries and novitiates; Orders and Religious Congregations in a state of total relaxation; secular clergy in a state of moral ruin and abandonment, although not as bad as religious clergy; the loss of faith and the secularization of religion; declining Mass attendance that tends to zero,/; the almost total abandonment of reception of the sacraments; youth separated from the Church; Catholic teaching vanished; the disrepute of Church Hierarchy; the great multitude of those who call themselves *theologians* and oppose the Magisterium with complete impunity; the legislation of almost all States inspired by Masonic principles; etc., etc.

In current times, the last Pontiffs have started the custom of the so-called *World Youth Days*. Hundreds of thousands of young people meet in some important city of the planet, ready to show their faith in tumultuous acts of worship presided over by the Holy Father and attended by innumerable Cardinals and Bishops from around the World. A spectacular *show* and a magnificent indicator of the flourishing some attribute to current Catholicism. Furthermore, since the Holy See promotes and organizes such acts, and given their objective, faithful Catholics cannot but applaud and congratulate themselves on the success attributed to them.

Nevertheless, a serious reflection concerning these events must be made, always based on rational and just arguments. In point of fact, some days after the last of the *Youth Days* (in Sydney, Australia, July 2008), His Holiness Benedict XVI declared in an address that *in Australia he had the opportunity to meet the youthful face of the Church.* A beautiful phrase, without a doubt, given the Person who pronounced it, deserving of complete acceptance.

Nevertheless, as everyone knows, in civil life (which, unlike what happens in Church life, gives the impression of being *the only territory of reality*), both in large (or small) businesses as well as in the undertaking of any large sociological movements, *results analysis* does not usually factor in as a base either the content or the charm of beautiful words. Certainly, it does not feel bound by Literature or Poetry. Quite the contrary. It makes conscientious studies, including the input of thorough calculations of economic, financial, mathematic, and statistical data whose alterations are delicately scrutinized to the last hundredth, trying to surmise, as a matter of vital importance, if the management has ended with a balance of gains or losses.

Without a doubt, *Youth Day* is not a part of this type of activities, which also should not be an obstacle to examining diligently its effects. In the end it is also a *business*, though referring in this case exclusively to the good of the Church and the salvation of souls. And in this sense it is well known that *Youth Day* has lent itself to negative sorts of observations, which deserve to be taken into account since, apart from being well intended, are founded on clear facts that cannot be denied.

We know, for example, with all certainty that, among the young attendants, there were a number of activists organized by very determined groups that promote homosexuality and lesbianism, along with proselytizing Protestant sects and apologists of Judaism, that carried out tireless efforts, often very fruitfully. Equally evident was the circulation and abundance of contraceptives, as well as sex and drug consumption (there is graphic documentation that removes all uncertainty). Also, since at these tumultuous acts of worship the custom is to receive the Eucharist indiscriminately, mass profanation of the Body of Christ is more than a mere possibility. On the other hand, neither in this last event nor from any other *Youth Days* have there been any noticeable results regarding an increase in the Christian fervor of the youth: things have continued, when returning to their respective countries, *exactly the same as before*; and even a notable regression in the faith has been observed that no one has even tried to conceal.

But this is not even the most important thing.

Everything seems to indicate that there is general satisfaction simply from the mere fact that the event took place; as if this and no other had been the intended outcome. There is always, of course, somebody who may try to call into question the negative data we have just mentioned. But there is an absolutely indisputable fact: *the overwhelming reality that no one seems to have cared to examine the effect produced by Youth Days.*

Could it be that (consciously or unconsciously) they had not thought of any objective other than simply celebrating this event...? What would have been reasonable, as well as logical, is to take for granted the existence of sufficient pastoral motives concerning the spiritual benefit of the young people. But if this is true, have the Pastoral analysts, when the event was accomplished, thoroughly examined its results (favorable or not, also considering the negative aspects at the same time)? In any case, where and when have the results of such inquiry been published? The truth is that the few who have dared, almost always with good will, to voice objections have been silenced immediately: labeled as pre–conciliar, traditionalists, enemies of progress and, above all, foreign to the *spirit* of the Second Vatican Council. And everyone knows that any appeal to the *spirit of the Council* is the secret (though quite effective) weapon *progressive* theology brandishes to disqualify people who try to present any objections.

Those who receive the true mission of Shepherding in the Church (Heb 5: 1–4), must transmit to the sheep entrusted to them the Message of the Good News. For which, first, it is necessary to know it. The delegate should maintain a strict relationship with Him Who sends him and know His instructions. And only afterwards is when he is prepared to contact the recipients: *That which we have seen and heard we announce also to you.*[25]

---

[25] *Quod vidimus et audivimus annuntiamus et vobis* (1 Jn 1:3).

But the mere study of the Revealed Word by the Shepherd is not enough for handing out the Gospel Message. In order to carry out his mission effectively, he needs the graces given by the Holy Spirit, Who leads to the knowledge of Jesus Christ and to the whole truth (Jn 14:26); graces which are transmitted ordinarily through prayer, though never without it.

It must be stressed again how urgent and imperative it is for the Shepherd, or the apostle, to make prayer an important part of his life. Which supposes an intimate relation between one and the other and a mutual interdependence. Thus, as the exercise of Christian virtue makes prayer possible and steady, so the practice of prayer is essential for the functioning of a Christian existence.

Prayer life for the Shepherd of sheep is but a consequence of his need to hear the voice of God. The messenger must know the content and meaning of the message to be able to transmit it. On the other hand, it is impossible to reach the hearts of men if he does not have a familiar interaction with the heart of God. Any attempt at dialogue with men, in order to establish their salvation, lacks the possibility of success if it is not previously supported by dialogue with God.[26]

---

[26] We say *establish their salvation*, though you could say the same about any type of dialogue among men, as events are clearly demonstrating..., though only for those who want to see it. When man dispenses with God to construct his own Paradise, with the intention of raising himself to heaven in his own Tower of Babel, the final outcome is none other than making any mutual understanding impossible. Of course, the bottom line of this issue goes beyond a simple failure of communication. It is a verified fact that each person, when he limits himself to speaking his own language, at the same time does not usually have much interest in understanding others. *Personalist* philosophies would say, of course, that this fact is irrelevant, once we have established that any dialogue among men should strive to respect *the truth* of the other. The problem arises the moment it is stated that everyone possesses *his own truth*, which is tantamount to saying that the truth as such does not exist anywhere.

Luke 10: 38–42, which narrates the reception that the sisters Martha and Mary gave to Jesus, is an important reference concerning this topic. The text is quite profound, though simple at first glance, and has been commented on often throughout the History of Christianity. Studies on Spirituality have dedicated special attention to it, for easily understandable reasons. Moreover, the text raises many and profound problems for which definitive solutions still have not been found that satisfy everyone and end the debate.

And though the Bible is not a book of puzzles, it is evident that some of its teachings are difficult to understand, as Saint Peter himself recognized (2 Pet 3:16), although it is also true that human nature's weakness has a lot to do with the problem, as it always resists accepting what seems arduous or difficult.[27] At first sight at least, the text only purports, on the one hand, to praise the importance of prayer, with special emphasis on greater intimacy with God and, on the other, to insist on its precedence over action.

In spite of this, throughout the History of Christian Spirituality, this passage has been the object of diverse and conflicting interpretations.

One of which has to do with the reaction caused against a classic and seemingly too literal reading of the text which gives primacy to prayer in detriment to action.

---

[27]Depth of content does not mean necessarily difficulty of comprehension. The words of the Lord, which according to Him are spirit and life (Jn 6:63), are often extremely profound and at the same time exceedingly clear. But it is not unusual that human nature frequently resists accepting them. Maybe because they deal with hard–to–put–into–practice teachings, very different from the possibilities that the easy way offers (Mt 7: 13–14). On the other hand, the Devil has been able to spread the idea that holiness is against human nature; at the same time, he has taken good care to present the most heinous vices as natural, pleasurable, and praiseworthy.

This second interpretation, opposed to the one that opts for the superiority of prayer, is supported by the clarity of texts that prompt apostolic action. As can be seen, for example, in the conclusion of the Gospel of Saint Matthew: *Go therefore and make disciples of all nations..., teaching them to observe all that I have commanded you.*[28] To which we must add, among others, the content of certain parables; like the one about those sent to work in the vineyard or the *Parable of the Sower*. On the other hand, it is well known that *apostle* means *one who is sent*.

But the truth is that the classic interpretation never claimed to devalue an *active apostolic life* in favor of prayer. Observing clear facts that took place through the history of the Church in general and the Missions in particular are enough to confirm this. Regarding Christian Spirituality, the *priority* of prayer never led to taking for granted a disregard or contempt for action.

The problem could have been the focus of an objective study able to reach helpful conclusions. But, once again, facts and critical history had to yield to preconceived notions. A matter that, in general, usually appears with greater acuteness when the prejudices are the fruit of ideologies antagonistic to Christianity, aggravated in this particular case by its contemptuous attitude towards prayer. The result was starting a campaign against contemplative life, which grew in intensity from the moment that Marxism began acquiring more influence in the life of the Church.

The campaign was unleashed on both theoretical and practical fronts. Regarding the first, they spread arguments against the principle of the primacy of prayer. Without even bothering to insist on New Testament texts that glorify evangelization,[29] they emphasized more the convenience of abandoning a supposed *contemplation*, until now seemingly useless or of scarce effects, to urgently undertake

---

[28] Mt 28: 19–20.

[29] *Go out to the highways and hedges, and compel people to come in, that my house may be filled* (Lk 14:23); etc.

the *action* that would reform the world and its structures. It is easy to appreciate in these tenets the effect of the Marxist principle, which states that pure Philosophy has served no purpose until now; thus, the urgency of resorting to activity as the only thing that can transform the world.

Clearly, we can see here the influence of Marxist philosophy, which had acquired relevance in the life of the Church since the middle of the twentieth century. Maybe not for the majority, whose *laissez faire* attitude facilitated the plans of a well-organized minority aware of its objectives. According to Marx, faithful follower in this matter of the doctrine of Engels, Philosophy had been until now a useless and even harmful science, since it had been concerned with *contemplating* the world when its true job should have been *its transformation*.[30] It is clear that the Worker Movements of the time and the obsessive fever unleashed in the Church about the *Social Question* had a lot to do with the development of events.[31]

The idea of the necessity of action reached extensive propagation, though accompanied this time by another new one which was to give testimony.[32] Slogans that tried to justify if not the abandonment at least the withdrawal of prayer to a second plane, or maybe a

---

[30] Perhaps the decisive work by Marx on this subject is known as *Thesis on Feuerbach*, written in the spring of 1845 and published for the first time by Engels in 1888. The work had then the form of an appendix to the edition of Engels's book, *Ludwig Feuerbach and the End of Classical German philosophy*.

[31] It seems that, at least regarding the social aspect, the fever has died down some. For example, few remember the six thick volumes of Cardenal Herrera Oria, Bishop of Malaga († 1968), dedicated entirely to the Social Question (the latest edition of his work: Angel Herrera Oria, *Complete Works,* Biblioteca de Autores Cristianos, Madrid, 6 volumes, 2002-2006).

[32] Old and traditional ideas, that had always made up the structure of Christianity, were presented as marvelous discoveries unknown until then. Of course, now they appeared in a completely secularized attire.

third, became of common use; *Action itself is already prayer,* was one that circulated most among the clergy. And, as expected, soon the missing step was taken to set aside a life of prayer. Taking things to its ultimate consequences has always been a behavioral pattern of human nature.

That is how the abandonment was produced in the life of the Church, in the form of a full–on retreat. In this regard, the California Gold Rush, unleashed in the middle of the nineteenth century, was left far behind and greatly diminished. Almost all religious, friars as well as nuns, including cloistered nuns, hurried to altogether abandon convents and the contemplative life. Moved, as they said, by the necessity of *giving testimony* to the world. Which seemed to be saying that we had been without testimony during twenty centuries of Christianity. Meanwhile, secular priests abandoned the practice of the Divine Office, the rosary, and almost all *pious* practices which were carefully avoided as taboo. The necessity of being present in factories and activities of the working man's world was accepted without question, as well as in suburbs, and in general all the places where the world could be shown that the clergy *were with the poor.* From here came the abundance of priests who became plumbers, electricians, and involved in other trades.[33] It was not important that the solidarity with the working class translated into a spiritual abandonment of the upper class, the middle class..., and of course also of the working class: in general, of all the Fold which, presumably, Christ had commended to such Shepherds. It was necessary to show that the priest was a man capable of *being*

---

[33]This gave rise to a remarkable phenomenon quite ridiculous and even farcical, depending on how you look at it. The local priest was frequently unable to attend catechesis or assist the sick due to finding himself *fixing up* some residence. Moreover, these things had their perks, since the benefits of such occupations were usually much larger than those produced by priestly ministry.

with everyone (except with the high- and middle-class people, at that time already for the most part demonized), though the facts showed, as we have just said, that he *was clearly with no one.*

This fever regarding the *need of giving testimony*, that originated in the clerical world and reached its peak from the middle of the twentieth century, is one of the most interesting and strange phenomena that have affected the life of the Church in all her History. And, of course, it also became part of the way of thinking that led to the abandonment of prayer.

As we consider this phenomenon, it seems necessary to ask an initial question: about what or whom was it necessary and urgent to give testimony?

At that time, asking the question did not seem to have a difficult answer, since any one of those who took part in that tumultuous flood of ideas would have been able to respond without hesitation. It had to do with showing that the Church was with the working class and that the priest, of course, apart from being a man like any other, felt himself entirely committed to those who suffer, victims of injustice, discrimination, etc.

It was evident that the answers lacked any supernatural content, presenting a purely political or sociological orientation. According to which, and after affirming that the Church had always been with the rich, it was necessary *to demonstrate,* circulating the same socio-political criteria, that the priest was with the poor and that he himself, at the same time, was the first (or the least) among them.

This is not the place nor is it worth arguing against the heap of absurdities which at that time acquired recognized status in the Church. What is most remarkable is not so much the fact that they spread with such profusion, but that they were accepted without hesitation, without the least criticism. Here we are going to limit ourselves to a brief examination of what happened, from the point of view of Theology and Christian life.

Current ecclesiastical, and especially clerical, language was filled with phrases that caused deep impact on people, even though no one knew (and still do not know) its exact meaning; neither those who spread them, and even less those who listen.

That the meaning of words in the modern age does not matter as much as the fact that they *sound* good is a well–known fact, despite attempts to make it go unnoticed. That is why theatrical *farce* has turned into a daily *farce,* once the sound or appearance have more relevance than the source from which they proceed. *Appearance* prevails over *being.* That is why theatre has acquired a profoundly interactive character, where the stage and platform are prolonged toward the spectators and include them. As with the *Passion plays* that were celebrated in certain towns in which local people would take part. Only, in modern life, the actor-spectators usually forget their condition and believe they are living within reality. It is not surprising that the Church of old was an enemy of the theater and conceded it only gradually, though with certain suspicion, until it was fully accepted in the present time.

All these things show the attempt to introduce to Christian People the idea of the coming of a New Era, considered in reality as the only authentic one in the History of Christianity. According to which, the priest would be the testimonial bearer of commitment to the workers, the poor, the oppressed, the underprivileged, minorities, and, in short, with all the marginalized of the world. In any case, and to summarize in a brief and succinct sentence, the priest would be a committed man called to give a shining testimony of poverty. Charity (another word that became taboo) lost its pride of place among the virtues, giving way to poverty and its monopolized value in giving testimony.[34]

All this has caused great confusion. The truth is that the priest has never had the mission of giving testimony of *something*, but of *someone*;

---

[34]It is well understood that the System has never considered poverty in the meaning it has always had as a Christian virtue, neither as a situation of destitution or misery. Poverty is really nothing more than the repository for all elements that fight against capitalism, according to the purely socio-political tone it has been ascribed. Moreover, the *poverty* of the System is at the opposite pole to Christian poverty. The latter lacks everything, including its own reputation. The former loves to dress itself with all the characteristic elements of show business; consequently, it wants to call upon the people with abundant illumination and deafening acoustics, so that they come in a hurry to applaud, admire, and, of course, help it out.

namely a Person, who is none other than Jesus Christ. The mistake in this point has led to tragic consequences, just as an old American saying goes: *the over emphasis on the work of the Lord may lead to forgetting the Lord of the work.*

The priest's mission consists in being *another Christ*. That is why he must give testimony of Him and must act *in persona Christi* at all times. This is a fundamental truth upon which all Christian Pastoral work revolves and from which it draws its sense. We must not forget that the priest is sent to the world with the same mission with which the Father sent His Son Jesus Christ: Jesus said to them again, *As the Father has sent me, even so I send you.*[35] Jesus Christ Himself carefully conveyed this with the utmost clarity, which would later be confirmed by the apostles: *you shall be my witnesses in Jerusalem and in all Judea and Samaria and to the end of the earth.*[36] That is why the work of the priest must revolve around his identification with Jesus Christ, so that He is *the only thing* the faithful perceive, even though it must be done through the person of the disciple: *He who hears you hears me, and he who rejects you rejects me.*[37] Saint Paul, meanwhile, insisted that he was only interested in giving testimony of Jesus Christ, however his preaching was received: *For Jews demand signs and Greeks seek wisdom, but we preach Christ crucified, a stumbling block to Jews and folly to Gentiles: but to those who are called, both Jews and Greeks, Christ the power of God and the wisdom of God.*[38]

---

[35] *Sicut misit me Pater, et ego mitto vos* (Jn 20:21).

[36] Acts 1:8. Cf. 2:32; 3:15; 5:32.

[37] Lk 10:16.

[38] 1 Cor 1: 22–24. It is important to observe that the capital event of Christ *crucified* is still scandalous for many. Protests against social injustice, supposedly in favor of the marginalized of this world, are usually nothing more than a rebellion against suffering and the redemptive quality Christianity gives it. In these can truly be perceived a sense of rage and even hatred, together with the desire to eliminate the presumed causes of such injustices. However we look at it, there is no sense of love or any true desire to help those who suffer.

Everything is sufficiently clear: though Christian language has been conveyed by the same old words, the corresponding concepts have been entirely subverted.

We must keep in mind that poverty, like the rest of the virtues, *if it is not founded on Christ, does not make any sense.* Poverty as an end in itself lacks meaning, except as a sick sentiment of masochism. It is often said that Mother Teresa offered her life for the poor, though *simply for love of them in themselves,* without using them to obtain prestige as a saint, unlike others who did this. Nevertheless, such a way of speaking shows a serious ignorance of what constitutes the essence of Christian Existence.

That form of poverty *has nothing to do with the need of giving testimony of Jesus Christ.* Then what is it about...? Since being a Christian is, by definition, being a witness of Christ in every moment (Acts 10:39; 1 Jn 1:2), do they perhaps pretend to give testimony of poverty, but in an abstract form, without any reference to Christ? If that is so, what meaning does poverty have, *as poverty itself*?

Nevertheless, since Christian poverty is a virtue, it only makes sense from love and in Love: *If I give away all I have, and if I deliver my body to be burned, but have no love, I gain nothing.*[39] If there is something clear in all this business, it is the indisputable truth that mere poverty, disconnected from its foundation in Jesus Christ but still with the pretension of being a virtue, is nothing at all. What sense does it make to disconnect a virtue from all reference to love for a person? Can poverty, charity, or any other virtue exist *floating in a vacuum?* Regarding the topic of love of man for mankind, without the need to base it on the love for a God Whose nonexistence is taken for granted, we will allude to it later.

There is a gospel passage that contains important details regarding our topic. It is the passage about the rich young man, told by the three Synoptics.[40] According to this, regarding the request of the young man, after Jesus had responded that the way to the Kingdom of Heaven passes through the fulfillment of the commandments, and after clarifying that the requirement was fulfilled by the young man, Jesus adds a further observation, which is at the core of this passage: *And Jesus looking upon him loved him, and said to him, You lack one thing; go, sell what you have, and*

---

[39] 1 Cor 13:3.
[40] Mt 19: 16–30; Mk 10: 17–31; Lk 18: 18–30.

give to the poor, and you will have treasure in heaven; and come, follow me.[41]

If it seems convenient to pay attention to the two hemistiches of this sentence: *sell what you have, and give to the poor... Then, come, follow me*, everyone will agree that the first depends on the second. And, indeed, it is so, since the determining motive for leaving everything is none other than following Jesus Christ. If that were not so, why and for what purpose would the young man give away all his riches? It is evident that, for the revealed text, giving up everything only makes sense *when it is done with the spirit focused on Christ*, and only for that reason.

What Scripture really does is nothing other than prolong the dictates of common sense. Which maybe is not by chance. Giving away what you have for no reason that justifies it, or only to appear before the world as poor, is nothing more than the product of a type of dementia, hidden pride, or a penchant for ostentation. The human being, as a free and intelligent creature, only acts for *reasons*, whether natural or supernatural, or both at the same time. In this case, supernatural reasons would not exist. And regarding the possible natural reasons, we have to recognize that they would be difficult to find: whether the desire to give testimony of poverty to the world, or of solidarity with the helpless, or of protest against capitalism, or similar reasons, and taking for granted that it is about something like this, it is obvious that such conduct would recruit new reasons to justify it. Unless you only want to speak for the sake of speaking, accumulating words and expressions that have nothing to do with rational arguments but only with word games, which can go on for an infinite amount of time..., without ever going anywhere.

In some other place, Jesus even goes so far as to establish a *necessary* relationship between following His Person and abandoning all things: *So therefore, whoever of you does not renounce all that he has cannot be my disciple.*[42] In any case, renouncing all things has a supernatural meaning (since any other would lack relevance to the subject at hand), according

---

[41] Mk 10:21.
[42] Lk 14:33.

to Jesus, when it is motivated by the decision to follow Him out of love: and could there be any other reason to follow Jesus Christ?

Some, however, would be willing to object: of course love exists in that type of testimony, since it is about practicing poverty *out of love for the poor*, without needing to appeal to any other reference. Just like Mother Teresa of Calcutta did, according to popular opinion.

First, we must say that love for the poor merely for the sake of the poor, disregarding any supernatural consideration, is nothing more than an illusion. Perhaps the time has come for progressive theology to stop brandishing vain words, whose meaning and content never give reasons to justify them. Pure philanthropy, founded (by definition) on purely natural human reasons, is something too weak and fragile for anyone to put their confidence in. Is it true that the pure altruist, or the one who gives no arguments other than those that *are able to be seen,* besides maybe a pretended love for humanity in itself, is really not moved by other motivations? The multimillionaire who throws away millions happily to contribute, for example, to the fight against global warming, is surely not moved by any other reason than an ecological concern for the environment, maybe accompanied by the fear of the realization of a threatening future event?

But if we decide to do away with speculations based on suppositions, we still can lay hold of more convincing reasons surely well-equipped enough to undermine the bases of the theory of love for the poor merely because they are poor. Thus, for example, according to John the Evangelist: *By this we know that we love the children of God, when we love God and obey his commandments.*[43] Therefore, and always according to Saint John, we know that we truly love the sons of God (in this case the poor) *when we love God* and fulfill the commandments.

Clearly, this last reason, though conclusive, is only valid for Christians. Nevertheless, those that raise the flag of the theories we mentioned proclaim themselves as such, and even as the only ones that know how to interpret the authentic meaning of the Gospel Message. Unfortunately, nevertheless, it is evident that, for reasons known only to those initiated

---

[43] 1 Jn 5:2.

in *progressive* Theology, the *First Letter of Saint John* is one of the New Testament texts that most frequently goes unnoticed: maybe because of the problems it raises for some of the approaches of avant–garde Theology? Those that refer to Ecumenism, for example ...?

The world, as could be expected, has hurried to give its approval to all which, in a more or less explicit form, seems ready to discard the Cross of Christ. The intrepid fighters, bent on the cause against social injustices and heralds of their commitment in favor of the oppressed, will perhaps not offer any testimony in favor of Jesus Christ, though surely they will receive the applause and favor of the World. In any case, and since their testimony lacks any reference to Jesus Christ, it remains limited to themselves and provides them their fitting prestige: *Tibi soli honor et gloria!* In this way, the model of the worker priest, of the rebel nuns and monks, or of those committed to the underprivileged of the World whose cause they have embraced by adopting a voluntary poverty, appear with an aura of greatness in a society that looks upon them with admiration. Surely their conduct will not offer any opportunity for feelings of attachment to Jesus Christ to arise, though it will become very obvious that they are the undisputed champions of liberty, the daring detractors against social injustice, and the declared enemies of Capitalism. Or to say it more concisely: *they give a firm testimony for themselves* that is valid in a World which, from that moment, will be willing to applaud them with enthusiasm and not spare them any admiration.[44]

The only problem here, and not an insignificant one, comes from the perspective of Christian philosophy itself since, logically, the problem is supposed to revolve around a group of ideas directly concerned with authentic Christianity. Indeed, by an incredible contradiction, the approach

---

[44]Human existence is evidently filled with strange paradoxes. Because now is when these witnesses of poverty, self-proclaimed champions of the oppressed, are going to receive recognition and awards from the World. A recompense that may range, according to a wide variety of possibilities, from a mere aura of prestige, capable nevertheless of opening many doors that provide access to the abundance of possibilities the World offers, to paving the way to fame, influence..., and even to the reception of a Nobel Prize.

by which the champions committed to the poor, to the oppressed, etc., achieve prestige for themselves *seems to be entirely incompatible with Christian Existence*. Jesus Christ Himself disowned the idea and put things in their place: *If I bear witness to myself, my testimony is not true; there is another who bears witness to me, and I know that the testimony which he bears to me is true*.[45] It's true that Jesus specifies also in another passage: *Even if I bear witness to myself, my testimony is true, for I know whence I have come and whither I am going* (Jn 8:14). But He adds afterwards: *I bear witness to myself, and the Father who sent me bears witness to me* (8:18). The teaching is clear enough: though His testimony of Himself is true (because He knows well where He comes from and where He is going), He always counts on the testimony of another (the Father, the Spirit, the Baptist...) as if he is trying to establish that mere *testimony of Himself* is insufficient. Jesus, of course, considers the testimony of oneself in order to receive the approval of the World is null and reprehensible: *Not that the testimony which I receive is from man* (5:34). Regarding the testimony of the Baptist (1:7), it must be integrated in the collection of revelation that comes from on High, as the episode of the Baptism in the Jordan and the Spirit descending in the form of a dove shows. Apart from that, it was Jesus Christ Himself who took it upon Himself to confirm that the entire mission of the Precursor was something that proceeded from Heaven (Mt 21:25).

The doctrine that supported abandoning prayer in favor of action was indeed rejected as false and dangerous; nevertheless, the idea of the need for a compromise remained alive among Catholics who had not lost their head. On the other hand, the catastrophic results of renouncing prayer called for a reaction that finally appeared around the middle of the past century, though only partially and timidly..., to be abandoned again, this time definitively, after a short time; a trend that has continued relentlessly in the twenty-first century, in the midst of a full *Ecclesiastical Springtime* Thus, around the

---

[45] Jn 5: 31–32.

years that preceded the Second Vatican Council until the death of Pius XII (1958) and even during the Pontificate of John XXIII, the so–called moderate approach remained in effect.

According to this viewpoint, there is no incompatibility between a life of prayer and a life of activity; even more: both are necessary and depend on each other; with one proviso: a life dedicated exclusively to prayer is conceivable (contemplative life), but it would not be possible even to think of a fruitful apostolic action whose vitality is not founded on prayer.[46] Indeed, almost all authors of Spirituality, just like those of the History of the Church, have always agreed on the possibility of a symbiosis of both lives.

The most perfect paradigm is offered by Saint Teresa of Jesus and Saint John of the Cross, two shining stars of the mystical life. The Saint from Avila, or the nun of contemplative prayer par excellence, is known also by the nickname the *Wandering Nun*; her book *The Foundations* is but a brief summary of her intense wanderings through the roads of Spain, visiting and founding convents and confronting a multitude of incidents.[47] Regarding the poet Saint of Fontiveros, his constant trips through the lands of Castille and Andalucía along with the many vicissitudes and persecutions that marked his life, did not stop him from becoming the most qualified Doctor of the Church regarding contemplative prayer.

---

[46]Later we will have to return to the interrelation that exists between contemplative and apostolic life. The principle to be established is firm: just as an apostolic life without a previous foundation on prayer lacks coherence, neither is it imaginable to have a purely contemplative life that is fruitless for the life of the Church.

[47]*The Foundations* book is but a pale reflection of the many works and trips of the traveling, bustling, convent-founding nun, Saint Teresa of Avila. Its comparison to *Las Moradas or The Interior Castle*, and her autobiography is surprising. She analyzes in depth the problem we are talking about here: the perfect conjoining between a life of intense activity and the total immersion in the depths of contemplative prayer.

The problem was resolved, apparently at least. Active life is as necessary as contemplative life, both bound together in perfect syncretism and beneficial unity. Nevertheless, simplistic solutions usually ignore problems with difficult or unconvincing answers. In this case, difficulties appear immediately when you examine it, both in the theoretical and in the practical domain.

Regarding the practical domain, the fact that the doctrine has ended in a *debacle,* as we have said above, gives a clue about the possibility of its containing some error. The *perfect conjoining* of both sides of the coin (active and contemplative life), as usually happens in an overly perfect (and maybe unstable) balance, is something easier *thought about* in a theoretical universe than *observed* in the real world of praxis. Concerning Saint John of the Cross and Saint Teresa of Avila, and like people, we must recognize that they do not usually abound as normal and ordinary examples. And it is evident that what appears only as extraordinary cannot be established as the normal rule for ordinary living. We do not need to be experts in human nature to realize something very manifest: the facility with which we are inclined to the easier side of things..., overlooking instead the harder or more uncomfortable side. Sanctity is only attainable by those who, in addition to receiving a deluge of graces from on High (or precisely because of this), have demonstrated that they are capable of practicing a heroic degree of virtue. Or at least it was like that before the time following the Second Vatican Council.

The difficulties in the theoretical domain have even greater consistency. You can talk, as extensively as you want, about the ideal of perfect harmony and complementarity between the active and contemplative life. And doubtless it is an ideal to which all Christians, and especially those of a consecrated life, should aspire. But we know well that ideals, as their name indicates, point more to goals we must achieve than to realities that frequently are not reached. For example, what Christian, worthy of the name, would not aspire to the ideal of perfection or sanctity as the goal of their life? *Be perfect as your heavenly Father is perfect,*[48] proposed Jesus to His disciples. Here is a path we must follow whose end will never be reached. Among other things, because the purpose of such a command *is not to arrive at its effective culmination, but simply to encourage us to make the effort to put it into practice.* And once this has been fulfilled, *the objective has already been achieved.*[49]

Indeed, as extensively as you want —and it is even possible to adopt conclusions that satisfy intellectual concerns, if only momentarily. In this sense, the doctrine (otherwise so useful as an ideal to achieve) of the perfect union between contemplation and action fulfills its objectives.

At the same time, the above–mentioned doctrine cannot ignore such a clear and resounding gospel text:[50] But the Lord answered her, *Martha, Martha, you are anxious and troubled about many things; one thing is necessary. Mary has chosen the best part, which shall not be taken away from her.* So according to Jesus Christ, if we want to indicate what is essential in this case, *only one thing is necessary.* And if we establish a hierarchy of values, *Mary has chosen the best part.* Regarding indicating what Jesus is specifically

---

[48] Mt 5:48.

[49] This is another aspect in which gospel teaching is different from a utopia. The latter are unrealizable and deceitful, since they are presented not as true possibilities that should be reached, but as goals to which we must necessarily aspire.

[50] Probably, at least in this case, there is no intention of hiding or manipulating the text. But it does seem that there is a certain will to *skip over* the words of Christ; a light *forgetfulness,* more or less unconscious, that has the power to solve the problem, or at least to lead to thinking it has been resolved.

referring to as the best and only necessary thing, it is sufficiently expressed in this passage.

It is always possible to blur the differences the text establishes, of course; or to claim that they have at least lost their relevance and have become nearly imperceptible, and even to pretend that they have disappeared. But it is a risky maneuver, one that would induce some people to think of a possible manipulation of the text.

The final solution? The doctrine of the perfect conjunction can doubtlessly be admitted, at least as a working hypothesis and as an ideal to be achieved, as long as the *absolute necessity of* prayer and its primacy over apostolic activity is clearly established; hence the *relative necessity* of Pastoral activity and Apostolate. Well understood that their relativity never indicates that they are accidental; on the contrary, their undeniable necessity cannot go unrecognized: their accidentality would only be admissible when compared with the life of prayer.

Things are not good because God commands us to do them; God demands we do them because they are good. And something similar could be said about this particular issue. Without a doubt, the primacy of prayer and recognition of its greater necessity do not obey a mere divine precept. Some *ontological reason* must exist here that causes it to be this way. Maybe because God is Pure Act, or Loving Dialogue, *before* any *ad extra* activity.

We should have in mind that the *ad extra* works of God, like Creation or Incarnation-Redemption, depend on His most free will, where there is no necessity at all as far as God is concerned. The Nature of God (the Triune God), on the other hand, is inherent to His Being by strict necessity: God *Is* and cannot *not be*; and He is *how He is* and could not be any other way.

If we leave out the priority of time and focus on that of nature, we must conclude, as we have said before, that the Dialogue of Love in God is *before* His *ad extra* works. These exclude any concept of necessity, which is just the opposite of what happens in the *Being* of God. Hence Jesus' address to His Father in the Farewell Sermon on the night of the Last Supper: *Father, I want those you have given me to be with me where I am, and to see my glory, the glory you have given me because you loved me before the creation of the world.*[51] The love-dialogue, therefore, that here we could compare to *prayer,* always precedes any *action.* Even more, it is absolutely necessary, as we have seen; whereas any action depends by nature on free will.

This is how the words of Jesus to Martha, which have preoccupied scholars of Christian Spirituality for centuries, acquire their full meaning: *one thing is needful: Mary has chosen the best part, which shall not be taken away from her.*[52] If you start from the premise that human beings have been created in the image of God, destined furthermore to participate in the same divine nature, it is not difficult to conclude that Martha's *activity* is of the order of things that depend on *contingency*; while the love dialogue of Mary with Jesus, which, taking into account analogy, we may call prayer, is of the order of *necessity.* Jesus Himself confirmed this doctrine in other places: *"I cannot of myself do anything. As I hear, I judge; and my judgment is just, because I seek not my own will but the will of him who sent me."* [53]

The saints also understood it in this way. Maybe by intuition more than clear understanding, but it is undeniable that it was a

---

[51] Jn 17:24.
[52] Lk 10:42.
[53] Jn 5:30; cf 8: 26.40; 15:15.

certain experience for them. Hence the beautiful stanzas of Saint John of the Cross:

> *My soul is occupied,*
> *And all my substance in His service;*
> *Now I guard no flock,*
> *Nor have I any other employment:*
> *My sole occupation is love.*[54]

It is true that, according to the Saint, all of his being, during his whole life, was used *in His service*. But now, at the decisive moment, or having found the place where the authentic truth of existence can be perceived, is the occasion to give way to *the only necessary thing*. That is why, *I guard no flock, nor have I any other employment; my sole occupation is love.*

And also, the well-known stanza that closes his poem *The Dark Night:*

> *I remained, lost in oblivion;*
> *My face I reclined on the Beloved.*
> *All ceased and I abandoned myself,*
> *Leaving my cares forgotten among the lilies.*

In short, a time came in which *everything ceased* for Saint John. Though what is important is the fact that all his cares are not very essential for him, since he has no qualms at all in leaving them *forgotten among the lilies.* He has found, at last, the true meaning of his existence and that which is the only thing *that is truly necessary.*

Now we can better understand the real aberration of the phrase *action itself is already prayer.* Since not only are they absolutely

---

[54] *Spiritual Canticle.*

different things, but they also pertain to distinct orders of reality: one, that of necessity, and the other contingency. From here we can conclude that only prayer, apart from being important, is absolutely necessary. To abandon prayer, therefore, in favor of action or a supposed need to give testimony, only manifests the capacity of the human spirit to accept the lies and falsehoods of the Evil Spirit. And those who support this approach, which is causing such great havoc, can be termed, if it were possible to use irony, as ignorant fools.

As the Spirit of the Angel of Ephesus did, the Shepherd's job is to address the Flock that has been entrusted to him, to correct it, to lead it by the good path. But the term *correct* has here a more general character that normally includes, as we saw at the beginning of this commentary, a collection of instructions of a doctrinal character, without leaving out possible praise, reprimands, or even threats. Keep in mind that the office of the Good Shepherd includes two types of actions regarding the sheep themselves: first of all, to lead them to good pasture with which to nourish them; secondly, to free them from the threats of the wolf and other dangers that surround their lives. This twofold task will require him to lead and encourage them at certain times, as well as to reprimand and threaten them at others.

Up until now, this teaching is clear and doesn't offer any difficulty. But what would happen if the members of the Sheepfold were not willing to listen to the Shepherd and even less to follow him? And what if, additionally, there were a mass desertion of the Shepherds? Truly speaking, it would not really make much practical sense to try to figure out which of these two events came about first: the overall crisis of Faith in Christendom or the desertion of the Shepherds. In fact, the situation appears as a homogenous and simultaneous *whole*, though it would not be difficult to lay the blame at the feet of the Shepherds.

Anyone would say that these questions, formulated as possibilities in a time like the present one in which it is declared as categorical the existence of an *Ecclesiastical Springtime* and a post–conciliar revival, sound pessimistic and consequently false. Nevertheless, *the formulation of both questions reflects exactly the situation in which the Church finds herself nowadays,* which, on the other hand, is completely new in her history. Until now, it was always a question of evangelizing pagan (*pre–Christian*) Societies or continuing to shepherd already Christian ones; currently, it is totally different. For now it is about re-evangelizing *post–Christian* Societies which, after having known Christianity, have formally rejected it. Consequently, the work of the Shepherd wishing to be faithful to the mission that has been commended to him is, in these moments, extraordinarily difficult: an arduous and delicate job which, in a certain way, can be considered a novelty in the History of the Church and categorized, without exaggeration, as an *almost impossible mission*. Saint Peter already warned: *For if, after they have escaped the defilements of the world through the knowledge of our Lord and Savior Jesus Christ, they are again entangled in them and overpowered, the last state has become worse for them than the first. For it would have been better for them never to have known the way of righteousness than after knowing it to turn back from the holy commandment delivered to them. It has happened to them according to the true proverb:*

> *The dog turns back to his own vomit,*
> *and the sow is washed only to wallow in the mire.*[55]

---

[55] 2 Pet 2: 20–22.

The situation is serious enough, whatever the smokescreen and contrary propaganda tries to make believe, to encourage the thought that the predictions of Saint Paul are being fulfilled: *For the time is coming when people will not endure sound teaching, but having itching ears they will accumulate for themselves teachers to suit their own likings and will turn away from listening to the truth and wander into myths.*[56] We cannot deny the *possibility* that these words of the Apostle may be relevant in this moment, even if it does not seem likely. Everything seems to indicate that the prophecy could refer to any of the great crises the Church has suffered throughout Her history. Some of which, being as serious as the Arian heresy of the fourth century or the Protestant Reformation of the sixth century, are not even comparable to the actual tragedy. Those heresies centered on problems with the Faith, while the current crisis affects the sense of the very existence of the faith. On the other hand, while those Movements tore apart Christianity, the current ones are leading to a state of devastation bordering on *destruction*.

It seems more likely that we find ourselves near to the situation announced by the words of Jesus Christ: *And Jesus answered them, "Take heed that no one leads you astray. For many will come in my name, saying, 'I am the Christ,' and they will lead many astray. And you will hear of wars and rumors of wars; see that you are not alarmed; for this must take place, but the end is not yet... For nation will rise against nation, and kingdom against kingdom, and there will be famines and earthquakes in various places... And many false prophets will arise and lead many astray. And because wickedness is multiplied, most men's love will grow cold.*[57] There is not the least doubt that these words refer to a *universal desertion* from

---

[56] 2 Tim 4: 3–4.
[57] Mt 24: 4–6.7.11–12.

Christianity: *For false Christs and false prophets will arise and show great signs and wonders, so as to lead astray, if possible, even the elect... And if those days had not been shortened, no human being would be saved; but for the sake of the elect those days will be shortened.*[58]

According to the well-known American writer and analyst Christopher A. Ferrara, *It can hardly be a mere coincidence that immediately after the Council's conclusion in 1965 the Church suffered the ecclesial equivalent of a world war: a catastrophic decline in every aspect of her life, from the number of religious vocations to Mass attendance to baptisms and conversions.*[59] *Within a few years of the Council seminaries and convents emptied, while tens of thousands of priests and nuns defected from their vocations. According to the Vatican's own statistics, published in* L'Osservatore Romano *in 2006, in 1965 there were 455,000 Catholic priests in the world, but by 1975 there were only 400,000. That is, 55,000 priests left the priesthood within ten years after the Council. Such a mass defection of priests had never been seen before in the Church's history. To this day the Church has not recovered. There are now only 406,000 priests in the world, 49,000 fewer than there were 42 years ago, when the Catholic population was much smaller.*[60]

These data are years old. And it is difficult to avoid a sense of *euphemism* when we read the statistics published by the Vatican. In any case, it is evident that the situation has considerably worsened these last years. The crisis of faith has become practically universal in the Church.

Of course, this can all be denied and, in fact, many do deny it. Though we must recognize, given the evidence of the facts, that such a denial comes

---

[58] Mt 24: 24.22.

[59] For a definitive statistical analysis see Kenneth Jones, *Index of Leading Catholic Indicators: The Church Since Vatican II* (Oriens Publishing, 2003).

[60] *L'Osservatore Romano,* April 30, 2006, pp. 8–9, reporting on the publication of the *Annuarium statisticum Ecclesiae* 2004 by *Libreria Editrice Vaticana.* Christopher A. Ferrara, *The Secret Still Hidden,* Good Counsel Publications, Pound Ridge, New York, 2008, p. 25.

from assuming a voluntary blindness or a clearly ill will. It can also be denied that two plus two is four; or that the night follows day and vice versa. Faced with the crushing reality on display for the whole world, we can only think that the text cited above by Ferrara is but small evidence.

That is why it might be convenient to end this topic with much more authoritative testimonies, that may in some ways be called irrefutable. In 1968, Pope Paul VI said that *The Church is in a disturbed period of self–criticism, or what could better be called self–demolition.*[61] Similarly in 1973, the same Paul VI admitted that *the opening to the world became a veritable invasion of the Church by worldly thinking. We have perhaps been too weak and imprudent.*[62] A year earlier, in perhaps the most astonishing remark ever made by a Roman Pontiff, Paul VI declared that *"from somewhere or other the smoke of Satan has entered the temple of God. In the Church too this state of uncertainty reigns. It was believed that after the Council a sunny day in the Church's history would dawn, but instead there came a day of clouds, storms, and darkness.*[63]

Of course, such words of the Lord, or similar ones contained in the New Testament, do not authorize us to affirm that we are at the end of History: *But of that day and hour no one knows, not even the angels of heaven, nor the Son, but the Father only.*[64] Words of Jesus Christ that were also confirmed in the moments immediately preceding the Ascension: *It is not for you to know times or seasons which the Father has fixed by his own authority.*[65] It is not strange, therefore, seeing the warnings repeated throughout the Gospels: *Watch therefore, for you do not know on what day your Lord is coming.*[66]

---

[61] Speech to the Pontifical Lombard Seminary, December 7, 1968.

[62] Speech from November 23, 1973.

[63] Christopher Ferrara, *o.c.*, pg. 28.

[64] Mt 24:36.

[65] Acts 1:7.

[66] Mt 24:42; *passim*.

But using exactly the same argument and without needing to resort to any other, *we cannot either say that we are not fully in the Last Times*. It is something we cannot affirm or deny. The only sure thing, therefore, *is that of that day and hour no one knows..., and that because of that we must be prepared.*

On the other hand, it is also obvious what we are witnessing with our eyes. We are referring to the situation we alluded to before: the universal desertion of Christians, though many insist on denying it. The fact is that we are spectators, as well as members, of a Christianity that, no longer being such, tries to cover its agony with a profusion of *shows* and spectacular fanfare which, in the end, are empty. A Christianity that is all the time begging for acceptance from the World by way of a new Doctrinal Gospel. Characterized, above all, for having substituted supernatural values with ideologies and projects that never go beyond a purely human horizon.

By the way, one of the most impressive and alarming aspects of the crisis is the silence in which the Ecclesiastical Hierarchy seems to be immersed. In Spain, for example, at the end of Francoist Spain —when it was no longer dangerous— there were numerous *prophetic indictments* (as they were called) of a political nature; in sharp contrast, the Spanish Hierarchy, when confronted with the present situation of absolute [religious, social, economic, and political] decay, seemingly has nothing to say.

The intention of giving certain indictments a *prophetic* nature, lacking grave and serious reasons that could justify the action of the Holy Spirit, requires prudence and utmost care. Unfortunately, in current times, such requirements tend to be forgotten and the Holy Spirit is *conjured* everywhere, at any time, and without any special reason. As if He were a *self–service* dispensary, the Spirit frequently is thought to be found at the disposal of whoever desires to invoke Him.

During the late Francoist Spain, *prophetic indictments* were given the role represented by the prophets of the Old Testament, who denounced with God's voice the sins of the People of Israel or of its Kings and Governors. Indicting the People was totally baseless —*absit!*—, since it was supposedly downtrodden by the oppressive Dictator. In modern Spain, in spite of the absolute deterioration of the situation, there are no prophetic indictments. Surely, because of the lack of prophets, the Spirit seems to find Himself unable to make His voice heard in defense of the oppressed, despite the unfortunate chaos and emptiness in which the current society is immersed.

In contrast, so-called *charismatic, catechumenal, etc.* movements have proliferated abundantly throughout the Church, all united by the common denominator of referring to an intimate connection to the Spirit, Whom they claim to control at their whim; not only His charisms and His presence, but also His direct influence.

Those claims can be the object of controversy, if you will, but I am not the one called to judge that activity attributed to the Spirit and which, seemingly, keep Him continually dynamic in those Movements. If such actions are good or bad, legitimate or illegitimate, justified or illusory, respectable or reckless, *the Church has her Doctors*. For it is She to whom the judgment and ultimate responsibility corresponds regarding this issue; ours is but a respectful compliance, and, if nothing else, maybe the feeling of perplexity, for both feelings are not incompatible.

Our perplexity is based on the fact that the judgment regarding the action of the Spirit in the Church, which no one can doubt nor in fact does doubt, has always been studied with the highest prudence when referring to concrete actions and determined declarations. The Popes, for example, have declared *with all certainty* that they have been assisted by the Holy Spirit *only* when they exercise *ex cathedra* the solemn and extraordinary Magisterium.[67] Besides, the fact that a certain person attributes to himself the same assistance or inspiration of the Spirit, pretending (even implicitly)

---

[67] *Certainty* here refers to the assistance of the Spirit in a particular case, not to the normal and undoubted assistance of the Spirit to the Extraordinary or Ordinary Magisterium.

the compliance of others, is something the Church has always considered with such prudence that she refuses to give any official *confirmation*. Pope John XXIII attributed his initiative to convoke the Second Vatican Council to an inspiration of the Holy Spirit. But, as everyone knows, even in the case of the existence of an authentic *private revelation* received by the Pontiff, its official verification would have been impossible, and the faithful would not be obliged to make it their own, notwithstanding the reverential respect willingly professed to the Pope, of course. Although, we must recognize that the events that accompanied the History of the Council, both during its duration and mainly afterwards, all of them duly verified and universally known, did not precisely help maintain an attitude of good will among the faithful toward the possible authenticity of the *source* from which the undoubtedly pious wishes of the Pope proceeded.

Nevertheless, the issue we are confronting here is strictly theological in nature and deserving, therefore, deeper analysis.

The New Testament contains some very relevant words from Jesus Christ Himself in this context: *Spiritus, ubi vult, spirat, et vocem eius audis, sed non scis unde veniat et quo vadat; sic est omnis, qui natus est ex Spiritu.*[68] From where we get that the Spirit blows *where He wills* and furthermore, always according to Jesus Christ: *thou hearest his voice, but thou knowest not whence he cometh, and whither he goeth*. Which probably means that, since the Spirit is sovereign and infinite Freedom —*Ubi autem Spiritus Domini, ibi libertas*—,[69] His conduct is absolutely *unforeseeable*, apart from *unpredictable*, by human understanding. There cannot exist a relation of proportionality, and even less compulsion, between any human initiative and a *necessary* response by the Spirit. An invocation is not an incantation.[70] Any actions or invocations done by man, no matter how much they are really his and truly meritorious, are also the work of

---

[68] Jn 3:8.

[69] 2 Cor 3:17.

[70] Catholic Liturgy in its worship of the Holy Spirit contains examples of unfading beauty and such deep theological content as the invocational hymn *Veni, Creator Spiritus*: which is more than sufficient, by itself, to clearly distinguish between a humble and beautiful *invocation* and what could seem like an *incantation*.

Grace.⁷¹ In such a way that Grace is always Grace, always present even in the authentic merit merited by man. Though the human creature can (and should) *invoke Him* with humility and reverence, the Spirit *ubi vult, spirat*: blows where he will and when he wills. The truth is that a created intelligence cannot ever know the limits, nor the extension, nor the purposes of an Infinite Freedom. That is why it would be truly imprudent, to say the least, to say things like *the Spirit is going to blow here or there or in this place at that time.* Confusing a humble invocation with something comparable to conjuring suggests Pelagianism. Infinite and Perfect Freedom, which is an attribute inherent to Infinite Goodness with Whom Freedom identifies, is totally unpredictable for men, infinitely exceeding the capacity of a created being: *For who has known the mind of the Lord, or who has been his counselor?*⁷²

On the other hand, the claim that today's Church enjoys a new *downpouring of charisms*, as it happened in the primitive Church, would require a serious confirmation if it does not want to be considered as a meaningless anachronism. So far, the reasons or grave motives sufficient to give some credit to the authenticity of such a downpouring of charisms has not been given.⁷³

And even if those claimed charisms are authentic, we must keep in mind that the presence of charisms does not necessarily suppose the action of the Spirit (Ex 7: 11–12; Mt 7:22).

On the other hand, in the *First Letter to the Corinthians*,⁷⁴ Saint Paul seeks to regulate the abundant profusion of charisms in the beginning Church, to which end he insists that they should proceed with order and pursue the edification of all. At the same time, he leaves it well established that the most important thing is charity, without which all the other charisms lack value.

---

⁷¹*Now everything is grace*, said the Country Priest of Bernanos at the moment of his death.

⁷²Rom 11:34.

⁷³The approval by the Church of the Statutes of a certain Movement does not carry with it a confirmation of the authenticity of alleged charisms.

⁷⁴Chapters 12, 13, and 14.

The doctrine on the Holy Spirit, as we conclude from the Sermon of the Last Supper,[75] describes the action of the Paraclete acting as a *Messenger*, Whom the faithful are waiting for without knowing nor discerning the exact moment of His coming. Apart from that, His mission is none other than to bear witness to Jesus Christ and remind His disciples about the teachings they had received. Reducing His role to the mere promotion of charisms —which do not necessarily suppose His presence, as we have said above—, would minimize His Work to almost nothing. Truly, the unequivocal proof of the action of the Spirit is the presence of His *fruits*: *charity, joy, peace, patience, benignity, goodness, longanimity, mildness, faith, modesty, continency, chastity*.[76]

The Spirit is the *Sanctifier,* and His function is none other than to sanctify. It is He Who speaks with authority about Jesus, Who calls to mind and makes understood His teachings, and the only One that can lead souls to the Savior. No one comes to the Father except through Jesus Christ (Jn 14:6). And no one, save only the Spirit as we have already said, can bear authentic witness of Jesus Christ (Jn 14:26; 15:26; 16: 13–14) and speak fully of Him to make Him known. Regarding the sanctifying role fulfilled by the Spirit in the Church, it is too serious a thing to try to reduce it to a circus act: *The kingdom of God is not coming with signs to be observed; nor will they say, 'Lo, here it is!' or 'There!' for behold, the kingdom of God is in the midst of you.*[77]

The true *interior* Christian life is incompatible with any manifestation or anything noisy like drums and cymbals, just as authentic sanctity has always abhorred anything that could resemble show or performance as something purely satanic. And it is also convenient to remember the philosophy of one of the temptations proposed to Jesus by the Devil: a

---

[75] Jn 15 and 16.

[76] Gal 5: 22–23.

[77] Lk 17: 20–21. *Ecce enim regnum Dei intra vos est* (Nova Vulgata); *The kingdom of God is within you* (The New Jerusalem Bible); *Le Royaume de Dieu est au milieu de vous* (La Bible de Jérusalem). The Greek ἐντὸς acts here as a preposition, and means *inside of* or *inside* (cf. Mt 23:26). In any case, it excludes the idea of exhibition or outward performance.

spectacular wonder that would solicit a successful applause from the crowd and, at the same time, would provide an easy triumph for the fulfillment of His mission as the Messiah (Mt 4: 5–6). The fruits of the Holy Spirit, which are those that truly configure the framework of a Christian existence, have never sought applause or recognition from the World. This is why it has been said that our God is a *Hidden God*[78] as even the Prophets from the Old Law have recognized: *And a great and strong wind before the Lord overthrowing the mountains, and breaking the rocks in pieces: the Lord is not in the wind, and after the wind an earthquake: the Lord is not in the earthquake. And after the earthquake, fire. But Yahweh was not in the fire. And after the fire, a light murmuring sound. And when Elias heard it, he covered his face with his mantle, and coming forth stood in the entering of the cave.*[79]

The problem that afflicts a large part of current Christianity is more serious than it seems. We are not referring to hypocrisy carried out by men to be seen and recognized, as Jesus energetically denounced (Mt 6: 1–6). The crucial issue now is that *being* has been replaced with *appearance* at the core of Christian existence. Man has substituted the veneration and love for God in exchange for self-seeking, self-esteem, and consideration of others. We are encountering the elimination of an interior life animated and moved by the Holy Spirit in favor of psychological feelings which, by their nature, are nothing but purely human. In other words, the profound mystery of the love dialogue between God and the soul, known only by each other, has now been eliminated:

> *And then we will go on*
> *To the high caverns in the rock*
> *Which are so well concealed;*
> *There we shall enter*
> *And taste the fresh juice of the pomegranates.*[80]

---

[78] Is 45:15.

[79] 1 Kings 19: 11–13.

[80] Saint John of the Cross, *Spiritual Canticle*.

It is true that Jesus instructed His disciples: *Let your light so shine before men, that they may see your good works and give glory to your Father who is in heaven.*[81] But it is evident that the conjunction *that*, does not have in this case a sense of finality but purely of *causality.* The light does not shine so that it can be seen; it simply shines and so fulfills its function. The fact that Christians do not work to be seen is something that becomes sufficiently clear in the serious warnings of the Lord quoted before (Mt 6: 1–6). The light is a witness of Jesus Christ, well understood that the witness, by its own nature, never refers to the one who is giving it, but only to the other: *and you shall be my witnesses in Jerusalem and in all Judea and Samaria, and indeed to the earth's remotest end.*[82]

One of the serious problems the current Church is confronting is her frequent resorting to theatrical activity; or to describe it with more accuracy, the modern phenomenon of the *Church–spectacle.* We are referring to the Church of the large mass gatherings, of the massive World Youth Days, of the spectacular outdoor canonizations, of the large Assemblies and lavish parades of Bishops, of the Papal ministry obsessed with a continuous international itinerant bustle, of the universal downpouring of *Congresses* whose utility and practical outcome has never been known by anyone, etc. Not to mention the *Liturgy–spectacle*, practiced in so many places and which no longer seeks divine worship and the spiritual edification of the faithful as its main goal, but psychologically arousing the congregation in an assembly of purely human feelings without any supernatural content.[83] It is helpful to say it once again: Divine worship has been replaced by the

---

[81] Mt 5:16.

[82] Acts 1:8.

[83] It would be interesting to compare the spectacle that the last Ecumenical Councils offered: Trent, Vatican I, and Vatican II. The spectacular nature of this last one, even discarding the incredible effectiveness of the *media*, contrasts extraordinarily in magnitude and depth with that of the other two. Regarding the results, although they were important in all of them, not all agree as to their character: for some the Council of Trent deserves to be condemned like *delenda est Carthago*, while others, on the other hand, think that Vatican II has been the cause of the great crisis the Church is currently suffering.

worship of man, theocentrism by anthropocentrism, and what used to be sacred Liturgy has now been reduced to mere pop–psychology, very hard to recognize as part of what was Catholic Theology.

Confronted with the undebatable reality of the *Church–spectacle* there are three possible explanations:

a) This reality is nothing more than a manifestation of an exuberant vitality: the celebrated *Springtime of the Church* as a result of the Second Vatican Council. As Pope Benedict XVI said at the last World Youth Day in Sydney, *I have had the chance to meet the youth of the Church.*

b) It is a useless attempt to mask the state of crisis in which the Church finds herself. Ridden with a downpour of desertions, both in the ecclesiastical and in the lay area; having abandoned her supernatural mission and content; being concerned with a discredited Hierarchy in many places; attempting to give evidence of her vitality to the world in the only way that she is still capable and that the world is willing to recognize.[84]

c) Even accepting as true the good faith of some part of the Hierarchy and a great number of the faithful, the promotion and rise of spectacle–like activity in the Church is nothing more than the culmination of an intelligent and savvy maneuver by her enemies, specifically Masonry, that has shrewdly taken advantage of the desertion of the Company of Jesus and the infiltration of Marxism in the Ecclesiastical Organism.[85] Either way, undoubtedly, sooner or later, this phenomenon will break the faith of many Christians, as in fact is already happening.

The first hypothesis is entirely discarded by the facts. The intent and capacity to deceive, aided by the workings of an immense propaganda and the willingness of many to be deceived, also has its limits. In the

---

[84]Recognized according to worldly criteria, of course. The things of the Spirit are not able to be known (nor even recognized) by the carnal man of modern society (Jn 14:17; 1 Cor 2:14).

[85]Masonry has probably been the one which mostly influenced the desertion of the Jesuits and their Marxist infiltration; nevertheless, there is an interrelation of main causes and contributing causes: that the Society of Jesus was the inventor and propagator of Liberation Theology in all Hispano–America is a well–known and documented fact.

end, reality becomes undeniable. Every day we know better the history of the Church of the second half of the twentieth century, with sufficient and abundant documentation capable of undoing the maneuvers that have attempted to disguise the truth in many ecclesiastical circles.

The second explanation could be accepted with reservations. It possibly is accepted by many, and it may be quite close to the truth; nevertheless, it cannot be considered the most profound reason for a crisis the like of which the Church has not seen until now.

The third one remains, therefore, the most plausible explanation of all; but it is not the ultimate reason, merely the second to last in any case. Indeed, how was it that the activity of Secret Societies was present in the Church? What happened for the Ignatian Order, ancient and eternal defender of the Church, to deny its principles and even its Faith in the Church? How was it possible that Popes John XXIII and Paul VI could believe in good faith in the possibility of a sincere dialogue with Marxism? And the questions could continue. But the complete history of the Church, even that which remains simply *on the side of men*, is still to be written and certainly will never be written. Regarding the real and definitive history, or that which remains *on God's side* and is contemplated by Him, it will become clear someday, though as Meta History and not as History. Which means that the Book that contains the truth of all things will only be opened to the eyes of men at the End of Time, when everything will have occurred to give way to the *Ecce nova facio omnia*.[86]

Meanwhile, and in the sight of what is happening, Christians have no other way out than to realize in their lives the words of Saint Paul: *my righteous one shall live by faith*.[87]

And rightly so, because the true Christian knows that he is a son of the Church and cannot establish himself outside of Her. Though often the human part of Her is more visible than the divine; and the Hierarchy, or a good part of it, is corrupted, in a state of decomposition, and entirely absent to its duties of Shepherding. The true Christian knows the

---

[86] Rev 21:5.

[87] *Justus autem ex fide vivet* (Rom 1:17; Heb 10:38; Gal 3:11). The Apostle, in turn, is quoting Habakkuk 2:4.

need of being faithful to Christ and the demands of the Faith received in baptism and has in mind the adage *Ubi Petrus, ibi Ecclesia.* From there, the incontrovertible truth by which someone separated from Peter remains separated from the Church. For the Church, even when She becomes too human, is still the Church, just as the corrupt Hierarchy is still the Hierarchy. No one, outside of Peter (and his legitimate successors) has received the command to constitute himself as the foundation of the Church, or to found another that pretends to be the only true one. However just or right the reasons may be that one could brandish to disassociate himself from the Hierarchy (and for sure they are in full or in part), he loses his legitimacy the exact moment in which the separation takes place. He who separates from Peter, even admitting the possible depth and truth of the reasons (in full or in part) which he claims to support his attitude, *he loses all truth* when he separates from the legitimate Hierarchy, which is the same as saying to separate from the Church.[88]

Hence the need, today more urgent than ever, for the Christian to see the Church as She really is, namely: a true *Mysterium Fidei,* as is explicitly professed in the *Credo.* Configured at the same time as Divine and Human, the divine part is only observable through faith, while recognizing the human part depends on the simple fact that Christians have eyes and ears, which runs the risk of scandal for those who, incapable of transcending their senses, do not come to be grounded in the faith.

And returning to the *reasons for credibility:* was it really necessary for Pope John XXIII to sign the Pact of Metz with Nikita Khrushchev in August of 1962, by which the Church pledged to not condemn Communism at the Second Vatican Council nor even name it? A pact that was then ratified and maintained, in turn, by Pope Paul VI until the end of the Council...?

---

[88]That is why the rehabilitation of Luther makes no sense at all, for example, in spite of the many ecumenically convenient reasons that there may be to do it. *Ecumenically convenient* reasons would not be, in this case as in others, more than *politically convenient* reasons. And History is witness to the nefarious results produced when the Church has let herself be led by this type of reasoning.

We are not going to judge intentions. It is not our task, and we are convinced that the intents of the Popes were good. But *good intentions* have never been sufficient in themselves, neither were they in this particular case to prevent the immense damage the Pact inflicted on the Universal Church. The launch of *Liberation Theology*, along with the planned invasion of Communism in all Hispano–America, are only some of the direct consequences greatly facilitated by the Pact of Metz.

Moreover, it is historically demonstrated that both John XXIII and Paul VI were convinced of the universal and irreversible triumph of Communism. Thus the necessity (maybe this could be some of the *good intentions*) that the Popes probably felt to arrive at an *entente,* with the purpose of ending the persecution suffered by Christians in the Countries subject to the Marxist yoke. Everything seems to show that such good Pontiffs forgot that the Church has never done well speculating about History (present or future), since this science, just like Politics (interior and even more so exterior) are fields of knowledge and human activity that find themselves *outside of their jurisdiction.*[89] In fact, for example, the events that happened after the end of the Council sufficiently proved that the purpose of ending the persecution of Christians was never achieved. In fact, we know no one, absolutely no one, who has achieved anything good from a pact made with the Devil. On the other hand, the previous Church Magisterium (uninterrupted until Pius XII) had condemned Communism forthright.

An example regarding Spain is extraordinarily clarifying. What pressed Pope Paul VI so much in his passionate effort to establish the Christian Democratic Party in Spain towards the end of Francoism, to start the destructive and hidden (and not so hidden) campaign to bring down Franco? As we have said before, political maneuvering never ends well for the Church. The Pope's resorting to electing Auxiliary Bishops (almost all nominated were Philo Marxists) in following years, is visible to everyone, with the consequent disaster for the Spanish Church, whatever people may say. Christian Democracy did not work out. Fortunately, of course, for it

---

[89] We do not refer here, of course, to the *moral judgment* that does in fact correspond to the Church regarding events of History.

has been well established that the *Party of the Church* (mainly in Italy) is very prone to corruption and extraordinarily adept at leading countries to political disaster.[90]

There is a case still covered in historical mystery, if only in part, that has affected profoundly the life of the Church after the Second Vatican Council:

Archbishop Annibale Bugnini, Secretary of the Commission for Liturgical Reform at the Second Vatican Council, was accused at that time of belonging to Masonry. Though he denied the charge, the topic was the object of discussion often during the years of the Council and afterwards, especially considering that the Archbishop was the author of the revolutionary reform of the Catholic Liturgy and everything regarding the rites of the Mass. Michael Davies is one of the historians that defend the truth of the fact, arguing that the dossier that contained the proof against the Archbishop had been put into the hands of Paul VI.[91] Whatever may be, it is a fact that the Pope deposed him of his position and sent him as Nuncio to a far–off third world country. Which makes it difficult to dissipate doubts about the masonic condition of our character.

But Paul VI maintained the new liturgy of the Mass as it had been designed by Bugnini; probably because the Pope considered it valid and convenient for the reform that the Council was pursuing, though certain inexplicable aspects of this papal behavior cannot be easily cleared away.

It goes without saying that no one (or almost no one) doubts the validity of Paul VI's Mass, imposed on the whole Church since the definitive approval of the liturgical reform of the Second Vatican Council. Which, as is logical, has nothing to do with the fact that a large group of priests, in addition to having suspicions against Archbishop Bugnini (never fully dissipated), have lived in the nostalgia of the depth and grandeur of the

---

[90]The mission of the Church is not to found Political Parties. Her task is to ferment the dough, but in no way to organize the form and size of the bread, *marketing*, and giving timely instructions to the bakers. Regarding the problem of Paul VI and Christian Democracy in Spain, you may benefit from consulting Ricardo de la Cierva, *La Hoz y la Cruz*, Fénix, Madrid, 1996, pp 230 ff.

[91]Cf. note 24.

rite of the Mass of Saint Pius V. However, the priests who were ordained before the Council did what we were supposed to do, namely: *obey faithfully, without the least protest, the Church mandate.* And that's how for more than forty years, we have celebrated faithfully and uninterruptedly the new liturgy of the Mass. Always with a lacerated heart filled with nostalgia for the sacrificial sense of the Mass of Saint Pius V, so difficult now to *infer* in Paul VI's Mass. Convinced also that there could be no better *sacrifice* for us, and therefore no more complete Mass, than to submit to the dictates of legitimate Hierarchy.

Currently Pope Benedict XVI has authorized, as an Extraordinary Rite, the possibility of celebrating once again the Mass of Saint Pius V. The same one in which so many of us priests had found the pristine sacrificial meaning of our priesthood. After so many years it is as if we were young once again. In short, God has desired to give that Mass back to us before we can gloriously collect its fruit in Heaven.

Conclusions? The undeniable truth is that, the Church being a Mystery of Faith, there is nothing else to do but believe in Her and live according to Her commands. Without a doubt it is all part of God's plan for a true Christian —become a grain of wheat that immolates itself in the hope of tomorrow's seasoned fruits. For this and nothing else is Christian existence.

I remember a tense (though respectful on my part) conversation that I had with one of the various Bishops under whose jurisdiction I have lived. The Prelate in question, who was certainly a good person, suffered the weakness of not easily receiving suggestions of any kind; apart from tending to think that his knowledge, which included almost all fields of learning, knew only the limits that he himself had imposed; difficult to determine, in reality, given how far off those limits were.

We were conversing about the situation of the Church of the time and my concerns about it. My beloved Bishop, who as usual in such cases had a reputation for being *conservative* but actually was a complete *progressive*, expressed rather sourly his disconformity with my opinions. Not surprising, on the other hand, since he was a diehard fan of Karl Rahner.

Knowing what I was getting myself into, I wanted to make my Bishop aware of the profound uneasiness I had regarding the doubtful orthodoxy of the Theology of Rahner, which, in my modest opinion, had largely contributed to the enormous confusion and unrest that distresses the Church in these times. As could have been foreseen, my hierarchical superior became scandalized and even indignant about my opinions, too stale and conservative, apart from being entirely against the *spirit of the Council*, according to what he said.[92]

On my part I tried a timid counterattack, even though I was aware of my foreseeable failure. Indeed, Rahner was universally known as the Maximum Pontiff and Supreme Definer of all Post Conciliar Catholic Theology, after having been established as definitive Arbiter in the deliberations of the Council. I ventured to tell my Bishop that, nevertheless, it would be convenient to have in mind the life and conduct of the *Definer*, known publicly on the other hand and very little in conformity with the teachings of the Gospel. In the end, sincerity and honor of the opinions of men are backed by their life and works.

At that very moment, my Shepherd's patience ran out. With an irate and powerful voice, he warned me that meddling in the private lives of people was no business of mine. *Do not judge and you will not be judged.* Apart from the fact, he continued saying, that the private life of a person has nothing to do with his teaching; especially when it has the depth and richness of Karl Rahner's theology.

Respectfully I did not want to contradict my Bishop. I was older than him by a good number of years, and probably more experienced also; which could have been enough to deserve a more friendly treatment, in spite of my condition as a subordinate. And though I know that there was no

---

[92]This *spirit of the Council,* as I have come to find, is the secret weapon used by the *progressive* Movement to disarm possible opponents. Since everyone ignores what it consists of and how it works (it is a secret weapon), no one dares to oppose those who wield it. The users, as has been said, do not know anything either regarding the composition or handling of the weapon, and they really do not need to know, since its mere mention, as it happens to children regarding the *boogeyman,* is enough to cause panic.

cowardice on my part, it is now, with the passing of time, that I recognize that my conduct was not very wise. After all, respect (which I would never lack) is entirely compatible with the truth. According to which, I could have argued that, regarding a person that was recognized as the *Definer* of all Theology of the time, it was perfectly logical and normal to have in mind his conduct and his life. *You will know them by their fruit.* It is true that Jesus Christ forbade His disciples to judge a person as bad *without basis*, but in no way did He want to abolish the faculty of having opinions; without which any coexistence among men would be impossible. When, besides, according to Jesus Christ Himself, the only way to know people with certainty is by their works, or *fruits*. On the other hand, I had in mind Saint Paul's advice to Titus: for there are many, says the Apostle who *profess to know God, but they deny him by their deeds; they are detestable, disobedient.*[93] Where presumably, Saint Paul would not have intended that the life and conduct of such doctors might be ignored.

The Church is truly a *Mystery of Faith*.

We who are now old had known her as she was up until the death of Pius XII. After him came John XXIII, and he *opened the windows of the Vatican*, by which perhaps he let in the winds that afterwards made up the so–called *Springtime of the Church* —or maybe the *smoke of Satan*, according to the words Paul VI would use a few years after. We do not know the reason why the current moment of the Church is considered a *Springtime,* when what we who are already old really see is a Catholic Church in a state of desolation and decomposition. Even less do we understand why we are listed as pessimists and defeatists. Of course, if seeing things as they are is pessimism, then we can certainly be called pessimists.

However, we will be defeatists according to the language and thought of the world, but by no means according to our Faith; which, as is well-known, never admits pessimism: *Have confidence, I have overcome the world.*[94] And we count on two important promises of Our Lord: *Behold I am with you all days, even to the consummation of the world,*[95] and

---

[93] Titus 1:16.
[94] Jn 16:33.
[95] Mt 28:20.

specifically as referred to the Church: *And the gates of hell shall not prevail against it.*[96]

Nevertheless, at present we live in obscurity, immersed in a kind of *Kenosis* where it seems as if the Spirit has abandoned His Church.

This is why we embrace our Faith with more strength and confidence than ever before, knowing that Faith is *the substance of things to be hoped for, the evidence of things that appear not.*[97]

The assurance of things hoped for. And if hoped for, it is because we do not possess them now, and that is why detecting a devastated Christendom does not fill our spirit with fear. Since, indeed, we do not now possess what we feel nostalgia for and for which we ardently yearn. But we firmly know, by faith, that a time (or an end of Time) will arrive in which there will be a new heaven and a new earth, in which we may contemplate the Holy City, the New Jerusalem descended from Heaven, dressed up for her Bridegroom, and that will be the definitive dwelling place of God with men (Rev 21: 1–3). That is why, without Hope it would be impossible for us to go on living. Since nothing would make any sense if the World were simply what we are seeing, without being able to hope for anything else.

Now we better understand the fact that the Church is a Mystery of Faith. The same state of desolation in which we now see her is, at the same time, the *foundation* and guarantee of what we hope. In us is fulfilled to the letter, perhaps more fitting than in them, what is said of the Patriarchs in the Letter to the Hebrews: *These all died in faith, not having received what was promised, but having seen it and greeted it from afar, and having acknowledged that they were strangers and exiles on the earth. For people who speak thus make it clear that they are seeking a homeland.*[98]

We also know that we will die without having received what was promised. At least what relates to the possession of a Holy Church, as if in some way we knew her and had seen her in our dreams. We know that things will not be any other way: the current Church will not be

---

[96] Mt 16:18.

[97] *Est autem fides sperandorum substantia, rerum argumentum non apparentium* (Heb 11:1).

[98] Heb 11: 13–14.

followed by a Holy Church measured according to the present age: but only the new Celestial Jerusalem and the definitive Dwelling Place of God with men. And what we now see as the ruins and remains (which does not mean total destruction) is the certain announcement of her arrival.

From now on things will go from bad to worse with no turning back. Though never to such a degree as to make the Church disappear. A remainder will always endure —the *pusillus grex*—, that will be more and more purified in the crucible of suffering.

But thanks to the present desolation we have better understood and felt our condition as *travelers and foreigners on earth*. The truth is that we were always in danger of establishing ourselves as sedentary people, forgetting that we do not have a permanent city here and that we are rather looking for the one that is to come (Heb 13:14). If this were not the case, why would God have permitted the current situation...?

But Faith is also *proof of the existence of realities that are unseen.*[99] Or of the things that are not seen... and which would be convenient or necessary to see. Or also of the things that we see... and which would certainly be preferably not to see, since the definition of the *Letter to the Hebrews* could be understood in any of these ways.

And a Holy Church, truly concerned about Her *supernatural mission* of salvation for men, is now one of the things *we do not see*. Maybe because it is hard to see or perhaps to find here or there. The true Christian, who lives in the Church and forms part of Her, often finds himself in a truly difficult situation when trying to recognize Her; and more so when oftentimes almost everything around him seems to be an obstacle. This is why Faith is necessary, without which, his apostasy would be assured. Understanding well that Faith is not something for him like a remedy to a difficult and unfavorable situation, but a true *ontological necessity*: the breathing ground or the necessary environment in which he has to live (Rom 1:17) and the only way to please God (Heb 11:6).

Regarding the things we see and would preferably not see, they are too many and we don't need to make lists again that would fill thick catalogs.

---

[99] Heb 11:1.

Everything becomes complicated the moment we realize that we need supernatural awareness to be able to recognize the Church as Holy and Divine; whereas to see her Human part all we need are eyes and ears.

The issue here is not so much that the Christian must accept the content of Mysteries *that he doesn't see*, like the Holy Trinity or the Real Presence of Christ in the Eucharist. The real problem, today, is included in the contents of the Faith: *the mystery of the things that we do see.* For example, to name one of many, accepting that Bishops, as we know them, were selected by the Holy Spirit (Acts 20:28). The Christian now, as in all times, lives by Faith. But a Faith which accepts not only the mystery of things unseen —*rerum argumentum non apparentium*—, but most especially the things that we can see... and that it would be necessary to not see, namely: those that provoke pain when one sees the frozen winter into which they have converted the current Church, and, at the same time, have given rise to the Hope for the arrival of the true Springtime, whose moment is known to God alone —*substantia rerum sperandorum*.

Facing the state of desolation in which we find the Church, whose solution is removed from merely human means, what can a good Shepherd do who contemplates with anguish the confusion and waywardness of his sheep...?

He must, of course, adopt some attitude and undertake some determinations. First and foremost, he cannot allow distress to dominate him, so as to not fall into the sin of hopelessness, in the belief that *nothing can be done*. The lack of confidence in the final victory of the Lord, is a grave sin for any Christian and even more so for a Shepherd.

But regarding the specific way of acting, how must he proceed?

Preaching (content, style, fidelity and adaptation at the same time, frequency, etc.) is undoubtedly one of the most important activities he must face. Saint Paul's instruction must receive more relevance and actuality than ever: *preach the word, be urgent in season and out of season, convince, rebuke, and exhort, be unfailing in patience and in teaching.*[100] It is remarkable that the Apostle bases the seriousness of the exhortation to his disciple Timothy precisely on the gravity of the situation: *For the time*

---

[100] 2 Tim 4:2.

is coming when people will not endure sound teaching, but having itching ears they will accumulate for themselves teachers to suit their own likings, and will turn away from listening to the truth and wander into myths.[101]

And there is something very important the Shepherd must keep in mind in the present times: the possibility that his word (the Word) will be heard and followed by very few; and even that, *at least apparently, is not echoed by anyone.* Maybe it is good to repeat more insistently: *by absolutely no one.*

Any pastoral, and modern, planning needs to accommodate its strategy to the time in which it exists. That is why the Shepherd must know that, as we get closer to the end Times, the number of false Christs and false doctors and prophets will increase. *Difficult times will arise in the last days.*[102] And if one must always heed the advices given by Scripture, this verse deserves special attention, since current events make it strangely relevant. The Shepherd should not allow himself to be led by a confident security based on the words of the Lord according to which no one, except the Father (and only He) knows the moment of the Second Coming (Mt 24:36, Acts 1:7). Such words are in fact true, for they have been uttered by Him Who said that He is Truth itself. But equally true are His very words of warning about the tribulations of the end times, in that *we can sense their proximity in some way:* as with the fig tree, as soon as its branches becomes tender and put forth their leaves, you know that summer is near (Mt 24:32). For this purpose, and as a confirmation of what has been said, we must pay special attention to one of the most mysterious sayings of the Lord, precisely in connection with the events of the end times; we are referring to the strange expression, taken from the prophet Daniel, of the *abomination of desolation* (Mt 24:15). Of which Jesus Christ says that, in the Last Days, will be *standing in the holy place* (Mt 24:15). To what or to whom is Jesus referring with such an enigmatic expression? After twenty centuries of exegesis and commentaries on Scripture, no one knows. Nevertheless, we must have in mind that, immediately after this expression and in the same breath, the Lord adds another warning, no less interesting

---

[101] 2 Tim 4: 3–4.
[102] 2 Tim 3:1. Cf. Mt 24: 5.11.24.

for this purpose. Jesus expressly says *let the reader understand.* It is clear, according to this, that though it may be difficult (or very difficult) to guess what the expression refers to, *in no way will it be impossible to have at least some glimpse or sign that gives us the key to its meaning.* So, *let the reader understand.* The thing is that we are very used to disregarding Scriptural expressions that are either too difficult to understand or possibly too risky if interpreted correctly. We cannot imagine Jesus talking in hieroglyphics or with the intention of not saying anything; something that seems to have been reserved for the language of many members of the Hierarchy of the Church. It is true that at times the Master speaks apparently to not be understood by many, as we can see in the parables (Mt 13: 11–13); but in no way do we sense the intention that His words should remain a mystery forever: Why would Jesus want to do such a thing? Regarding this, for example, Saint Mark is careful to warn us that *With many such parables he spoke the word to them, as they were able to hear it; he did not speak to them without a parable, but privately to his own disciples he explained everything.*[103]

Maybe we should pay more attention to certain words of Saint John in his First Letter: *Children, it is the last hour; and as you have heard that the Antichrist is coming, so now many Antichrists have come; therefore, we know that it is the last hour.*[104] It is true that almost two millennia have gone by since the moment this text was written. Nevertheless, we know that the concept of *time* in Scripture is extremely delicate and hard to manage. Not in the sense that it has nothing to do with reality, nor in the sense that Scripture is using, in this point, a symbolic or metaphorical figure of speech. Quite the contrary: it is *real language,* even though we have not come to perceive it —probably because it exceeds the capacity of our understanding during our worldly pilgrimage— in all its mysterious depth. Accordingly, such an extreme difficulty resides only in us and not in the language of Scripture. Hans Urs Von Balthasar has already drawn attention to the apparent ambiguity of the concept of *hour* in the Gospel; in the sense that it is used, by Christ Himself, encompassing an advanced

---

[103] Mk 4: 33–34.
[104] 1 Jn 2:18.

future that nevertheless is capable of rolling back to the present: *But the hour is coming, **and now is**, when the true worshipers will worship the Father in spirit and truth.*[105] It is very probable, therefore, that the text of 1 John 2:18 is indicating to us that, though the action of the Antichrist will reach its climax in the moments immediately previous to the Second Coming, He is truly *already acting among us*.[106]

The informed Shepherd should have in mind the requirements that the loving care of the sheep entails. And that the Wolf, as a synthesis and compendium of the dangers that lie in wait for the sheep (He actually is the origin of them all), must be taken very seriously, with the consequent obligation to be vigilant and forewarned. The Word of God is one of the great concerns of a Shepherd because the Devil has a vested interest in distorting It by influencing those who proclaim It. And we must not underestimate the power and influence of him who, in the end, is the *Prince of this world* (Jn 12:31; 14:30).

This danger is extremely serious because Christ's statement that the Devil is the Lord of this world has never been taken seriously by Christians. They have simply considered this remark a type of warning about the watchfulness we should maintain towards Evil, along the lines of the advice of being vigilant given by Saint Peter in his First Letter (1 Pet 5:8). But we are not dealing here with a mere warning, but with the outright affirmation about who is the Lord of this World, endorsed also by Saint John in an even more forceful way (if possible) than the one uttered by the Master: *the whole world is in the power of the evil one*.[107] And if we add to this the words of the Apocalypse, according to which the Devil is the *deceiver of the whole world,*[108] we have a solid base, provided we are ready to grant the words their proper meaning, to fully explain the situation in which the current Church and world find themselves. Christ Himself

---

[105] Jn 4:23.

[106] The relationship between time and eternity, and even the concept of time itself, belongs to the order of many mysteries which are still to be researched and which, very probably, man will never fully clarify in the present eon. Scripture cannot help but use them indiscriminately, even though it is aware that its understanding by men will always be reduced to the most superficial levels of the arcane.

[107] 1 Jn 5:19.

[108] Rev 12:9 cf. 20:10.

warns us expressly about the negative influence of the Evil One regarding the preaching of the Word; He seems to indicate that the Devil can succeed, not only in distorting the Word, but even in impeding It, reducing It to nothing: *I will no longer talk much with you, for the ruler of this world is coming. He has no power over me.*[109] What is called, ironically by some though not without reason, *episcopal speech* is one of the manifestations of this phenomenon. If the Evil One gets Shepherds to never or almost never speak to the sheep; or that they do speak using empty and unintelligible words, or also perhaps foreign to the true problems of the Sheepfold, He has truly achieved a victory.

When the Shepherd of the sheep *has brought out all his own, he goes before them, and the sheep follow him, for they know his voice. A stranger they will not follow, but they will flee from him, for they do not know the voice of strangers.*[110] Here we notice the forceful declaration of Christ that the sheep do not follow a Shepherd *whose voice they do not know,* in a cause-and-effect relationship. It is not merely the fact that the sheep will not follow the Shepherd, they will even *flee from him*, because they do not know his voice. Statements that should lead us to reflect more intensely upon the extreme importance of preaching: *Quomodo credunt ei, qui non audierunt? Quomodo autem audient sine praedicante?*[111]

In this text from Saint John the concept of *stranger* applied to the Shepherd refers to the sheep that are commended to him. According to Christ's very words, the sheep stop following the Shepherd when they consider him a *stranger.* Which happens, according to the text, the moment *they do not know his voice.* And what may be the cause or causes for them to not recognize his voice?

There seem to be fundamentally two: Either because they never, or almost never, hear it, and consequently the sheep never get used to it. Or because they surmise that the voice is not the expression of the true Shepherd.

---

[109] Jn 14:30. Is the Devil able to block the fruitful result of the Word, or even to silence It, through his presence and action?

[110] Jn 10: 4–5.

[111] Rom 10:14.

Let us delve a little into this second cause:

First, how do the sheep perceive the falsehood of that voice that does not belong to the Shepherd? The Lord Himself gives the key to the problem. It has to do with the fact that who leads the sheep does not care about them, precisely because they are not his: *He who is a hireling and not a shepherd, whose own the sheep are not, sees the wolf coming and leaves the sheep and flees; and the wolf snatches them and scatters them. He flees because he is a hireling "and cares nothing for the sheep"* (10: 12–13). And the sheep notice that they mean nothing to the hireling beyond the benefit that they can bring to him. The hireling does not love them, and that is why, in a situation of danger, he will only look after himself without bothering about what might happen to the sheep.

There is something important here, which we already know but which may go unnoticed: the fact that all creatures of the animal kingdom, rational or not, *know how to perceive the presence of true love: when they are truly loved and when they are not.* That is why the sheep are conscious that they mean nothing, or maybe very little, to the bad Shepherd.

Truly speaking, the hireling does not even deserve to be considered a bad Shepherd. For the scriptural text, *he is not a Shepherd* (10:12). Something that many Shepherds in the Church should have in mind, but about which they usually forget when they accept the office only *as a position acquired, with guaranteed perks*; or, if the post is not important enough except as a steppingstone to achieving a better one.[112]

To this group we must add those Shepherds who stop giving pasture to their sheep for selfish, purely human, reasons. For example, either because they, simply out of cowardice, stop denouncing situations that hurt the good of the souls or even put their salvation in danger; or because they do not want to deal with possible complications; or because they want to keep receiving certain benefits or subsidies; or because, when all is said and done, they do not dare to confront the System and its powerful Propaganda Apparatus.

---

[112] Not a few Shepherds in the Church use the greater part of their time (including travel) searching for and managing possible influences, with the sole purpose of rising in rank.

In this regard, it is convenient to remember the terrible invectives from the Prophets of the Old Testament against bad Shepherds. Like Ezequiel, for example.[113] Or the irate sermons of the Fathers, like Saint Augustine, also full of strong words against them.[114] Rebukes that only follow the teachings of Jesus, echoing His Words, perhaps even more strong and more severe: *thieves and robbers* (10:8)... *comes only to steal and kill and destroy* (Jn 10:10)... *leaves the sheep and flees* (10:12).

Supposing that we do not find ourselves already in the Last Days, in which case the spiral of Evil will grow without anything to stop it until the very instant of the Second Coming; it is time to ask ourselves for possible solutions. The current crisis demands them, but many may never find them: either because we do not know (or do not want to know) how to find them, or because they simply do not exist. Nevertheless, given God's universal desire for salvation, we must admit that there must be some answers to confront this situation, seemingly heading towards despair.

Unfortunately, it is unlikely that such a solution will come from Church structures. Taking for granted that the Church finds Herself in a flourishing time called by many the *Ecclesiastical Springtime*, there is no reason to think about the need for reform. And that is exactly what is happening. The first thing a sick person needs to do, to get on the road to recovery, is to recognize that he is sick. But regarding the Church as a whole, one cannot see at present, whether in short, medium, or long term, a purposeful will to be faithful to the wishes of her Founder and a Tradition of more than twenty centuries. The last true reform that took place was the one started by the Council of Trent. Which, with the greatest irony called itself *Counter Reformation,* and that is why many have thought about the need of some *Counter–Spring*, capable of curing the Church of its current misfortunes. The first Vatican Council, whose internal history shows quite an agitated environment, was more worried about eradicating conciliarism and ensuring the authority of the pope. While Vatican II, with a much more agitated internal history than the former, did worry about giving a strong *impulse* to the Church; though, according to some, exactly in the opposite direction to the correct one. As for us, we do not think the

---

[113] Ezek 34: 2 and ff. Cf. Is 56: 9–11.

[114] Cf., for example, is very strong *Sermon 46*.

events happened exactly in this way, but it is only just to recognize that Powerful Lobby Groups, once the Assembly was finished, were very careful to turn the steering wheel a couple of times in order to correct the vehicle's direction at their will. And then...? This is the moment when the words of Saint Peter come to memory, as impelled by the wind, *Lord, to whom shall we go?*[115]

Here we see something similar to the problems that the Ecumenical Question poses and the solutions being given. Such difficulties can only be solved by the Lord Himself and *only by Him*, according to His own clear words: *And I have other sheep, that are not of this fold; I must bring them also, and they will heed my voice. So there shall be one flock, one shepherd.*[116]

Once again, the issue at hand is that salvation is not going to come without prayer and holiness. Solutions will actually be given, once again, by the *pusillus grex* of the poor of the world, as the authentic lovers of Christ will always be, and not by the High Ecclesiastic Policies nor the laboratory of Pastoral Planning. Which leads to the need for trustworthy Bishops full of Faith and love for Christ, as a previous and indispensable starting point. Their appointments will require that the selecting team —the Vatican, the Nunciatures, and Episcopal Conferences— give special priority, before any other thing, to what true Pastoral work and the good of souls demands. A measure which would be certainly followed by an extraordinary resurgence of both holy priests and laymen convinced and firm in the Faith of Christ.[117]

---

[115] Jn 6:68.

[116] Jn 10:16 It is important to note the fact that Christ speaks here in first person, referring clearly to Himself (*illas oportet me adducere*). It is He, according to His words, Who is going to bring the sheep back, and it will be *His voice* —His voice!— that the wayward need to hear to return to the fold. Once again, we see the tendency of human nature, generally too *natural*, to forget, or at least put in parenthesis, the words of the Lord. That is why we should not expect much of Mixed Commissions, nor of the policies of many Hierarchs of the Church.

[117] Although utopias remain always, or almost always, in the kingdom of *ideas* and fantasy, some of them, like this one for example, are the *only way* to seriously confront the problem we are dealing with. We may be before the only case in which

For the Lord reproves him whom he loves, as a father the son in whom he delights.[118] The Letter to the Church of Ephesus, as we have already said, contains grave admonitions and even threats: *Remember then from what you have fallen, repent and do the works you did at first. If not, I will come to you and remove your lampstand from its place, unless you repent.*[119]

Reprimands, by their very nature, are the fruit of Love more than of mere Justice. Above all they are acts of love toward the person who is being corrected; a condition that is not lost even when they add due punishment. We must keep in mind that, during man's earthly pilgrimage, God distributes mercy with open hand more than dealing out justice upon him. Unlike what happens when the time of trial has ended, in which mercy ends and gives way to justice. And since in God justice and mercy coincide, everything depends on the heads or tails of the coin that determines man's destiny before or after the moment of transit.

The *loving* character of correction is very clear in the texts quoted above, taken from the Book of Proverbs and Sirach. The same happens with each of the Seven Letters to the Churches in Asia in the Apocalypse, where feelings of tender charity take precedence over their repressive character.

---

a utopia, without losing its quality as such, represents an indispensable condition to reach the end. What we are saying is the present case would lose its utopian character if men really wanted to face the difficulty. We must have in mind that the concept of utopia is not a synonym for *impossible* to carry out, as Marxism has fully demonstrated. Someone may ask why then we continue to qualify the case we are considering as a utopia, and the response is obvious: *Because we do not hope that the problem at hand will come to be resolved...*, at least regarding the present eon.

It is curious that utopias rooted in perversion are capable of becoming real situations, contrary to those animated by goodness, which are always confined to the land of fantasy and dreams: *for the sons of this world are wiser in their own generation than the sons of light* (Lk 16:8).

[118]Prov 3:12. Cf. Prov 13:24; 23:13; Sir 30:1.
[119]Rev 2:5.

What is curious and interesting about this is that rebuke, even when accompanied by punishment, becomes part of the love relationship, sometimes as a necessary ingredient. Clearly, we would be dealing then with a condition of *still imperfect*, or not complete, love; where reproach, or maybe simple occasional complaints, by either lover still has a place.

As for God regarding His creature, the problem does not entail any difficulty. Given the weakness and imperfection of human beings,[120] it is logical, and even necessary, that God must frequently correct them. Though in diverse ways and different degrees of intensity.

The relationship between God and man is always a relationship of love. It was the reason for his creation and for the end to which he was destined: by Love and for Love. A different thing is whether man responds to the summons to love which God presents to him. But if the response is affirmative, then the degree of perfection achieved by the love relationship becomes relevant; which depends in turn on the generosity of the creature. To an ever more perfect relationship corresponds a different and peculiar aspect of correction which is more and more informed by love. Which means, in an apparent paradox, that it acquires greater degrees of intensity as love becomes more perfect, precisely for that reason. The mystics would talk here of the need for *Purification*, of the *Night of the Senses* or *of the Spirit* and similar terms, though the problem seems to go beyond such realities. To a more generous response of love by the creature corresponds a greater degree of *purification* or of suffering brought about by God, Who corrects man and directs him by the only way that leads to true Love.[121]

---

[120] Cf. Ps 78:39; Sir 18: 7–13; Job 4: 17–21, Rom 7: 14–25; *passim.*

[121] The narrow path of Matthew 7:14. If in addition to narrow it is steep and difficult, it is due to the fact that it is a means to *correct*, which amounts to the same as *straighten* or *put straight*. For the object of correction is to make something *straight*; or maybe *correct* it, which is the same. Hence, the path that leads to life, in addition to being narrow and steep is also straight; or what would be defined in geometric terms as the shortest path to arrive at a given destination. Divine *correction* is nothing more than another manifestation of the love of God for man.

What we are going to say now is based on the fact that the divine–human relationship has already reached a high degree of perfection. We are, then, on the path of true Love.

And since we are dealing with *correction* (whose end, as we already know, is to intensify and perfect Love), it is logical that an element of *suffering* may appear regarding the creature, as we have mentioned before. However, what precisely makes a person in love suffer most...?

In a relationship of true Love,[122] what makes the person in love suffer most is the absence of the person he loves.

But the *absence* which we are talking about here gives rise to the period the mystics and Spiritual authors would call *purification*, which is but the consequence of divine *correction* of the creature. A phase of the spiritual itinerary that also appears in the form of concealment or *kenosis* of the beloved, which in this case would be God Himself.

That God uses this type of correction, especially painful, with those He loves, and even more intensely with those He makes special objects of His Love, is something known and universally accepted:

> *Whither hast thou hidden thyself,*
> *And hast left me, O beloved, to my sighing,*
> *Thou didst flee like the hart, having wounded me:*
> *I went out after thee, calling, and thou wert gone.*[123]

This type of *absence* is opposite to that which those who have rejected God experience. This is a loving absence that causes nostalgic anxieties, lively hopes, and even, ultimately, an indefinable joy.[124] Whereas the ab-

---

[122]Regarding the manner of writing this term in this present work, whether lower or upper case, attention to the context will resolve any doubts. When the word refers to God (God is Love) it appears with upper case, and also when it refers to both the Love that has reached a high degree of perfection and the divine–human relationship of love, which is the only setting where such degree of love is achieved.

[123]Saint John of the Cross, *Spiritual Canticle*.

[124]The antithesis of suffering–joy is kind of a fundamental part in the divine–human Love relationship during the trial period. Remember the peculiar case of

sence of God, caused by the express and voluntary rejection by men, is but a foretaste of that which must occur, in a total and definitive way, in eternal damnation. Its essence, which cannot be described or perceived by human understanding in this life, is what Catholic Theology has always termed *pain of loss*. Regarding the loving absence, the pain and suffering produced by the concealment or disappearance of the Beloved, even with the presence of the suffering–joy antithesis, also surpasses any explanation framed in purely human parameters.

It is well understood that the absence of God, motivated by the express desire of men to *get Him out of the way*, should not be considered as merely referring to one or a few individuals, independently from their number. It *also includes a good part of the Institutional Church* as such: and here are included an undefined, though numerous, number of Cardinals, Bishops, Priests, and, in general, officially Catholic people who work and have influence in positions of grave responsibility.

The *Holy* Church, or Mystical Body of Christ, formed by the part of the Militant Church that has remained faithful, by the Suffering Church of Purgatory, and the Triumphant Church of Heaven, should not be confused with the *human* (too human) part of the Earthly Church: the one whose members have either clearly deserted their Faith (though many times they do not expressly admit it) or do not dare to proclaim it before the World because of cowardice (Mt 10:33, Lk 12:9, Rev 21:8).[125] The promise of Christ regarding the Gates of Hell that will never prevail against the Church (Mt

---

the stigmatized, in which Love seems to have reached a high level of perfection. Regarding the text of Saint Paul in Galatians 6:17, in which the Apostle asserted he was bearing in his body the marks of the stigmata of Christ, its meaning continues to be debated; though, whatever the apostle was referring to, undoubtedly, he was trying to express his profound sufferings and, at the same time, the intense joy he was feeling because of his intimate relation with the Lord.

[125]The *deserters* continue to form part of the Church unless they have expressly denied their Faith or have clearly fallen into formal heresy. But it is probable that the promise of indefectibility, made to the Church by its Founder, refers rather to the *living* Church, or Mystical Body of Christ, formed by those who in some way find themselves in communion with Him; as we will say afterward.

16:18) seems not to refer to this last one: *Super hanc petram aedificabo Ecclesiam meam*; where seldom do we notice the possessive adjective *my*, that accompanies the substantive Church. For it is *His Church* that will prevail, and not the merely human part formed by those who, in fact, have substituted love for Gospel principles with love for those of this World (2 Tim 4:10).

The episode of the people of Gadara is instructive in this regard.[126] The pigs of the Gadarenes were drowned in the lake at the intervention of Jesus in favor of a possessed man; because of which the Gadarenes asked Him to go away from their land: *they begged him to leave their neighborhood.*[127] Jesus acquiesced without adding a word. And what happened in Nazareth was even worse.[128] When Jesus finished preaching in the Synagogue, He was violently rejected and they even wanted to throw Him off a cliff; though He *passed through the midst of them* also in silence.

The bride of the *Song of Songs* also expresses her pain due to the absence of the Bridegroom. These arrays of feelings cannot be lacking in a Poem of divine–human Love. They manifest themselves in a discreet way when the remoteness of the Bridegroom is still not felt in all its bitterness, coinciding thus with the moment in which the bride still finds herself in the initial phase of merely searching.

> *Shew me, O thou whom my soul loveth,*
> *Where thou feedest, where thou liest in the midday,*
> *Lest I begin to wander*
> *After the flocks of thy companions?*[129]

---

[126] Mt 8: 28ff; Mk 5: 1ff; Lk 8: 26ff
[127] Mt 8:34.
[128] Lk 4: 16ff.
[129] Song 1:7.

Other times, however, since the absence of the Bridegroom is felt with greater severity, an immediate and anguished search by the Bride is provoked:

> *Upon my bed by night*
> *I sought him whom my soul loves;*
> *I sought him, but found him not;*
> *I called him, but he gave no answer.*
> *Will rise now and go about the city,*
> *In the streets and in the squares;*
> *I will seek him whom my soul loves.*
> *I sought him, but found him not.*
> *The watchmen found me,*
> *As they went about in the city.*
> *Have you seen him whom my soul loves?*[130]

The lamenting and complaining caused by the absence of the beloved, since Love has not been yet consummated in the Homeland, are inherent to this Love and their presence is mandatory in love literature of all times. Regarding divine–human Love, it is impossible for it to reach its perfection without walking the way of the Cross, the only way to share the existence of Christ and to consummate mutual Love. For, how could mutual love become perfect without previous communion of lives? From there comes the need, in this special love relationship, for purifications on the part of the bride, among which we must count in a special way what the mystics call *Nights,* caused ultimately by the purifying *absence* of the Bridegroom.

Nevertheless, a thorny problem makes its appearance here.

---

[130] Song 3: 1–3.

God Corrects Those He Loves

The Bridegroom, led by His passion for the bride and desiring a total Love, corrects her and *punishes* (purifies) her. So that she, a human being after all and also in love, expresses the pain of her heart through anguished lamentation. Nevertheless, as we have been insisting repeatedly, in Love everything is reciprocal and bilateral. According to which, and once we have established as evident that the bride needs to be the object of purifications, the question arises if we should expect also, from the Bridegroom, complaints and lamentations, possibly motivated, for instance, by the intentional absence or loving disdain of the bride.

We can go a step further and ask if some of these lamentations and complaints, in some way at least, could be blamed on the Bridegroom as caused by His own actions. The question could be posed in this way: the bride laments the absence and (apparent?) disdain of the Bridegroom, of which she herself is ultimately the cause. And yet, can it be stated, in possible reciprocity, that the lamentations and complaints of the Bridegroom can be based on His own conduct? The bride laments and cries out of pain and because of the absence that she has caused, as we have said. Nevertheless, when it is the Bridegroom Who laments and suffers, is it possible to say that such sufferings can be charged to Him? In other words: if the bride is the object of necessary purifications, could we say also that the Bridegroom must take over the suffering and pain that the business of love usually entails —at least as a previous phase?

And the response to both questions is undoubtedly affirmative. In the first place, for what we have already said: In the relationship of Love everything proceeds according to the promptings of bilaterality and reciprocity. From which we infer, if we admit that we are before a true love relationship (and in this case the most archetypical example), that it cannot lack such qualities, in the end considered as fundamental to the essence and concept of Love. And every relationship affects both parties.

In the second place, because Scripture proclaims it. The Sacred Poem, the *Song of Songs,* speaks of the divine–human Love relationship as a true combat: *and let his banner over me be love*, the bride says referring to the Bridegroom.[131] Remember also Jacob's wrestling with the angel, Who is none other than God Himself according to some texts which precisely tell the *victory* of Jacob.[132]

That the idea of *combat* appears contained in the concept of Love should not be surprising, and it even looks very familiar. Many times has divine–human Love been spoken about as the commencement of a real–life tournament, in which the question of *which of the lovers gives more to the other* is settled. And we have also shown, alluding to the parables of the talents and the minas, that man is capable of returning to God even more than he received: *Master, you delivered to me five talents; here I have made five talents more.*[133] On the other hand, if the tournament of Love we speak about here were not real, the divine–human Love relationship would not transcend beyond the realm of pure ideas.

The key to the problem, with its possible solution, has to do with the fact that God wanted to maintain a *perfect* Love relationship with man. For which, *it was necessary to place Himself on the same level and in the identical state as man.* By which we are affirming that man must rise..., or God must descend; or maybe both at the same time. And this is how another fundamental mark in the concept of Love appears: Since *a disciple is not above his*

---

[131] Song 2:4.

[132] Gen 32: 25–29 and Hosea 12: 4–5.

[133] Mt 25:20. Also we don't need to point out that such an incredible capability for man is also the work of grace. Which grants gifts that are real and that have nothing to do with figurative language.

teacher, nor a servant above his master; it is enough for the disciple to be like his teacher, and the servant like his master.[134] Words of Jesus that we can already see are just as piercing and difficult to comprehend in its complete meaning by human understanding. Actually, we are not dealing now with the disciple being more than the master or the servant than his lord, or vice versa; but that the disciple or the servant *may be equal to his master or to his lord*. Thus these other words of Jesus: *For which is the greater, one who sits at table, or one who serves? Is it not the one who sits at table? But I am among you as one who serves.*[135]

Such a sublime plan from God was made possible by Jesus. Once God became Man, taking on a human nature as His own, we can already say that He is on the same level and in the identical situation as His creature. Both placed in a parallel condition, it made possible an *I–you* dialogue, and reciprocity became a reality. Man can now love his God with a super–naturalized Love, but from and according to his human nature, the only way *for him* to love perfectly since everything must act according to its own nature.[136] And that is not all. When the Word took to Himself a human nature, He also *made His own* the situation of the weakness of this nature because of its own fault. Which means that, even though Christ is the *Innocent Lamb*,[137] He appears burdened with the weaknesses and miseries of all men. A passage of the prophet Isaiah is of capital import to this issue: *Surely he has borne our griefs and carried our sorrows;*[138] *yet*

---

[134]Mt 10: 24–25; Lk 6:40; cf. Jn 13:16; 15:15.

[135]Lk 22:27.

[136]The fact that supernature in this case is necessary does not nullify what was just said. The well–known saying: Grace does not destroy nature but elevates it.

[137]Cf. Jn 1: 29.36; Heb 7:26.

[138]*Languores nostros ipse tulit*. The Greek word corresponding to *languores* is ἁμαρτίας, which means sin or *sinful action*.

we esteemed him stricken, smitten by God, and afflicted. But he was wounded for our transgressions, he was bruised for our iniquities; upon him was the chastisement that made us whole, and with his stripes we are healed. All we like sheep have gone astray; we have turned everyone to his own way; and the Lord has laid on him the iniquity of us all.[139] We should keep in mind that the statement: *has borne our griefs and carried our sorrows,* must be understood in a true and strong sense, namely; not *as if* he had taken on our griefs, but as *truly making them his own.* If there were any doubt, Saint Paul is even more explicit: *For our sake he made him to be sin who knew no sin, so that in him we might become the righteousness of God.*[140] According to Saint Peter, *He committed no sin; no guile was found on his lips*[141]*...He himself bore our sins in his body on the tree...*[142]

Clearly, two things, at the same time different but important, are emphasized together in the texts. In the first place, that the sins are *ours.* And in the second, *that He* [Jesus] *Himself bore them and made them His.*

However, one might ask how it is possible that an Innocent Man, Who is also the Son of God, can make *His own* the sins of His brothers to the point of appearing guilty before them and before His Father?

The response to this question will lead us to the unfathomable abyss of the mysteries of Love, of even Divine Love Himself in this case, or just Love. If catching a glimpse (just a glimpse) of *the deep things of Satan* (Rev 2:24) is already a mystery unfathomable

---

[139] Is 53: 4–6.

[140] 2 Cor 5:21.

[141] 1 Pet 2:22, quoting Is 53:9.

[142] 1 Pet 2:24.

for men, what could be said about the mystery much greater and more inaccessible to the creature that is the unknown depths of Infinite Love? Is it possible that Infinite Holiness, out of Love, has been willing to bear the imputability of infinite Malice?[143] Only an Infinite Love can consent to the extreme of an *infinite folly,* entirely incomprehensible for man both in this life as in the other.[144] Hence, when Scripture speaks of *the stumbling block of the Cross* (Gal 5:11) it is alluding to this mystery.

All things considered, we must reach the following conclusion: the penultimate reason that explains the fact that Jesus bears the sins of all men is the reality of the Mystical Body; and Love is the last reason.

The fact that Jesus assumes the responsibility of the human race is better understood when we realize that, in the end, it is His own Body: *Then as one man's trespass led to condemnation for all men, so one man's act of righteousness leads to acquittal and life for all men. For as by one man's disobedience many were made sinners, so by one man's obedience many will be made righteous.*[145] A mystery that at the same time depends on another: the relationship between the first and the new Adam. *The first man Adam became a living being; the last Adam became a life-giving spirit.*[146] That Christ assumes sins affects the whole human race and not only Christians:

---

[143] The evil of grave sin is infinite in a certain way, *ratione termini,* because of its object and the dignity of the offended Person, Who is God, infinite by nature.

[144] Only an Infinite Love can forgive an infinite offense inflicted on Itself; but not without satisfying at the same time Infinite Justice. Though in God infinite Justice and Mercy are identical in His Infinity.

[145] Rom 5: 18–19; cf. 5: 12–21.

[146] 1 Cor 15:45.

Ipse est propitiatio pro peccatis nostris, non pro nostris autem tantum sed etiam pro totius mundi.[147]

Modern Theology is somewhat reluctant to clearly recognize the relationship between the Mystical Body of Christ and the Mystery of the Incarnation–Redemption. Hence, it tends to prefer to explain the assuming, by Christ, of the sins of all men as *solidarity*. Christ, new Adam, exercises His role as head of the whole human race by means of His solidarity with all men, carried out by the Incarnation and completed in the end, as fruit of Salvation, through the Redemption or death on the Cross. It is possible that modern theological schools have been influenced by theories of the universal salvation of *all* men and of *the anonymous Christian*, since both more easily agree with the salvation *of all the human race* of which Christ becomes solidary by His Incarnation, than with the doctrine of the Mystical Body of Christ, in which only those who pertain to Him *in actu* are saved.

In the Textbook of Christology written by Mateo Seco and others[148] it is said that *the headship of Christ over all mankind, His union with all men, is the perspective in which what is said about Redemption must be located.*[149] *In this headship the supreme de-*

---

[147] 1 Jn 2:2. Christ is the Savior of all, though more specially of the faithful: *Salvator omnium hominum est, et maxime fidelium* (1 Tim 4:10). Here is where the danger of interpreting the salvation *of all men* wrongly is hidden. Christ assumes the sins of all and is in fact the Savior of all, *but not all men are saved*, as we will soon see.

[148] F. Ocáriz, L.F. Mateo Seco, J.A. Riestra, *El Misterio de Jesucristo*, Eunsa, Pamplona, 1993, pp. 421–423.

[149] Undoubtedly Correct. In a footnote the headship of Christ over all men is distinguished from His headship over the Mystical Body. Explaining that the first is *a presupposition* of the Redemption by way of satisfaction; while the second is a *consequence* of the first regarding men who receive in themselves the fruit of the Redemption already realized. It is the only time the Mystical Body is expressly

gree of solidarity with all men is shown, which is a mystery whose existence is clearly affirmed in the New Testament (Rom 5: 12ff; Col 1: 13-20),[150] *and in whose depth we can get closer to the mystery itself of the Incarnation.* Then there is a quote by Pope John Paul II: *"The subsistence of the divine person of the Son in Christ, which at the same time surpasses and embraces all human persons makes possible the redemptive sacrifice 'for all.'"*[151] Which gives the impression that we are dealing with an ambiguous statement from the Pope, since it does not seem correct to say that the Word or the divine Person of the Son, *subsists* in Christ. The Word does not *subsist* in Christ, but Christ *is* the Word; the Word made man of course. The meaning of the word *subsist* in Spanish (still exist, live), as well as the Latin word *subsistere* (subsist; to still be in effect, in Late Latin) makes the use of this word ill-advised in this place, since it can lead to interpretations that are in little agreement with the Faith. It is difficult to understand the opportuneness of the quote in the textbook, unless to emphasize the *for all*; an expression that, used incorrectly, can lead to ambiguities and even to assertions that part from the Faith, as we see in Rahnerian theology. And the textbook continues: *The solidarity and headship of Christ over all men is, then, the consequence of the Incarnation of the Word Himself: from the eternal Word in Whom the Father "utters" all creatures (creation "by" and "in" the Word, according to John 1:3 and Colossians 1: 16-17), and Who, becoming man, "embraces," before the Father, all men.*

---

mentioned in connection with this question, though afterwards the book talks about the members who benefit from the grace achieved by the Head.

[150] Here is a reference to Saint Thomas: *Sum. Theol.*, III^a, q. 8, a. 3, in which his conclusions regarding the Mystical Body do not clearly seem to be accepted.

[151] John Paul II, Speech, 26.X.1988., n. 5, *Insegnamenti*, XI, 3 (1988), 1332. The *for all* of the end of the quote is underlined in the textbook.

The assumption of the sins of mankind, thanks to its *solidarity* with Christ as another human being or as a new Adam, is an explanation that may be in need of improvement. Indeed, the idea of *solidarity* is sufficiently evanescent as to deserve mistrust; it seems preferable, therefore, to use a *reference and a clear relationship* to the reality of the Mystical Body; which could possibly bring us closer to the doctrine of Saint Thomas.

Love as an unfathomable abyss can only be known by man in the same way (limited) in which he can know God, Who is Love (1 Jn 4:8). Hence, being Love Totality or Fullness, such marks or qualities pertain also to the concept of created love, at least as a participated and analogical form of divine Love.

Knowledge of God means knowledge of Love and vice versa; since God is Love (1 Jn 4:8). In such a way that renouncing Love is the same as ceasing to know God. The Devil was deprived of the true knowledge of God the very instant in which, shutting in on himself and choosing his own self, he deprived himself of the possibility of giving himself to another; and in totality, since Love does not understand anything short of totality. Since then, the Devil, even though he cannot stop believing in God (Jas 2:19), actually knows him only through hate, which is most opposed to Love. Hence, now *he cannot understand* what Love is.[152] His knowledge of this reality is exactly the same as the one he has of God: a *backwards* and de–naturalized knowledge.[153]

Stopping believing in Love is much more than alarming, it is *absolutely the worst* that can happen to a human being after having turned against his own nature and against that for which he was created.

And here we must mention a chilling reality. If the Church, after twenty centuries and against a precept of divine Law, has admitted divorce

---

[152] That is why Saint James said that devils believe in God and tremble. But we know well that such trembling, produced by hate and fear, cannot proceed from Love (1 Jn 4:18).

[153] Let us not forget that Saint John establishes a connection between the knowledge of God and the knowledge of Love (see quoted text).

(though it is called something else), it is because she has stopped believing in Love; and Love is a total and perennial reality, very reluctant therefore to admit conditions of any kind since, in the end, created love is also a participation in Divine Love, Who, after all, is identical to God Who is Love (1 Jn 4:8). Divorce becomes possible the moment this idea of Love is no longer accepted. However —and this is truly serious—, if the Church has stopped believing in Love, then she has stopped believing in God. *Which would mean that the Church has lost the Faith.*

Of course, we could always say correctly that the Church as such can never disappear nor lose faith. This is true if we refer to the Church Herself, and not to so many members who, having fallen into an apostasy that could well be called universal, have effectively lost the faith. So, it would be more correct to say that *Faith has been lost in the Church.*

The New Order of *universal brotherhood*, advanced by Freemasonry as a substitute for Love, is another utopia. You cannot say that it is going to fail, since for that it would have to have seen the light first. Which is something that has never happened nor ever will happen. If, for Freemasonry, Religion is no more than a vulgar superstition befitting times gone by which were full of darkness and ignorance, it is certain that, in one way or another, Religion has existed during a time that coincides with the history of humanity..., and highly likely will continue existing despite the depression that she currently suffers. Whereas universal brotherhood, despite being considered as the storehouse of all good things and the panacea for all evils, has never gone beyond being just another of the many farces imagined by freemasons in their aprons...; without any prospect on the horizon that things may become any different. Proof of which, among other things, is the failure of the so–called *solidarity*, a new magic trick, universally accepted even by the Catholic Church, invented to replace the concept of *charity*, but that is nothing more than a mere *flatus vocis* whose effectiveness does not go beyond its sound when pronounced. Actually, Saint Paul already had alluded to how anodyne is the noise produced by instruments like bells and cymbals: it affects the eardrum for a few seconds and immediately fades away (1 Cor 13:1). In modern society, the word *solidarity* has been reduced to an empty voice, used primarily by politicians to trick fools. And also by Theology and *progressive* Church Hierarchy, most likely obeying the demands of its well–known inferiority complex and fear of the World; something which, unfortunately, they feel incapable of giving up. But, truth be told, no one believes in the famous solidarity except to talk about it. Just like Santa Claus: no one knows who he is or what he means, but he serves as a way to increase sales in department stores, to trick silly people, and to distract children. By the way, he also uses a bell that he rings tirelessly; maybe to achieve that, fleeing the annoyance of the noise, pedestrians roaming the sidewalks might circulate more quickly.

Jesus shed His blood for all men (1 Tim 2:4), though in fact not all are saved: *qui pro vobis "et pro multis" effundetur...* (Mt 26:28; Lk 22:20). With which neo-modernist theology does not seem to agree, neither with the Scripture text nor with the Magisterium and the teaching of the Church throughout twenty centuries. That is why it exchanged the words *pro omnibus* (all) for *pro multis* (many), a substitution whose basis no one has explained satisfactorily. Some insinuate that it is nothing more than a corollary of the Rahnerian theory of universal salvation (everyone is Christian and everyone is saved); and they even go so far as to doubt the validity of the consecration of wine in the New Mass of Paul VI (now called Eucharist). This is a worrisome conclusion because, although it seems farfetched, many serious people affirm it. In connection with this, it is interesting to notice that, according to the testimony of Father Malachi Martin, former professor at the Pontifical Biblical Institute, official exorcist of the Holy See for years, and recognized expert on the topic, those who perform satanic rites, with derision and grave profanation of the Holy Mass and of the Eucharist, always use the Roman Rite and never the one from Vatican II or Paul VI, since they do not consider this last one as the true Mass.[154]

---

[154]In fact, the Holy See granted a term of two years for the Bishop Conferences in each country to correct the corresponding formulas (October 17, 2006). A precept that, at least until now (early 2009), no one has gone along with and currently lies in complete oblivion.

The idea of the Mystical Body is different from the legal concept of *surrogacy*. The former is not about taking the place of another person, either physical or moral, both in its rights and its obligations, but to take upon oneself, as if they were his own, the crimes that others have committed. Understanding well that we are not dealing merely with *taking on the responsibilities of some alien person's acts*, but assuming them as one's own. Which is possible in the History of Salvation thanks to Jesus Christ, given that the guilty are members of the same Body whose Head He is: *For just as the body is one and has many members, and all the members of the body, though many, are one body, so it is with Christ. For the body does not consist of one member but of many... If all were a single organ, where would the body be? As it is, there are many parts, yet one body. Now you are the body of Christ and individually members of it.*[155]

Where two things are to be emphasized in the Pauline text:

In the first place, the fact that all those who belong to the Church integrate and form *only one Body*. Which is known as the Mystical Body of Christ.

In the second place, the reality that, despite forming only one Body, the members are distinct one from another and each one endowed with his own individuality (personality).

It seems that the Apostle desired to insist on the peculiarity of both things: it is about *only one and the same Body* (a); though formed by different and distinct members, constituted *each one as a person* (b).

Regarding the first (a), the fact that Christians are part of only one Body with Christ as the Head legitimizes the doctrine according to which Christ *assumes* as His own the sins of men, since they are *members of His own Body*. Those who do not pertain to the

---

[155] 1 Cor 12: 12.14.19–20.27.

Mystical Body are called nevertheless to integrate themselves in Him (1 Tim 2:4), always maintaining the fact that not all men are saved.

For Saint Thomas, all men from Adam belong to the Mystical Body, at least *in potentia*. Yet only those are saved who *in actu* (in fact) belong to Him and while they remain in Him: *I answer that, This is the difference between the natural body of man and the Church's mystical body, that the members of the natural body are all together, and the members of the mystical are not all together —neither as regards their natural being, since the body of the Church is made up of the men who have been from the beginning of the world until its end— nor as regards their supernatural being, since, of those who are at any one time, some there are who are without grace, yet will afterwards obtain it, and some have it already. We must therefore consider the members of the mystical body not only as they are in act, but as they are in potentiality. Nevertheless, some are in potentiality who will never be reduced to act, and some are reduced at some time to act; and this according to the triple class, of which the first is by faith, the second by the charity of this life, the third by the fruition of the life to come.*

Hence we must say that if we take the whole time of the world in general, Christ is the Head of all men, but diversely. For, first and principally, He is the Head of such as are united to Him by glory; secondly, of those who are actually united to Him by charity; thirdly, of those who are actually united to Him by faith; fourthly, of those who are united to Him merely in potentiality, which is not yet reduced to act, yet will be reduced to act according to Divine predestination; fifthly, of those who are united to Him in potentiality, which will never be reduced to act; such are those men existing in the world, who are not predestined, who, however, on their departure from this world, wholly cease to be members of Christ, as being no longer in potentiality to be united to Christ.[156]

---

[156] Saint Thomas of Aquinas, *Sum Theol.*, III\u1d43, q. 8, a. 3, *Respondeo*. Translation from newadvent.org. According to Pius XII's Encyclical *Mystici Corporis Christi* (n. 12), Christ was established the Head *of all the human family* from the bosom of the Virgin; though it was by the power of the Cross that the Savior made His office of Redeemer fully real.

Salvation is a free *request* made by Love that, as is logical, waits for an accepting free response, given that freedom belongs to the essence of Love (2 Cor 3:17). But the possibility of a free acceptance supposes unequivocally the possibility of rejection, also free.

If men do not form a same and only body with Christ, but maybe they are united to Him by a kind of solidarity (even with Christ as Head of the human race), it would be harder to explain the fact that Christ bears the sins of men as His own.

Regarding the second (b), Saint Paul is careful to emphasize the individuality and particularity (personality) of each member of the Body. The Body is in fact *one,* but the members are *many.* The texts from Chapter 12 of the *First Letter to the Corinthians* are clear: *For the body does not consist of one member but of many* (v. 14); *but as it is, God arranged the organs in the body, each one of them, as he chose* (v. 18); *that there may be no discord in the body, but that the members may have the same care for one another* (v. 25); *Now you are the body of Christ and individually members of it* (v. 27); *For as in one body we have many members, and all the members do not have the same function.*[157]

The fact that each one of the members of the Mystical Body is a person makes it possible for them to be recognized individually, in their condition as sinners firstly and saved afterwards. The good or bad *actions* are always imputable to *persons* and never to things or to Organisms as such.[158] Before, only the race and descendants of Adam existed, of which Christ also was part, as Head and as true Man that He is. But now, thanks to Him and *through union*

---

[157] Rom 12:4.

[158] In the end the entire human race will be judged, though not globally as an Organism, but individually and personally each one of its members: *I will give to each of you as your works deserve* (Rev 2:23. Cf. Eccles 11:28; Ps 62:13; Mt 25:15; 1 Cor 3:13; Gal 6: 4–5; 1 Pet 1:17).

with Him, men have been established moreover in a true Organism or Body whose Head also is precisely Him; and now more than ever, since we are dealing with a true Organism or Body. At the same time this Body acquires its full effectiveness once those who make it up have been redeemed. If before, only a race of men, descended from a common father, existed without any other bond of union besides what is derived from that condition, now that race has been constituted in one same and only Organism whose members are something more than solidary: *that there may be no discord in the body, but that the members may have the same care for one another* (1 Cor 12:25). At last true Love has been made possible, originated in the Head and diffused to Its members; and at last the evanescent and volatile substitute called solidarity has been left behind definitively.

We must have in mind that Christ *carried*, as if they were His own, the sins and misery of all men. He became sin for us, according to the expression of the Apostle, *but he could not take upon himself the condition of sinner*.[159] And that is why the same Apostle adds that Christ never knew sin: *Eum, qui non noverat peccatum, pro nobis "peccatum fecit," ut nos efficeremur iustitia Dei in ipso*.[160] Saint Peter also emphasizes that Jesus Christ never was a sinner: *Qui peccatum non fecit, nec inventus est dolus in ore ipsius*.[161]

They are two clear assertions apparently contradictory. Christ became sin for us; though He never knew sin. The problem here consists in explaining, as far as possible, the mystery of Faith: Christ became sin for us, though He never knew even the shadow of sin. Or, in a more accessible presentation, how can we bear the sins of

---

[159] *Quis ex vobis arguit me de peccato?* (Jn 8:46).
[160] 2 Cor 5:21.
[161] 1 Pet 2:22.

others, to the point of *becoming sin*, without being a sinner? What can the Pauline expression *became sin* mean?

Before all else, it may be helpful to insist on the fact that we are dealing with a mystery of Faith; one more of those that make up the part of theological science called Christology. And that is why we can only pretend to find approximations to the problem, in the hope that they may bring us closer to the knowledge and Love of our Savior.

We must keep in mind that each one of the members of the Mystical Body, including Christ, is a person, and, therefore, absolutely responsible for his good or bad actions; he and only he: *Actiones sunt suppositorum* (actions are attributed to persons), as taught in classic Philosophy. From where we deduce that Christ, as Head of the Body and Person at the same time, can take the sins of the members of His Body (after all, it is His own Body), but never the *authorship*, in the sense that every sin is imputed to the person who committed it and only to him. Nevertheless, this assertion, at least apparently, would explain the fact that Christ bore the *responsibility* of the sins of men, but not that he became sin for them. And the revealed texts seem to go beyond what a mere assigning of responsibility would mean.

The explanation, as far as we can possibly find or fathom it, would lead us maybe again to the Mystery of the Mystical Body, insisting on what we have already said. Since it is His own Body, the sins committed by its members *are really His*, in the sense that they belong to Him, which goes far beyond what the concept of mere responsibility demands. Such *responsibility* is not the *action*, but inherent condition of the action. At the same time responsibility makes *merit or demerit* possible, but neither of them identifies itself with the action; and the same can be said of the *prize or punishment* to which they lead. The action itself can be taken on by another person, but never the *authorship* (which would suppose a lie), the responsibility, the merit, or demerit, which are all untransferable and personal. When the action is destroyed, the responsibility that derived from it is no longer imputable to him or them that performed it. So, it is not possible to assign sins to Christ as their author, since each one of the members of the Body is a distinct person (Christ as well) and the only one responsible, therefore, for his own actions. That another takes upon himself the negative burden that may derive from them does not remove the reality that the actions *pertain to* each one and are *untransferable* as such.[162] If anyone would take them upon himself for Love, to save the guilty, he does nothing but submerge them *personally* in that Love and turn into justice and glory, by the strength itself of the act of love, what was sin and misery. Something more than possible when we are dealing with infinite Love.[163] For just as Hate can do nothing against the creative and transformative power of Love (just like That–Which–Is–Not is incapable of acting on or influencing Being), so too because of this, Love is the Creator of all things, from the moment in which all were made by Him, for Him, and from Him.

The World, subdued as it is by Satan, Father of Lies and Liar from the beginning, incapable therefore of seeing things as they are, always views them *backwards*. It exalts and praises the evil man as highly as possible, for example, presenting him as the ideal to which one should aspire. Conversely, it disparages the honorable man and calls him vile, considering him an aberration. And the most extraordinary thing is that he (the World) ends up completely convinced by his own lies. That is why he can never appreciate the reality of

---

[162] And here the philosophical concept of person would come into play.

[163] [Christ] *having loved his own..., he loved them "to the end"* (Jn 13:1).

things and less still the true being of man. Thus, he finds himself prevented from knowing, or even suspecting, the *infinite sadness* in which he lives, namely: fully submerged in *Falsehood*, like the air he breathes or the breeding ground in which he feeds, convinced that he alone has the *Truth*. But living in contradiction is living de–natured or even worse, since it is acting against its own nature (*contra natura*). That is how the wicked man or Liar (which ends up being the same thing), by choosing as an enemy and declaring war on *Being,* has definitively opted for the *Opposed–to–Being.* Nevertheless, the Contradiction and Absurdity stops here; for Being is contrary to Nothing; Nothing, on the other hand, cannot be contrary to Being, for the simple and easy reason that it is not anything. Consequently, he who has made an option for a Lie[164] finds himself on the dividing line between Nothing and that which is Opposed to Being; though for that we would have to suppose that such a dividing line exists. If then the attitude of him who has chosen a Lie is far from being a mere illusion, it is necessary to recognize in it a reality, whatever kind it may be. And what kind of entity would we recognize in a position contrary to Being? Since it seems certain that it has it. A possible answer can be found in the fact that Being (Infinite) is God; and God, as we know, besides being Infinite Truth, is Infinite Love, or simply Love. Then what is contrary and opposed to Being must surely be what is Opposed–to–Love, better known as Hate, and in this way we would have explained the loathing of the wicked one for the divine. And thus the problem is reduced to the need to attribute an entity to Hate: surely an unsolvable proposition for a human being, in so far as it has to do with an abysmal mystery framed in another even greater Mystery included in what the Bible calls the *deep things of Satan* (Rev 2:24).

---

[164] *They exchanged the truth about God for a lie* (Rom 1:25).

To get to the bottom would suppose something like reaching the depths of its antithesis, which is Infinite Love. And equally it can be said that, since Being is *Absolute*, the wicked man has made his option for what is *Relative*; which, also by nature, is nothing in itself and even less in Totality, and hence the sense of emptiness and anguish that always accompanies evil. For the same reasons, the wicked man is the mortal enemy of *facts* (reality), which he absolutely hates (...*and if the facts are against us, so much for the facts*, as Lenin said), choosing rather a fantasy world of imagination about things that do not exist (utopias), knowing that they are not real. It is not surprising that part of the torment corresponding to the punishment to be suffered in eternal condemnation in Hell consists in this: forcing the reprobate, who always chooses a Lie, to admit and recognize the unyielding Truth: that he finds himself, now and forever, rejected and an absolute failure and compelled to recognize this as his *Only Truth*, unable now *ever* to embrace Falsehood. A startling and frightening punishment for him for whom putting up with the Truth involves a far greater torment than suffering Fire. Now the reprobate understands that *his truth* was nothing but *his Lie,* which is most contrary to Being, understanding that his life has not been such a life and that neither has his existence been such an existence. As for the reality of that thing that is contrary–to–being, since it is not Nothing, in what can it consist and which is its own entity? Evidently, whatever it is, it will have to do with Hate and only with Hate. Hate that, *ratione termini* (since it is against God), is also infinite; about which it only remains to say that its mystery is as impossible to explain, *sensu contrario*, as the mystery of Infinite Love. And in what would consist of an existence eternally fed by the inextinguishable flame of an Infinite Hate? Of course it is not possible to know, though we can affirm this for sure: since Infinite

Hate is also Anti–Love, and since Love consists in leaving oneself to surrender oneself to another and receive that person at the same time, such an existence must necessarily remain in a maximum security jail in which the condemned could never get out of himself, nor be able to address someone pronouncing *you*. He becomes actually enclosed in an eternal solitude in which he would not be able to think of himself as an *I*, which, as a person, either does not exist as such or has become eternally de–natured.[165]

Regarding the disciples and followers of Jesus...?

Theirs is to share the life and existence of their Master. Their life is no longer really their own, or the one they would have lived, but that of their Master: *He who finds his life will lose it, and he who loses his life for my sake will find it...*[166] *He who eats my flesh and drinks my blood abides in me, and I in him...*[167] *As the living Father sent me, and I live because of the Father, so he who eats me will live because of me...*[168] *It is no longer I who live, but Christ who lives in me.*[169] Living their Master's life has to do also with the fact that Christ *became sin* for men, and the necessity for His disciples to follow Him in this as well.

At this point it would be good to caution about the weak consistency of doctrines centered on *Being yourself*, so in fashion now. As we have seen, man reaches his full maturity and identity when he lives not his own life but that of Jesus Christ. The slogan *be*

---

[165]The question of the personality of the condemned is more than doubtful, insofar as the person was made for love. But, even without denying it, it is evident that it must consist in a misshapen, or *contra natura*, entity, and to call it schizophrenia or something torn apart would be to do it a favor.

[166]Mt 10:39.

[167]Jn 6:56.

[168]Jn 6:57.

[169]Gal 2:20.

yourself seems to lead rather to shutting oneself up in one's own self as a means of self–fulfillment, disengaging everything else.[170]

That the disciple of Jesus lives his own life only when he renounces it to live the life of another, in this case of his Master Jesus Christ, should not seem strange since from the first it is a consequence of the demands of Love. *We only reach the truth of our own life when we live the life of another.* To understand this, we must keep in mind that the nature of man has been created for love; thus, *leaving himself* and giving himself voluntarily to another. And since Love is reciprocal and bilateral, at the same time that the one who loves gives his life, he receives one from the opposite member of the Love relationship. In such a way that, since it has been created precisely for that, his existence only becomes authenticated when it is not his own. Understanding here as *his own* what the individual would have become if, after having received it, with its corresponding gifts, he would have disposed of it in his own way according to his own will. By which, not only would he have put his own will before that of the other, but also would have put it aside, dispensing with it.

That the Christian is called to share in the existence of Jesus Christ and therefore in His sufferings and death, is clearly declared by Saint Paul in an extremely strong tone: *Now I rejoice in my sufferings for your sake, and in my flesh I complete what is lacking in Christ's afflictions for the sake of his body, that is, the church...*[171]

---

[170] This doctrine seems to remind us of the French or German *personalists*, according to whom one's *own truth* is the only sure foundation of existence.

[171] Col 1:24. As we can see, what is said here is none other than the application of the doctrine of the Mystical Body of Christ: the members participate in the destiny of the Head.

that I may know him and the power of his resurrection, and may share his sufferings, becoming like him in his death[172]

Therefore, the disciples are also called to *become sin* for their brethren in connection with the doctrine of participation. But, in what way do they share that condition with their Master Jesus Christ?

Christians live today, perhaps, the most turbulent period the Church has known throughout her history. If we do not find ourselves now in the End Times, events seem to insist on making us believe we are.[173] The Church is suffering a profound crisis: heresies, more or less expressed or more or less concealed, march on everywhere; the Magisterium is headed by almost no one and frequently seems to remain silent; confusion is spreading; desertions and apostasies continue in an increasing number, while Falsehood and Evil spread their power everywhere as the Great Liar, or Satan, seems to have finally established himself at last as the only Lord of the World (Rev 13:7; 20:7).

The Good is rejected constantly almost everywhere. The few Christians who still remain firm in the faith are fighting in retreat in a spirit of defeat. We know however that the Church will not disappear (Mt 16:18), though at the end of History she will find herself reduced to its minimum expression (Lk 18:8). It is certain that for now, *at least outwardly,* all her Institutions and ranks exist; and even with more splendor and effectiveness than ever, according to many (the *Ecclesiastical Spring*). But serious thinkers, not allowing

---

[172] Phil 3:10.

[173] We already know that the End Times is somehow a relative event in History. The truth is that the *Novissima Hora,* according to the expression of Saint John (1 Jn 2:18), is already here, as the Evangelist expressly recognizes. If anything, we could talk of the culmination of the End Times, or of the moment of the Parousia, or the end of History.

themselves to be fooled, know that is merely stage decoration; simple appearance facing the spectators but without anything behind; pure and abundant *show* with little or no content. Small groups do in fact remain, small bodies of true Christians here and there which by and large feel helpless. *Christian life* and Gospel preaching have faded. And all this to give rise to the careful language of innocuous speeches, which try by all means not to upset the world: The Proclamation of the Beatitudes, together with the Promulgation of the New Commandment, have been substituted by the Announcement of *Dialogue*, of *Solidarity*, and of *Tolerance*...! Everything to make one think that Jesus Christ probably got His Message wrong.

Still, or maybe because of this, there is a truly happy note: the few Christians that still remain are the most fortunate in Church History. It is true that the World despises them and that they are afflicted everywhere with more intensity than ever; and precisely for that same reason they are the most blessed. In them are fulfilled, but now more truly than ever, the words that Saint Paul applied to his contemporary Christians: *in honor and dishonor, in ill repute and good repute. We are treated as impostors, and yet are true; as unknown, and yet well known; as dying, and behold we live; as punished, and yet not killed; as sorrowful, yet always rejoicing; as poor, yet making many rich; as having nothing, and yet possessing everything.*[174]

Tamquam nihil habentes, et omnia possidentes. Here are some of the most beautiful and profound words written by the Apostle; and which have filled the World with puzzlement.[175] A World that cannot understand that the Christian is the only human being capable

---

[174] 2 Cor 6: 8–10.

[175] We have often said that Christianity is full of paradoxes; but they are only realities which, by exceeding in marvel and magnificence poor human understanding, seem *baffling* to it.

of reaching *all* (the only meaning of his existence and the exclusive key to his happiness), once plunged into *nothingness* after having surrendered the totality of what he was and what he had. *He that shall lose his life for me, shall find it.*[176]

Here is the reason for their Joy. For if they have reached the *All* it is because it has been given to them to share with greater intensity than anyone else in the Passion and Death of Christ. For the secret of the greatest Happiness always passes through the previous and mandatory way of the Greatest Pain.

Which, at the same time, would lack any sense if, when all is said and done, that pain had nothing to do with *sharing the existence of the Beloved.* For in that, and in no other thing, consists Perfect Happiness: in living the same life of the Beloved. Which means for our heart to beat with His, to live His own feelings and share His own sense, to be with Him (it matters little if in joy or in suffering) and, definitely, to give oneself to Him and receive Him at the same time: *life for life.* Regarding giving up everything, we might think that it would be an even more marvelous thing than receiving it, according to the *beatius est magis dare quam accipere,* which is a precept that urges Him to do the same. Since Love —must it be said again?— is always bilaterality and reciprocity: for He too wants to love in addition to being loved…! The bride of the *Song* always speaks with this necessary sense of reciprocity, *for you cannot love without being loved*; and that is why she says:

> *My beloved is mine and I am his.*[177]
>
> *I am my beloved's and my beloved is mine.*[178]

---

[176] Mt 10:39.
[177] Song 2:16.
[178] Song 6:3.

The Beloved could not be for her if she, in turn, were not for the Beloved. And if man were not made for love it would not be worth having been created. But Love necessarily supposes the *loss* of the self, to make possible —in the only manner and way— the *encounter* with the Beloved:

> *If, then, on the common land*
> *From henceforth I am neither seen nor found,*
> *You will say that I am lost;*
> *That, wandering love–stricken,*
> *I lost my way and was found.*[179]

---

[179] Saint John of the Cross, *Spiritual Canticle.*

...To him who conquers I will grant to eat of the tree of life

(Apoc. 2:7)

IV

CHRISTIAN VICTORY

Victory is the normal consummation of Christian existence: *in reliquo reposita est mihi iustitiae corona, quam reddet mihi Dominus in illa die...*[1]

But *normal* does not mean that it always happens. Rather the opposite; in the sense that if victory is the happy culmination of combat in favor of someone, it is necessary to admit also that the risk of a possible defeat exists as well. *Normal* means, thus, that it can or cannot happen, but is more fitting to the nature of the case in question that victory, in fact, happens. According to Saint Augustine, there is no crown without victory, and there is no victory without a fight; and he adds in one of his treatises that *the crown of victory has been promised only to those who fight.*[2] Hence the promise of the Spirit to the Angel of the Church of Ephesus: *To him who conquers I will grant to eat of the tree of life, which is in the paradise of God.*[3]

---

[1] 2 Tim 4:8.

[2] Saint Augustine, *De Agone Christiano*, 1.

[3] Rev 2:7. A similar promise is made also, in other terms, to the Church of Pergamum (Rev 2:17).

But if victory, for which the Christian is destined, is the happy outcome of a previous combat, then we have to say that combat is the *necessary* circumstance for every man coming into this world. *Is not human life on earth just conscript service? Do we not live a hireling's life?*[4] And even more especially for the Christian. As Saint Paul expressly recognized, noticing in passing that the weapons used by the disciple of Christ are not of the World or worldly: *For though we live in the world we are not carrying on a worldly war, for the weapons of our warfare are not worldly but have divine power to destroy strongholds.*[5]

That the situation of man, especially the Christian during his earthly pilgrimage, is constant fighting, appears throughout the whole New Testament; and thus the continuous exhortations to be vigilant.[6] The *homo peregrinus* is still part of the state of the Church called *Militant* or *Fighting Church*; while the *Triumphant* Church is made of those who definitively were victorious after having fought.

Vigilance is, therefore, a permanent state of the Christian without which his Faith could not survive and therefore he be saved. Saint Peter's warning regarding this (1 Pet 5:8) is quite expressive. Hence the great sin of the foolish virgins of the parable consisted in that they were negligent, since they fell asleep and *did not prepare* for the arrival of the Bridegroom (Mt 25). And the same thing happens in the parable of the good seed and the weeds, where the enemy took advantage of the moment in which men slept —*cum autem dormirent homines...*[7]— to sow the bad seed.

---

[4] *Nonne militia est vita hominis super terram, et sicut dies mercenarii dies eius?* (Job 7:1).

[5] 2 Cor 10: 3–4.

[6] Mt 24:42 and parallel verses; 26:41 (parallel: Mk 14:38); Acts 20:31; 1 Pet 4:7; 5:8; 1 Cor 16:13.

[7] Mt 13:25.

Without constant vigilance and struggles, the Christian cannot survive as such, nor can the Church. The warning comes from the Lord Himself: *But know this, that if the householder had known in what part of the night the thief was coming, he would have watched and would not have let his house be broken into.*[8]

These truths became part of the doctrinal heritage of the Church for centuries. One of the functions that was given to it by its Founder was continued vigilance to protect the Flock. The Good Shepherd, unlike the mercenary who does not care about the sheepfold, takes care of His sheep, He separates them from dangers and leads them to good pastures. Always trying not to neglect, even for a moment, His duty of vigilance (Jn 10):

> *Watchman, what of the night?*
> *Watchman, what of the night?*[9]

This is why the Church has always been conscious of her duty to be vigilant regarding the Faith and of the need that each one of her members has to fight if he wants to be saved. And without the least hesitation about it.[10] The Church has always thought of herself as the *Barque of Peter*, shaken unceasingly by the waves and the random fluctuations of the World, so that she has never had doubts about her condition as *Militant Church*. Nor did she forget the words of warning of her Founder: *Simon, Simon, behold, Satan demanded to have you, that he might sift you like wheat.*[11] As well

---

[8] Mt 24:43.

[9] Is 21:11.

[10] One does not need to know much History of the Church to know that her Shepherds, *at least from the doctrinal point of view,* never doubted this. Another thing is that, *in fact,* they often failed to put it into practice.

[11] Lk 22:31.

as the words of the Apostle: *Do you not know that in a race all the runners compete, but only one receives the prize? So run that you may obtain it. Every athlete exercises self–control in all things. They do it to receive a perishable wreath, but we an imperishable one.*[12]

A doctrine that for centuries stayed constant... until the twentieth arrived, in an historic moment that came to coincide approximately with the death of Pope Pius XII.

Later, a great *change* in the way of understanding Pastoral practice happened. Pope John XXIII was the first who decided that the Church should abandon her belligerent attitude against those who fought against her. From now on, the *Militant Church* would become the *Dialoging Church,* or the *Church of the Outstretched Hand.* The Pontiff thought, seemingly, that the job of arguing with heretics and schismatics, or denouncing them to warn the faithful, had been a failure. So, it was preferable to choose *dialogue, comprehension,* and *tolerance.* From now on she would no longer attempt the *conversion* or the *return to the Fold* of those who, in one way or another, had separated themselves from her, but only the *reunification* of all in a common place. Though no one knows yet where such a common place is or the possible outcome of the new resolve to *smooth over* positions.

Once such a decision was made, the tasks of mission, conversion, apostolate, and catechumenate gave way in their priority, as functions of the Church, to a new attitude: of dialogue, tolerance, and an ardent ecumenism. This last one, it must be said, included a certain dose of syncretism. The duties of vigilance and fighting against errors against the Faith were put in parentheses to adopt an attitude of dialogue, pacifism, and comprehension. Hence some

---

[12] 1 Cor 9: 24–25.

gave way to the suspicion that the new Pastoral practice was influenced by personalist doctrines of French and German philosophers; founded, as we know, on the recognition of *everyone's truth* in an atmosphere of coexistence and mutual respect.

Everything points to the fact that fear had a lot to do with this change of attitude. A good number of Senior Hierarchies of the Church, among whom doubtless were numbered John XXIII and Paul VI, felt very fearful about the events of the time. Especially about two things that set the tone of the era: scientific advances, on the one hand, and the extraordinary rise and expansion achieved by Communism on the other.

Two important events derived from this state of mind: The Pact of Metz of compromise with Communism and the passive attitude of inaction (tolerance) regarding the wave of Neo–modernism which, in the wake of the Council and continuing afterward, was invading the Church.

Despite the undoubted good will of the Popes, the consequences of these changes in attitude, far from being what they expected, led to a catastrophe regarding the life of the Church and the Faith of the faithful.

This is not the place for a documented analysis of the events that took place in those turbulent times which were transcendent to the trajectory of the Church and whose repercussion still endures. Here we are going to limit ourselves to sketch an analysis of the theological basis that the new situation introduced: did they effectively legitimize the change or, on the contrary, were they the cause of the confusion and damage done to the Pastoral practice of the Church?

We must keep in mind that here we are talking about *Pastoral* practice and not *Dogmatic* Theology. The Church cannot change or contradict herself regarding her dogmas. Just remember the well–

known proverb, which has practically become law: *nihil innovetur, nisi quod traditum est*; or the warning of the Apocalypse: *I warn everyone who hears the words of the prophecy of this book: if anyone adds to them, God will add to him the plagues described in this book, and if anyone takes away from the words of the book of this prophecy, God will take away his share in the tree of life and in the holy city, which are described in this book.*[13] The Magisterium of the Church has always presupposed homogeneity, unity, continuity, and fidelity to itself.

But here we are dealing with Pastoral work, trying to explain the reasons that could have motivated the fearful, and seemingly cowardly, mindset that appeared at the time of Vatican II in so many hierarchs of the Church, since that was, without a doubt, one of the main causes of the great change of orientation in the Church regarding Pastoral work in general and the Liturgy in particular. This very mindset meant the abandonment of a fighting spirit in order to adopt in its place another, more complacent disposition: one of tolerance and dialogue, whose practical results materialized in an attitude of surrender.

It is very hard to explain how a Christian could be scared of the advances of Science. And even more so when we are dealing with members of the Hierarchy.[14] How is it possible that Christians, and above all members of the Hierarchy, can believe that there are incompatibilities between Faith and Science? A wavering faith as well as a scant knowledge of science are

---

[13]Rev 22: 18–19.

[14]The fear started mostly at the middle of the last century. The beginning of the Space Age, with the arrival of satellites, the Moon landing, plus the advances in computing, in communications, and, in general, in the world of technology, caused tribulation and shock in many believers. Though it seems incredible, the famous Russian *Sputnik* (1957) had a debilitating effect on the faith of many. However, as a whole, the strangest thing undoubtedly was the fearful reaction of the Hierarchy.

preconditions for the advances in the field of technological investigation, admirable on the other hand, which are able to make the Faith stumble. It is amazing that enlightened Christians, including those in places of great responsibility, have hesitated in their faith because of such advancements. Anyway, maybe the key to this issue can be the relationship that exists between fear and a doubting faith. Something that the Lord Himself has expressly recognized: *Why are you afraid, O men of little faith...?*[15] *Where is your faith?*[16]

An even greater problem would be to explain the paths by which certain people, more prone to and comfortable with questioning their faith, as events have proven, have reached positions of great responsibility in the Church. The question gets worse when we realize that they were not isolated cases, but quite a general phenomenon in the ecclesiastical world. Maybe someday the Church will see in herself the need to seriously reflect, either on the very *existence* of some of its ecclesiastical Centers of formation, or on the *criteria* upon which they function. Especially those located in Rome, capital of Catholicism and its central nucleus of irradiation. Doubtless the problem lends itself to a careful study that could raise questions. Like, for example, the following: up to what point can an *elite ecclesiastical Center* (one, for example, that exists for the formation of future Bishops) feel legitimized regarding the doctrine of the New Testament? Is there a possibility that a candidate to the priesthood can receive the proper training, according to the gospel teachings and Christian spirituality, *with an expectation of receiving a future episcopate*? Experience has proven that the preparation for a future priesthood, into which in some way the possibility of purely human aspirations may creep (as those expecting positions of relevance could be), is dangerous and disastrous. Examining coldly and objectively the facts would be enough to be convinced of this.[17] Of course, the judgment of Saint Paul in 1 Timothy 3:1 (*si quis*

---

[15] Mt 8:26.

[16] Lk 8: 23–25. Apocalypse (21:8) cites cowards, followed immediately by the incredulous, in the list of those destined to the second death.

[17] It is interesting to observe that the Church is the only human Institution that is not in the habit of undertaking, hardly ever, a serious *results analysis*.

episcopatum appetit, bonum opus desiderat) could always be brought up. But it is one thing to consider the Episcopate as the culmination of Christian Priesthood and another as a motivation to positions of influence and power. If no one should dare to have access to the Priesthood *if he has not been expressly called* (Heb 5:4), with more reason it seems daring to aspire at the very outset to the Episcopate. One of the greatest misfortunes the Catholic Church suffers in this postmodernist phase she is going through, is the great number of clergies, devoid of interior life and supernatural spirit, lacking any other intentions beyond reaching positions of influence.

The profound change in attitude undertaken in the Pastoral work of the Church needs to be well studied to be understood; probably interesting conclusions will be reached. For example, was it probable that the fearful attitude of various members of the Hierarchy and not a few theologians of the moment gave rise to the attitude that Maritain would later define as *kneeling before the World*?

Let us consider, for example, the very fashionable issue today of peace, which its detractors, alluding to its most extreme formulations, have given the name *pacifism*.

There is no doubt that the doctrine about peace, as it is being taught in today's Church, has suffered a noticeable change in relation to its meaning in the New Testament.

When current Pastoral work and Theology refer to peace, they are really referring to it *in the sense the World understands it* (absence of wars). Which is something that no one would dare deny, since the written and oral records on the topic are so numerous that they would fill libraries. Nevertheless, in a serene study of the topic, problems do not cease to arise that make accepting such a doctrinal orientation difficult.

In the first place, the concept of peace according to the World is not only alien to the teachings of the New Testament but is even opposite to it; and, in the end, it becomes a pure utopia, which makes it as false as it is unrealizable.

The concept of worldly peace *has nothing to do* with the peace that Jesus Christ wanted to leave as a legacy to His disciples: *Peace I leave with you; my peace I give to you...*[18] Our Lord begins, as we can see, telling His disciples that He leaves them *peace*. Just like that, in a general sense. But such a generic concept of peace cannot be different from the way the Master understands it since His vision of peace is the only one possible and the only that deserves such a name. That is why He speaks immediately afterwards of *my peace,* where the possessive adjective is quite eloquent and sufficiently clear. Jesus Christ refers thus to *His peace,* and no other: what He understands as the *only peace.* And just in case there was still some doubt, He is careful to mention expressly in the same verse that His peace is not what the World understands as such: *not as the world gives do I give to you.*[19]

According to which, and apart from the fact that the classics have always linked the idea of peace with that of justice,[20] it is evident that the Christian concept of peace is not only different from that of the World, but probably even contrary to it. Regarding peace according to the World, we should note that the mere absence of war is far from being considered as an absolute value, since the doctrine of just war and legitimate defense have always been admitted as

---

[18] Jn 14:27.

[19] Jn 14:27.

[20] Psalm 85:11; Is 48:18, Rom 14:17. May 22, 1982, Pope John Paul II celebrated a Mass, *Pro Pace et Iustitia Servanda,* with Argentinian and British Bishops because of the Malvinas War. By uniting both concepts, the Pope was doing nothing more than following a centuries–old tradition, continued by Saint Augustine, and that reached its high point with the great Spanish jurists of the Spanish Golden Century.

valid. On the other hand, neither can we discard the fact that teachings and beliefs according to the World are usually contrary to Christian ones: *For my thoughts are not your thoughts, neither are your ways my ways, says the Lord.*[21]

How, then, can we explain that Catholic Pastoral theory and Theology have stopped insisting on the idea of Christian peace and adopted instead the concept of World peace?

And once again fear appears as a possible motive for certain behaviors: Fear that Christian proposals may not be accepted by the World and, consequently, acceding to its proposals to achieve, by any means, a coming together...?

If true, we could only conclude that such decision making, defended by even part of the Hierarchy of the Church, is liable to lead to dire consequences.

First, because the World will never accept a *consensus* with Christian points of view. It will never agree with any doctrine that contains even a trace of Christian content, as it has demonstrated many times. Whenever the Church has attempted a certain *coming together* or has propitiated a *dialogue* (either with the World or with other *Churches*), it has been She who has yielded without receiving anything in return. On the other hand, we cannot accept the possibility of a *consensus* among teachings which have different and even contrary content (2 Cor 6: 14–15) unless it begins with the premise of admitting the truth of all religions; just like the syncretistic Ecumenism influenced by idealist and personalist philosophies. In short, unity above all; even if it must be achieved at the expense of truth.

We have already said above that aspiring to an extreme pacifism, with a total absence of war, is a utopia. Or if you want to say it another way, it is a falsehood and an attack on the beliefs of the

---

[21] Is 55:8; cf. Rom 11: 33–34.

Christian People. There will always be wars in the world, as the experience of History and common sense of anyone who thinks have well proven. Serious historians would smile at the idea that efforts for peace, as an objective certainly achievable in a more–or–less distant future, had any value. On our part, we are not going to make forecasts nor elucidate regarding the future. But it is Scripture itself that clearly states that there will always be war among humans, and even more intense and frequent as we approach the End Times (Mt 24: 6–7; Mk 13: 7–8; Lk 21: 9–11; Rev 13:7). Saint Paul laughs at the *pacifists* who at that time will still be calling for peace: *When people say, "There is peace and security," then sudden destruction will come upon them as travail comes upon a woman with child, and there will be no escape.*[22] And many a year before, Jeremiah the prophet already rebuked those who tried to fool the People with promises of a peace that, in reality, would never arrive: *They have healed the wound of my people lightly, saying, "Peace, peace," when there is no peace.*[23] And just in case anyone still would have a doubt, regarding the historic moment in which we find ourselves, we may refer to the ever increasing business of weapons trafficking, the wild race to get nuclear weapons, borderless terrorist activity, the imminent danger of a new Cold War, the reality of hot conflicts in many parts of the world, etc. etc.

Presented with these premises the Church cannot dedicate herself to defending utopias doctrinally, and even less to *surrender* to the World; otherwise, she would betray her own mission, which is to proclaim the truth, whatever many happen, for the salvation of men.

---

[22] 1 Thess 5:3.
[23] Jer 8:11.

It would be a grave error to think that this modern attitude of the Church is not a mere tactical or strategic error on the part of the pastoral directors of the Church.

The current state of the Church —very delicate and complex, carefully and intelligently laid out towards a point of total destruction— could not be produced by chance nor by a strange aleatory conjunction of certain historic circumstances, as if it would have arisen by magic. In reality, it is the result of a well-thought-out plan by educated minds that have known how to put it into practice, step by step, toward a foreseen and sure end. And here we must refer to Freemasonry, the main agent introducing this conspiracy, using Modernism and Marxism as its most important tools to infiltrate the ecclesiastical Organism.

It has also resorted to disseminating confusion, alluding to presumed obligations of believers, like that of obedience (very well manipulated and instrumentalized in this case) or appealing to a supposed spirit of the Council, referring to Vatican II. Both used against everyone who does not submit to the claims and approaches of these manipulators.

The use of such procedures has brought about great confusion among believers and has given rise to a delicate situation. The criticism against the Magisterium prior to the Second Vatican Council, which is real even if disguised, has not only weakened the foundation of the centuries-old Magisterium of the Church before Vatican II. By the requirements of the most basic Logic, this criticism has also put into question the Magisterium of this last Council. In effect, if you defend that the previous Magisterium, either for being obsolete or depending on its historical circumstance which at this time are no longer relevant, has lost its authority and cannot continue to demand the assent of the faithful, the same inescapable logic can be applied to the current or a later Magisterium. If previous councils are no longer considered valid, arguing from this last one, it doubles that this last one can also be disqualified arguing from previous ones..., or from those that will be convoked in the future. The result is the destruction of all Magisterium. At this point, it is difficult not to remember personalist teachings: the truth is only valid, alternatively, for *me*, for *you*, or for *another*; moreover, *here* and *now*, but nothing more.

Natural consequences inevitably have arrived. The Church has found herself divided, and schisms have even appeared, some which have been formal and according to law, such as with the French Archbishop Marcel Lefebvre, and others merely de facto, as with large sectors of the North American Church, not to mention the ones in South America caused by Liberation Theology. Consequently, a strange division has taken place in the bosom of the Church capable of delighting the Prince of Darkness; namely, traditionalist Christians on one side and conciliar Christians (of the conciliar Church) on the other. Outlandish denominations that contradict the perennial belief that all Christians are traditionalists, since Tradition is one of the sources of Revelation without which authentic Christianity cannot exist. *Conciliar Church* is a term which may lead to as many interpretations as there are numbers of individuals.

Of course, different groups of dissidents have not been treated in the same way, according to the preferences and taste of the System. The case of the followers of Archbishop Lefebvre has been intriguing. Compared to the stance of current Theology regarding Luther, the situation is comic at least, if not tragic. Luther is the heretic through whom more damage has been done to the Church than in all her history.[24] Nevertheless, the current position of Catholic Theology and Pastoral theory is that he was right *in almost everything he said*. Or maybe in everything, according to some;[25] and that is why the campaign arose in the bosom of Catholicism in favor of his rehabilitation. Moreover, it is a fact recognized by many theologians and well-known prestigious thinkers that Lefebvre really was

---

[24]He managed to divide the Church in such a way that the schism continues after multiple centuries, apart from the definitive end of Europe as a union of nations under one faith and common values, among other things.

[25]His Holiness Benedict XVI has lately said, concerning the delicate problem of the dogma of justification, that Luther was right in his *sola fides* doctrine (Address November 19, 2008) though we have to qualify it with the necessary complements. The problem, nevertheless, arises when you keep in mind that Luther expressly rejected such qualifiers.

right in the totality of his complaints regarding the state of the Church after the Council; or at least in a large part of them. Nevertheless, it is a fact which *no one has taken into consideration*; the dissident bishop was charged with incurring schism, which appears to be true. In which case, could it maybe be recognized as the only mistake of someone whose good will and desire to stay faithful to the Church cannot be denied?

Either way, it is necessary to admit that complaints against the Church, made in a determined historic moment, can be true in part and even in their totality, as appears to have occurred in this case. Nevertheless, it is not lawful for anyone to separate himself from the legitimate Hierarchy, according to *Ubi Petrus, ibi Ecclesia*.[26] In fact we are facing another aspect of the inevitable destiny of the followers of Christ: to be obedient to a Hierarchy, maybe corrupted, as something that is part of the Cross that their vocation imposes as a necessary condition. A Cross, maybe as tremendous as it is heavy, but which the disciples of Christ, in imitation of their Master, must bear. Once again, a truth imposes itself —*Extra Ecclesiam, nulla salus*—, reminding us of the words Saint Peter directed once to Jesus Christ, *where will we go...?*

It seems that none of this would have taken place if the Church had been less complacent and had not renounced her duty of vigilance over the Flock commended to Her, or the combative mind set against the criteria of the World. How could the Church forget, or even put in parenthesis, Saint Augustine's warning that there is no crown without victory, nor victory without a fight?

The most serious thing is that this fearful attitude, translated into a fatal and skittish surrender, is against postulates of Christian living clearly expressed in New Testament Revelation and that have been part, for centuries, of the doctrinal heritage and the tradition and soul of the Church.

---

[26] It seems that this expression was first used by Saint Ambrose, *Enarrat. in Ps.*, 40, 30.

Christianity is not a religion of comfort, nor has it ever been its norm to run away from difficulties. It does not lead its members by the wide way, or that which according to Jesus Christ leads to perdition, but by the narrow and steep one that leads to life, also according to the Master (Mt 7: 13–14). That is why he who decides to live according to the Gospel assumes an existence burdened with difficulties; he will be compelled to maintain a continuous fight against constant contradictions liable to turn into persecutions of all kinds; which can become so serious as to cause death (Mt 5:10; 2 Tim 3:12).

The attitude of surrendering and giving up the fight is opposed to a fundamental point of the Gospel Message, *precisely for which Jesus Christ, according to His own assertion, had come to the Earth*:

> *Do not think that I have come to bring peace on earth;*
> *I have not come to bring peace, but a sword.*[27]

Of course, it is a metaphor; a figure of speech that the Master would use sometimes (Mt 5: 29–30; 18: 8–9; Mk 9: 45.47; Mt 18:6; Mk 9:42). He did not come to promote wars. Nevertheless, as is proper to these tropes, *in this case too the metaphor is intimately related to reality;* a literary usage but with a base in reality. And as it was not the mission of the Master (Who wrote nothing), nor of those who wrote down His teachings, to elaborate literary frills, it is evident that a serious assertion is contained here: *The words that I have spoken to you are spirit and life.*[28] Besides, regarding this case, and precisely because what is said is important, it must be expressed with sufficient clarity.

---

[27] Mt 10:34.
[28] Jn 6:63.

As it is, indeed. The incredible invitation that Jesus Christ proposes, supposes for man the risk typical of a great Adventure. Great in its importance, difficult to realize, and even fearful in its results.[29] Since it involves for him decisive consequences that will have to be decided in a unique alternative: either Perfect Happiness forever, or its loss, also forever. With the consequent failure of his existence for all eternity, in this last case.

The words of Jesus Christ referring to the destiny of His disciples during their earthly pilgrimage are *disturbing* at least. The presence in the world of God made Man, along with the mission for which He came, tend to provoke among men, disciples or not, an attitude which can be described as *disturbing, difficult, and challenging.* He did not come to bring peace to Earth. At least not as the World understands peace, which envisions it only as a condition of tranquility and wellbeing but imagined in a human way. A situation which, even without having in mind any supernatural content, was already made impossible forever by man himself, since it was sin that introduced pain, disgrace, fear, insecurity, suffering, and ultimately death itself into the world. We have already said above that the search for this world idealized by human understanding, which will never achieve its ends by itself, is a utopia. And the Church cannot adulterate the content of her Message nor hide or cover with euphemisms the words of Christ, nor change their meaning. In the end, for all parts concerned, He is:

> *the cornerstone;*
> *a stone that will make men stumble,*
> *a rock that will make them fall,*

---

[29]Regarding the difficulty to fulfill it, the help of grace will not be lacking to men. While, about the unsureness of its results, there is always the appeal to live from Christian hope; that produces sufficient confidence in God to live in the Joy that Christ left to His own.

according to Saint Peter.[30] Because of that, right after affirming that He has not come to bring peace but the sword, in order not to leave the least doubt and despite the possibility of increasing the uneasiness in the hearts of men, He then adds:

> *For I have come to set a man*
> *against his father,*
> *and a daughter against her mother,*
> *and a daughter–in–law against her mother–in–law;*
> *and a man's foes will be those of his own household.*[31]

These are also figures of speech. Of course, no one has thought that Jesus Christ wanted to disseminate enmity, and even less among loved ones and very close ones. His first commandment that summarizes the rest is that of Love: *A new commandment I give to you, that you love one another; even as I have loved you, that you also love one another. By this all men will know that you are my disciples, if you have love for one another.*[32] It is worth asking, then, about the meaning of what He uttered before. For it is evident that the Master *is talking seriously.* And that is why the content of His thought, profound and essential, possesses a scope that goes beyond what a superficial interpretation would suppose. As we are going to try to see.

However, it is fitting to first emphasize another important aspect. For the meaning of the words of Jesus Christ is found on the opposite side of the *decaffeinated* and faded Christianity currently in use by Catholic theologians and pastoralists. Understanding well

---

[30] 1 Pet 2: 7–8.
[31] Mt 10: 35–36.
[32] Jn 13: 34–35.

that the term *pastoralists* encompasses Church Hierarchy also (or at least part of it), which is ultimately who puts Pastoral activity into practice. We position ourselves far from certain stances of surrender and desertion that are a consequence of an inferiority complex and fear, of opportunist interests, and even of more or less hidden apostasies.

The words of the Master reveal that Christianity is not a religion of eclecticisms, syncretisms, half–truths, accords among religions (achieved generally by means of a *consensus* that dispenses with truth), hands stretched out to error, concessions to those who do not hesitate to shamelessly attack the Church, incomprehension and even persecutions of those who, for not playing the game, have heroically chosen fidelity to the immovable principles of the Faith. Christianity is not a doctrine of weaknesses or of conformism. Precisely because it is a religion of clarity, it does not do well with ambiguous words —*God is light and in him is no darkness at all*—[33] or with the lack of decision and firmness.[34] This is where the apparent *hardness* of its demands and the rigor and strength of its teachings comes from. In short, Christianity is the proclamation of an *intimate Love relation between God and men*, with everything that derives from it. Therefore, it has nothing to do with contrived doctrines of oriental religions: the search for *nirvana*, the dissolution of man by his transformation into the All, the dominion of the mind and of pain, the stoicism before the inescapable ends of men that are destiny and Nothingness... The surrendering position betrays the most fundamental relationship that God has wanted to maintain with man.

---

[33] 1 Jn 1:5.

[34] Here we speak of error, without referring to those who err. Étienne Gilson said that there are many who confuse the respect due to persons who err with the respect for error itself.

Ambivalent, ambiguous, and equivocal language is an effective weapon used today by Neo–modernism inside the Church, in Dogmatic and Pastoral Theology. It usually uses traditional terms, though with the possibility of being interpreted as Modernism does. In this way they become *bulletproof* concepts, immune to possible reactions from sound doctrine. Afterwards, it is up to praxis, intelligently handled, to orient them in modernist fashion. In this way those terms can be used as offensive and defensive weapons at the same time. Which means that the modernist sense spreads among most Christians, while the traditional sense is reserved in case any type of response might appear. This procedure uses many variants, each one studied and opportunely used and whose detailed description would require a textbook. It is used in daily Pastoral activity with all normality, though its greater influence is exerted through multitudes of Documents emitted by various sources, starting with the Second Vatican Council. It seems unnecessary to add that it has achieved its purpose to confuse a multitude of the faithful.

Only few realize that the manipulation of language undertaken by means of an intelligent operation of cloak and dagger —carried out both by political Powers and progressive Theology— apart from being an effective means to destroy the Faith of the Christian People, also supposes a direct attack on the Gospel's didactical methods.

Gospel language is indeed firm, clear, and, at the same time, deep; but *deep* does not mean *dark*. The Gospel faces problems directly and does not hide from them; it calls things by their name and shows what paths to follow without hesitation. That is why it often produces a certain feeling of hardness and rigidness. Therefore, it is susceptible, given the weakness of human nature, of being interpreted either with excessive softness (blurring and reducing its content like decaffeinated coffee or fat free milk) or passing over it in an apparently negligent way (as if its teachings were not there or had not been noticed).

Whereas the language used by Modernism is dark, ambiguous, and especially apt to produce confusion. Progressive language, unlike the concise and plain language of the Gospel, is clothed in a pseudo–cultured, pompous, flowery, and baroque vocabulary with airs of scientific seriousness and an insinuating pretension of its ability to be fully understood only by people of culture. Such a tone of *highly scientific* seriousness gives it a mark of notoriety and an effective endorsement of certainty; with a result in naive people that is almost infallible. In this way it muddles questions and produces the desired confusion as an essential step, in the end, to cause the Faith of the weak to tremble.

Jesus Christ, always according to His own assertion, has come to the world to *set a man against his father, a daughter against her mother*..., etc. Clearly, this gospel language is not that of the modern Pastoral practice nor of the current Magisterium of the Church. And yet, since this Magisterium is confronted with the greatest crisis the Church has suffered, now more than ever before clear instructions and energetic corrections in course would be necessary. If this is not done, the Flock of Christ is liable to suffer a spiritual starvation of devastating consequences as the alarming number of desertions and apostasies the current Church is enduring is clearly showing.

Authentic Magisterium is urgently needed, well founded on supernatural values and New Testament doctrine, sufficiently valiant to not fear confronting the World. Neither the Magisterium nor Pastoral practice can exercise their functions looking at the World, but only *to Him Who is the only Master* (Mt 23:8; Jn 13:13) and the *Great Shepherd of the sheep* (Heb 13:20). Adopting another role model can only lead to failure and the loss of souls.

Fortunately for men, Jesus Christ never saw the need to have diplomatic relations with any country. Nor did He feel compelled to be careful about His reactions and measure the scope of His words when speaking to the *media*, attitudes that, in the end, are causing the nullification of modern Pastoral care and Catechesis. Or even worse, if possible, since empty–of–content or misguided peaching causes extraordinary damage to souls: *I tell you, on the day of judgment men will render account for every careless word they utter* (Mt 12:36; cf. 2 Cor 2:17). What some people call *episcopal language* had still not appeared in the Church in Jesus' times, and He was not too concerned about the negative reactions that proclaiming the truth might arouse. Now we understand why the language of Jesus Christ, as forceful as it is incisive, seems extremely likely to shock modern Pastoral practice,

> *He who loves father or mother more than me*
> *is not worthy of me;*
> *and he who loves son or daughter more than me*
> *is not worthy of me.*[35]

The Fathers of the Church frequently used the expression *Adversus Haereses* as a generic title for their writings: true diatribes directed against the heretics of their time. But since today the attitude of acting, speaking, or writing *Against Anyone* is intolerable, they would be firmly condemned.[36]

---

[35] Mt 10:37.

[36] The absolute interdict of condemnation includes an important exception: when we are dealing with enemies of the System. In which case every kind of excommunication, anathema, condemnation, interdict, injunction, and damnation would be thrown against them.

Many are those who do not seem to care too much about the wolves who disperse the sheep and devour the flock. They are convinced that it is better to go out to meet them with an outstretched hand and unconditional openness to dialogue. The problem is that it is difficult to believe in the ability of wolves to dialogue, as the daily experience of its obstinate attitude against any kind of reasoning testifies.[37]

It is quite difficult to accept the existence of bad faith in certain people, or in their disposition to believe in the convenience of striking pacts with the Devil. How was it possible that the Church would promise, by an expressed Pact, to not condemn Communism, not even mention it, in the Second Vatican Council? Were Pope John XXIII and his successor Paul VI really convinced that Marxism was going to respect the Accord? On the other hand, it is always possible to allege, in favor of both pontiffs, that it was a good option because of the possibility of alleviating the sufferings of the persecuted Church... though highly doubtful in its fulfillment, as the facts widely confirmed. Nevertheless, even in the case that the Pact would have been respected by Communism (a rather unlikely event), it would seem necessary to have had in mind, through a serious balance of pros and cons, the confusion and scandal that the Pact, in all probability, would cause in the whole Christian world. Not forgetting either that suffering is the inherent and consubstantial quality of all Christians, considered individually or as the Flock or the Body of Christ. Suffering cannot, therefore, be characterized as a disgrace to be avoided at all costs. All the efforts in the world made in obedience to charity in order to mitigate suffering or make it disappear will not be sufficient. Besides, sharing in the Pas-

---

[37]What daily experience does demonstrate is that the *disposition to dialogue* is not a synonym for *disposition to give in* regarding one's own points of view.

sion and Death of our Lord belongs to the foundations of Christian existence.[38] History offers few surprises. And if we cannot doubt the good intentions of the Hierarchy, we must recognize, confronted with the evidence of historical truth in this case, that the result was a failure that caused a lot of damage.

In any case it is hard to extend the presumption of good faith to other cases whose implications are well known. It is an arduous task trying to believe the *naivety and innocence* of well–educated people in positions of grave responsibility. We have alluded to this topic above: it is not possible not to call into question the true intentions of the ambivalent language of Neo–modernism, used today by so many theologians and Pastors of the Church. God alone is the judge of what is in the hearts of men, though sometimes facts seem to be quite eloquent. Let History study this thorny issue.

Though it is scandalous for some who try to ignore it, Jesus Christ insists on an ever more incisive language:

> *If anyone comes to me*
> *and does not hate his own father and mother*
> *and wife and children*
> *and brothers and sisters,*
> *yes, and even his own life,*
> *he cannot be my disciple.*[39]

These words do not refer to merely *confronting* but also to *hating*, which is even more difficult. And what does modern Pastoral theology say about this...? But before we attempt a response and

---

[38] This is the main reason to oppose euthanasia.
[39] Lk 14:26.

examine the words of the Master, it is convenient to call our attention to an important question as a precaution necessary to avoid committing an error in historical assessment.

One may possibly think that renouncing fighting and practicing surrender instead would not be anything more than a tactical error committed by a very naive Catholic Hierarchy and Pastoral practice; even if, in the end, animated by the best good will. We must keep in mind that the attitude of surrender usually conceals itself by using many subterfuges. One of them, usually the most common of all, consists in using slogans which, in addition to *sounding good*, possess an extraordinary aptitude to confuse naive people: the convenience of dialogue and tolerance in the name of unity, recognizing *the truth of the other*, the consideration of changes according to historic circumstances... and many more.

But even though we could admit the truth of such pronouncements, the presence of methods and procedures *not only alien to but contrary to the content of the Gospel and didacticism peculiar to Jesus Christ* is evident; as can be seen in the quoted texts and in those we still will see later. Which does not stop giving us a serious reason for concern.

It seems logical to think that the precept of Jesus to His disciples to teach *all that I have commanded you* (Mt 28:20) would also include the way to do it. Even more so when, as everyone knows, the method can affect the content of the teaching. Reality shows every day that, far from being about a mere *modus loquendi* without consequences, the method used supposes an adopted stand which is very capable of falsifying the doctrine.

Someone invented the expression *episcopal language*, with irony not exempt from malice, to refer to the art of speaking without committing oneself or actually saying anything. Unfortunately, there are reasons that support, in not a few cases, the justification of this acrimony. The main distinctive trait of the new Pastoral practice is characterized by the refusal to fight, as a result of the praiseworthy practice of implementing a policy of an outstretched hand. Its practical philosophy could be summarized in an ideology including things like these: not offending anyone; above all, we must not bother the *media*, current Government, the general System, or anyone who can inflict negative consequences to the speaker; and we cannot forget this other mantra: the need to respect the truth *of each person*. Unfortunately, this last expression introduces us to a chapter of existentialist and personalist philosophies whose final result is to always end up denying absolute truth and, consequently, God.

Ignoring the subjective aspect of the question, about which we spoke before, it does not seem necessary to insist on the fact that the didactical method of Jesus Christ does not go that way. We just saw this in the expressions used by the Master; the same ones that some do not hesitate to characterize as excessively strong, sharp, harsh, and disproportionate.

As we will see promptly, what we clearly find out from certain expressions of Jesus Christ, seemingly too harsh, is nothing but the fact that He is *saying it seriously*; because the topic requires it due to its transcendence. The Gospel is not a joke, nor is the way of life that it advocates a triviality. And Christianity is far from a *business* or way of living (1 Tim 6:5) from which to get some advantage, as some seem to think. From all of which follows that superficiality, on the other hand the least of the sins identified among those that correspond to this topic, is at odds with the Christian life:

> *The kingdom of heaven has suffered violence,*
> *and men of violence take it by force.*[40]

Once again, the unusual and unexpected. Jesus Christ speaking of *violence*..., and moreover to say that it is necessary if you want to enter the Kingdom of Heaven. The list of words and expressions that modern Pastoral practice would reject as abominable taboos is growing alarmingly. And since the word *violence* is among the most demonized, its indiscriminate use —and even discriminate— is quite capable of provoking unprecedented scandal.[41]

Those who desire to see things serenely, and as a rule use common sense, do not need to be advised that Jesus Christ does not advocate violence; He simply *is serious*. He cautions those who desire to follow Him that the task to be done is not only far from being a triviality, it also is reserved for the daring and those gifted with a heart able to fall in love. In the end, loving is the task among tasks and the adventure among adventures, in so far as it is exactly what man was created to do.

I had the opportunity to visit, not long ago, a painting exhibition organized by the NGO *Manos Unidas* with the purpose of, according to the signs that were on the walls and the pamphlets lying on the tables, promoting fundraising (an unusual thing for NGO's) within another of the so–called Hunger Campaigns. After contemplating with astonishment human stupidity, plastered this time on the ridiculous *futurist* paintings shown there, I started reading some of the numerous pamphlets and slogans that were spread on the walls and tables. Most of them reflected themes

---

[40] Mt 11:12.

[41] Here we cannot appeal to the metaphor. It is evident that Jesus Christ is referring first and foremost to a situation of moral force, which obviously does not exclude physical constraint: *Indeed, all who desire to live a godly life in Christ Jesus will be persecuted* (2 Tim 3:12).

elaborated on the basis of utopias; or if you prefer, they were about utopias elaborated on the basis of cliches. The list of topics was divided, half and half, between pacificism and hunger in the world. One of them said: *if you want peace, avoid violence.* A phrase, seemingly very appropriate, which sounds agreeable to many, and which gave me a chance to remember, as by contrast, one of the lines professed as common currency by the ancient Romans: *Si vis pacem, para bellum.* Which of the two should we keep...? Of course, the mere question would suffice to scandalize many, put in the position of needing to make a choice. As for me, I have always thought that preparing for war, if you sincerely want peace, does not seem so crazy. It certainly is a thing that seems to contain much more common and practical sense than the ditty about avoiding violence. Apart from that, the Roman adage enjoys the advantage, over the current slogans of the NGOs, of being based in reality and, because of that, is truer whether one wants it to be or not since pacifism is nothing more than a utopia and a means of seducing the naive..., besides being an instrument for making money.

And we are even able to give another warning, particularly to those simple people, or maybe those gifted with a good dose of candor, for whom the above–mentioned slogans and topics seem to be well-intentioned, simple-minded phrases: it is simply not true; far from it. We are dealing more with an extraordinarily *realist* matter, as those who use them know very well, *in the sense that, as we have said, they are an effective way of making money*, about which no one asks for accounts and whose use often remains in the aura of mystery.

Undoubtedly, it is not true, and would be rather absurd, that Jesus Christ wants to counterpose fathers against sons or vice versa. And the same thing can be said about His being in favor of war or violence.

Keep in mind that Jesus Christ *is clearly referring in those texts to Love.* To the Love of God and the will to follow Him out of Love. And since Love is the most elevated and sublime thing in the Universe, the thing *by* and *for which* man was created, and with him all things —*One thing is needful. Mary has chosen the best part*—

[42] there are more than sufficient reasons to understand His word. Because of the decisiveness of the issue, Jesus Christ uses language that is appropriate to make us understand its importance. And, in fact, Love is the most fundamental and only necessary thing:

l'Amor che move il sole e l'altre stelle.[43]

Strong language is fully justified in this case because of the importance of the topic. In our thought's judgment of things upon which everything depends, including life and death, it is necessary to use special language, ordinarily metaphorical and even hyperbolic, but which everyone understands in the right circumstances. It is the normal human and universal way of speaking, used quite frequently, as we can verify in the gospel texts: *If your hand or your foot causes you to sin, cut it off...*[44] *Whoever causes one of these little ones who believe in me to sin, it would be better for him to have a great millstone fastened round his neck and to be drowned in the depth of the sea.*[45]

And Jesus Christ is clearly referring to Love. Everything that refers to Him is worthy of any lofty name no matter how magnificent it might be, if it contributes to confirming His essential and fundamental quality. Nothing exists that can be compared to Love, nor is it possible to assess Him by any human measure:

---

[42] Lk 10:42.
[43] Dante, *Divine Comedy*, Paradise, end.
[44] Mt 18:8.
[45] Mt 18:6.

> *For love is strong as death,*
> *jealousy is cruel as the grave.*
> *Its flashes are flashes of fire,*
> *a most vehement flame.*
> *Many waters cannot quench love,*
> *neither can floods drown it.*
> *If a man offered for love*
> *all the wealth of his house,*
> *it would be utterly scorned.*[46]

He is entirely incompatible with a hesitating *yes* or *no*, and incapable of knowing what the World usually understands by *half measures*. Consequently, He does not admit anything other than *everything* or *nothing*. As we can also attest in scripture texts. One whom Jesus invited to follow Him was willing to do it, though he asked first to bury his dead father: *But he said to him, "Leave the dead to bury their own dead; but as for you, go and proclaim the kingdom of God."*[47] And in the same way he answered another person who wanted first to go and say farewell to his family: *No one who puts his hand to the plow and looks back is fit for the kingdom of God.*[48]

If modern Theology and Pastoral practice use a *soft* language, often equivocal, full of euphemisms, and always with the fixation to *not hurt* and *not bother*, it is due to the degradation to which the idea of Love has been subjected. To the intended universal Super Church created by man, advocated by Freemasonry, corresponds an appropriate language: purely earthly, drab, dull, and at an infinite distance from the celestial one: *He who comes from above is above*

---

[46] Song 8: 6–7.
[47] Lk 9:60.
[48] Lk 9:62.

all; he who is of the earth belongs to the earth, and of the earth he speaks; he who comes from heaven is above all.[49]

The most evident and painful proof of the corruption of the concept of Love among Catholics is found in the new dispositions concerning the sacrament of matrimony.

The *indissolubility* of Christian matrimony is from divine institution, as is clearly documented in Scripture, Tradition, and the constant twenty-centuries–old Magisterium. Conjugal love is an analogate to the Infinite Love Who is at the bosom of the Trinity and the only source of all true Love. He is the mutual *total and unconditional* surrender of Two Who love each other. *Total* and *unconditional* are actually two essential characteristics without which true love is not even possible. Accordingly, the Church has never admitted divorce, since love *ad tempus* is nothing more than love *ad libitum*, which turns out to be the same as saying *while it lasts* or *in so far as we feel like it*. Which has nothing to do with Love.

Though the indissolubility of Christian matrimony is from divine institution (Mk 10:9; Mt 19:6), it is really based on the nature of love itself. Indissolubility has been a hallmark of marriage ever since its institution in Paradise. Jesus Christ affirms it expressly, responding to the question proposed by the Pharisees about the libel of repudiation permitted by Moses: *For your hardness of heart Moses allowed you to divorce your wives, but from the beginning it was not so.*[50] Its elevation to the category of sacrament by Jesus Christ reinforces and substantiates even more this condition. It is evident that God is not a supporter of Love *for a limited time*.

The Church lacks the authority to admit divorce, which would also be going against her own Tradition and her own Magisterium. And nevertheless, Catholicism has chosen to accept it..., though changing the name; she has dispensed with the term *divorce* and has introduced the expression *declaration of nullity of the bond*.

---

[49] Jn 3:31.
[50] Mt 19:8.

The gravity of this situation quickly becomes clear, especially when taking into account that *nullity* is achieved by practically all marriages that solicit it. The proportion of more than ninety percent of nullities achieved supposes an actual totality, since the small quantity of petitions rejected can still go to higher agencies, where they are always taken care of and favorably served.

But the case raises serious issues: is it enough to change the name of a thing to assert that it is something else, despite its essence being the same? It is the case of *abortion*, for example, that now is usually known by the name *interruption of pregnancy*.

The acceptance of divorce is a grave issue, but not as serious as admitting the use of *adulterated language*. Which, as everyone knows, is used to cause confusion, by way of concealment or disguise, in realities that may turn out to be dangerous or may produce undesired consequences. By making people believe that certain realities are not what they seem, or by causing them to go unnoticed, the danger of untimely reactions is avoided, and the desired ends are produced.

Manipulation of language, wisely used by modernism, is one of the most disturbing consequences of the Church of the Second Vatican Council and its aftermath. As much as it may be bitter to admit it, it is necessary to accept the evidence of the ambiguous language of many texts of the conciliar Documents and of the new Liturgy.[51] The fidelity and obedience any Catholic owes to the Church cannot be an obstacle on the path to the truth: *Amicus Plato, sed magis amica veritas.*[52] Though the most worrisome feature of this practice is that it is opposed to the Tradition and the Magisterium of the Church, whose clarity and certainty of language have always been proverbial. Not to mention the doctrine of Scripture,

---

[51] Texts like *it will become "for us" the bread of life*, in the offering of bread to be consecrated in the Eucharistic Celebration, cannot hide its ambiguity. In fact, what does the expression *for us* mean exactly? More than a few are convinced of the presence of double meaning here, one of which has a noticeably Protestant taste.

[52] A saying quoted by Ammonius in his *Life of Aristotle*, though others attribute it to Cicero, in his *De Amicitia*.

which has never been hesitant, indecisive, or irresolute: *Let what you say be simply 'Yes' or 'No'; anything more than this comes from evil.*[53] Saint Paul was also a fervent supporter of clarity: *So with yourselves; if you in a tongue utter speech that is not intelligible, how will anyone know what is said? For you will be speaking into the air....*[54] *I thank God that I speak in tongues more than you all; Nevertheless, in church I would rather speak five words with my mind, in order to instruct others, than ten thousand words in a tongue.*[55]

The problem of the double meaning of ambivalent terms consists in that one of them, generally the one that points to error, tends to be imbedded in the addressees more strongly than the other; while the latter, on the other hand, usually goes unnoticed and almost always ends up disappearing. With the climate of perversity and paganism that the System has spread to all areas of society, together with the already weak human nature, choosing falsehood is the mature fruit that usually falls by itself. Jesus Christ attributes the option for darkness to a previous human wickedness: *Men loved darkness rather than light, because their deeds were evil.*[56] In other texts He relates the abundance of evil with the cooling of charity (Mt 24:12) as cause for the loss of Faith (Lk 18:8). According to which, it is possible to consider an *option for evil* prior to the *option for error*; and it is surely evident that choosing falsehood is the result of a previous perverse choice of the will.[57] Either way, the *sons of this earth* know the problem well; being always more astute than the sons of the light (Lk 16:8), they strive to foment the corruption of society by all means possible as a previous and even necessary phase to facilitate the achievement of their ends.

On the other hand, an ambiguous term used according to this context leads to error *by its very nature*. Since it contains in its bosom a lie that has the possibility of being accepted, which turns that term into something

---

[53] Mt 5:37; cf. Jas 5:12.

[54] 1 Cor 14:9.

[55] 1 Cor 14: 18–19.

[56] Jn 3:19.

[57] Carlos Cardona, *Metafísica de la Opción Intelectual.*

intrinsically evil. Either way, we must be careful not to confuse the deep (and sometimes obscure) language used by Scripture with ambivalent forms of discourse, often used deliberately.

We have said before, paraphrasing the Book of Job, that the life of man on this earth is a continuous fight and combat. But the word combat also includes a sense or meaning of *competition* or *contest*.[58]

The term taken in the sense of *fight* or *combat*, reflects indeed the situation of man on earth as a result of an unfortunate accident, though voluntarily sought out: sin; which gives him his new condition of fallen nature. But taken in its sense of *competition*, it is possible to conclude that the concept relates to the human being as something proper to it and as a consequence of its human nature.

To understand it, let us just recall that man has been created by Love and for Love. Or to put it more clearly, he has been made by God to love and to be loved.

But created Love possesses another essential characteristic, namely it is configured as a tournament or competition: two contenders — the two lovers— *fight* or compete with each other to decide *which one gives more to the other:*

And his banner over me was love.[59]

This characteristic is exclusive to created Love and does not exist in Infinite or Uncreated Love. In the bosom of the Great Trinity, the Father *could not give more* to the Son, nor the Son to the Father, since both give themselves to each other mutually *in totality*. Infinity, contrary to what happens in created or divine–human Love, cannot increase or decrease.

---

[58] In the text of 2 Tim 4:7 (*bonum certamen certavi*), the noun (ἀγών) refers more to an athletic or sporting competition; cf. 1 Tim 6:12; Heb 12:1; *passim*.

[59] Song 2:4.

The problem is posed here in the following way: created Love in Its diverse forms of true Love, is always a participation in and an analogate of Uncreated Love. But it was established that *competition* or *contest* corresponds to the very nature of Love, therefore we must admit that this characteristic must be found, at least in some way, in Uncreated Love.

Remember that the Divine Persons are configured as relations of *opposition* that in no way are accidents, since they are truly identical to the Divine Essence. The existing relationships between the Father and the Son are those of paternity and filiation. Maybe we can understand such *opposition* as a competition or contest; though in a state of *total perfection*, and thus without beginning or end, without increment or diminishment; only infinite totality. Nevertheless, this total perfection *does not eliminate the reason for opposition between those two Persons,* Who, because they are Infinite and love each other in totality, give everything mutually, in an eternity that knows no beginning or end. If the contest were to have reached totality and fullness on both sides, it would have reached total perfection; but even then, the essence of contest would not disappear. Precisely because this divine relationship lacks beginning or end, and no change at all exists in it, maybe we can consider that *it always has kept its essence as a contest.*

This *contest* between the two lovers —in the case of divine–human Love, God and man— is not a figure of speech, but something absolutely real. Otherwise Love, Who is at stake here, would not be real.

A mysterious episode in the Book of Genesis speaks of Jacob wrestling with God: *A man wrestled with him until the breaking of the day.*[60] *When the man saw that he did not prevail against Jacob, he touched the hollow of his thigh; and Jacob's thigh was put out of joint as he wrestled with him. Then he said, "Let me go, for the*

---

[60]The narration presents God in an anthropomorphic form. But besides the fact that the text itself recognizes it expressly, all of Tradition has unanimously identified this figure as God.

day is breaking." But Jacob said, "I will not let you go, unless you bless me." And he said to him, "What is your name?" And he said, "Jacob." Then he said, "Your name shall no more be called Jacob, but Israel, for you have striven with God and with men, and have prevailed." Then Jacob asked him, "Tell me, I pray, your name." But he said, "Why is it that you ask my name?" And there he blessed him. So, Jacob called the name of the place Phanuel, saying, "For I have seen God face to face, and yet my life is preserved."[61]

Whatever interpretation we give the text, it is evident that it refers to *real* relationships framed in an intriguing *contest* between God and man where the key is surely found in the sense that is given here to the idea of contest.

The first thing we notice, as a remarkable thing, in this text of Genesis, is the fact that God puts Himself at the level of man and, moreover, *is defeated*. However much anthropomorphism is supposed here, it is evident that man is the one who prevails. From where we seem to learn that the contest spoken of here, far from referring to some metaphor or allegory, is pointing to something real.

The New Testament sheds light on this problem since it is, regarding the Old, the definitive revelation of the Love of God for man. In connection with this topic, the parable of the talents (Mt 25: 14–30) and of the pounds (Lk 19: 11–27) are telling and even surprising.

From them we get that man can give back to God not only the quantity equivalent to what he has received from Him *but also double the amount.* As we can see, Scripture presents here a situation that should logically be susceptible to some explanation fully intelligible

---

[61] Gen 32: 25–31.

by divine understanding and comprehensible, in some way at least, though not in all its depth, by human intelligence.

We are dealing, therefore, with a situation that occurs between two —in this case God and man— and in which there is some sort of dispute at stake. Doubtless because there exists between both a certain and previous *opposition*, however peculiar it may be, where the combat is so real that *man is capable of emerging victorious*.

To shed some light on this problem, to the extent possible, it is worth remembering that God has wanted to establish a true Love relationship with man. So, the elements necessary to set it up must also be real and authentic. For God loves truly and has wanted to be loved by man, also truly. And hence the necessity, respected by God from the moment He wanted to Love, *to be faithful to the rules of the game*. If He wanted to see His creature truly in love with Him, necessarily He would have to take a chance and *play for real*. However, it is evident that the more proper sense to give to the *rules of the game* is none other than to respect the nature of things. Ultimately, pure Logic. And God is infinitely logical since He is Infinite Truth.

Therefore, in the case of the *game of Love*, it is necessary to follow Love's own rules. So that, either the *game* is configured with all its ingredients, nothing other than the qualities that are essential to it, or there cannot be Love at all. And one of the important rules that sets the tone in this topic is the one that establishes the need for each lover *to be at an equal status with the other*. Since everything that belongs to one also belongs to the other. As the beloved of the *Song of Songs* says:

My beloved is mine and I am his.[62]

---

[62]Song 2:16; 6:3.

For a contest or competition to be considered fair, which is the same as to say true, it is necessary that neither contestant holds any advantage over the other. Otherwise, it would no longer be a true contest, but at most an exhibition. Indeed, if the contest is not carried out under conditions that are fair to both opponents, without any advantage or favor for either of them, it cannot be considered a true combat.

But God wanted *to be truly loved* by man. Which would mean that He would have to love as a human being, which is man's only way of loving, though in this case elevated also by grace, otherwise a true Love relationship would not exist between God and him. Indeed, each lover must act according to his nature, even though in man's case it be elevated to be *supernatural*. But such an elevation, fashioned by grace, neither destroys nor decreases nor prescinds with human nature, but purifies, elevates, and empowers it. And an *empowered* human nature does not cease to be human nature.

And Love, as we have been saying, is a competition. Which is another of the motives for the Incarnation: if God wanted to face man in a combat of Love, and in just conditions, that is to say true ones so that the competition be real, He had to become man.

The New Testament addresses this issue explicitly. From the Old we could still infer a general theory about Love; though with difficulty, or not at all, the authentic divine–human Love, since God made Man in Jesus Christ had not appeared yet. But now Jesus Christ Himself, stating previously a general approach to the subject, puts things in their place and gives way to the only possibility for divine–human Love to be a reality:

> *No longer do I call you servants,*
> *for the servant does not know what his master is doing;*
> *but I have called you friends,*
> *for all that I have heard from my Father*
> *I have made known to you.*[63]

Where it becomes clear that God does not want to have a simple Lord–servant relationship with man, but of friend to friend, of absolute intimacy and affection. For *when Jesus knew that his hour had come to depart out of this world to the Father, "having loved his own who were in the world, he loved them to the end."*[64] So He loved them *to the end...* Certainly, now the cards are on the table, and we only need to start the contest.

One of the events of the Last Supper, from which we usually do not draw the entire depth of its meaning, is narrated in John 13: 1–15 and describes the washing of the disciples' feet by the Master. The fragment is usually interpreted as a manifestation of humility by Jesus Christ. Which is true, as long as we do not forget that the Word of God, contained in revealed texts, is living and active (Heb 4:12); and that, having been pronounced for all men, of all times and places, is subject to interpretation in depths that are never exhausted. The climactic moment of this scene is surely when Saint Peter, considering himself unworthy and on an inferior level to his Master, refuses to have his feet washed by Him. Whereupon Jesus admonishes him in a strict tone: *If I do not wash you, you will not have part with me.* Now, it would be possible to believe that both, the refusal of Peter before the gesture of his Master, meant as an act of humility that ends in a situation of affectionate rebellion,

---

[63] Jn 15:15.
[64] Jn 13:1.

and, at the same time, Jesus Christ's intention to show His love and humility to His disciples indicating a way of conducting themselves, would offer a sufficient explanation of the passage: *If I who am the Lord and Master have washed your feet...*

But as often is the case in gospel texts that refer directly to Jesus Christ, the ultimate reasons that motivate His words or conduct can be more profound. Jesus, having loved them *to the end* (13:1), wanted consequently to put Himself on the same level as His disciples. Which was actually necessary if He wanted to be reciprocated in the same way; for though the personal condition of the lovers is still specific to each one of them, since the love relation requires the *I* of each one as essential, it is true that Love places both in a situation of being *on the same level.* Which seems normal when we consider that in Love *everything* of one is also of the other:

> *My beloved is mine and I am his.*[65]

The bride, for her part, speaks of her intimacy with the Lover. Though in such a way, nevertheless, that seems to imply that any type of inequality, regarding the dignity of one or the other, would be as if erased, if not at least forgotten:

> *O that his left hand were under my head,
> and that his right hand embraced me!*[66]

This is what the Apostle Peter was opposing, with good intention but mistakenly; consequently, he received a serious warning from

---

[65] Song 2:16; 6:3.
[66] Song 2:6; cf. 8:3.

Jesus Christ: *If I do not wash you, you will have no part with me.* In which we need not see a simple recrimination directed to the disciple, but a warning to make him understand that, in this case, he could not have part with his Master. We are not dealing then, with a reproach toward the refusal of Saint Peter, but an admonishing founded on the need imposed by the nature of things: if there is not a situation of equal condition, there cannot be a relationship of Love.

One could think that the act of humility of Jesus Christ before His disciples exceeds what is normal, to the point of seeming excessive. So disproportionate and even exaggerated if you want, that it could be considered a humiliation.

And it is true that it could be construed as an exaggerated act. If for *exaggerated* we understand here what exceeds what is normal and passes the limits of what is reasonable. That is why it should be qualified more as *excessive*, in the sense of surpassing the petty and limited human measures, which is understandable when we have in mind the infinite distance there is between the Person of the Master and that of the disciple. Maybe that is what Saint Paul wanted to express when he said that the Word *semet ipsum exinanivit*,[67] or that he became *nothing* for the sake of men. Since the distance between God and His creatures is infinite and absolutely immeasurable, it is reasonable to say [an apparent absurdity] that the Infinite Being became Nothing. The fact that God wanted to make man a participant in His own nature, to give to him and receive His Love, and make him His son, intimate friend, and His conversation partner, is inconceivable for the creature; but sufficient for God to have wanted to be so close to him as to become similar to him and even equal to him: *And the Word became flesh and dwelt among us.*

---

[67] Phil 2:7.

The problem raised here is the apparent antinomy that God decided to enter into something like a tournament or contest, as an equal to an equal, between Himself and His creature; and, what is most strange, that He allows him the possibility of defeating Him.

Nevertheless, we must have in mind that God does not like to deal with things as if they were imaginary; nor does He grant gifts that do not correspond to any other reality than that of metaphoric or figurative language. If He grants man the gift of competing with Him and places him on an equal plane, such a grace supposes a condescendence of *real* significance. And because it is real, we understand that man enjoys the possibility of winning.

What happens is that such a possibility for man is, of course, as we have already suggested, the work of grace. Which always grants gifts that are real and do not end up resolving themselves in pure wordplay. According to which, in the end, everything is a gift from God. Concretely, in this situation that we are talking about, two things can happen. Either God is the winner of the contest, in which case we are before an ineffable display of grace; or it is man who wins the victory, in such a way that then he will find himself before a magnanimous and incredible reality... also from among the marvels of grace. At the end of it all, what Bernanos said through the mouth of the Country Priest would remain: *Everything is grace*. Indeed, it is evident that grace is something ineffable.

What seems unfathomable remains to be explained: the possibility of God being defeated by man in the combat of Love. Indeed, we are confronted with a very difficult thing to understand. In any case, in absence of an exhaustive explanation, it may be possible to find hints capable of giving some response to the curiosity of human understanding. It is evident that to even attempt any *kind of explanation,* we would need to enter into the study of the mysteries of Mystical Theology and to go deeper into the profound secrets of contemplative prayer. Consequently, it is possible that we will get to know very little; and even most probably nothing at all.

Additionally, the language used here alludes to real things and not dreams as we have already mentioned above; therefore, extreme precaution should be in order because, although the language deals with real things, it not always should be interpreted according to ordinary human understanding and ways of expression. We find ourselves inside the scope of supernatural mysteries —in fact before the greatest of all mysteries, which is that of Love— which is inaccessible for man, except at levels of understanding that do not exceed superficiality. It will be necessary, therefore, to walk as if over lit charcoal, with a scrupulous care to avoid numerous obstacles, always being mindful of analogy; without forgetting, for instance, to be careful to avoid any hint of anthropomorphism, *theomorphism*, or other attempts to improperly transpose to the supernatural realities or expressions that pertain to the natural and mundane.

First of all, it must be clearly stated, without discussion, that, since God is Infinite Love, no one can pretend to love more than He does.

Having established this, we must insist on the question: How is it possible then to talk of competition in the divine–human love relationship?

Since God is Infinite Being, He is identical to Infinite Love or Essential Love (1 Jn 4:8). But Infinite Love, or simply Love, is an unfathomable bottomless well before which man can do nothing other than to *lean out* over the rim. It is impossible for the human being to come to understand the degree of profound liberality by which Infinite Magnificence is capable of pouring Himself out to His creature. It happens however that acting in this way, God does nothing other than manifest His greatness, lavishing His generosity infinitely; or, in any case, to the point in which the creature is able to receive it. Using a human way of speaking, we could say that the divine munificence *is actualized even more* when it becomes real in creatures. It would be licit to call imprudent the man who, daring to put limits to Love, would try to determine to where Infinite Love is capable and to where Infinite Love is not capable of reaching.

If we admit that God has wanted that His love relationship with man be composed under the form of contest or combat, presumably there would be the necessary conditions so that it could be qualified as an authentic and just contest.

For which it is necessary for both contestants —God and man— to find themselves equipped on equal terms. Avoiding what would suppose an advantage for either of them, as required by the rules to be kept in the competition among noble contenders.[68]

But in this specific case, man could not place himself at the level of and according to the situation of God. From where it was necessary that God should *descend* to the level and condition of man. In this way it is possible to understand that the difficulty to comprehend this situation —that of a competition of Love between God and man— is no different, in the end, from those that arise when accepting the mystery of the Incarnation.

That God has wanted to make man His *partner*, which is to say His companion, His friend, His associate, and, therefore, His competitor and adversary in the Love relationship to be carried out with Him, is easy to admit if we accept the revealed fact that God really has wanted to make man His friend (Jn 15: 14–15), His son (1 Jn 3: 1–2), and even a participant in His divine nature (2 Pet 1:4). And of course, it is easier to understand the former than the latter. If God has elevated man to the category of His *true* son, why not admit that He has accepted him as an antagonist in the competition of Love that the lovers (God and man in this case) undertake?

The condition of being equalized to the same status between God and man is clearly witnessed in Scripture. The fundamental and most important text is the Prologue of the Gospel of Saint John: *And the Word was made flesh and dwelt among us.*[69]

The first of the two parts of the verse —*And the Word was made flesh*— is read without difficulty in the proper sense. Regarding the second —*And dwelt among us*—, it is more susceptible to interpretation in a *soft* sense; namely according to the literal and superficial meaning that he lived *in our midst*. Nevertheless, everything seems to point to the fact that the text should be read equally in a *strong* sense, since its intention to emphasize

---

[68] *An athlete is not crowned unless he competes according to the rules* (2 Tim 2:5).
[69] Jn 1:14.

that the Word became *one of us* is evident, exactly the same as what the first part of the verse states.

But it does not seem necessary to insist on the topic about which Scripture texts abound. From the *semet ipsum exinanivit*, of Philippians 2:7, to others of interest for the topic at hand. Like the one that puts in the mouth of Jesus Christ the certainty that those who confide in Him will do greater things than He did: *Truly, truly, I say to you,*[70] *he who believes in me will also do the works that I do; and greater works than these will he do, because I go to the Father.*[71] Or the one that contains the consoling and emotional promise stated also in the farewell Sermon: *And when I go and prepare a place for you, I will come again and will take you to myself, that where I am you may be also.*[72]

As we can see, the challenge of love on equal terms, that can even end in an advantage for man, is not a topic that is foreign to Sacred Scripture.

We find ourselves, consequently, before the loving confrontation between God and man, as we have repeatedly said. Though we have also said that Love is an unfathomable abyss of mystery. If man already has difficulty delving into the reality of created and participated Love, what can we say about his possibility of understanding when he encounters the depths of Infinite Love? Furthermore, man is incapable of explaining —for the simple reason that he never has come to understand it— the mysterious attraction that Greatness experiences toward Smallness, Infinite to the finite, Being in Essence to created being, Magnanimity to weakness and destitution, the Highest Holiness to weakness and frailty... For it is evident that God is seduced by the humble: *In that same hour he rejoiced in the Holy Spirit and said, "I thank thee, Father, Lord of heaven and earth, that thou hast hidden these things from the wise and understanding and revealed them to babes; yea, Father, for such was thy gracious will.*[73] So there is nothing unusual that, as some theologians have assured us, God moved forward the time of His Incarnation feeling fascinated by the humil-

---

[70] Pay attention to this initial emphasis.
[71] Jn 14:12.
[72] Jn 14:3.
[73] Lk 10:21.

ity and purity of the Virgin of Nazareth. Regarding the statement about the joy experienced by Jesus Christ when He pronounced His enthusiastic exclamation contained in the text of Saint Luke, *it is not said incidentally nor as a circumstantial detail*; but rather it is the demonstration of what we have been saying. The overflowing rejoicing it mentions is the result of the seduction experienced by the Creator for the smallness and weakness of His creature. A rejoicing about which and by which Jesus Christ also feels completely in tune with the Father.[74]

After all we have said, we still must deal with the most difficult aspect of the problem: Is it possible, since it seems contradictory, that man could end as the winner in the contest of Love undertaken between him and God? The decision to respond affirmatively, with the support of texts such as the parable of the talents or of the pounds, without insisting more on the topic and going on, would be too simple. But since our understanding would not be satisfied, it will be necessary to outline an explanation, if that be possible and to the extent it is possible.

First and foremost, it must be clear, though it is not necessary to say so, that Infinite Love cannot be exceeded in intensity of Love by any creature. To state anything else would be contradictory, apart from absurd, and no one would be willing to support it.

In which case, if we still insist on configuring the divine–human love relationship as a tournament or competition of Love, with the possibility

---

[74] The fascination and seduction that Smallness has over Greatness is another mystery. Without a doubt, in Humility there are sufficient glimpses of Beauty and Goodness to be capable of attracting Majesty. Maybe it is all due to the fact that, in contemplating what is small, the Supreme Magnanimity finds an opportunity to become what It is Itself; which is the same as to say that the infinitely Magnanimous Being finds a chance to love. It is true that Infinite Love does not need love outside of Himself. But, in the case that He decide to do so, led by His own Love, in order to extend it to other beings and elevate them in that way to the condition of co–participants, *there is no reason at all to qualify such a decision as unreasonable*. That is why it seems logical that Scripture places the Spirit of God at the beginning of time itself, presiding over the first instant of Creation (Gen 1:2). After all, the created Universe is the product of Love.

of man being the winner, we should try to search for an explanation. That being said, does such an explanation exist?

Of course, the decisions and judgments of God are absolutely immutable *ab aeterno*. A truth of faith that human reason itself can easily understand. But the fact is that the decisions of God, about cases and occasions in which, according to the magnificence of His Grace, He has decided to allow that *the will of man prevail over His own, are also equally "ab aeterno."* They are circumstances in which the infinite divine Liberality is going to give man's will the chance to *break* and impose itself on the divine. It is true that if someone in the act of condescension would let himself be defeated out of love, it is possible to think that, in the end, both the result and the combat itself, would be close to fiction.

Which seems true with regard to creatures, but in no way in the case of God Whose gifts, always given by grace, are *absolutely real* and, because of that, far from any aspect of fantasy or imagination. If God granted the faculty that, in a certain case, the human will should prevail above His own, such a gift has nothing to do with fiction. The will and word of God do what they say, nothing more: *so shall my word be that goes forth from my mouth; it shall not return to me empty, but it shall accomplish that which I purpose, and prosper in the thing for which I sent it.*[75]

On the other hand, Sacred Scripture, both in the Old and in the New Testament contain examples that ratify the truth of what we have been saying.

During the period of the Old Law, the cases in which Moses repealed the will of God to punish the Jewish People are well known.

Regarding the New Testament, we will limit ourselves to quote two characteristic examples.

The first, and maybe more important, refers to the narration of the episode of the wedding at Cana, contained in the Gospel of Saint John 2: 1–12. According to the Evangelist, the Virgin Mary, who had been invited to the nuptial banquet with her Son, intercedes for the bride and groom about the difficulty they were in. The Mother realized that the wine had run out and, doubtless moved by compassion, she discreetly let her Son

---

[75] Is 55:11.

know. Who responds to her, not without a certain indifference, that the problem had nothing to do with them: *Woman, what does this have to do with you or me? My hour has not yet come.* An affectionate rebuke to which, by the way, the Mother pays no attention and, instead of that, gives instructions to the servants to do what Jesus tells them. With the happy result we know and that is detailed in the narration.

The other episode refers to the case of the Canaanite woman,[76] and it is even more surprising, if possible, than the previous. The Master denies granting her request and responds with words that do not fail to contain a certain hardness and acrimony. After saying that He had been sent personally only to the House of Israel and not to foreigners, he says to the woman: *It is not good to take the bread of the children and give it to the little dogs.* But in turn, the response of the stranger is a surprising show of wit, humility, and loving affection: *It is true, Lord, but the little dogs also eat the crumbs that fall from the table of their masters.* Whereupon the reaction of the Lord, disregarding His own will, is as moving as it is understandable in a Heart like His.[77]

As usual in any combat, each one of the combatants aims to win victory, for there is no other objective of the fight. In the one the Christian fights throughout his earthly life, in which the victor has

---

[76] Mt 15: 21–28. Others say Syrophoenician. Saint Mark clarifies that she came from the territory of Tyre and Sidon (7:24).

[77] The doctrine about the Saints as *intercessors*, so deeply rooted in the Church since her very origins, abounds on this topic. The Christian People always professed deep devotion to these champions of Christ, whom they considered as models to imitate and as powerful advocates before God on their behalf. The Saints were champions to achieve good things for those who still militate, as well as to annul God's decrees punishing the sins of His militant children. Unfortunately, surely due to the torrential *rain of Saints* which fell on the Church after the Second Vatican Council, devotion to the Saints is one more of the pearls that the treasure of popular devotions has lost.

been promised a crown, it is no different: *To him who conquers I will grant to eat of the tree of life.*[78]

But especially in combats on the scale of a multitude, the outcome does not depend only on the contenders as such, but we must also have in mind the weapons and instruments used in the confrontation. Which can vary from one to the other in their quantity and degree of perfection. The previous study of the set of elements that intervene in the fray, along with previous and careful consideration, is what strategy is about; whose correct approach before combat is fundamental if one does not want to be defeated (Lk 14:31).

Nevertheless, the combat that the Christian has with God *is entirely different from the one he fights against the World*. This last is no longer a combat of love, but a confrontation of true enmity and even of hatred by the World.

The hatred by the World for Christians is a consequence of its hatred for Jesus Christ, which extends to the disciples. *The world cannot hate you, but it hates me because I testify of it that its works are evil.*[79] Of course, as we could expect, the consequences of the hatred for Jesus Christ do not take long to appear, since *a disciple is not above his teacher, nor a servant above his master; it is enough for the disciple to be like his teacher, and the servant like his master. If they have called the master of the house Beelzebub, how much more will they malign those of his household.*[80] The feelings of the World toward the disciples are always the result of those experienced towards the Master, corresponding to the intimate relationship and dependence that exists between the Head and His members: *If the*

---

[78] Rev 2:7.

[79] Jn 7:7. Thus, in this order. The World does not hate Jesus Christ because of its contempt for Christians, but the other way around. First comes the hatred for Jesus Christ; later, and by extension, hatred for His followers.

[80] Mt 10: 24–25.

world hates you, know that it has hated me before it hated you...*[81]* If they kept my word, they will keep yours also.*[82]*

The strong relationship of dependence by Christians on Jesus Christ gives meaning and relevance to their existence. According to the demands of Love, human life, made to love and be loved, only develops as such *when it identifies with and is changed for that of another*; understanding the *other* as the loved one. To become an authentic existence it must go out of itself, since otherwise *it remains alone and does not bear fruit* (Jn 12:24); which means that it would not go beyond being sterile and useless.[83] Be that as it may, *the disciples follow their Master and share His existence*. For them, following the loved Person and participating in His life is what gives meaning to their existence, in addition to true Happiness. In this way, the suffering and joy of the Master is the suffering and joy of the disciples. At this point, do successes or failures matter much, when the only thing that is worthwhile is being with Him and staying next to Him, experiencing the Joy of hearing His voice (Jn 3:29) and leaning close to His breast (Jn 13:23)? It is in this sense that we can say that the *following* is consubstantial to Christian life (Mt 16:24):[84]

> *Following thy footprints*
> *The young girls run along by the way.*
> *At the touch of a spark,*
> *And at the spiced wine,*
> *Flows forth the Divine balsam.*[85]

---

[81] Jn 15:18.

[82] Jn 15:20.

[83] We must note the relationship existing between solitude and infertility. The human being, created by Love with the end purpose of loving and being loved in turn, is not at all destined to find itself alone; which would be nothing other than an egotism in the path that is contrary to Love. That is why Hell is defined as eternal solitude.

[84] Cf. Mk 8:34; Lk 9:23.

[85] Saint John of the Cross, *Spiritual Canticle*.

We must take into account that *following* Christ is not the first phase that the Christian must face in his spiritual life, nor the definitive one. The first step that the disciple must take on this path consists in abandoning everything in order to make following the Master possible (Mt 19:21). In the business of Love the lover *is not satisfied with following the beloved person* but, above all, looks for reciprocal and mutual belonging. The attitude of the formerly blind man of Jericho, filled with thanks and affection, is still far from what would be perfect Love: *immediately he received his sight and followed him on the way.*[86] But in divine–human Love we are not trying to walk the same path, but to become one and only with Him, since, ultimately, Jesus Christ Himself is the way: *I am the Way, the Truth, and the Life.*[87]

Thus the three phases that compose the framework of Christian perfection become clear: abandoning everything, following Jesus Christ, and achieving at last, in that way, an identification and interchange of lives.[88] Therefore, there is a previous phase whose mission is to make possible the second one or an intermediate that serves as a link until we reach at last the definitive moment in which the process of mutual possession in Love culminates.[89]

It is logical that this should be the case, since following would make no sense without a reference to the final point or arrival. The path only serves to arrive at a definitive place, and not to stay on it. Its mission is to serve as an instrument to those who still find themselves as pilgrims or *in via*, searching for a final destination not yet reached. And, therefore, the way always involves a period of effort and anxiety.

---

[86] Mk 10:52.

[87] Jn 14:6.

[88] It is important to insist that the identification of lives does not mean the disappearance of either lover or the transformation of either lover into the other. The absolute identity of each one of the persons, as such person, is an indispensable condition for Love to exist.

[89] The classical text in this sense is Matthew 19:21: *If you want to be perfect* (last phase) *go and sell everything you have* (first phase) and then *come and follow me* (intermediate phase).

> *Whither hast thou hidden thyself,*
> *And hast left me, O Beloved, to my sighing?*
> *Thou didst flee like the hart,*
> *Having wounded me.*
> *I went out after thee, calling, and thou wert gone.*[90]

Even the intermediate, or following, phase is subject to the ups and downs that are present in the first one, where one must abandon everything. This initial stage is never easy but overcoming it is indispensable for going on to the next. Saint Peter, for example, had still not understood that the true following of the Master would mean for him, as a previous requisite, the hard test of his own cowardice and betrayal which he would have to assume and overcome. Only afterward he would find himself able to clearly and openly follow Him: *Where I am going* —Jesus Christ told him— *you cannot follow me now; but you shall follow afterward.*[91]

The final or *last* part of the process does not exactly match, therefore, with following the Master. But rather with the moment of His final return, when He will come again to be forever with His own: *Father, I desire that they also, whom thou hast given me, may be with me where I am.*[92]

It is interesting to note that Christian Spirituality has shown, in general, a tendency to put the emphasis more on the intermediate phase than the last one. Frequently it has insisted more on the phase of following or of imitating Christ (Thomas à Kempis), as if this were the definitive one. According to some, this issue leads to no practical result. Others, on the contrary, are inclined to question the alleged lack of consequences: Is there any theoretical conclusion that lacks practical consequences...? And there are even some who have intended to see here, for example, a certain connection with the problem of the relationship between active and contemplative life. In any case, the imitation of the life or virtues of Jesus Christ *cannot be an end in itself*; since that which Christian existence is

---

[90]Saint John of the Cross, *Spiritual Canticle*.
[91]Jn 13:36.
[92]Jn 17:24.

directed to is union with Him, through participation in His own life. Or in other words, Asceticism is not the end, but the path toward Mysticism.

The fight that the Christian has to wage against the World and the Power of Darkness is unique and atypical. By which we mean that the norms that govern it are not the ones that govern fights among men. And even less those that preside over the challenge of love with God.

In the fight against the World there is a first rule which, even though fundamental, is forgotten by Christians with more frequency than desirable: *the weapons and means to be used by one side and the other are completely different.* Or rather we must say that they should be so, for Christians usually insist on using in the struggle the same means as the Enemy.

Saint Paul clearly said: *for the weapons of our warfare are not worldly but have divine power to destroy strongholds.*[93] Where two important statements are made. First, and always, according to the Apostle, the weapons the Christian should use in the fray have nothing to do with those used by the Power of Evil. Second, as he then adds, those specific to the disciples of Jesus Christ are powerful enough *to destroy strongholds.* In another place he is even more explicit: *Stand therefore, having girded your loins with truth, and having put on the breastplate of righteousness, and having shod your feet with the equipment of the gospel of peace; above all taking the shield of faith, with which you can quench all the flaming darts of the evil one. And take the helmet of salvation, and the sword of the Spirit, which is the word of God. Pray at all times in the Spirit, with all prayer and supplication.*[94]

---

[93] 2 Cor 10:4.
[94] Eph 6: 14–18.

In fact, Saint Paul does nothing here other than to apply the doctrine clearly expressed in the Gospel. Meaning, in the end, that the content of the Christian Message *is not only different from the criteria of the World, but it is the opposite of them*. A different and contrary message, which is the Gospel, that leads to a Life that is distinct and contrary to the World.

The Apostle expresses this doctrine in all of his exhortations. Regarding his preaching, for example, he gives a discourse that seems to be done on purpose. In it he inserts a series of apparently incongruent and paradoxical norms that doubtless would be categorized by the criteria of the World as nonsense: *When I came to you, brethren, I did not come proclaiming to you the testimony of God in lofty words or wisdom. For I decided to know nothing among you except Jesus Christ and him crucified. And I was with you in weakness and in much fear and trembling; and my speech and my message were not in plausible words of wisdom, but in demonstration of the Spirit and power, that your faith might not rest in the wisdom of men but in the power of God.*[95] As we can see, we find ourselves here in the diametrically opposite place to the ways of acting used by modern Pastoral practice.

The Pauline procedures, as we can surmise, are none other than those advocated by Jesus Christ about how to evangelize: *Take no gold, nor silver, nor copper in your belts, nor bag for your journey, nor two tunics, nor sandals, nor a staff; for the laborer deserves his food.*[96] Where it is noteworthy that it is not just a question of the absurd attempt to use natural means to achieve supernatural ends; but also it is quite clear that the madness of the World can only be fought by the Wisdom of the madness of God (Rom 8:7;

---

[95] 1 Cor 2: 1–5.
[96] Mt 10: 9–10; cf. Lk 9:3; 10:4.

1 Cor 1: 21.23; 2:5; 2 Cor 1:12; Gal 5:11; Eph 3:10). Ultimately, it is about confronting the whirlwind of madness into which the World has fallen with the scandal of the Cross.

The current crisis caused by the modernist heresy that has invaded the Church, after and as a result of the Second Vatican Council, has given rise to the important shift in Pastoral practice and the Liturgy of the Spouse of Christ. All of which, in turn, has created enough confusion to cause a quite widespread questioning of the faith. Christians are *no longer in a position to believe* that their own specific weapons, which are those that should be used in the fight against the World, are powerful enough to destroy fortresses, in spite of the promise of Scripture. So it would be a mistake to attribute the current situation to a *simple strategical error*. For what has actually happened is something very different. The attitude that the *World is right* has been received with universal acceptance. Whether it is said or not, the current moment contemplates a large-scale crisis of Faith. Since Pastoral practice and Liturgy do not enjoy specific autonomy, but are a practical application of Dogma, everything depends on the set of beliefs in Faith the latter includes..., or maybe of disbeliefs.

In fact, the practice of almost all Religious Families in the Church, especially since the Modern Age, has followed this path. Doubtless, with the best imaginable intentions. The problem arose when the method of seeking Power was adopted, in addition to the suitable use of human means possible to spread good *from and by them*. The situation has even created a great danger for the Church, which is why we have called it by the term *Great Temptation*, whose dire consequences are before our eyes.[97] Unfortunately, though inexplicably

---

[97] Cf. my book *Waiting for Don Quixote*, Shoreless Lake Press, New Jersey, 2007, pp. 385–477.

no one apparently considered it, Power and Money always lead to corruption and disaster (Mt 6:24; Lk 16:13); no matter how much men, including Christians, are determined not to see it this way.

This being the reality, how should Orders, Families, Congregations, Religious Institutes face the problem? Because the problem undoubtedly exists, and denying it would make it worse. And yet, this issue is part of another more general one that includes the urgent necessity of a General Reform —*in capite et in membris*— of the whole Church, which undoubtedly must be undertaken by the Church herself, sooner or later, if she wants to make real the promise of her Founder about her permanence till the End of Time.

Of course, we are not going to make the mistake of denying the need and usefulness of Religious Families in the Church; we simply want to raise awareness about the need of facing the problem. Looking for, especially, a better orientation of Religious Families, capable in turn of leading to a reshaping of their structures. A task to be performed by an extensive reform, whose main objective would be to safeguard the Spirit; namely: the way of living gospel teachings in community in today's world, in the way that most benefits the Church. A hard task, in which men of the stature of Saint Francis of Assisi or Saint Ignatius of Loyola, along with others that came after, failed: *Historia est Magistra Vitae...*, if we are willing to listen to her.

But an arduous and difficult task does not indicate the impossibility of carrying it out. As for what we are referring to here, the need to confront it is evident. To which end we will have to start by giving it due importance, compared to other topics that are maybe given too much attention at the present time. Which can be of greater or lesser transcendence, like the need for dialogue, tolerance, Ecumenism, etc., but that do not reach the seriousness of the one we are talking about and about which, oddly enough, is hardly ever talked about. And either way, how can we pretend to organize someone else's house without fixing our own first? Saint Paul already warned that one of the qualities of a Bishop must be to know how to govern his own house (1 Tim 3:4). Adding in another place: *For what have I to do with judging outsiders? Is it not those inside the church whom you are to judge? God judges those outside. "Drive out the wicked person from among you."*[98] As if the Apostle believed in the need of fixing one's own business before aiming to organize another's.

As we can see, the problem centers again on the apparent opposition between Faith and Reason. Nevertheless, the confrontation between the criteria of the World and those of the Faith is inherent to Christianity. Recognizing that the teachings contained in the gospel Message, if considered with only the light of human reason, can seem nonsensical. So deep is the opposition between the Gospel and the World, or between the thoughts of God and those of Men (Is 55: 8–9; Rom 11:33).

Something we can see more clearly, for example, in reference to another teaching of Jesus Christ. Precisely one that affects the way human beings live and the way society is organized. But which, examined merely with the light of human reason, sounds like madness: *"You know that the rulers of the Gentiles lord it over them, and their great men exercise authority over them.*[99] *It shall not be so among you; but whoever would be great among you must be your servant, and whoever would be first among you must be your slave.*[100]

---

[98] 1 Cor 5: 12–13.

[99] We must recognize that there is no better overall description of practically *all* forms of government among men. Notice that Jesus Christ expresses here a generalization that seems to have no exceptions.

[100] Mt 20: 25–27.

The key to the problem lies in that progressive Theology accepts essentially none of the tenets of the Faith. It aims to develop a more *reasonable* religion, convinced that it would be the only one acceptable to the modern world and modern men. Additionally, this Theology understands as *reasonable* only that which human understanding is capable of elaborating and explaining. For progressive Theology, the *Dark Ages*, far from being limited to History's Middle Ages, endures to our time... until we reach its definitive extinction at the moment that coincides with the celebration of the Second Vatican Council. This Theology normally offers itself to believers as being the blossoming of authentic Christianity. To which end it presents insistent mantras to the community of Christians, like the so often displayed *Springtime of the Church.* It knows well the strong impact value of slogans and platitudes repeated unceasingly, and that the falser they are the wider acceptance they receive. This phenomenon can only be explained by the general increase of evil, which in turn has led to a cooling of charity (Mt 24:12), a weakness of Faith, and the consequent disposition of people to prefer and love falsehood (Rev 22:15). Whereby numerous people of good will are being deceived, despite the difficulty of fully exempting anybody of any responsibility. Either way, it is well known that, throughout History and especially in more modern times, Humanity has been controlled and guided by astute, hidden minorities.

Progressive Theology, interpreting Hebrews 11:1 in a restrictive way —*Now faith is the assurance of things hoped for, the conviction of things not seen*— identifies *things not seen* with what is irrational and false. For this Theology, *things not seen* equals what transcends and exceeds human understanding. That which does not fit in it or is not its own product and which, therefore, cannot be admitted. It is an assumption that ignores the fact that Faith and truth mutually condition each other, namely: Faith is founded on truth and truth, in turn, is supported and authenticated by Faith.

On the other hand, this Theology confuses the *content* of the Faith, which does indeed exceed human understanding, with the *motives* to accept and believe it (reasons for credibility and preambles of the faith), that are entirely rational and reasonable. Hence it infers that Faith is irrational and that it has nothing to do with the truth.

Jesus Christ relates Faith with the truth and makes the former depend on the latter: *If I tell the truth, why do you not believe me?*[101] According to His words, regarding He Himself, the reasons for credibility are based on evidence itself: *If I am not doing the works of my Father, then do not believe me; but if I do them, even though you do not believe me, believe the works.*[102] So the works and the facts provide evidence and, therefore, deserve credibility. It is reality perceptible in itself and put before our eyes..., unless we chose to close them to not see.

If Faith lacked reasons upon which to base itself, it would indeed be irrational; but, in the end, the fundamental determining reason for the assent of faith is the authority of a revealing God.

But modern man has decided that *there cannot be any truth* other than his own, truth he himself has elaborated. To which when someone asks *why* it must be that way, he will respond that he himself *has decided it*. Which does indeed seem irrational.

The act of Faith is at the same time an act of the intellect and an act of the will. It is not merely an act of reason, nor simply an act of the will; it is an act of a human being. Therefore, neither the human reason nor the will separately are what adhere to God, *but*

---

[101] Jn 8:46.
[102] Jn 10:37; cf. 5:36; 10:25; 15:24.

the complete human being, who gives himself to God and grants Him freely his confidence. Whereby once again we see on the horizon the old problem of intellectualism and voluntarism, each of them trying to understand man on its own without achieving it. For it is the condition of human nature to be endowed with both intelligence and will in the unity of a whole.

What has been said explains that the act of Faith resolves itself in being an act of Love; as always happens in all the relationships between God and man. For the unconditional surrender and the total submission is only given to him in whom you believe and in whom you fully confide; or said in another way, to him whom you love. For it is well known that true Love does not impose conditions nor indicate restrictions: *it does not rejoice at wrong but rejoices in the right. Love bears all things, believes all things, hopes all things, endures all things.*[103] The fact is that true Love does not understand anything that is not *totality*.

It does not correspond to this place to address the delicate topics of the relationship between Faith and Reason, the nature of Faith as a free act, the dark nature of Faith, or the role of the reasons for believing in relation to the freedom of the act of Faith. All these questions are dealt with in Theological treatises.

Consequently, we will limit ourselves to briefly summarizing some of the issues established as certain by Catholic Doctrine. From which we will advance some conclusions, always subject to debate, to the problem that we have been dealing with.

(1) First and foremost, the act of Faith *is a free act.*

The scripture basis for this truth, settled and definitively defined in the First Vatican Council,[104] is very clear (Mk 1:15; 16:16; Jn 3: 18–19;

---

[103] 1 Cor 13: 6–7.
[104] Ses. III, cap. III, c. 5.

1 Jn 3:23). Not forgetting that the act of Faith is meritorious and infused with Grace since it is a supernatural virtue.

Saint Augustine said that *credere non potest, nisi volens.*[105]

(2) It also should be noted that the *irresistible "evidence" of the preambles of Faith is not contrary to the freedom of Faith.*

A problem widely debated by theologians, though everyone agrees about the conclusions. The *evidence* of the preambles of Faith is not that of the principles of science. The way of reconciling the *evidence* of the preambles with the freedom of the act of Faith is always a live issue in theological debates, though we have already said that the conclusions are held to be certain. It is noteworthy that many Church Documents referring to this topic avoid using the word *evidence*.

A very interesting problem, very much to the liking of theologians and open to deeper investigation.

(3) *Faith is an obscure knowledge (the dark nature of Faith).*

A truth based on texts like John 20:29, 2 Peter 1:19 and, above all, on Hebrews 11:1, where it says that Faith is the proof of things *unseen*. It is usually said that this statement has never been defined because it also has never been doubted by anyone.

The *Dictionnaire de Théologie Catholique,* in its article *Foi,* takes on the issue saying that *to speak of "things unseen" is to point to the lack of evidence of the object; and consequently, to the obscurity of its knowledge; therefore, it follows that the knowledge of Faith is dark. The word "see," in the broader sense of "knowing," is indeed used for the act of Faith, but with certain restrictions that attest to the darkness of this knowledge (1 Cor 13:12).*

The darkness of the Faith does not exist in Science.[106] The fact that the Documents start with the premise of admitting the darkness in the definition itself of Faith (Heb 11:1), is already quite significant.

---

[105] Saint Augustine, *In Joa.,* XXVI, 2.

[106] For Saint Thomas Aquinas, it is not possible to have Faith and Science at the same time about the same thing (II^a–II^{ae}, q. 1, a. 5).

But Modernism rejects Faith or dispenses with it. Its effort centers on introducing in the world a *reasonable* religion, in no way needing to resort to transcendence or the supernatural and capable, therefore, of being accepted by men of the *New Age,* in which the worship of God will be substituted with the worship of man. The final station of an *intellectual* route in which either God does not exist (atheism), or it is impossible to know Him in the case that He does exist (agnosticism).[107]

A significant part of modern Catholicism, as if it had decided to commit suicide, has chosen this orientation and has practically dispensed with Faith. A statement that is not usually proclaimed in a strong categorical way. But the stark fact is that the contents of the new Liturgies, and most notably those authorized in the Neocatechumenal, charismatic, etc. movements, openly lead to attitudes of skepticism about the Faith.

And yet, according to Scripture, *without Faith it is not possible to please God,*[108] and, therefore, there is no room for salvation. Even though this statement is only admitted by those who still believe in Scripture as the Word of God.

Since Faith is an act of the understanding, if it is denied or disregarded, the power of human reason is weakened, for it would not be possible for reason to open itself to new fields of transcendence which, thanks to Faith, elevate it and preserve it from error. It is certain that, for some, admitting Faith means in fact removing reason

---

[107] Notice that agnosticism is an even more irrational doctrine than atheism. The God of the agnostics, incapable of making Himself known to His creatures and to ask for their fidelity in the case that He did exist, would be a perfectly useless God. Which would be equal to proclaiming the *impossibility* of God's existence. And hence we infer that, if for atheism God *does not exist,* for agnosticism on the other hand *God cannot exist.*

[108] Heb 11:6.

from its own scope. Nevertheless, the truth is that the denial of the possibilities that Faith can grant human reason, in the double sense of preserving it and empowering it, has never been demonstrated.

It should be noted again that we do not intend to introduce a philosophical or theological debate here about this topic; neither corresponds to this place. But let us stress the fact that the reduction of the idea of man, disguised absurdly as an alleged exaltation of human reason and human nature, is maybe one of the number of reasons that explain the crisis that the world and the Church herself suffer today.

Europe, for example, seems overdetermined on dispensing with any trace of rationality. An advanced culture, rooted in many centuries, promoter of the most elevated culture, moral and spiritual values, has been thrown overboard. That is why there are those who say that the European continent has placed itself on the verge of suicide. Either way it is interesting to find out that this *new culture*, embodied in doctrines that have such disastrous results as *Liberation Theology*,[109] has led American indigenous people, particularly in countries like Bolivia, Ecuador, and Peru, to impose aberrations like the return to the worship of *pre–Columbian gods*. Just like that. Hispanic America, in particular, had been, since the evangelization that followed its Discovery and for multiple centuries, the most populous bulwark of Catholicism; today, unfortunately, the Catholic Faith is alarmingly decreasing and practically devastated. If the diffusion of Marxist doctrine were not enough, all indications are that, once Pandora's Box has been opened, an easy path has been given for all errors, since it no longer seems possible to choose

---

[109]Liberation Theology is not a doctrine that originated in America, but that proceeds entirely from European ideologies.

undertaking one blunder while excluding others. Another obvious example of the advances of modern civilization.

The symptoms of this situation are quite numerous, appearing even in types of activity in which a superficial observer would never have noticed. This is what happens, for example, with the transcendent *beauty* in the life of the Church.

Since the object of the intellectual act is truth, and since truth and beauty are identical, the *disqualification* of reason leads unfailingly to an undervaluation, if not a complete disintegration, of the idea of beauty. A phenomenon that is very frequently found now inside the Church and particularly in the Liturgy.

Setting aside theological debates,[110] it is evident that we cannot compare the beauty and majesty of the so-called Traditional Mass or Mass according to the Rite of Saint Pius V, with the concise simplicity, verging even on vulgarity, of the Mass implemented by Pope Paul VI after the Second Vatican Council.

They invoke, in favor of the latter, practical reasons like its brevity and simplicity. But the problem consists in finding out if the closer approach to *ordinary life*, expecting to achieve a greater participation of the People, possesses indeed the virtue of promoting devotion in the community of Christians. For we cannot disregard the danger that the faithful might get used to considering the Mass as *another thing among many in the day*, which, precisely because of this, is incapable of transporting us to a different and superior World. Of course, those who side with modernist theories that do not admit a world different than the one built by man himself, will find in the new Rite a greater accordance with their ideas.

---

[110]We do not intend here to question the validity or legitimacy of the *Novus Ordo*, which we recognize as being settled, but only to reflect on its timeliness in contrast with the *Traditional Rite*.

Although it is true that the infinite Beauty of God is identical to His infinite Simplicity, man is not a simple being. So, it is not clear that simplicity, better even than complexity, can provide a more complete perception of beauty. Given the nature of his intellectual and volitional acts, man is more open to the idea of God through a multiplicity of visible things; whose complexity and mystery contribute to elevating him to a world which is superior and distinct from the one in which he moves among *everyday things*. Man does not reach the perception of beauty through simple intuition; moreover, created things only possess fragments of beauty in greater or smaller degree. On the other hand, human knowledge always starts with the senses: *Nihil est in intellectu quod prius non fuerit in sensu...* For Saint Paul, for example the invisible perfection of God becomes accessible to human intelligence *per ea quae facta sunt*,[111] where the plural indicating collectivity used by the Apostle is worthy of note. And it is the job of the Liturgy to introduce man to the *mystery* and the world of the supernatural, inaccessible to him through the mere use of his senses. Nevertheless, it does not seem that what is vulgar and ordinary, stripped of almost any quality of transcendence, could be the better way to introduce him to the mystic and numinous universe of the worship of God. Regarding *brevity*, which is usually invoked also as a practical reason justifying the liturgical reforms, it is certain that the modern world lives at a quicker and more hurried pace than the old one; and that is why it is considered normal that the faithful have difficulty dedicating thirty minutes a week to Mass. It is important not to lose sight, nevertheless, that such faithful are the same ones that do not find it inconvenient to dedicate a good number of hours, either to watching

---

[111] Rom 1:20.

a movie, or maybe some sporting event, or simply sitting in front of the TV, without any worry about the time that goes by.

Regarding the Liturgy done by certain new Movements that have emerged inside the Church like the Charismatic, Neocatechumenal, etc. the problem worsens much more.

It is difficult to classify the worship ceremonies used by these Movements as *liturgical,* unless we use the term *Liturgy* in a broad and imprecise sense. If Liturgy is defined, in its traditional and strict sense, as *the collection of practices of divine worship and of the rules to which they are subject*, as the Spanish María Moliner Dictionary says, the term does not fit here. The Liturgy of these Movements, which completely disregards general rules in force in order to use its own, rather unique and picturesque ones, in no way emphasizes *divine worship*. What any impartial observer who sees this would infer is that the only motivation is to foment the *merely human feelings* of the participants.

It does not seem possible to deny that we can see in the worship practiced by these Movements a notable tendency to *ugliness*. We see the fact that the solemnity, gravity, and profound elevation of Gregorian chant, venerated by the Church for centuries, has been substituted by modern songs whose supernatural content and sense of the numinous is very doubtful; accompanied in turn by the strumming of guitars and other garish musical instruments which, together with the involvement of the assistants' voices and gestures, create a hectic assembly where, they say, the Spirit flaps his wings, which is very difficult to believe. Certainly, King David sang to God with the harp in his own way. Nevertheless, they still have to prove that the hustle and bustle and turmoil of such turbulent ceremonies in which the spontaneous occupies a pride of place —*the flowing of the Spirit,* according to them— are the best way to lead the soul to the interior life and to the serenity of dialogue with God: *And behold, the Lord passed by, and a great and strong wind rent the mountains, and broke in pieces the rocks before the Lord, but the Lord was not in the wind; and after the wind an earthquake, but the Lord was not in the earthquake; and after the earthquake a fire, but the Lord was not in the fire; and after the fire a still small voice. And when Elijah heard it, he wrapped his face in his mantle and went out and stood at the entrance of the cave. And behold, there came a voice to him, and said, "What are you doing here, Elijah?"*[112]

Despite all of which, it is not precisely here where we see the ugliness in the *worship* practiced in these Movements. Quickly we can notice, even with little observation, that in it they have dispensed with the solemnity, beauty, and the gravity of sacred ceremonies. And what has been used in turn to give rise to the ordinary and vulgar and even the profane.

Masses, called simply *Eucharists,* are celebrated outside of the temples, in venues or halls dedicated to ordinary activities: cafeterias, profane meeting halls, or the like; always seeking the absence of any reference to the sacred, to the sense of sacrificial liturgy according to what the Church has always practiced, and to anything that in some way might recall an altar. To which we must add that the role of the priest has been reduced to its minimum expression, when not completely annulled. Whose final reason that may explain it is unknown to laymen, as we see in all things relative to the spirituality of these Movements. When some explanation is given, something that rarely happens, it is impossible to find parallels in traditional doctrine and teachings of the Church.

Clearly, once again, the sense given to the Eucharistic celebration is of paramount importance here. The mere determination of these

---

[112] 1 Kings 19: 11–13.

Movements to avoid the term *Mass* at all costs, leads us to think that the change of terminology shows the purpose of changing the meaning of the celebration. In short, it seems evident they are making an effort to show that the Sacrifice of Christ on the Cross, truly present on the altar through the mystery of the Eucharistic celebration, has been substituted by the new meaning of simply meals of fraternity and solidarity.

Considering all pros and cons, the final balance is that we have lost sight of the notion of beauty. Worship and liturgy have been reduced to the level of today's man: ordinary, stunted in his faculties, without esthetic sense or sensibility to appreciate either the marvelousness or the splendor of being. In short, the faithful's incapacity to perceive beauty is the end of a path which, having begun by forgetting the notion of being, led, through strange but logical tracks, to the loss of the perception of the truth.

The marginalization of Faith carried out by the Neo–modernist trends, in force in the Church today, has produced disastrous consequences of a magnitude known only to God. Among which we must include the devaluation of the human being.

The two faculties most peculiar to the human being and which characterize him as a person, his intelligence and his will, were destined by God to be elevated and amplified through Grace, in a degree man himself could never have imagined (1 Cor 2:9): intelligence to the point of the contemplation of God and will to the point of feeling the joy of possessing Him.

Though both faculties are different, as appropriate in a creature, both integrate the unity that is man. Both destined by grace to reach supernatural elevation, neither of them makes sense without the other. Hence, the difficulty of understanding the final end of man as beatific vision or mere *satiating contemplation of truth*. For everything points here as well to the fact that the vision must precede desire and possession, even as a priority in nature: *nihil volitum quin praecognitum.*

Miguel de Unamuno[113] rejected this old and well–known scholastic aphorism which, according to him, constitutes the supreme principle of intellectualism. And it is interesting to note that the same position was adopted by the founder of *Opus Dei*, Saint Josemaría Escrivá.[114]

Nevertheless, it is hard to understand that the *contemplation* of God, already in the Homeland, could mean perfect happiness for man if it is not accompanied by the desire and the reality of His *possession*. If we examine the patristic and scriptural texts, it is easy to discover that all speak clearly of *sharing* divine life, with the corresponding and mutual possession. So that it is probable that neither intellectualism nor voluntarism, separately and independently, could be absolutely true. It is impossible to explain love without drawing upon the attraction felt at the contemplation of the good and the beautiful; in such a way that the feeling of love would seem impossible without that *previous* contemplation. In the bosom of the Trinity, the generation of the Son precedes (with a priority of origin, not time) the spiration of the Holy Spirit; a *spiratio* (or procession specific to the Holy Spirit) *follows* the mutual contemplation of the Father and the Son (relations of fatherhood and filiation). Regarding *cupid's arrow* to which the founder of *Opus Dei* alludes so humorously, or *love at first sight* as others say, it understands precisely as an indispensable element, that *first sight*; and it is rather unimaginable that love could spontaneously arise, as out of nothing, and without anything that provokes or arouses it. As

---

[113]In *Del Sentimiento Trágico de la Vida*. The position of Unamuno is not surprising given his enmity toward intellectualism.

[114]According to what appears in one of the historians of his life, Juan Ramón Gallo, in a biography from 1980: *Chatting, one day in February of 1960, with a group of philosophers and theologians about freedom as being better than knowledge, he surprises them with this reflection:* "The heart always goes further than the intelligence. Intelligence goes after. *And one of the philosophers will say:* And what about nihil volitum nisi praecognitum, nothing is desired if not known first? Well even with that! And if not, could you explain to me cupid's arrow that hits with only superficial knowledge?"

for the rest, everyone knows that Unamuno was a great thinker and good philosopher, though not a saint; just as Escrivá de Balaguer, who was a saint, was not, however, a philosopher.

The disqualification of human intelligence by Neo–modernist doctrines, by ignoring its potentiality to be developed through Faith, supposes a *devaluation* of the idea of man and an attack on his nature. It is also indirectly an attack against God, inasmuch as man is His masterpiece, now deprecated by man himself: *Gloria Dei est Vivens Homo*, as Saint Irenaeus said.[115] The consequence is that the attempt, so dreamed of by Freemasonry, of making a *reasonable* religion apt to be accepted by modern man, only results in diminishing him and dispossessing him of his most elevated qualities. Which, nevertheless, is still not the most serious thing.

As we have said above, the object of the act of Faith is dark, while the act in itself is essentially free. If, moreover, the principal determining factor of assenting to Faith is the authority of a revealing God, we can easily conclude that the act of Faith is, above all, an *act of confidence*.

And is, therefore, an act of loving surrender and submission. Looking past reason itself, and against all evidence, the act of Faith abandons itself in the arms of the beloved person and puts its confidence in him: *And Simon answered, "Master, we toiled all night and took nothing! But at your word I will let down the nets."*[116] But to voluntarily surrender *oneself* to the one whom you love, by giving what is most personal and intimate, as are one's own intelligence and will, is but the *act of love*. Saint Paul, referring to his sufferings, advised his disciple Timothy that they were well justified: *for*

---

[115] *Adversus Haereses*, IV. xx. 7.
[116] Lk 5:5.

which cause I suffer as I do. But I am not ashamed, for I know whom I have believed.[117]

And Jesus Himself reprimands the apostle Thomas: *Have you believed because you have seen me? Blessed are those who have not seen and yet believe.*[118] Thomas believed because of the power of the evidence, though for the Lord, blessed are those who have believed because of an act of confidence, without having seen. Such an act of surrendering one's own intelligence and will to the loved person becomes, because of that, a true act of love. Thomas adhered to his own judgment, while the true believers renounce themselves and confide in Jesus Christ out of love. The circumstance that the apostle Thomas repented of his conduct does not invalidate the situation, as the fact that he could not avoid the reproach of his Master proves. In this way, the proposal is as follows: Thomas *locked himself in* and confided in his own judgment; the believers in Jesus Christ, on the other hand, forgot about themselves and *broke out of their own selves.* And Love consists precisely in denying oneself, to surrender to the beloved person: *Beatius est magis dare quam accipere.* To give therefore, before receiving; lose one's own life, before receiving that of the other. More still: to give, without expecting to receive anything in exchange; to lose everything, knowing that no other thing is going to be found in remuneration: *Love is patient and kind; love is not jealous or boastful; it is not arrogant or rude. Love does not insist on its own way...*[119]

According to the Letter to the Hebrews, *By faith Abraham obeyed when he was called to go out to a place which he was to receive as*

---

[117] 2 Tim 1:12.
[118] Jn 20:29.
[119] 1 Cor 13: 4–5.

an inheritance; and he went out, not knowing where he was to go.[120] He did not know where to go, but confided fully in Him Who called him. And it is hard to believe that someone might infuse such a radical change to his own existence, in response to the request of another, if not done out of love.

And the *Letter to the Hebrews* continues, giving testimony to the Faith of the Fathers: *These all died in faith, not having received what was promised, but having seen it and greeted it from afar, and having acknowledged that they were strangers and exiles on the earth.*[121] So they could only see promises and greet them from afar. If they merely saw them *from afar* it is because they still found themselves too distant from the clarity about reality. And with all that, they believed firmly in them.[122]

From where we infer that putting Faith aside, as Neo–modernism does, is a direct attack against Love, and, in the end, against God Himself.

---

[120] Heb 11:8.

[121] Heb 11:13.

[122] There are abundant texts about this.

FINAL REFLECTION

As those who have arrived to this point might have noticed, I have intended to center in this last chapter on the topic of the culmination of Christian Existence insofar as it is linked to the promise of victory for those who, apart from fighting to the point of shedding blood (Heb 12:4), have believed in that victory to the end through hope. With the ineffable Prize as a recompense which Saint Paul called the *Crown of Justice*.[1]

And I say that I have tried because I have doubts that I have achieved it. Throughout the chapter, tangential questions have arisen that have made the result a little bit of everything. I must say in my favor, nevertheless, and as a weak justification, that when some topics did not seem to fit too well in the principal theme, I made an effort to at least try to make them relevant. Of course, as usually takes place in so many written works, the result will be very far from satisfying to many; and least of all, to me.

The confidence and sureness of Victory, as the culmination of the earthly existence of the disciple of Jesus Christ, is a subject of such vital importance that it is the only transcendental thing. Such confidence is now more necessary than ever for those who profess to follow Jesus Christ and who, because of that, find themselves harassed in a thousand ways by the World today and without any way out other than seeking refuge in hope.

---

[1] 2 Tim 4:8.

Fortunately, the concept of Christian hope does not coincide with human hope. The latter refers to the hope about something that can come to fruition..., but that can also fail; since often it goes beyond the possibility of those who hope. Christian hope, on the other hand, enjoys the certainty of reaching what it is waiting for, if it is accompanied by the fidelity that such promises demand (Rom 5:5).[2]

Though, in fact, Christian hope goes beyond what man can hope and take for granted. When failure seems to loom and you only perceive the darkness that surrounds everything, she gives the fortitude to continue holding on with strength; despite any obstacle that tries to stand in one's way. Like Abraham, who *believed against hope*.[3] The daily life of any human being is a mound of setbacks and suffering: pain in all its forms, sickness, various and diverse failures, not being understood by anybody, family problems, a feeling of loneliness, a sense of emptiness and uselessness of one's own life... If he is a Christian, then we must add more specific and proper sufferings, like the Night of the Spirit with its interior and exterior trials, the main one of which could be the apparent absence of God; temptations of all kinds; incomprehension and perhaps persecution by friends and enemies; one's own wavering in Faith; the diverse and subtle assaults of the World; the sharp feeling of not having responded to the Love of God, united to one's own sins... When some or all of that happens, the hour of Christian faith is at hand.

The attitude of *hoping against all hope* refers above all to the corresponding supernatural virtue, which has little to do with purely human hope. When the latter fails there is nothing to do except

---

[2]According to the Apostle: *as it is my eager expectation and hope that I shall not be at all* ashamed (Phil 1:20).

[3]Rom 4:18.

adopt the attitude of conformity and resignation. In contrast, when it seems that there is no place for anything else..., *not even for supernatural hope*; when the dense darkness appears that sometimes hovers over the *Night* of Christian life; when all seems to indicate that God has disappeared and abandoned His creature (Ps 22:2; Mt 27:46), the time to *fight against the impossible* has arrived: the time to continue trusting firmly in God and hoping against all hope. And we have said *against all hope*, that is, even apart from the supernatural virtue which also sometimes seems to have faded from the horizon of one's own existence. The same situation that Jesus Christ on the Night of the Mount of Olives and the Virgin Mary at the foot of the cross lived in an exceptionally intense way.

As we have said before, Christians of our time —and I refer particularly to Catholics, since we make up the True and Only Church— have to live in a situation in which resorting to hope is a matter of survival. And we are not without motive. For the Church finds herself going through maybe the most serious moment it has known throughout her history.

As for me, God has permitted me to know, throughout a long life, the fortunes of the Church through two very different periods of her History.

The first one, encompassing the greater part of the twentieth century, was a period of relative calm and stability for Catholicism. Though maybe we can talk of tranquility amid problems that, in fact, never have been completely absent in the life of the Church. It was in this period, for example, when the problem of the invasion of the modernist heresy appeared, which was easily and rapidly crushed by Popes Pius IX and Saint Pius X. In spite of all that, the Church expanded and prospered, conversions multiplied, the number of vocations to the priesthood and consecrated life grew, the prestige of the Hierarchy and especially the Popes increased, even some large countries, like the United States of America, came to know a time so prosperous for Catholicism that it promised a unique harvest of receptions into the Church.

The second period, in which we remain, is of such a different sign that it even can be qualified as the opposite. Beginning at the time of the death of Pius XII, it is marked by the words with which the new Pontiff, Pope John XXIII, stated that he had decided *to open the windows of the Vatican*. Besides that, John XXIII himself, inspired by the Holy Spirit —in his own words— was pleased to convene the Second Vatican Council.

Many times, considering the events throughout these years, I have thought about the possibility that the Pope, maybe victim of some error, had involuntarily opened Pandora's Box instead of the windows of the Vatican. I have also often asked, though logically without finding an answer, about the possible reasons that would prompt the Holy Spirit —if we believe the words of the Pope— to inspire the convening of a Council, bearing in mind the situation in which the Church was.

I hasten to caution that I do not pretend to undertake the task of judging behavior that does not concern me, *the Church has her own Doctors*; much less when that behavior refers to decisions possibly made by the Holy Spirit. I confine myself to mention factual situations, putting into words only what I have often asked myself about serious and transcendent issues, which is what any person who is worried about events that affect him deeply usually does.

During the time I am referring to —the last third of the last century and the first decade of the current one— we Catholics have been forced to confront very difficult times. I am referring naturally to those who have decided to maintain loyalty to the Faith and the principles which, at least until then, had been considered unchangeable.

It has been for me a long time in which I have seen myself affected by a multitude of events, many of which have been painful and have impacted my life profoundly.

I have seen my Homeland disappear as a Nation, reduced to a mere memory to be quoted by History. I have also had to witness the apostasy of Catholicism, with the resulting abandonment of its Faith, History, traditions, and glorious past. Menéndez y Pelayo[4] had already prophesied that Spain would disappear as a nation when it stopped being Catholic. Just as it has happened. The events seem to show that there is a necessary relationship of cause and effect between one and the other. And all in order to surrender to a foul paganism incapable of noticing that it finds itself on the brink of a precipice, in the face of the silence and passiveness of the whole society and even its own Church Hierarchy; as if both thought that nothing was happening: *For as in those days before the flood they were eating and drinking, marrying and giving in marriage, until the day when Noah entered the ark, and they did not know until the flood came and swept them all away.*[5]

That is how I have been hit with the pain of contemplating and suffering from inside, since I too am a member of the Church, the decomposition of Catholicism, being reduced to its minimal expression with a worse and worse outlook. I have seen myself forced to endure the strong attacks of the Modernist heresy, with all that it brought with it: general anarchy in the Liturgy, the appearance in Pastoral work of multitudinous theatrical *shows*, pretending to make believe in the existence of a prosperous Catholicism that no

---

[4]Menéndez y Pelayo, *Historia de los Heterodoxos Españoles*, Epilogue.
[5]Mt 24: 38–39.

longer exists; the crisis of Faith and the consequent questioning of almost all dogmas; the corruption of a good part of the Hierarchy, including the highest ranks that even sometimes have no problem in showing openly their lack of Faith or their mocking attitude toward Morality; the mass desertion of Catholics to other Christian faiths; the clear and expressed giving up by the Church of her missionary activity, an essential mission received from the hands of Jesus Christ Himself (Mt 28:19), not to mention the sad spectacle offered by the religious Orders in full retreat or of the Youth who have abandoned the Church, and the consequential almost total lack of vocations...

And if that were not enough, I have been pressured, hounded on all sides, to accept the Great Lie as valid. The one that consists in admitting, as an inconclusive truth, that the Church is in the best moment of her History, which has been called, I do not know if ironically or jokingly, the *Springtime of the Church.* I have not been forgiven because I have maintained the integrity of the Faith and the validity of the unchangeable principles. And I have only been permitted to subsist in exchange for being reduced to nothing, afflicted always by the pain of feeling the contempt of my own brothers.

And something even more painful. In addition to all of the above, I have found it necessary to accept, throughout my life, the unquestionable truth that a corrupt Hierarchy is still the Hierarchy of the Church. It was not possible for me to do without it, if I wanted to continue forming part of the Flock of Christ: *Ubi Petrus, ibi Ecclesia.* Wherefrom once again we find the proof that obedience is the test of fidelity, which is to say the same thing as Love: *Obediens usque ad mortem, mortem autem crucis.*[6] Because if it will not

---

[6] Phil 2:8.

always be possible, or necessary, to understand, it is still necessary to remain constantly faithful (Jn 20:27).

There are, therefore, ample reasons to adopt an attitude of hoping *beyond all hope*. A hope that, while taking for granted the reality of the fight, guarantees the certainty of the Prize to those who have confided and emerge triumphant in combat: *And to him who conquers I will grant to eat of the tree of life*. In this sense, the Christian knows well that he fights confidently: *I do not run aimlessly, I do not box as one beating the air...*[7]

And now the time has come to reflect on the mystery of the prize the victors receive.

According to what is said to the Angel of the Church of Ephesus, the winner in the conflict will be permitted to *eat of the tree of life*. Evidently, we are dealing with a metaphor into which we will have to take a closer look and try to find its meaning. At least to the extent possible.

As it could not be otherwise, if we are mindful of the unfathomable depth of revealed data, there are many cases in which the Word of God addressed to man resorts to using metaphor. Revelation contains a whole host of truths that *are there*, conveyed to mankind for his happiness and salvation; but given their mysterious nature, they cannot possibly be expressed in words understandable to man's limited understanding. Sometimes there is no other way than to present them like an insinuating whispering, allowing man the freedom, supported always by the light of the Spirit, so that he can try to *sense*, or maybe *grasp*, the depth of the mystery: *What no eye has seen, nor ear heard, nor the heart of man conceived...*[8] And we can already see that the apostle Saint Paul himself recog-

---

[7] 1 Cor 9:26.
[8] 1 Cor 2:9.

nizes that there is no way to discover, even in a vague way, what is waiting for those who complete the Christian life, since what is promised is too sublime to be described, even by angelic words —if they were to be addressed to man. Then...? Then there is no other remedy than what is normal in these cases, namely: to attempt to delve deep into the metaphor and compare it to other revealed data that are parallel or complementary.

And since the prize promised to the Angel of Ephesus speaks of the tree of life, it seems normal to suppose that it refers to Life. On the other hand, the recompense offered to the Angel of the Church of Smyrna insists on the same thing: *Be faithful unto death, and I will give you the crown of life.*[9] That said, Life, taken in its absolute meaning, which is surely how the text understands it, is Christ; according to what He Himself told us (Jn 11:25; 14:6). From where it seems licit to infer that what is promised to the Christian athlete is nothing less than *the possession of Christ*. A possession that is destined to be carried out in a profound intimacy and degree of intensity, since *I came that they may have life, and have it abundantly.*[10]

That that Life refers to Christ Himself, is something that is confirmed by the prize promised to the Angel of the Church of Thyatira. Which is none other than the *morning star*.[11] Which, likewise, is Jesus; according to what He Himself recognizes and proclaims: *I Jesus have sent my angel to you with this testimony for the churches. I am the root and the offspring of David, the bright morning star.*[12]

---

[9] Rev 2:10.

[10] Jn 10:10.

[11] Rev 2:28.

[12] Rev 22:16: *Ego sum radix et genus David, stella splendida matutina.*

And what prize could be offered to a Christian, once the trial of life is overcome, other than Christ Himself? Could the Christian desire anything else? Is there anything that could better provide the Perfect Happiness he desires? If the meaning of Christian existence and the ultimate goal of his happiness can only be Love —to love and be loved—, what other thing could more abundantly fill the desire to love and feel loved, which also is so connatural to man and so rooted in his heart? Could someone in love desire anything else —and man was born with a marked destiny, characteristic of *being in love*— than the possession, which is also reciprocal, of the beloved person...?

Saint Paul said that Christ is the life of Christians (Col 3:4). Which is as certain as the fact that He can turn death itself into gain (Phil 1:21). The death that now is revealed to be the necessary and definitive step to possess Him and be with Him (Phil 1:22).

As far as I am concerned, throughout my already long life, I have had the opportunity to confront numerous ups and downs, many of them very painful, as could have happened to anyone whose existence has been as long as mine. Nevertheless, I consider them all trivial or, even better, as nothing, before the hope of possessing what my battered heart has always anxiously desired. Contemplating now my life from its end is when I understand that without Christ it would not have had any sense at all. For through it all I have not desired anything else but Love, but true Love; which is the same as total Love, that only He can give me. I am not talking about any of the forms of Love that life offers that flow meandering, as streams through the wide plain of life; but only He Who, as the only and unique Love, and in the form of an impetuous flow, comes from the source itself of the waters and is identical to it. The truth is that I have never been able to understand Love any other way than as *totality*. And even recognizing that my heart has never come to fill its yearning, even now that my walking in search of the Homeland still lasts, I have always felt encouraged by the hope of completely satiating it after all. For as God is a *devouring fire* (Deut 4:24), I cannot help but recognize that He has *consumed* my soul to the point of turning it to ash.

That said, what sense does the promise made to the Angel of Ephesus have, according to which if he is the victor he will be given to eat of the tree of life? Is it a roundabout way of trying to explain something? Maybe an indirect way of expressing something, trying to convey greater clarity? But if for the Christian life is Christ, and doubtless that is what the promise refers to, why not indicate it directly and without roundabout verbiage. Is there any reason to not proclaim clearly, as the Apostle does, that there is no more vehement desire in the soul of the disciple than to *be with Christ* (Phil 1:23)?

Life is the possibility and condition for Love to exist. But *condition* here does not refer merely, as we may think, to Life considered as the previous origin that makes the unfolding of Love possible. But the fact that Life, with the range of possibilities and options it offers, is one of the fundamental elements that make up the concept of Love. As in the bosom of the Trinity itself, or the place of infinite Life and Love, where the fact that Love is structured through the mutual donation of lives of two who love each other appears (Jn 6:57).

Man has been created to love. But Love supposes the reciprocal giving of one's own life between an *I* and a *thou* who mutually love each other. If Love means the giving in totally of the *I*, with all that he is and all that he possesses, to the beloved person, it is understood that Life is the supreme value that can be given (Jn 15:13). That

Final Reflection 429

is why the texts that speak of the giving and loss of one's own life abound. It should be pointed out that, rather than loss, there is here an interchange of lives between lovers.[13] Or to say it more precisely, it is about the loss of life to gain the life of the other; for the ardent desire that Love puts in the soul points to no other thing. Beyond that, even common language expresses this with ease when it uses expressions like *my life* or *life of mine* or other sayings to refer to or address the beloved person. Such an exchange of lives between those who love each other, which in the purely human love relationship is reduced to little more than a metaphor, becomes real in divine–human Love; as we infer clearly from scripture texts (Jn 6: 56–57; 15: 4–5; 17:26).

The offer to the Angel of Ephesus of an *Abundant Life* as the prize for victory, means the promise of a Life equally Abundant and to the end: *usque in finem* (Jn 13:1). Which has no other final object, since we are dealing with absolute and perfect Love, than the Person Himself of Jesus Christ; and through Him to the Father. That is why it can be said, therefore, that promising total Love is to offer the possession itself of the Spouse. That is, in short, the form biblical and mystical language uses to speak of the possession of God.

What is the thing that makes the enamored lover feel *seduced*, to the extreme of rejoicing, by the idea of giving everything to the beloved person, including one's own life? Certainly, the lover does not do it to receive something in return; not even the life of the beloved person, as if this were the reason to make the exchange. The happiness of the one in love, more than in receiving something, whatever that may be, comes from giving everything: *There is more*

---

[13] To cite only a few texts by way of example: Mt 20:28; Mk 8:35; Lk 9:24; 17:33; Jn 10: 11.17; 12:25; Gal 2:20; 1 Jn 3:16.

*joy in giving than receiving.*¹⁴ The enamored lover feels *fascinated* in the presence of the beloved person; he does not think about anything but her and *does not desire anything else than her good*, in addition to forgetting himself. Here the moment of rapture has arrived, of the enchanting spell, of awe in the presence of the sublime and marvelous, of an irresistible attraction that the contemplation of Beauty and the Good produces: an array of feelings that are all summarized in the ecstatic and wonderful amazement in the presence of Being. We are not dealing here with the allure produced by the contemplation of the Beauty and Good of Being as *abstract* realities. What really draws the enamored and ecstatic spectator out of himself is the contemplation of such things *as the qualities of someone who is a person*; who, because of this, is capable of *responding* in turn. Or to say it in another way, it is the unfathomable admiration, of the lover, in the presence of the discovery of a *thou* who is capable of addressing him fully as another *I*; and who at the same time *also feels fascinated* and in love.¹⁵ By which we have come to the bottomless well of the mystery of Love, namely: to the enchantment produced by enraptured contemplation, the same that is anxious to go out of himself to give himself at the same time that he has found also a response equally seduced and in love. Certainly, that is why the mystery of Love is structured and founded according to a *relational reality which, of course, is personal*. The discovery of the *other* means the discovery of *Love*, as well as also of the *person* as the perfection of Being.¹⁶ The discovery and correct understanding of the concept of *person* supposes the definitive

---

[14] Acts 20:35.

[15] A *thou* in which shine to a high degree, or even to the highest degree, the attributes of Being.

[16] Maybe in this way we could trace a point of union with the Thomist principle of the *satiating contemplation of truth* as the object of *Beatitudo*.

Final Reflection

goodbye to solipsism, all forms of egotism, and the modern fantasies of *one's own truth* or of *being oneself*. The person is a subsisting entity and a reality that is complete in itself, unveiled as such in a true state of perfection; but destined to go out of himself to relate with *the other* and thus make his perfection extensive. Or to say it another way, the person is a being whose destiny and whose sense of existence are none other than Love.

Love is a relationship between persons. Wherefrom the person is not constituted by Love, neither by the *discovery* of the other; but, as such, is before them. In the bosom of the Trinity, the Persons are formed by *relations*, that are in no way accidents. Therefore, the perfection and individuality of each one of them is *absolute,* or better said *infinite*, since they are actually identical to the divine Essence. That is how we say that the Father is perfect God, the Son is perfect God, and the Holy Spirit is perfect God, without their being, because of this, three gods. In creatures, however, relations are accidents. That is why it cannot be said that the perfection of the created person is absolute in the same way it can be said about divinity. Which is not an obstacle that in creatures the person finds itself already constituted as such *before* the discovery of the other; though, in the end, it is *oriented* to the other, who ultimately serves as an element for the person to *discover* and make his own perfection extensive. If the created person depended on the other in its intimate constitution, it could not give itself to the other in *totality* and in absolute and complete *freedom*: if it does, it is precisely because it is a complete *I*.

The personal character of Love appears clearly at the promise to the Angel of the Church of Pergamum: *To him who conquers I will give some of the hidden manna, and I will give him a white stone, with a new name written on the stone which no one knows except him who receives it.*[17]

---

[17] Rev 2:17.

In the mysterious meaning of the Prize, promised in the form of a metaphor, it seems right to admit here that, both the *hidden* manna and the new name that *no one knows except him who receives it*, lead to thinking of the intimacy of love, in solitude, withdrawn, and forgotten by all, which happens in the special and unique relationship of the *I–thou* of the ones in love:

> *In solitude she lived,*
> *And in solitude now has built her nest;*
> *And in solitude her dear one alone guides her,*
> *Who likewise in solitude also was wounded by love.*[18]

True Love —as well as the collective love *to others*— is resolved always in the personal relationship of the *I* to the *thou* and vice versa, which is another exclusive quality of divine Love and divine–human Love. The Good Shepherd calls *each of His sheep by name* (Jn 10:3), and even thinks it is worth leaving ninety-nine in the field to go and search for the *one* that has been lost (Lk 15:4). The Love of God for His creatures, like the whistle or call of the Shepherd to his sheep, is always a unique and personal Love and call: *Ego Dominus, qui vocavi te nomine tuo.*[19] And again in the *Song of Songs*:

> *My dove, my perfect one, is only one,*
> *The darling of her mother,*
> *Flawless to her that bore her.*[20]

---

[18] Saint John of the Cross, *Spiritual Canticle*.
[19] Is 45:3.
[20] Song 6:9.

Final Reflection

That is why the bride addresses the Bridegroom insisting also on solitude and the secret *I–thou* dialogue, in which love words are said that only they know. As if this is the only thing that really matters:

> *My Love, Stars in the Heavens,*
> *Seas kissed by bows of a thousand ships below,*
> *Eyes of sweet youthful maidens,*
> *Songs of wood thrush and sparrow,*
> *Everything I told you and which you now know...*

And the Bridegroom answers her, making the saying come true that the love dialogue between lovers becomes, by far, the most beautiful competition that anyone could have imagined:

> *Come to me; be with me; stay.*
> *While brisk North winds gust over the high meadow;*
> *Leave the flock to find its way,*
> *Whisper to me, faint and low,*
> *That you feel wounded by my love's tender blow...*

The *new name that no one knows except him who receives it* expresses the intimacy in solitude that the lovers desire for themselves. It concerns the mystery of the love dialogue of the *I–thou*, established in solitude, in which they express feelings and say words that remain secret forever between them: *Everything I told you and which you now know.* The bride is something unique and singular for the Bridegroom: *My dove, my perfect one, is only one...*; in turn, the Bridegroom too is for the bride the only one among many:

> *As an apple tree among the trees of the wood,*
> *so is my beloved among young men.*[21]

Neither the Bridegroom nor the bride desire anything else than to mutually belong to one another. He is the only prize desired by the bride and she is the singular glory of the Bridegroom: *You are beautiful as Tirzah, my love, comely as Jerusalem...*[22] Hence the solemn declaration of the Bridegroom that the bride belongs to Him; recognizing, at the same time, that He is her property:

> *Set me as a seal upon your heart,*
> *As a seal upon your arm;*
> *For love is strong as death,*
> *Jealousy is cruel as the grave.*[23]

Unfortunately, the loss of the ideas of intimacy and solitude in the divine–human dialogue, a result in turn of the devaluation and forgetfulness of the love relationship between God and man, is one of the marks that characterize modern Catholicism.

For centuries the Church cherished, as a fundamental part of her patrimony, the idea of the importance and necessity of prayer. A topic that aimed above all, as to the ultimate standard, to contemplative prayer, which was thought to be the culmination of Christian life during the time of our worldly pilgrimage.

But the idea of the personal dialogue with God has weakened in recent times, as Christian Spirituality, which was always centered on the person, opted progressively for social issues. Saint John of the

---

[21] Song 2:3.
[22] Song 6:4.
[23] Song 8:6.

Cross and Saint Teresa of Avila were left behind and forgotten, as if they were, in the best case, glorious relics of former times, while Mystical Theology was exchanged for Social Doctrine.[24]

It would be useless to deny that the Catholicism of supernatural character and content has given way to a show-ridden Catholicism, rather sensational and for this world. The slow disappearance of the internal element has progressively given way to an increase in external factors, which in the end, as one may have expected, have been reduced to a mere show, putting on acts or behavior so as to attract attention to herself. In the present time, there are not a few Shepherds in the Church to whom the words of our Lord could be applied: *Beware of the scribes, who like to go about in long robes, and love salutations in the marketplaces and the best seats in the synagogues and the places of honor at feasts.*[25]

It even sounds naive to say that such conduct is contrary to the genuine teachings of the New Testament.

Everything suggests that, consciously or unconsciously, the continued effort to put the emphasis on the external, as appears especially in the progressive theatricalization of the Liturgy and the

---

[24] A notable phenomenon that usually goes unnoticed is the *drought* of treatises on Spirituality, starting in the last third of the past century. Their absence has been compensated by tons of Documents and Social Doctrine books. A whole bulky Body of Doctrine known in depth by few, due above all to its enormous complexity and its exorbitant length, though practiced by even fewer. In the period that goes until Vatican II, the doctrine of the Church as an Organism and as Mystical Body was not an obstacle for the traditional spirituality, centered on the *personal* relationship of the soul with God. The second commandment —love thy neighbor— was nothing more than a continuation and extension of the first —love God.

[25] Lk 20:46.

abundance of Mass events,[26] has no other objective than attempting to conceal the lack of content of modern Catholicism..., or to slow in some way the continued bleeding and desertion of the masses of the faithful. Where have those virtues gone, which someone described as *passive*, but in reality made up the beautiful painting in which you could admire humility, the desire to go unnoticed, silent sacrifice, the hidden life of prayer in sublime dialogue with God, authentic poverty (but not sociological poverty), the continued and often heroic suffering for the love of Jesus Christ, and so many things that made the Christian life shine in a sublime way...? Is it possible that people are still convinced that things like the search for influence and power, the accumulation of money, the desire to spread to the greatest number of countries, the effort to climb the career ladder and acquire name recognition and, in general, the indiscriminate use of purely human means by Religious Families that exist in the Church (Orders, different types of Institutes, Congregations, etc.) are going to produce fruit for souls? But that is how we have come to the abundant rain of incessant activities, of meetings and gatherings everywhere, and at all times, of the shameful dependence on the media and public opinion, of constant trips and traveling that leave no place or space to reflect, to have serenity, for study or prayer... *Bene curris, sed extra viam* as Saint Augustine said. It seems that works like *The Way of Perfection* of Saint Teresa of Avila have fallen into the most complete oblivion to be substituted with the new and enthusiastic feeling in favor of the *perfection of the way*, and that is why trips and continuous traveling have become irreplaceable;

---

[26]Understanding that the theatricalization of the Liturgy almost always brings *desacralization* with it. Appearing above all in the marginalization of the ministers of worship, to let lay people in (men and women); in the use of profane instruments and vestments (often falling into ridiculous outcomes); in the introduction of dances and indigenous rights; etc.

even for nuns, including of course cloistered nuns, who have left behind their convents and have considered it their duty to embrace Jesus Christ's instruction: *Go therefore and make disciples of all nations...*[27]

Pope John Paul II during his Pontificate made almost two hundred trips. A very considerable number especially if we consider the duration and length of the travels; and we do not doubt the pastoral fruit of such tireless pontifical activity. And although it is certain that the Apostle Saint Paul also made trips, we should not forget that, the world being much smaller then, his trips were much shorter in length compared to those of John Paul II.[28]

Arriving at the end of the road, having won in combat, it is the moment to receive the prize or Crown of Victory:

> *Arise, my love,*
> *My fair one, and come away;*
> *For lo, the winter is past, the rain is over and gone...*
> *And the voice of the turtledove is heard in our land.*[29]

And with the prize, the discovery that the reward had already begun to be received from the beginning. Before reaching the finish line and from the very beginning of the contest, the fact of having run for the Bridegroom and with the Bridegroom, sharing His destiny to the death, had meant supreme joy:

---

[27] Mt 28:19.

[28] Thanks to that limitation, current modest Tourist Companies can carry out their *Tours* without excessive expenses, with not a little satisfaction of those devout people who want to follow the so-called *Route of Saint Paul*.

[29] Song 2: 10–12.

> *Draw me after you, let us make haste.*
> *The king has brought me into his chambers.*
> *We will exult and rejoice in you;*
> *We will extol your love more than wine.*[30]

Running with Him is running with certainty (1 Cor 9:26), and walking next to Him and hearing His voice, sharing all the ups and downs of His life is already complete joy (Jn 3:29). Something that the workers of the first hour did not understand, according to the parable of those sent to work in the vineyard. For having been chosen, with the goal of being destined to support the greater weight of the day and the heat, was already a better prize than the small denarius agreed upon for the wage. The most beautiful part of the prize given to the winner of this combat, contrary to what it might seem to a superficial thought, is not found so much in the fact of having won, *but in having lived and suffered with Him.* Saint Paul, who insists on explaining the destiny of the baptized as a participation in the Death of Christ and, from there, also in the Resurrection, wraps both acts in a singular and unique destiny: *For as many of you as were baptized into Christ have put on Christ.*[31] Whereby, would suffering or rejoicing be as important as, in any case, being with Him? It was He Who wanted to preserve the stigmas of His Passion in His glorious body, just like His followers will wear in the Homeland, like victory trophies, the traces of the hardships suffered because of His cause. That is why we can ask, regarding the exclamation of the bride of the *Song of Songs* and the joy which, according to her, both are going to share: whether it refers to the moment in which they finally meet in the halls of the Bridegroom, or if those joys already count for her *from the very moment in which she runs with Him.*

---

[30] Song 1:4.
[31] Gal 3:27.

Final Reflection

That is how my life has unfolded. In the footsteps of the Master in a quest which, seeing what has been achieved, one could call unfruitful. Maybe I myself share this idea, at times at least. But things are not always as they seem, and sometimes we need to see them from the opposite point of view to how the World considers them; only in this way can we see them in their true reality. An apparent defeat, for example, can appear as a successful victory, examined from the right angle. And it is not rare for a fruitless quest to end in the most marvelous discovery. That is why the destiny of the Christian journey does not consist so much in reaping triumphs as in constantly starting new battles; nor in having found at last what the heart so desired, as much as the willingness to continue the search without tiring.

Sometimes —after all we are human—, in view of what we perceive in the World and in the Church and in the midst of the heat of the battle, it is difficult to avoid a sense of fatigue. These are the moments in which, maybe because we feel nostalgia for the Homeland, and also because we foresee the end of the path approaching, we seem to understand better —a lot better— the instruction of the Apostle: *Seek the things that are above... Set your minds on things that are above, not on things that are on earth...*[32]

---

[32] Col 3: 1–2.

Index of Quotations of the New Testament

Matthew

3: 11, **191**
   13–15, **103**
4: 4, **170**
   5–6, **295**
5: 4, **49**, **75**
   5, **28**
   8, **55**, **81**
   10, **361**
   11–12, **41**
   16, **296**
   29–30, **361**
   37, **378**
   48, **131**, **281**
6: 1–6, **295**, **296**
   24, **401**
   25–32, **184**
7: 7–11, **184**
   13, **44**
   13–14, **267**, **361**
   14, **79**, **84**, **184**, **194**, **316**
   15, **40**, **110**
   16, **155**
   16–20, **110**
   22, **293**
8: 26, **353**
   28, **319**
   34, **319**
9: 15, **46**
   16, **185**
10: 9–10, **399**
    14–15, **161**
    16, **40**, **184**
    21–22, **40**
    24, **204**, **229**, **230**
    24–25, **28**, **141**, **323**, **394**
    27, **21**
    28, **4**, **27**
    33, **318**
    34, **361**
    35–36, **363**
    36, **40**
    37, **367**
    38, **84**
    39, **170**, **200**, **223**, **237**, **253**, **339**, **343**
11: _, **79**
    11, **78**
    12, **372**
    27, **197**, **224**
12: 32, **70**
    36, **367**
    47–50, **218**
13: 11–13, **309**
    11–15, **13**
    25, **348**
    28, **244**
15: 8–9, **176**
    21–28, **393**

16: 18, **35, 45, 180, 305,
319, 341**
24, **84, 395**
25, **237**
18: 6, **361, 374**
8, **374**
8–9, **361**
19–20, **162**
19: 6, **376**
8, **376**
16–30, **274**
21, **396**
30, **231**
20: 16, **231**
25–27, **402**
28, **229, 429**
21: 25, **278**
22: 36–39, **219**
40, **138**
23: 8, **84, 366**
12, **103**
26, **294**
24: 4–6, **287**
5, **308**
6–7, **357**
7, **287**
11, **110, 308**
11–12, **287**
12, **17, 36, 125, 127,
182, 378, 403**

15, **308**
21–22, **36**
22, **288**
24, **36, 110, 288, 308**
32, **308**
32–33, **11**
35, **181**
36, **289, 308**
37–44, **12**
38–39, **423**
42, **289, 348**
43, **349**
44, **133**
25: _, **348**
1–13, **140**
6, **133**
14–30, **239, 381**
15, **333**
20, **228, 322**
29, **241**
26: 28, **330**
31, **37, 188**
41, **348**
27: 46, **80, 421**
63, **81**
28: 19, **424, 437**
19–20, **249, 250, 268**
20, **259, 304, 370**

Mark

1: 15, **405**
4: 33–34, **309**
5: 1, **319**
7: 24, **393**
8: 34, **84**, **395**
   35, **237**, **253**, **429**
9: 42, **361**
   45, **361**
   47, **361**
10: 9, **376**
   17–31, **274**
   21, **242**, **275**
   31, **231**
   44, **231**
   45, **229**
   52, **396**
12: 29–30, **131**
   30, **215**
13: 7–8, **357**
   31, **181**
   35, **133**
14: 27, **37**
   38, **348**
15: 34, **80**
16: 16, **161**, **405**

Luke

2: 34, **80**
3: 9, **239**
4: 16, **319**
5: 5, **415**
6: 26, **41**, **90**, **257**
   38, **15**, **241**
   40, **141**, **204**, **323**
7: _, **79**
   47, **15**, **241**
8: 23–25, **353**
   26, **319**
9: 3, **399**
   23, **395**
   24, **237**, **253**, **429**
   26, **182**
   60, **375**
   62, **375**
10: 4, **399**
   16, **252**, **273**
   21, **390**
   38–42, **267**
   42, **283**, **374**
11: 23, **80**
12: 9, **318**
   10, **70**
   27–30, **184**
   36–38, **134**

37, **229**
39, **133**
49, **191**
50, **206**
13: 30, **231**
14: 11, **103**
23, **268**
26, **253**, **369**
27, **84**
31, **394**
33, **253**, **275**
15: 4, **59**, **432**
16: 8, **315**, **378**
13, 401
17: 20–21, **294**
33, **429**
18: 8, **18**, **36**, **180**, **341**, **378**
14, **104**
18–30, **274**
19: 11–27, **239**, **381**
26, **241**
20: 46, **435**
21: 9–11, **357**
33, **181**
22: 15, **135**
20, **330**
27, **323**
31, **349**
32, **180**
23: 31, **186**

24: 16, **107**
32, 111
36–44, **204**

John

1: –, **84**
3, **327**
5, **235**
7, **278**
14, **84**, **389**
29, **323**
36, **323**
2: 1–12, **392**
3: 8, **54**, **292**
16, **207**
18, **161**
18–19, **405**
19, **378**
29, **85**, **395**, **438**
29–30, **78**
30, **253**, **255**
31, **376**
4: 14, **242**
23, **310**
5: 30, **283**
31–32, **278**
34, **278**
36, 404
40, **128**, **195**

6: 53–57, **170**
  56, **339**
  56–57, **223, 429**
  57, **97, 99, 339, 428**
  60, **189**
  63, **267, 361**
  63–64, **169**
  68, **314**
7: 7, **394**
  16, **250**
8: 14, **278**
  18, **278**
  26, **283**
  31–32, **211**
  32, **211**
  40, **283**
  46, **334, 404**
  58, **254**
10: _, **45, 188, 349**
  3, **62, 432**
  3–4, **245, 249**
  3–5, **62**
  4, **79**
  4–5., **311**
  8, **313**
  10, **128, 195, 313, 426**
  11, **429**
  12, **187, 312, 313**
  12–13, **312**
  16, **58, 179, 314**

17, **58, 429**
17–18, **230**
25, **404**
30, **252**
37, **404**
11: 25, **426**
  30–35, **209**
12: 24, **395**
  24–25, **237**
  25, **253, 429**
  31, **310**
13: 1, **48, 215, 336, 384, 385, 429**
  1–15, **384**
  2–16, **229**
  7, **101**
  8, **101**
  12–14, **103**
  13, **366**
  13–14, **230**
  16, **141, 229, 323**
  19, **254**
  23, **395**
  34–35, **363**
  36, **397**
14: 3, **102, 114, 134, 141, 225, 390**
  4, **28, 44**
  6, **28, 72, 84, 135, 210, 250, 294, 396, 426**

    10, **250, 259**
    12, **390**
    15, **211**
    17, **297**
    18, **114**
    23, **211**
    24, **250, 259**
    25–26, **73**
    26, **14, 84, 266, 294**
    27, **61, 355**
    30, **310, 311**
15: _, **294**
    4–5, **429**
    5, **210**
    11, **150, 224**
    12, **138**
    13, **82, 204, 205, 428**
    14–15, **389**
    15, **102, 114, 227, 260, 283, 323, 384**
    18, **41, 395**
    19, **90**
    20, **41, 141, 229, 395**
    24, **404**
    26, **73, 294**
16: _, **294**
    4, **41**
    8–11, **73**
    9, **86**
    13, **14, 86, 250**

    13–14, **55, 72, 294**
    15, **14, 197, 224**
    20, **113, 150, 234**
    22, **113, 150, 234**
    24, **113, 150**
    33, **184, 304**
17: 10, **14, 224**
    24, **283, 397**
    26, **135, 205, 429**
20: 13, **46, 47, 77, 150**
    15, **77**
    15–17, **64**
    21, **248, 273**
    27, **425**
    29, **406, 416**

ACTS OF THE APOSTLES

1: 7, **289, 308**
    8, **273, 296**
2: 16, **70**
    16–20, **70**
    19–20, **70**
    32, **273**
3: 15, **273**
5: 32, **273**
8: 20, **124**
10: 39, **274**
20: 28, **307**

    31, **348**
    35, **116**, **168**, **430**

ROMANS

1: 16, **182**
   17, **298**, **306**
   20, **410**
   25, **337**
4: 18, **243**, **420**
5: 5, **134**, **143**, **145**, **175**, **202**, **420**
   12, **327**
   12–21, **325**
   18–19, **325**
7: 14–25, **316**
   19–23, **141**
8: 7, **399**
   21–22, 10
   23, **131**, **232**
   24, **138**
   24–25, **132**
   26, **232**
   28, **47**
10: 14, **311**
11: 33, **402**
   33–34, **159**, **356**
   34, **293**
12: 3, 14
   4, **333**

13: 11, **140**
   12, **48**, **144**
14: 7–8, **99**, **139**
   14, **156**
   17, **355**

1 CORINTHIANS

1: 17, **83**
   18–28, **256**
   21, **83**
   22–24, **273**
   23, **257**, **400**
   25, **83**
2: 1–5, **399**
   5, 400
   9, **413**, **425**
   11, **160**
   14, **54**, **297**
   14–15, **160**, **251**
   16, **159**
3: 13, **333**
4: 1–2, **254**, **259**
5: 12–13, **402**
7: 5, **184**
   32–34, **222**
8: 1, **165**
9: 24–25, **350**
   24–26, **141**
   26, **79**, **145**, **425**, **438**

11: 7, **104**
    11–12, **105**
12: _, **293**
    12, **331**
    14, **331, 333**
    18, **333**
    19–20, **331**
    25, **333, 334**
    27, **331, 333**
    31, **71, 84**
13: _, **61, 293**
    1, **329**
    3, **274**
    4–5, **416**
    6–7, **405**
    7–8, **242**
    8, **123, 134, 244**
    10, **191**
    12, **102, 216, 406**
14: _, **71, 293**
    5, **71**
    9, **378**
    18–19, **22, 71, 378**
15: 19, **39**
    22–25, **74**
    45, **325**
16: 13, **348**

2 CORINTHIANS

1: 5, **42**
    12, **400**
    22, **44, 131**
2: 17, **367**
3: 17, **54, 55, 292, 333**
4: 2, **88**
    3–4, **15**
    5, **88**
    10, **128**
5: 2–5, **131**
    21, **324, 334**
6: 8–10, **342**
    14–15, **356**
10: 3–4, **348**
    4, **398**

GALATIANS

1: 10, **89**
2: 2, **145**
    19–20, **221**
    20, **96, 192, 253, 339, 429**
3: 11, **298**
    27, **438**
5: 11, **80, 83, 325, 400**
    22, **77**
    22–23, **110, 294**

6: 4–5, **333**
17, **318**

EPHESIANS

1: 14, **44**
3: 10, **400**
5: 22–24, **104**
   23–24, **223**
   28, **104, 222**
   32, **221**
   33, **222**
6: 14–18, **398**
   17, **21, 88**

PHILIPPIANS

1: 20, **420**
   21, **99, 132, 139, 427**
   22, **427**
   23, **132, 139, 144, 428**
   29, **29**
2: 5, **173**
   6–8, **229**
   7, **229, 386, 390**
   7–8, **103**
   8, **424**
   16, **145**
3: 1, **113**
   10, **341**

12, **131, 145**
4: 4, **113**

COLOSSIANS

1: 13–20, **327**
   16–17, **193, 327**
   24, **47, 79, 340**
3: 1–2, **439**
   4, **99, 427**

1 THESSALONIANS

4: 13, **132**
5: 3, **16, 357**
   19, **70**

2 THESSALONIANS

2: 3, **17, 57**
   7, **83**
   8, **74**
   10–11, **16**

1 TIMOTHY

1: 5, **138**
   6–7, **138**
2: 4, **330, 332**

3: 1, **353**
    4, **402**
4: 10, **326**
6: 5, **371**
    12, **141, 379**

2 Timothy

1: 4, **76**
    12, **416**
2: 5, **141, 389**
    9, **88**
3: 1, **308**
    12, **184, 361, 372**
    16, **11**
4: 2, **245, 249, 307**
    3–4, **147, 287, 308**
    7, **132, 379**
    7–8, **241**
    8, **133, 347, 419**
    10, **188, 319**

Titus

1: 16, **304**

Hebrews

1: 1–2, **55**
3: 7–8, **55**
    15, **55**
4: 7, **55**
    11, **79**
    12, **21, 88, 95, 169, 384**
5: 1, **258**
    1–4, **265**
    4, **354**
7: 26, **323**
9: 22, **83**
10: 32, **141**
    38, **298**
11: 1, **18, 305, 306, 403, 406**
    6, **138, 306, 407**
    8, **417**
    13, **417**
    13–14, **305**
    13–16, **138**
12: 1, **379**
    4, **419**
    7, **245**
13: 14, **306**
    20, **248, 366**

James

2: 19, **328**
5: 12, **378**

1 Peter

1: 8, **235**
   17, **333**
2: 7–8, **363**
   8, **80**
   22, **324, 334**
   24, **324**
   25, **248**
4: 7, **348**
5: 4, **248**
   8, **143, 187, 310, 348**

2 Peter

1: 4, **192, 389**
   19, **406**
   19–20, **11**
2: 1–3, **110**
   20–22, **286**
3: 7, **9**
   10–13, **9**
   16, **267**

1 John

1: 2, **274**
   3, **265**
   5, **364**
2: 2, **326**
   18, **309, 310, 341**
   27, **250, 251**
3: 1–2, **389**
   16, **429**
   23, **406**
4: 5, **88**
   8, **182, 328, 329, 388**
   9, **99**
   10, **228**
   18, **21, 181, 328**
   19, **207, 228**
5: 2, **276**
   4, **243**
   19, **310**

2 John

7–11, **160**

Revelation

1: 1–3, **3**
   8, **254**
   15, **85**
   17, **130**

2: 1–6, **52, 129**
    4, **121, 123, 127, 129, 212**
    5, **236, 315**
    7, 51, **53, 347, 394**
    8, **130**
    10, **426**
    11, 53
    17, **53, 347, 431**
    23, **333**
    24, **324, 337**
    28, **426**
3: 6, **107**
    15–16, **128, 236**
    20, **136, 225**
7: 17, **75**
12: 9, **310**
13: 7, **341, 357**
    10, **30**
19: 13, **84**
20: 7, **341**
    10, **310**
21: 1, **10**
    1–3, **305**
    4, **75**
    5, **298**
    6, **254**
    8, **318, 353**
22: 10–11, **48**
    13, **130, 254**
    15, **403**
    16, **426**
    17, **48**
    18–19, **352**
    19, **3**
    20, **48, 217**

Books of the Bible

Acts, Acts of the Apostles	**Jn**, John	**1 Pet**, 1 Peter
Amos, Amos	**1 Jn**, 1 John	**2 Pet**, 2 Peter
Bar, Baruch	**2 Jn**, 2 John	**Phil**, Philippians
1 Chron, 1 Chronicles	**3 Jn**, 3 John	**Philem**, Philemon
2 Chron, 2 Chronicles	**Job**, Job	**Prov**, Proverbs
Col, Colossians	**Joel**, Joel	**Ps**, Psalms
1 Cor, 1 Corinthians	**Jon**, Jonah	**Rev**, Revelation
2 Cor, 2 Corinthians	**Josh**, Joshua	**Rom**, Romans
Dan, Daniel	**Jud**, Judith	**Ruth**, Ruth
Deut, Deuteronomy	**Jude**, Jude	**1 Sam**, 1 Samuel
Eccles, Ecclesiastes	**Judg**, Judges	**2 Sam**, 2 Samuel
Eph, Ephesians	**1 Kings**, 1 Kings	**Sg**, Song of Songs
Esther, Esther	**2 Kings**, 2 Kings	**Sir**, Sirach
Ex, Exodus	**Lam**, Lamentations	**1 Thess**, 1 Thessalonians
Ezek, Ezekiel	**Lev**, Leviticus	**2 Thess**, 2 Thessalonians
Ezra, Ezra	**Lk**, Luke	**1 Tim**, 1 Timothy
Gal, Galatians	**1 Mac**, 1 Maccabees	**2 Tim**, 2 Timothy
Gen, Genesis	**2 Mac**, 2 Maccabees	**Tit**, Titus
Hab, Habakkuk	**Mal**, Malachi	**Tob**, Tobit
Hag, Haggai	**Mic**, Micah	**Wis**, Wisdom
Heb, Hebrews	**Mk**, Mark	**Zech**, Zechariah
Hos, Hosea	**Mt**, Matthew	**Zep**, Zephaniah
Is, Isaiah	**Nahum**, Nahum	
Jas, James	**Neh**, Nehemiah	
Jer, Jeremiah	**Num**, Numbers	
	Obad, Obadiah	

Contents

**SEVEN LETTERS
TO
SEVEN BISHOPS**

Introduction 1

I. The Voice of the Spirit 53

II. Lost Love 123

III. God Corrects Those He Loves 247

IV. Christian Victory 347

Final Reflection 419

www.ingramcontent.com/pod-product-compliance
Lightning Source LLC
Chambersburg PA
CBHW060414010526
44107CB00006B/684